AMAZONS,
ABOLITIONISTS,
AND ACTIVISTS

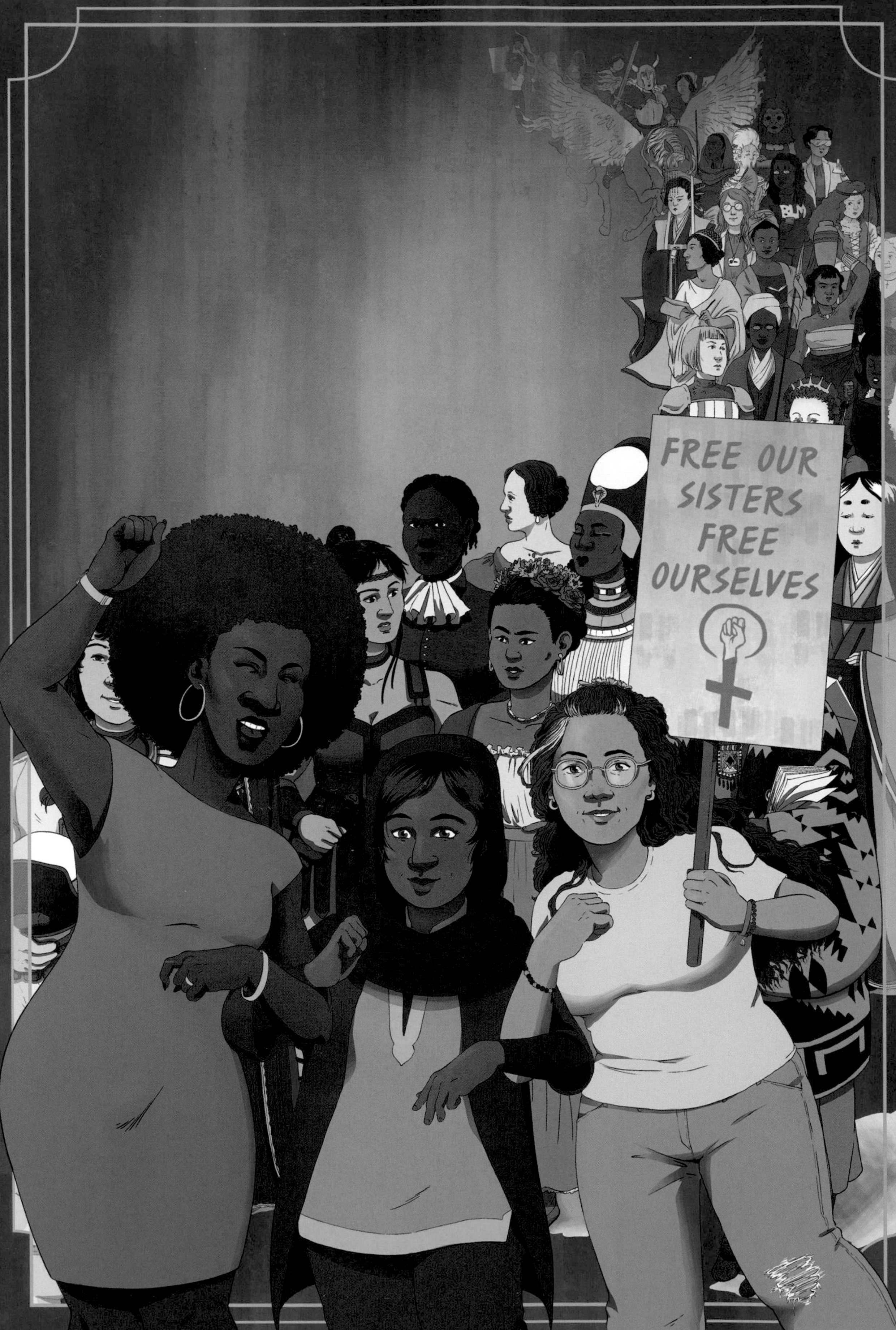
FREE OUR SISTERS FREE OURSELVES
BLM

AMAZONS, ABOLITIONISTS, and ACTIVISTS

A GRAPHIC HISTORY OF WOMEN'S FIGHT FOR THEIR RIGHTS

MIKKI KENDALL
ART BY **A. D'AMICO**
COLORS BY SHARI CHANKHAMMA
LETTERS BY ERICA SCHULTZ

TEN SPEED PRESS
California | New York

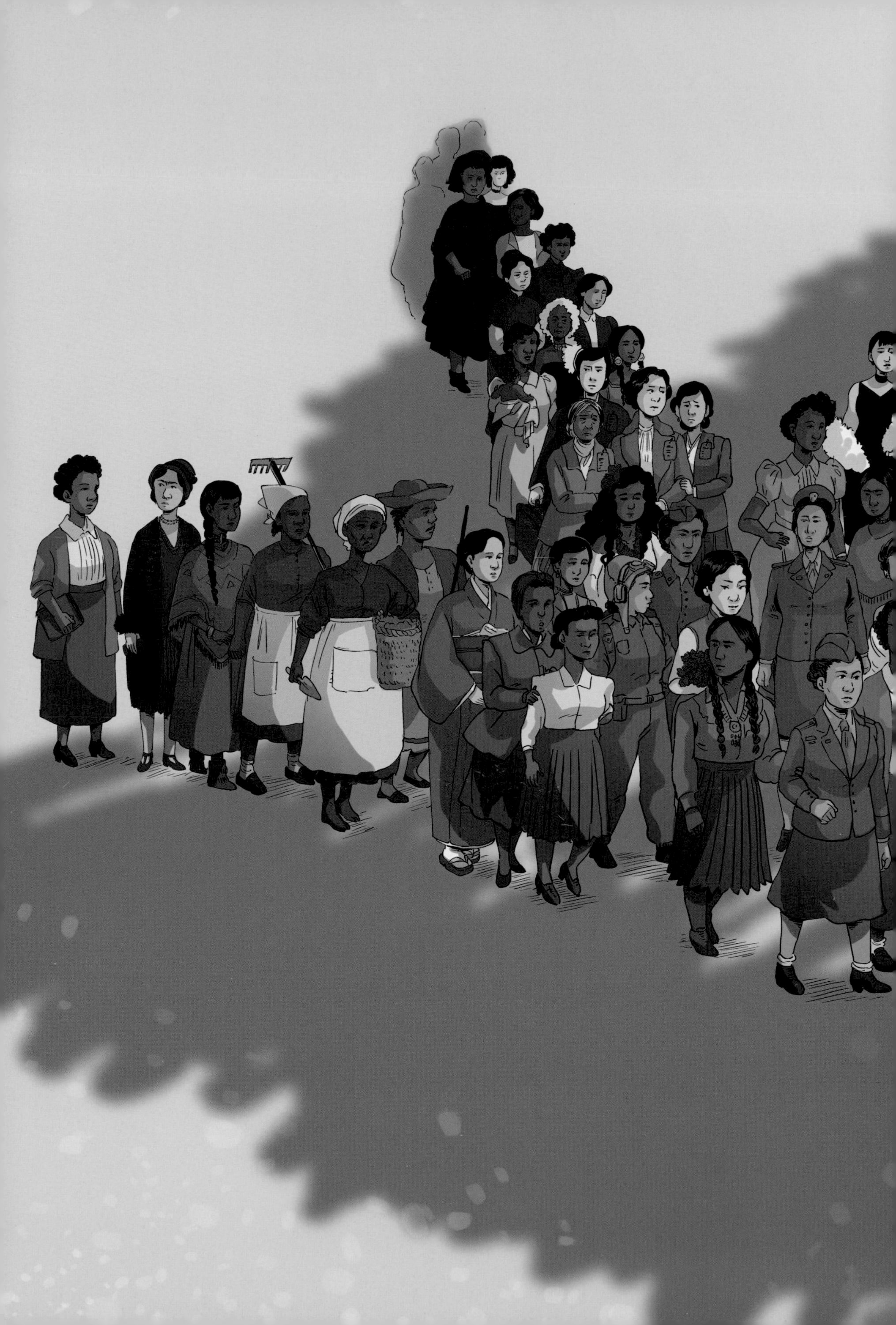

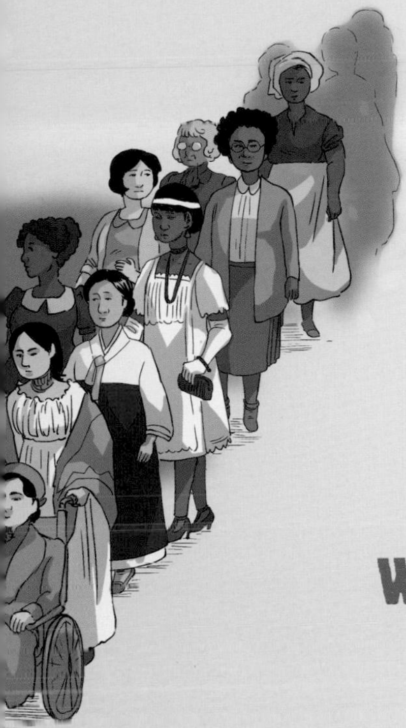

THIS IS FOR THE ONES WHO PAVED THE WAY, THE ONES WHO LEARNED TO MAKE A WAY, AND FOR THOSE WHO FACE ROADS YET UNKNOWN.

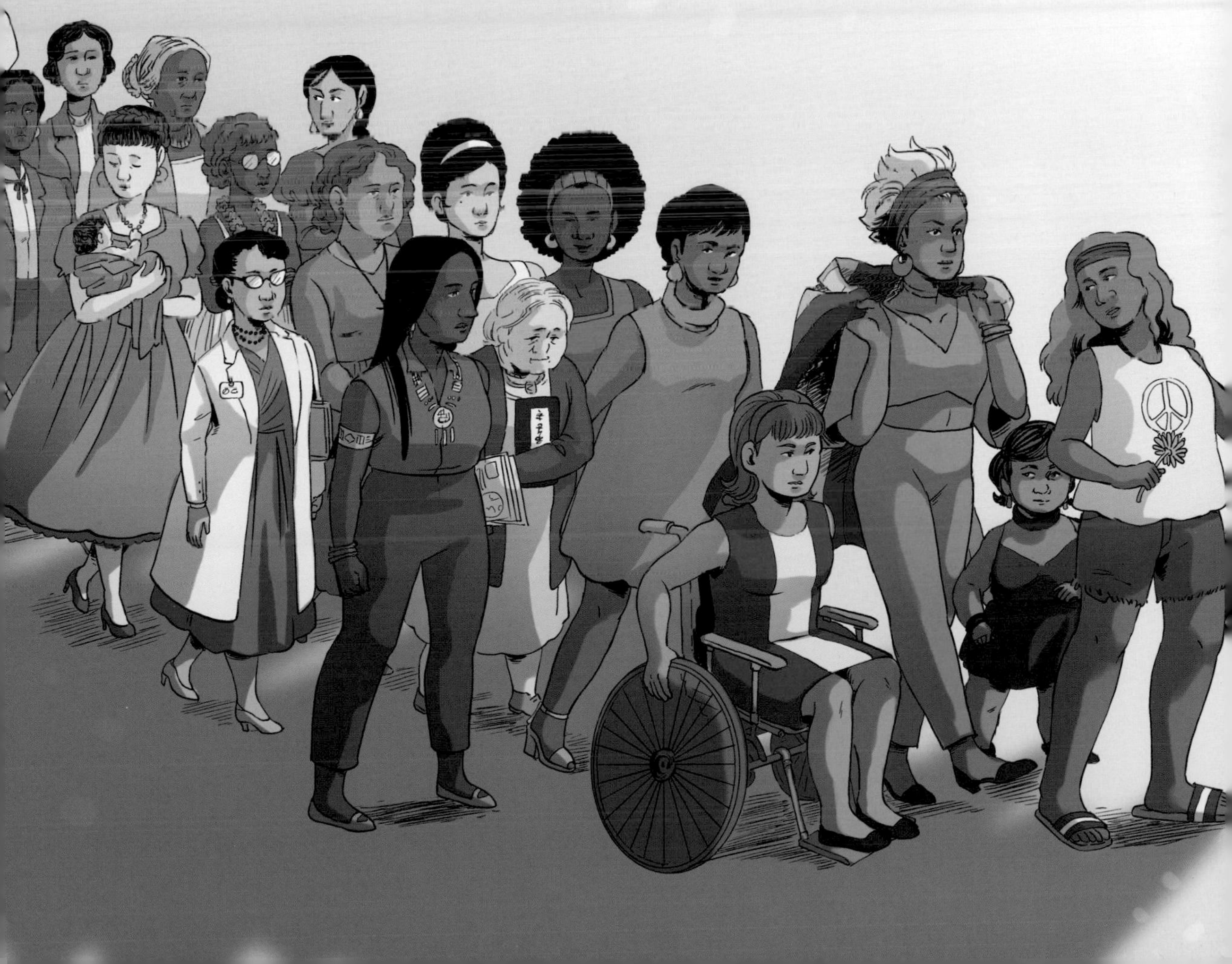

CONTENTS

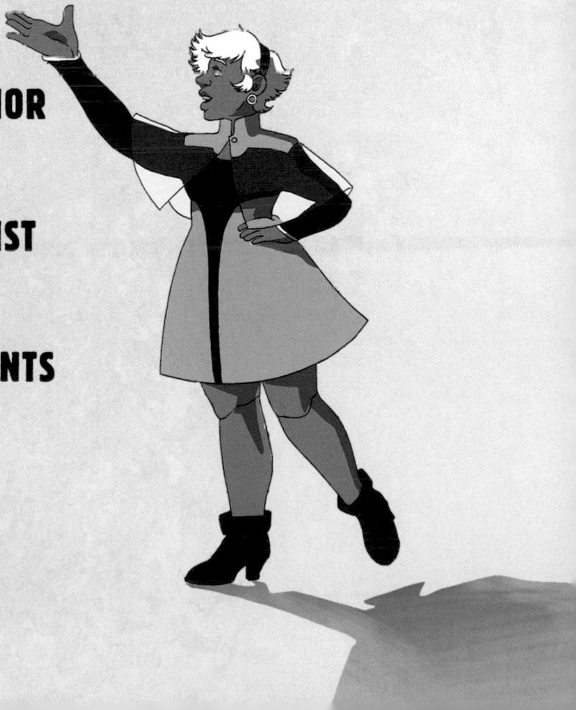

CHAPTER 1
WOMEN'S RIGHTS IN ANTIQUITY: THE SEED IS PLANTED

4500 BCE TO 859 CE

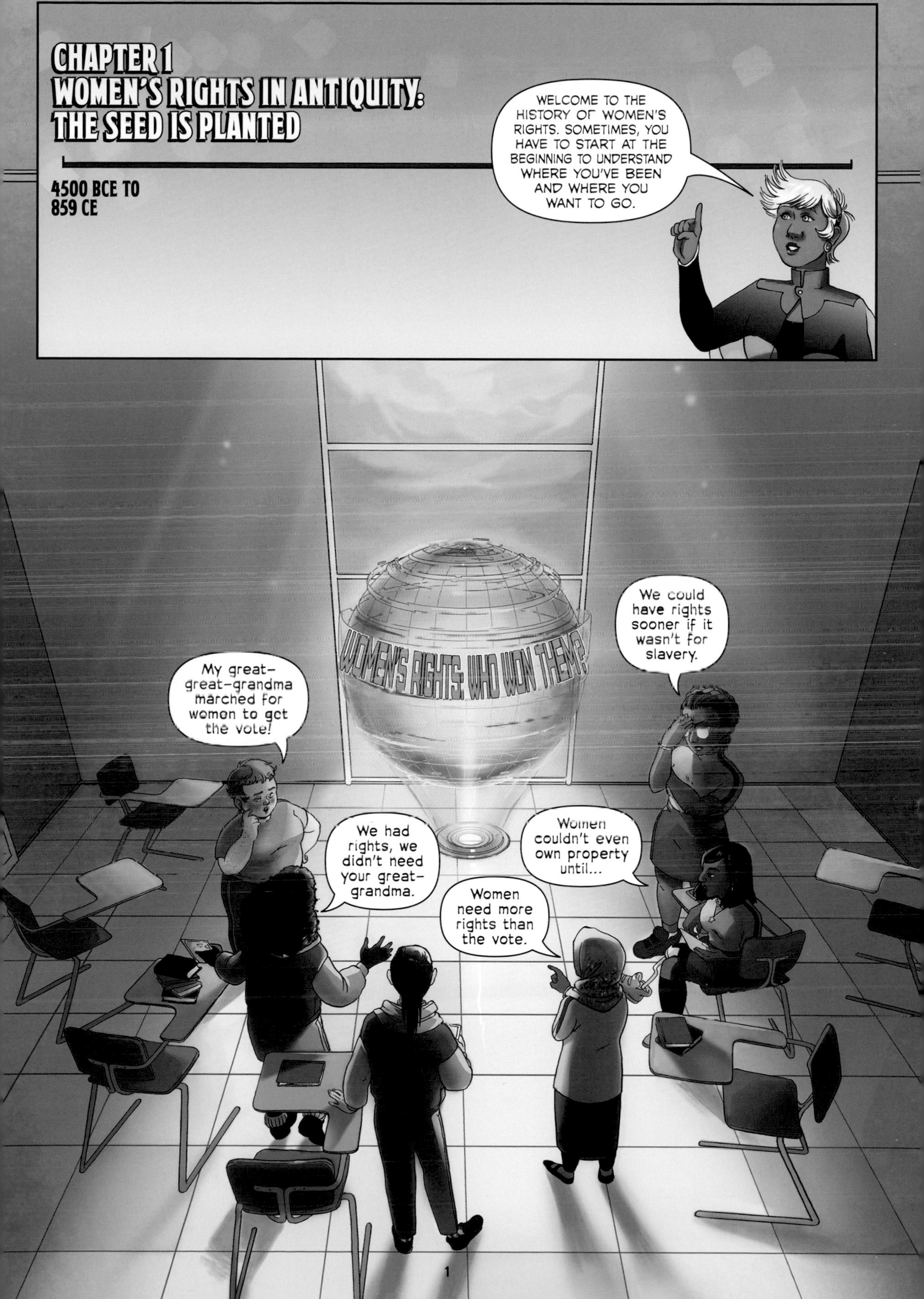

WELCOME TO THE HISTORY OF WOMEN'S RIGHTS. SOMETIMES, YOU HAVE TO START AT THE BEGINNING TO UNDERSTAND WHERE YOU'VE BEEN AND WHERE YOU WANT TO GO.
WOMEN'S RIGHTS: WHO WON THEM?
My great-great-grandma marched for women to get the vote!
We could have rights sooner if it wasn't for slavery.
We had rights, we didn't need your great-grandma.
Women couldn't even own property until...
Women need more rights than the vote.

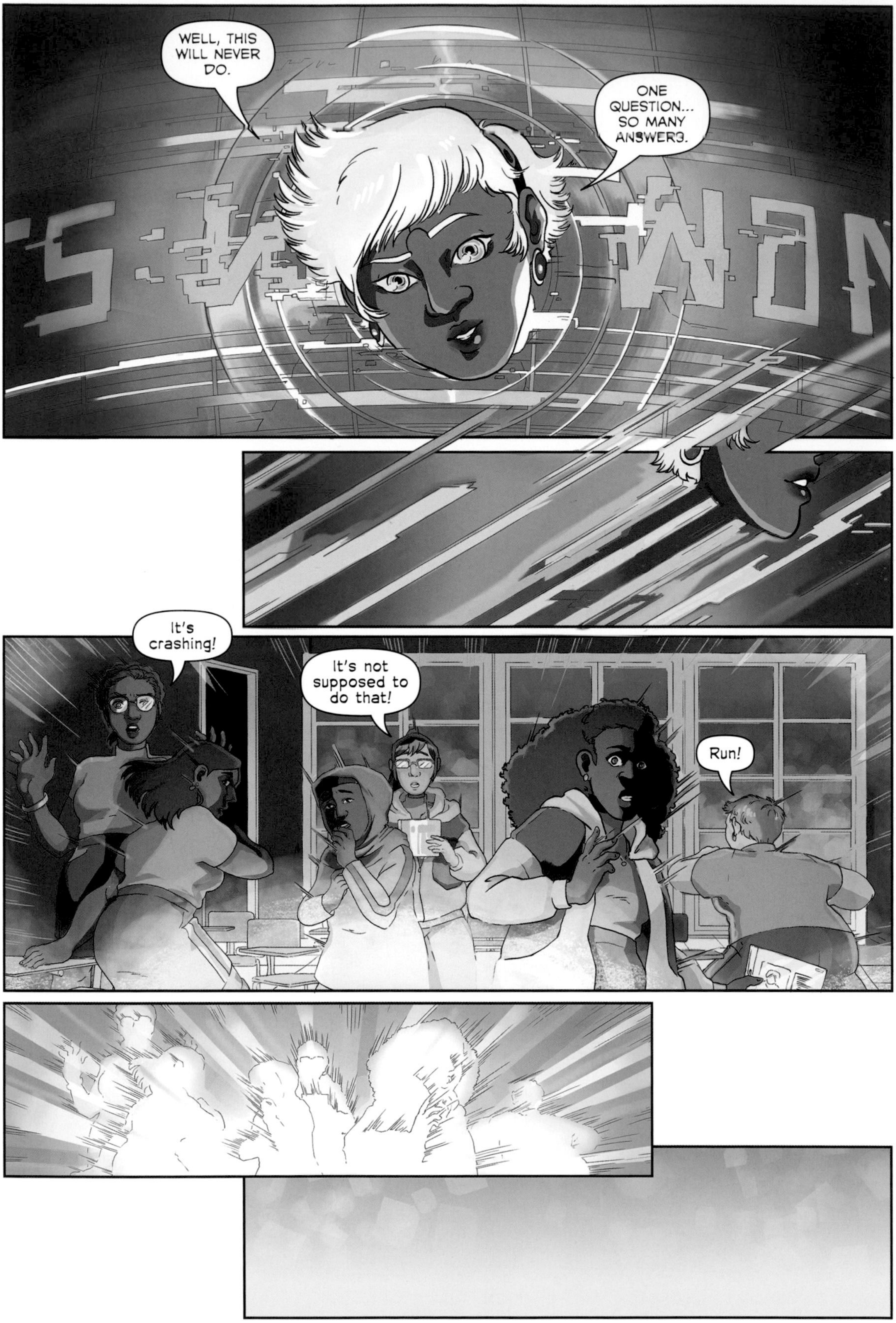
WELL, THIS WILL NEVER DO.
ONE QUESTION... SO MANY ANSWERS.
It's crashing!
It's not supposed to do that!
Run!

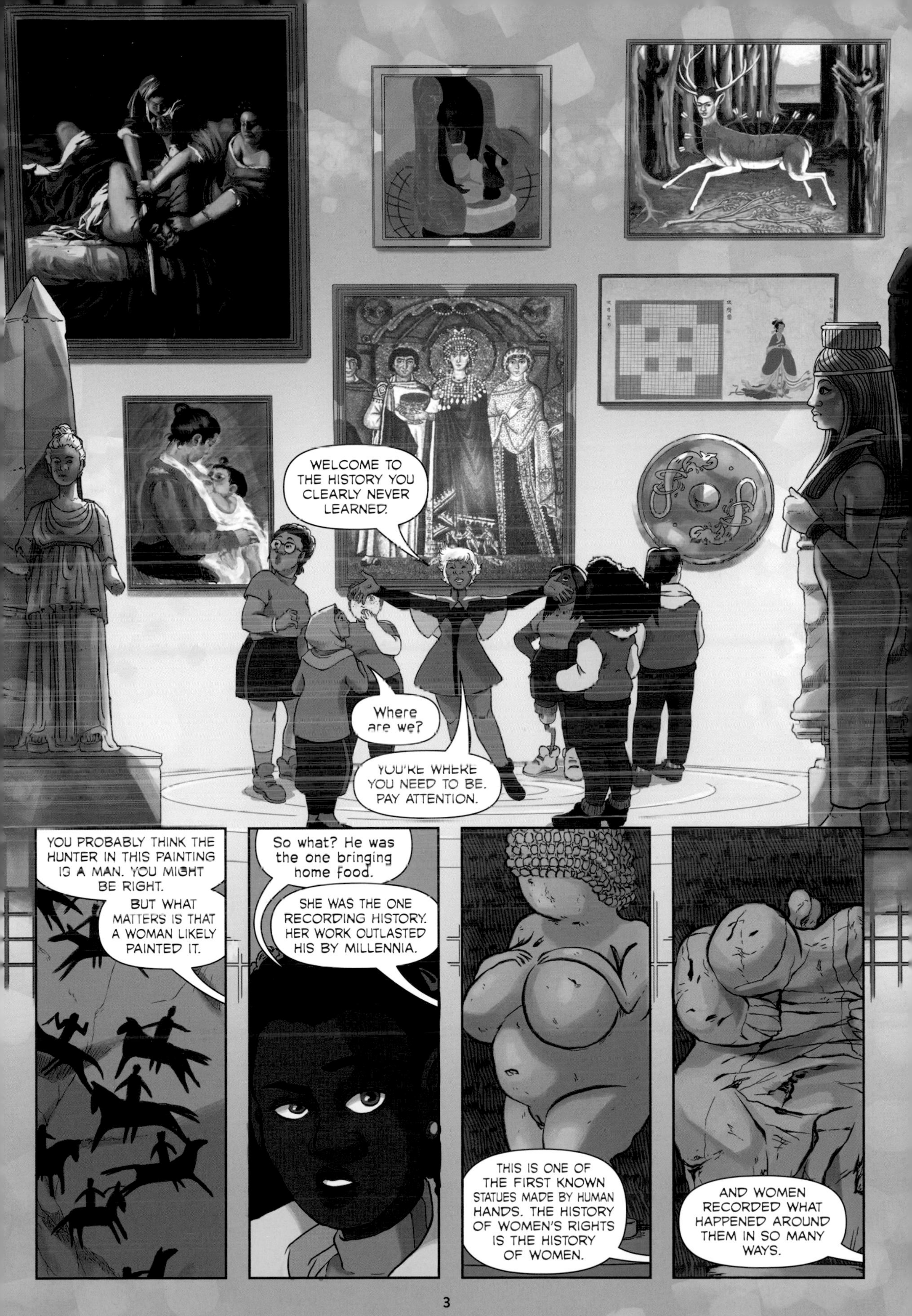

WELCOME TO THE HISTORY YOU CLEARLY NEVER LEARNED.
Where are we?
YOU'RE WHERE YOU NEED TO BE. PAY ATTENTION.
YOU PROBABLY THINK THE HUNTER IN THIS PAINTING IS A MAN. YOU MIGHT BE RIGHT.
BUT WHAT MATTERS IS THAT A WOMAN LIKELY PAINTED IT.
So what? He was the one bringing home food.
SHE WAS THE ONE RECORDING HISTORY. HER WORK OUTLASTED HIS BY MILLENNIA.
THIS IS ONE OF THE FIRST KNOWN STATUES MADE BY HUMAN HANDS. THE HISTORY OF WOMEN'S RIGHTS IS THE HISTORY OF WOMEN.
AND WOMEN RECORDED WHAT HAPPENED AROUND THEM IN SO MANY WAYS.

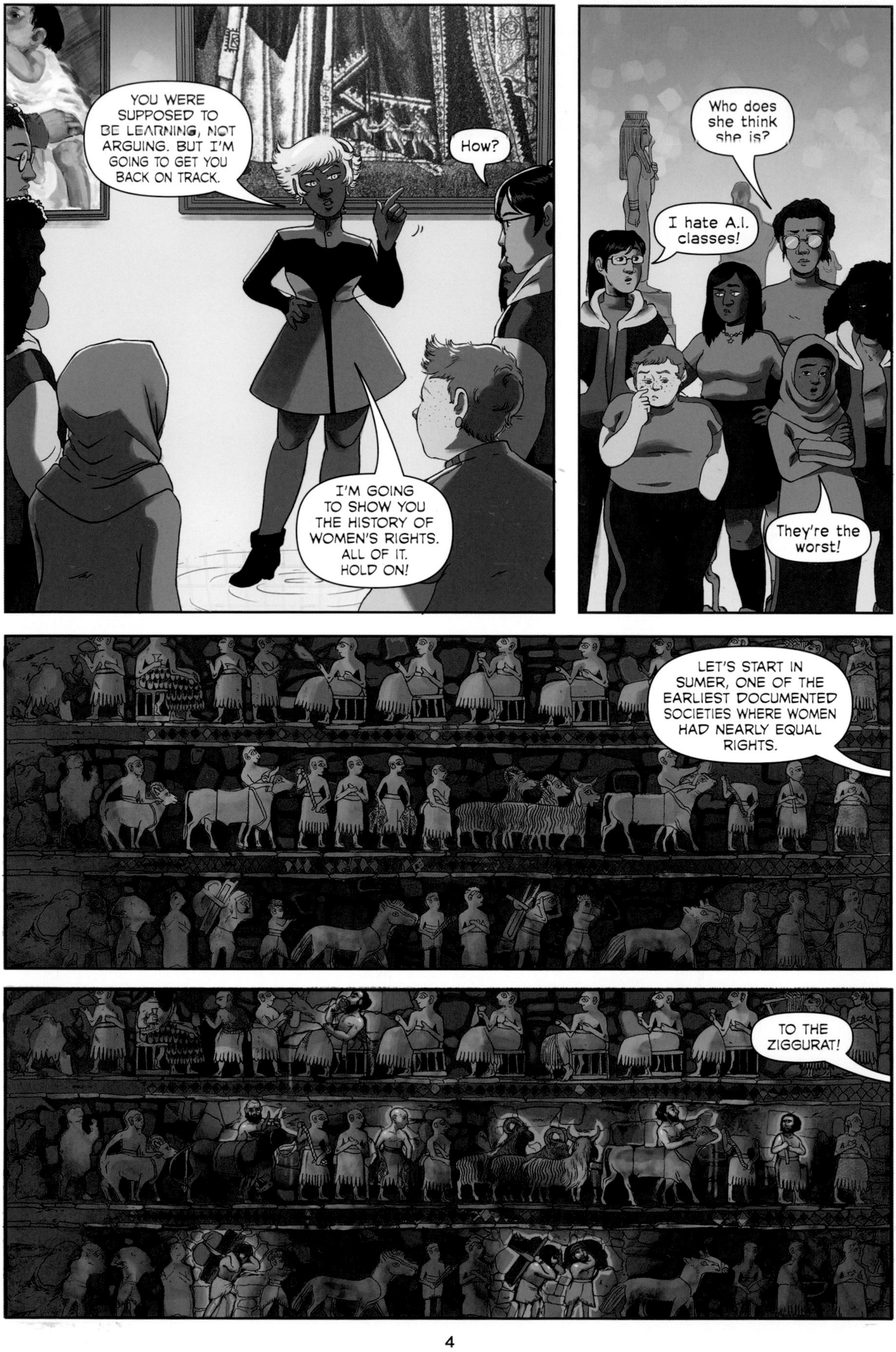
YOU WERE SUPPOSED TO BE LEARNING, NOT ARGUING. BUT I'M GOING TO GET YOU BACK ON TRACK.
How?
I'M GOING TO SHOW YOU THE HISTORY OF WOMEN'S RIGHTS. ALL OF IT. HOLD ON!
Who does she think she is?
I hate A.I. classes!
They're the worst!
LET'S START IN SUMER, ONE OF THE EARLIEST DOCUMENTED SOCIETIES WHERE WOMEN HAD NEARLY EQUAL RIGHTS.
TO THE ZIGGURAT!

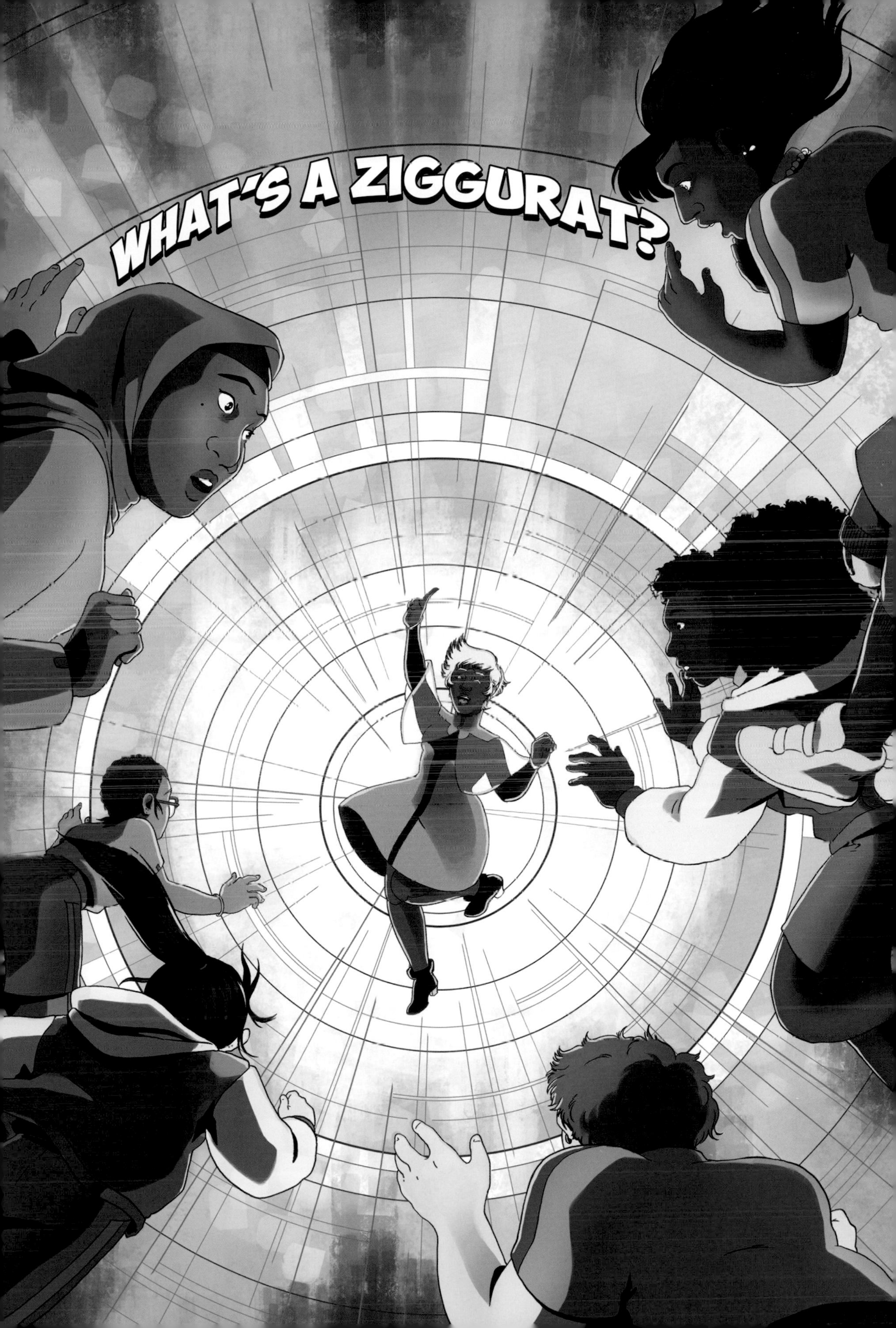
WHAT'S A ZIGGURAT?

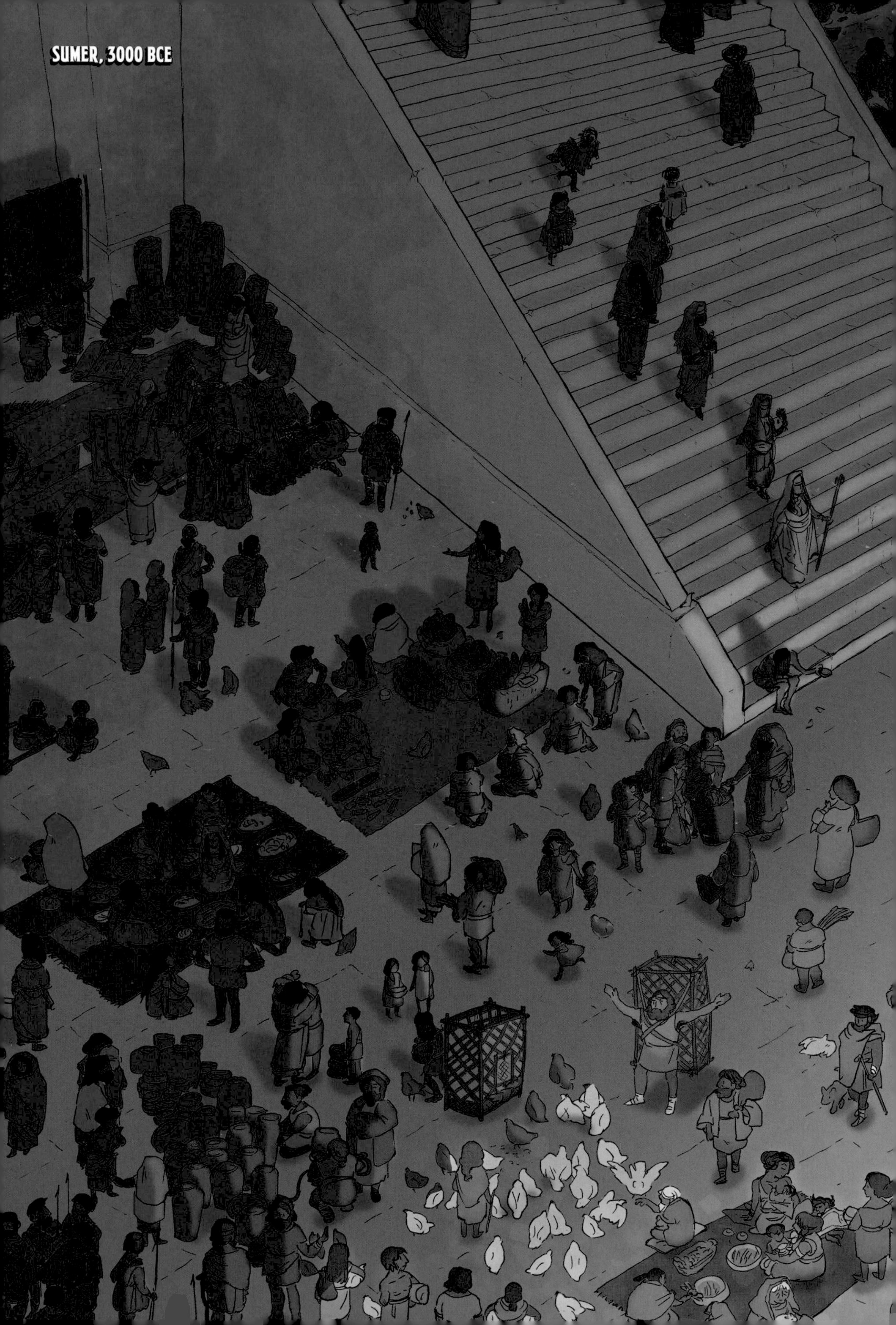
SUMER, 3000 BCE

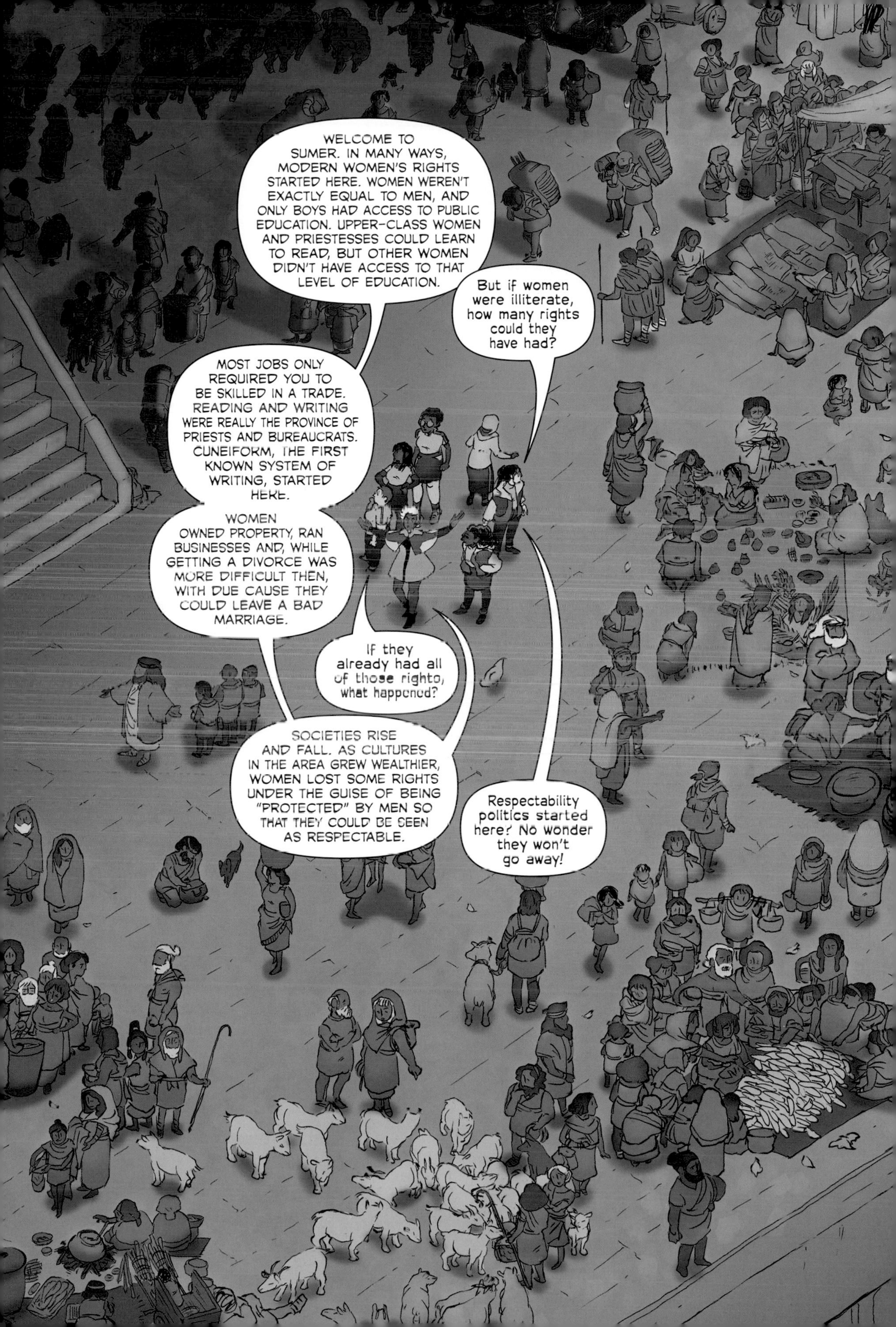
WELCOME TO SUMER. IN MANY WAYS, MODERN WOMEN'S RIGHTS STARTED HERE. WOMEN WEREN'T EXACTLY EQUAL TO MEN, AND ONLY BOYS HAD ACCESS TO PUBLIC EDUCATION. UPPER-CLASS WOMEN AND PRIESTESSES COULD LEARN TO READ, BUT OTHER WOMEN DIDN'T HAVE ACCESS TO THAT LEVEL OF EDUCATION.
But if women were illiterate, how many rights could they have had?
MOST JOBS ONLY REQUIRED YOU TO BE SKILLED IN A TRADE. READING AND WRITING WERE REALLY THE PROVINCE OF PRIESTS AND BUREAUCRATS. CUNEIFORM, THE FIRST KNOWN SYSTEM OF WRITING, STARTED HERE.
WOMEN OWNED PROPERTY, RAN BUSINESSES AND, WHILE GETTING A DIVORCE WAS MORE DIFFICULT THEN, WITH DUE CAUSE THEY COULD LEAVE A BAD MARRIAGE.
If they already had all of those rights, what happened?
SOCIETIES RISE AND FALL. AS CULTURES IN THE AREA GREW WEALTHIER, WOMEN LOST SOME RIGHTS UNDER THE GUISE OF BEING "PROTECTED" BY MEN SO THAT THEY COULD BE SEEN AS RESPECTABLE.
Respectability politics started here? No wonder they won't go away!

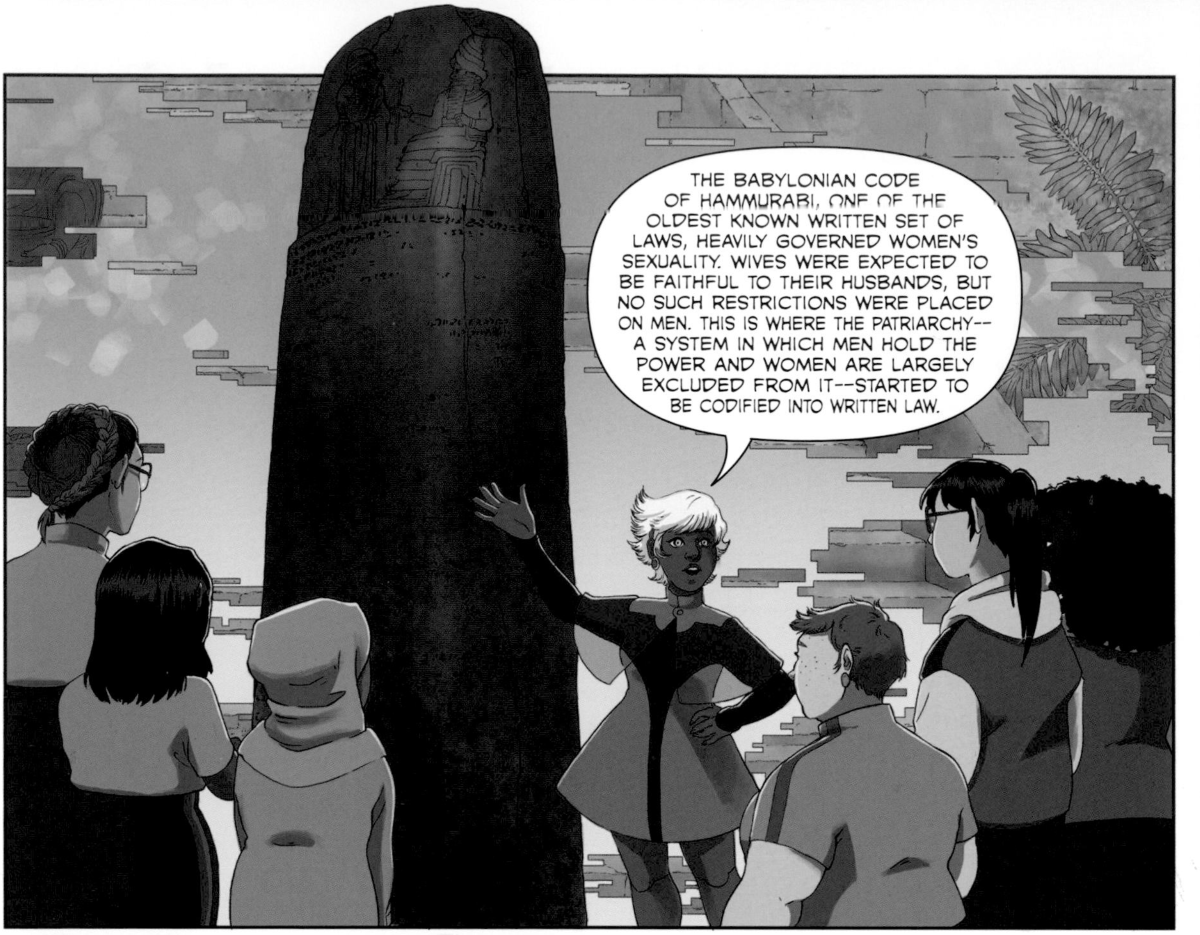
THE BABYLONIAN CODE OF HAMMURABI, ONE OF THE OLDEST KNOWN WRITTEN SET OF LAWS, HEAVILY GOVERNED WOMEN'S SEXUALITY. WIVES WERE EXPECTED TO BE FAITHFUL TO THEIR HUSBANDS, BUT NO SUCH RESTRICTIONS WERE PLACED ON MEN. THIS IS WHERE THE PATRIARCHY--A SYSTEM IN WHICH MEN HOLD THE POWER AND WOMEN ARE LARGELY EXCLUDED FROM IT--STARTED TO BE CODIFIED INTO WRITTEN LAW.

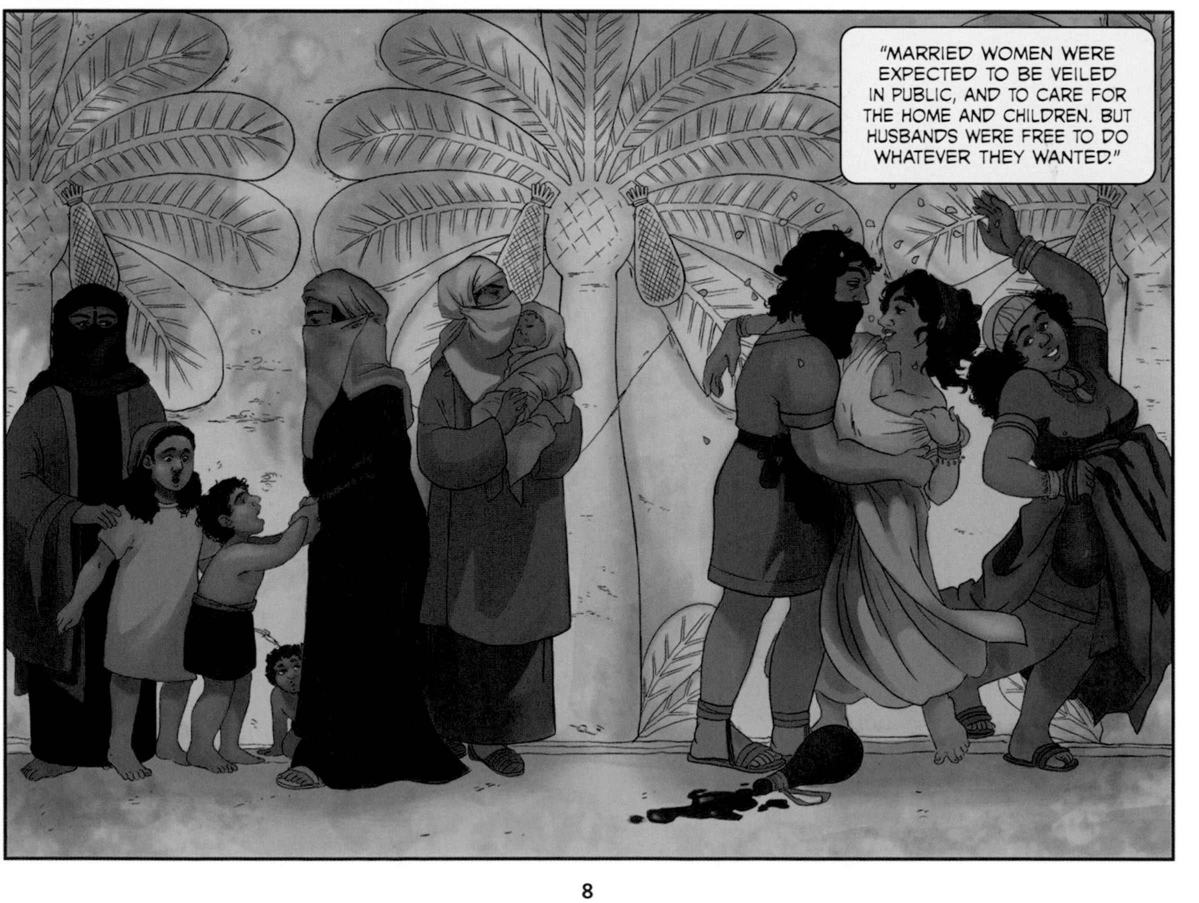
"MARRIED WOMEN WERE EXPECTED TO BE VEILED IN PUBLIC, AND TO CARE FOR THE HOME AND CHILDREN. BUT HUSBANDS WERE FREE TO DO WHATEVER THEY WANTED."

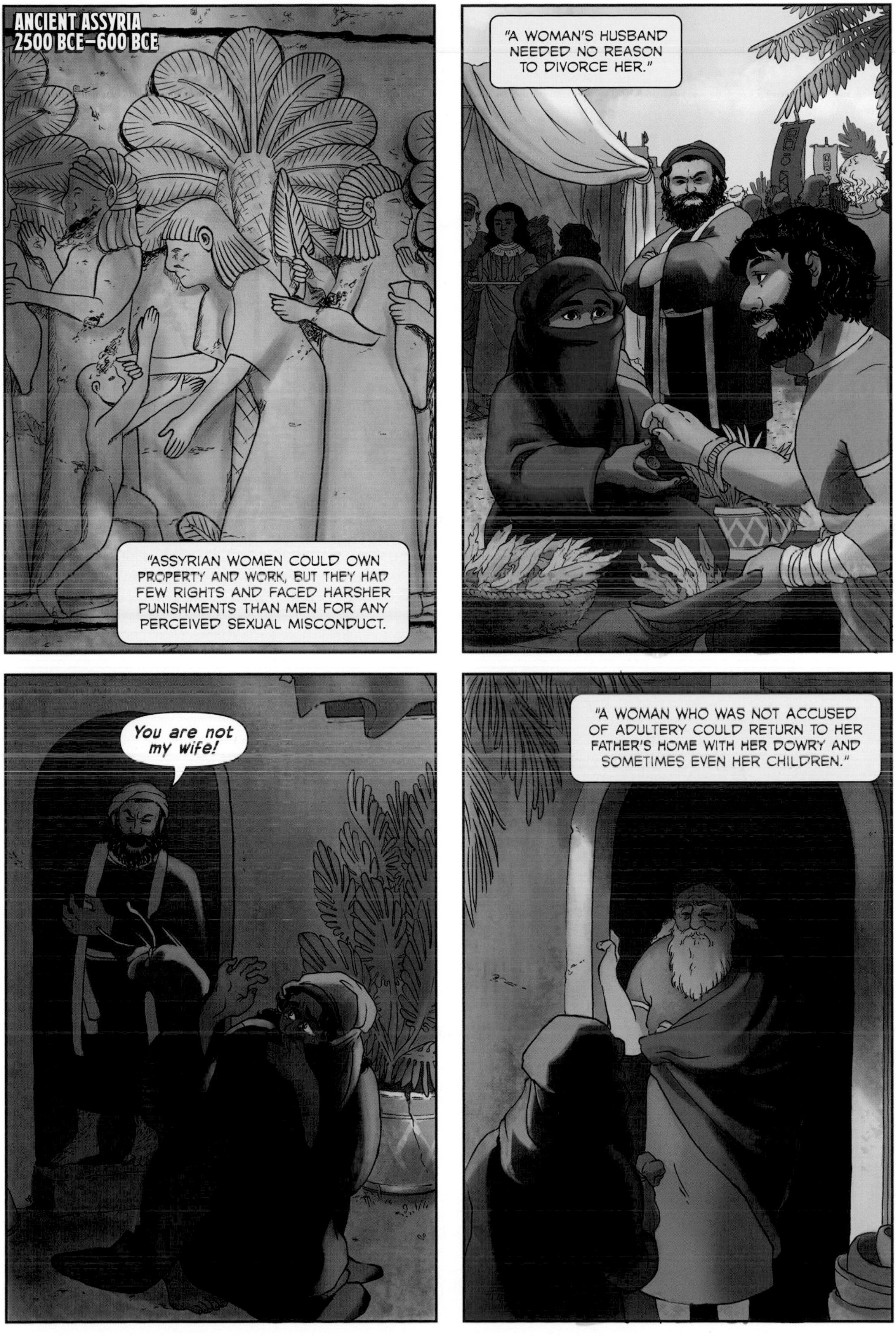
ANCIENT ASSYRIA
2500 BCE–600 BCE
"ASSYRIAN WOMEN COULD OWN PROPERTY AND WORK, BUT THEY HAD FEW RIGHTS AND FACED HARSHER PUNISHMENTS THAN MEN FOR ANY PERCEIVED SEXUAL MISCONDUCT.
"A WOMAN'S HUSBAND NEEDED NO REASON TO DIVORCE HER."
You are not my wife!
"A WOMAN WHO WAS NOT ACCUSED OF ADULTERY COULD RETURN TO HER FATHER'S HOME WITH HER DOWRY AND SOMETIMES EVEN HER CHILDREN."

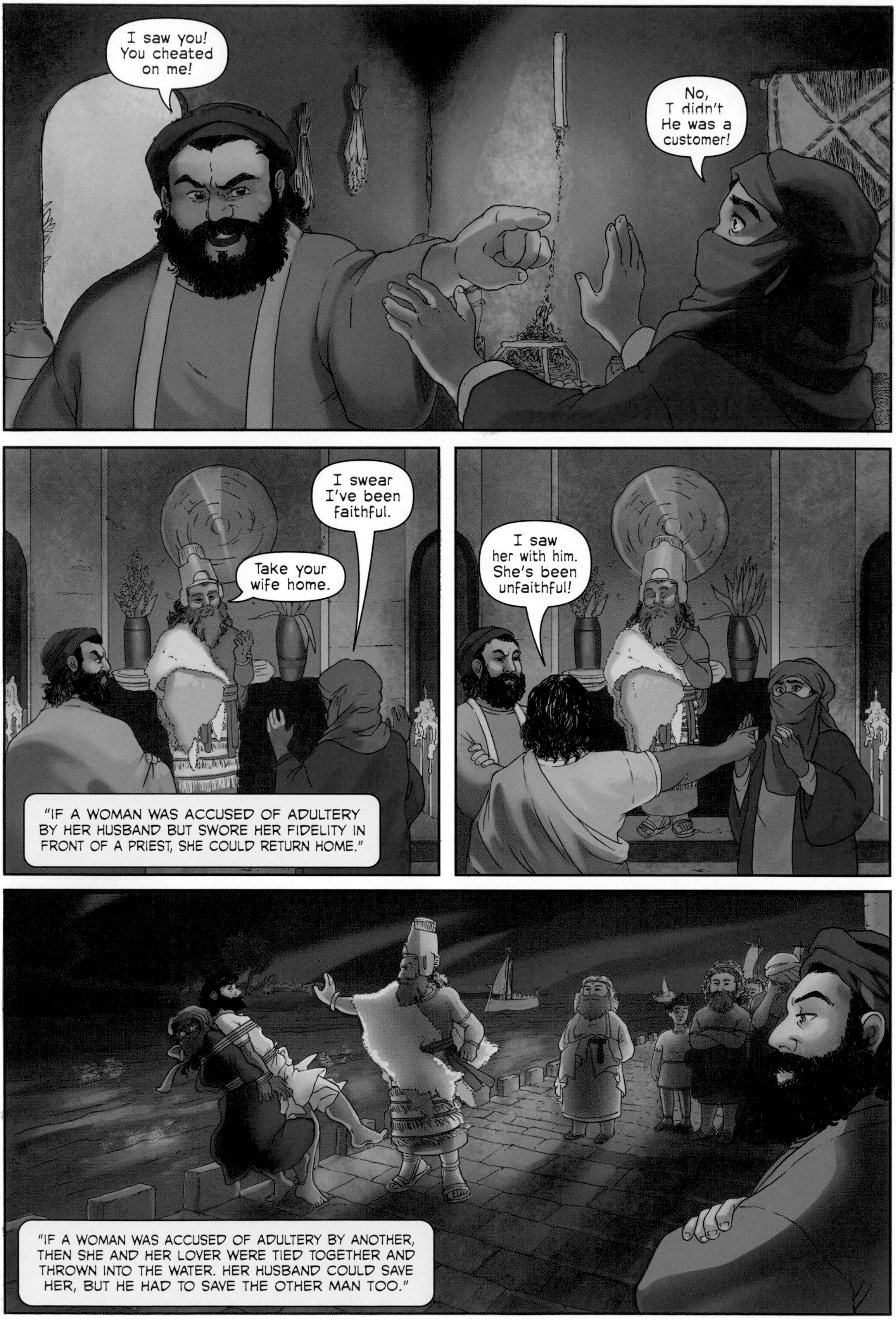
I saw you! You cheated on me!
No, I didn't He was a customer!
I swear I've been faithful.
Take your wife home.
"IF A WOMAN WAS ACCUSED OF ADULTERY BY HER HUSBAND BUT SWORE HER FIDELITY IN FRONT OF A PRIEST, SHE COULD RETURN HOME."
I saw her with him. She's been unfaithful!
"IF A WOMAN WAS ACCUSED OF ADULTERY BY ANOTHER, THEN SHE AND HER LOVER WERE TIED TOGETHER AND THROWN INTO THE WATER. HER HUSBAND COULD SAVE HER, BUT HE HAD TO SAVE THE OTHER MAN TOO."

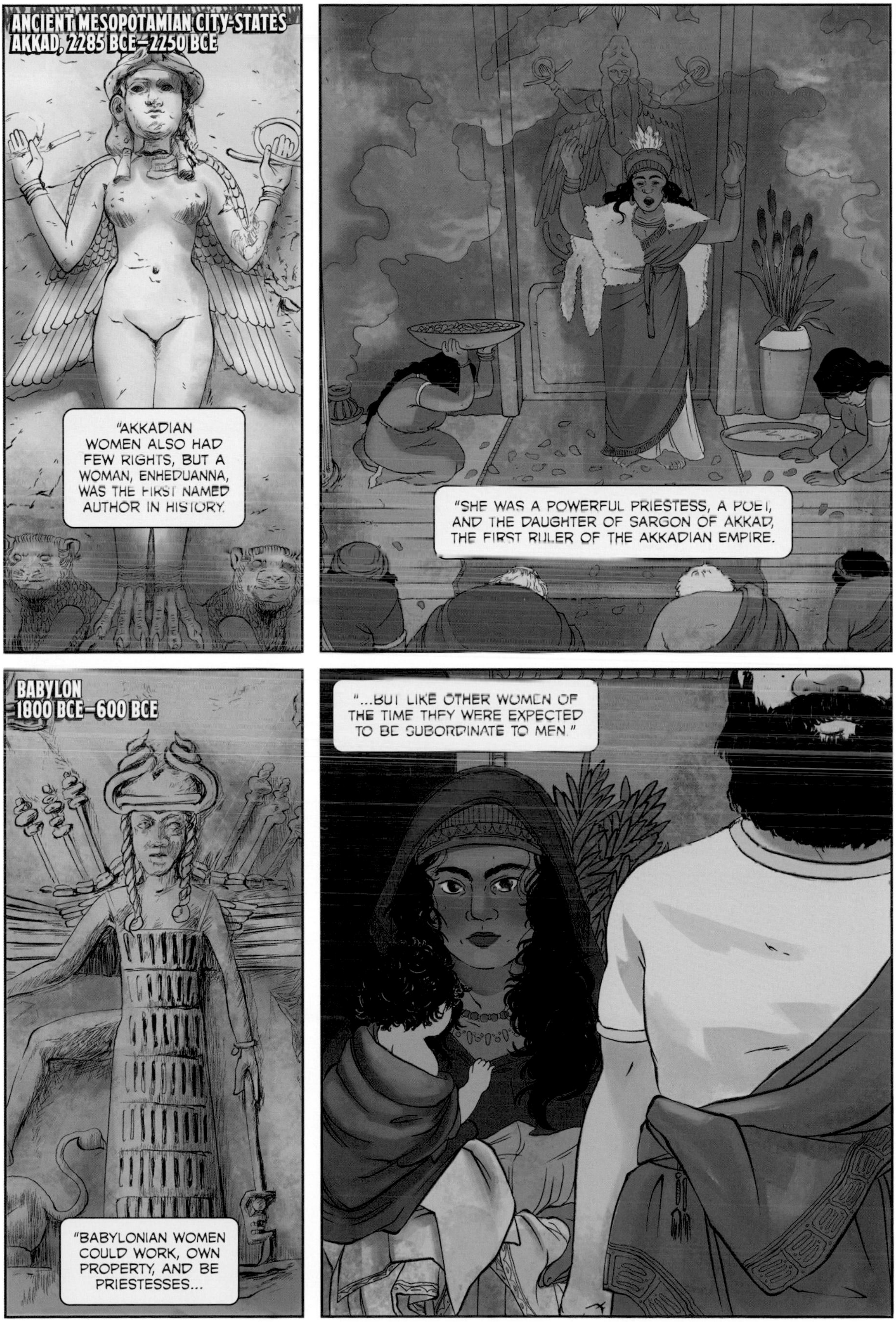
ANCIENT MESOPOTAMIAN CITY-STATES
AKKAD, 2285 BCE–2250 BCE
"AKKADIAN WOMEN ALSO HAD FEW RIGHTS, BUT A WOMAN, ENHEDUANNA, WAS THE FIRST NAMED AUTHOR IN HISTORY.
"SHE WAS A POWERFUL PRIESTESS, A POET, AND THE DAUGHTER OF SARGON OF AKKAD, THE FIRST RULER OF THE AKKADIAN EMPIRE.
BABYLON
1800 BCE–600 BCE
"BABYLONIAN WOMEN COULD WORK, OWN PROPERTY, AND BE PRIESTESSES...
"...BUT LIKE OTHER WOMEN OF THE TIME THEY WERE EXPECTED TO BE SUBORDINATE TO MEN."

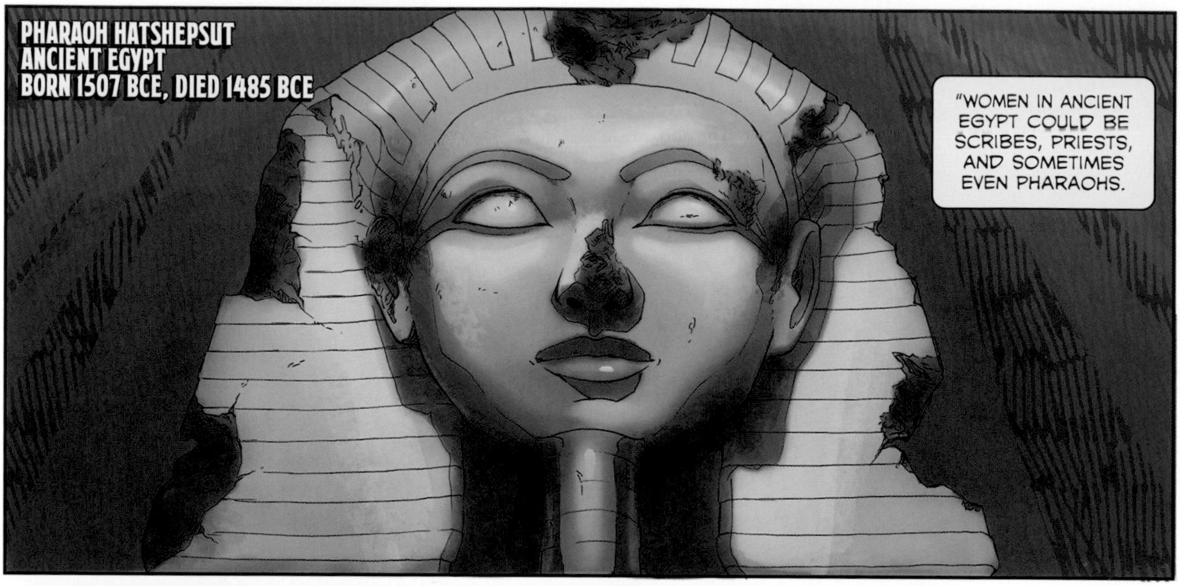
PHARAOH HATSHEPSUT
ANCIENT EGYPT
BORN 1507 BCE, DIED 1485 BCE
"WOMEN IN ANCIENT EGYPT COULD BE SCRIBES, PRIESTS, AND SOMETIMES EVEN PHARAOHS.

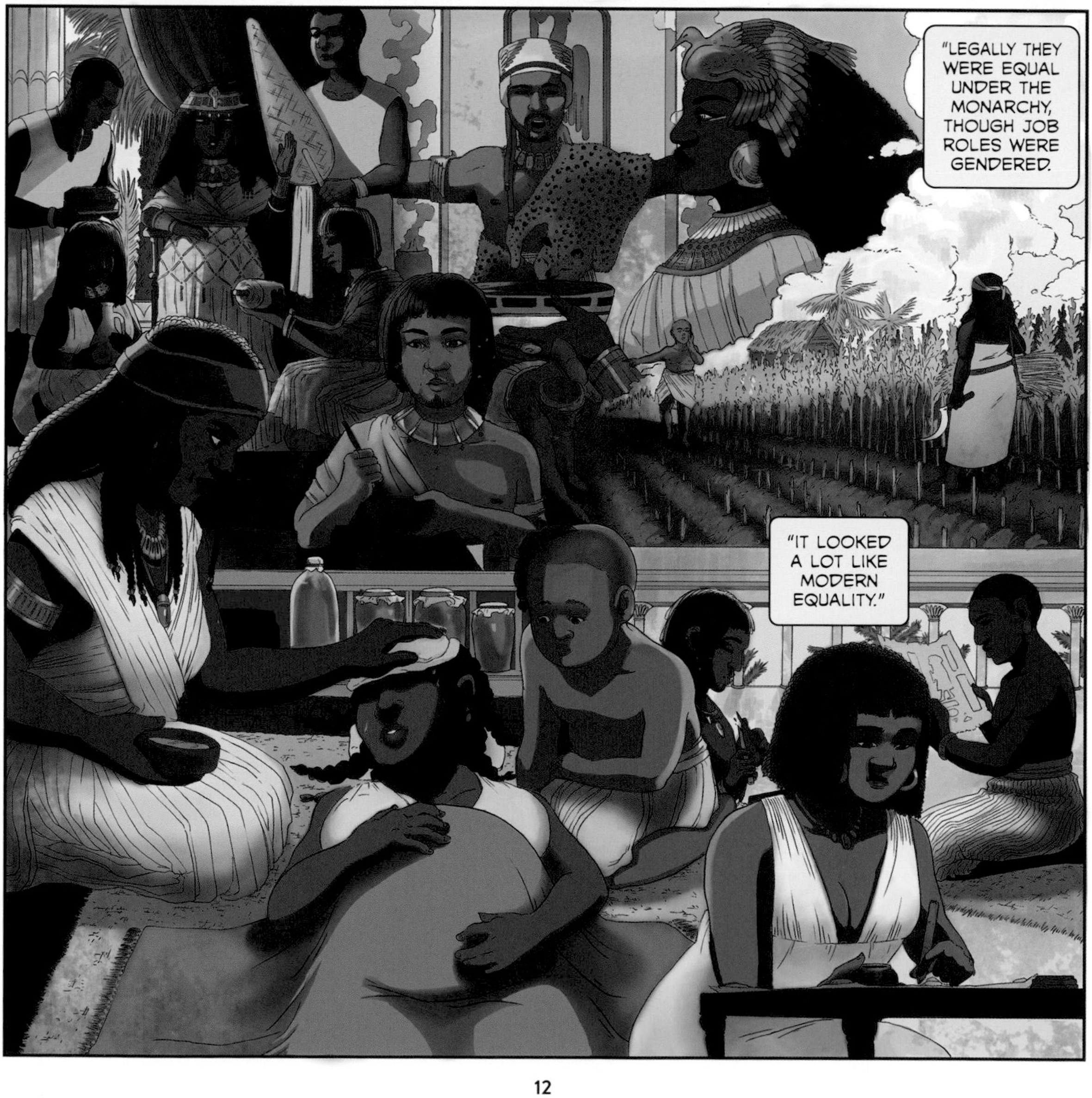
"LEGALLY THEY WERE EQUAL UNDER THE MONARCHY, THOUGH JOB ROLES WERE GENDERED.
"IT LOOKED A LOT LIKE MODERN EQUALITY."

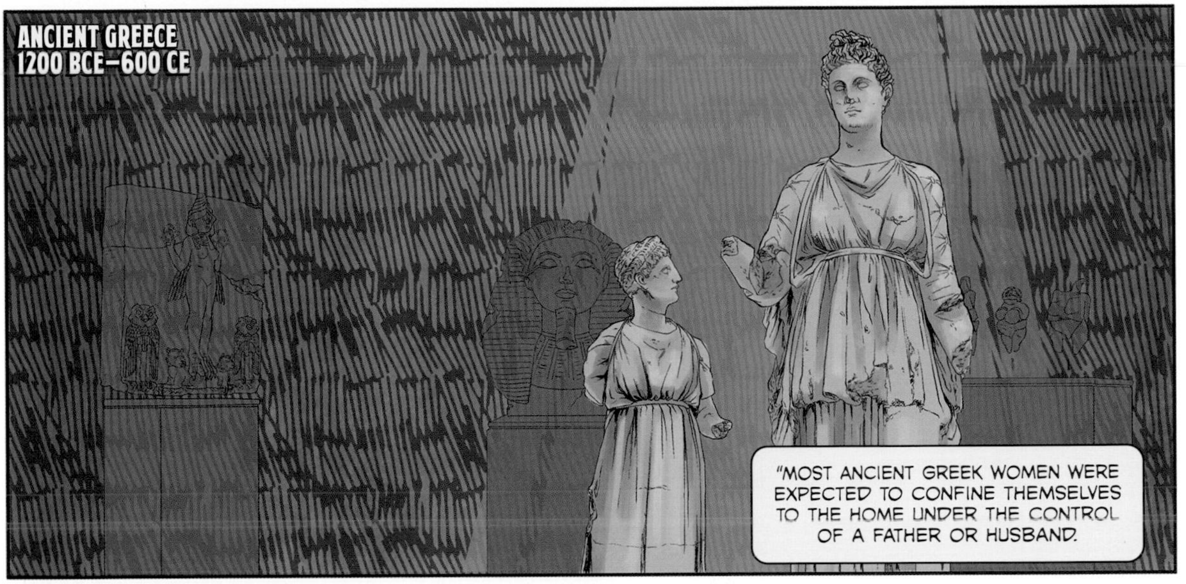
ANCIENT GREECE
1200 BCE–600 CE
"MOST ANCIENT GREEK WOMEN WERE EXPECTED TO CONFINE THEMSELVES TO THE HOME UNDER THE CONTROL OF A FATHER OR HUSBAND.

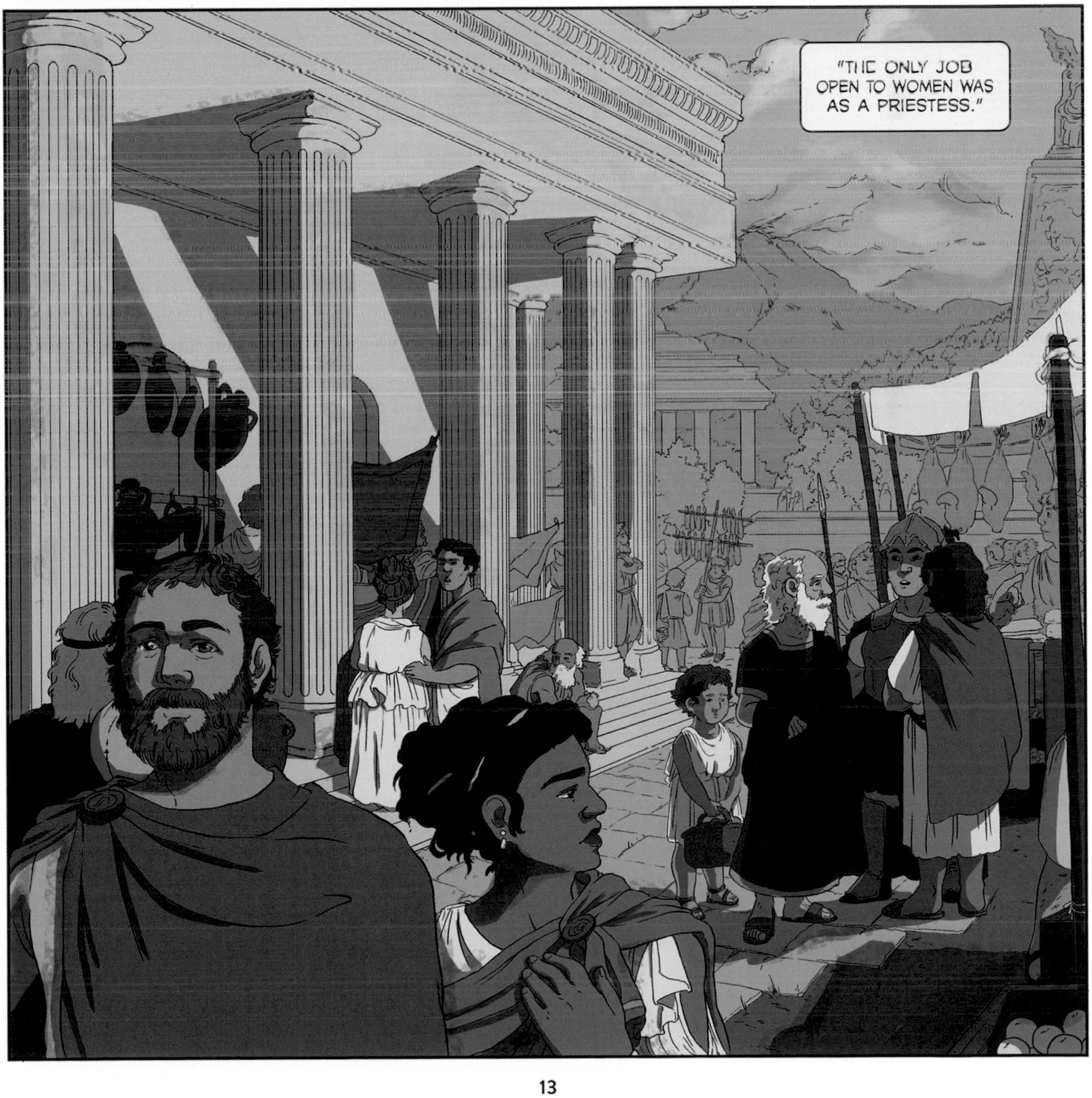
"THE ONLY JOB OPEN TO WOMEN WAS AS A PRIESTESS."

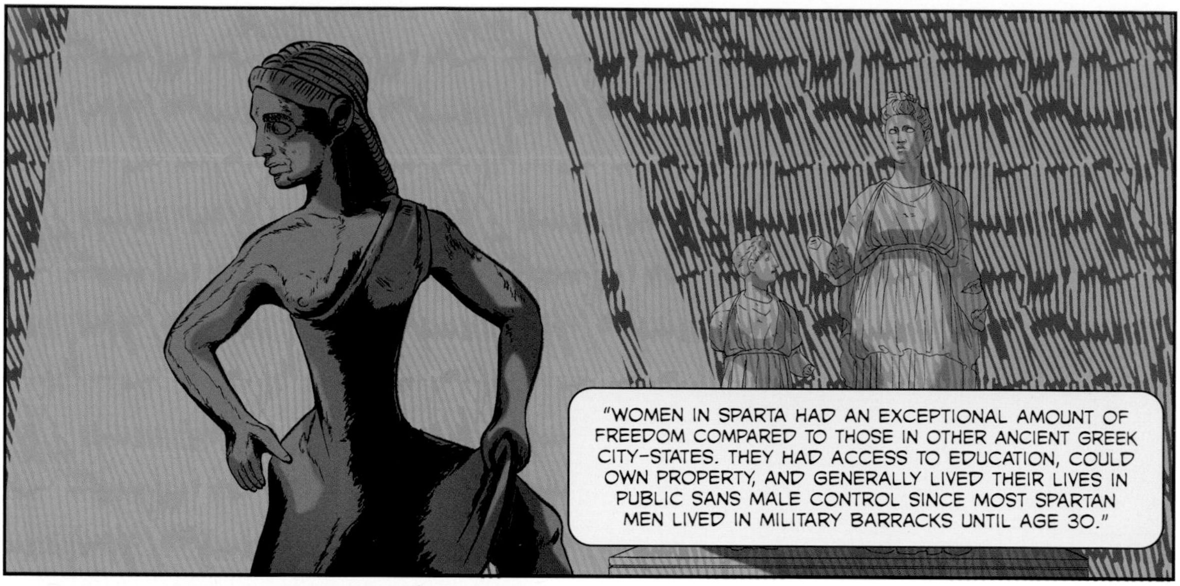
"WOMEN IN SPARTA HAD AN EXCEPTIONAL AMOUNT OF FREEDOM COMPARED TO THOSE IN OTHER ANCIENT GREEK CITY-STATES. THEY HAD ACCESS TO EDUCATION, COULD OWN PROPERTY, AND GENERALLY LIVED THEIR LIVES IN PUBLIC SANS MALE CONTROL SINCE MOST SPARTAN MEN LIVED IN MILITARY BARRACKS UNTIL AGE 30."

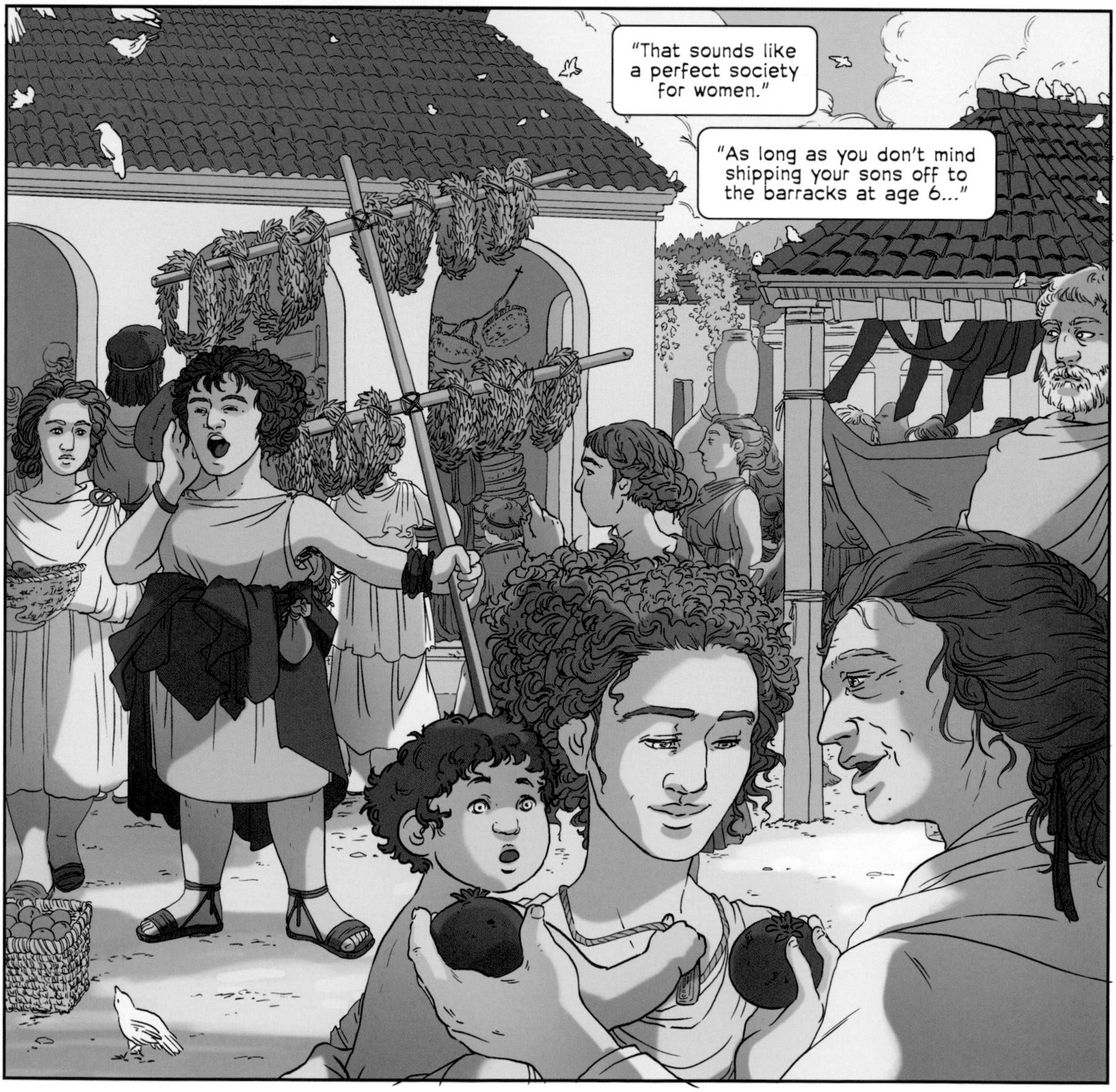
"That sounds like a perfect society for women."
"As long as you don't mind shipping your sons off to the barracks at age 6..."

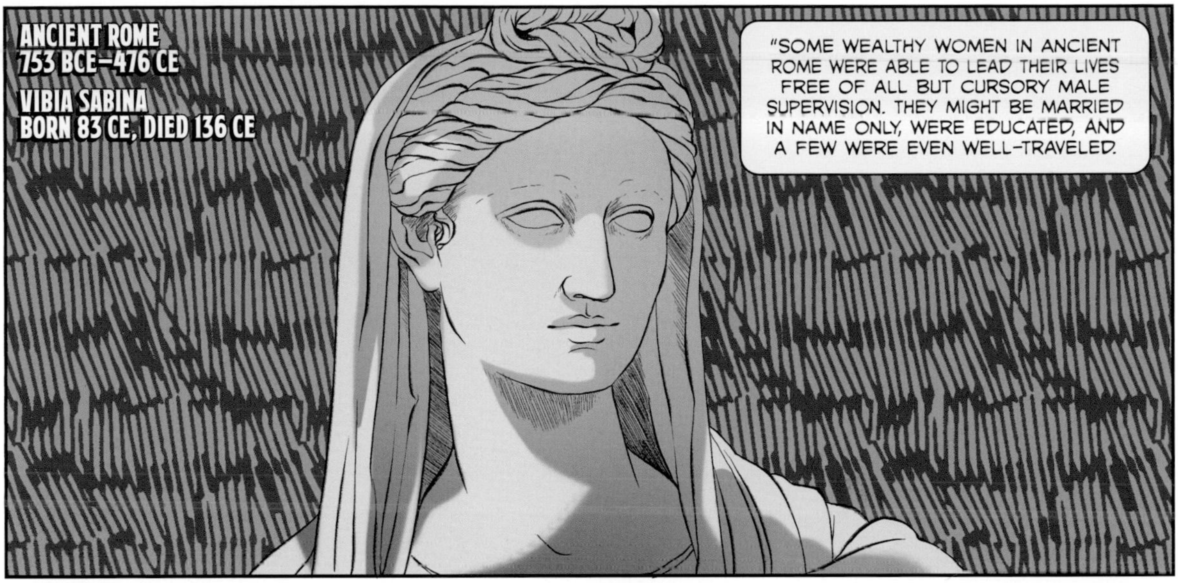
ANCIENT ROME
753 BCE–476 CE
VIBIA SABINA
BORN 83 CE, DIED 136 CE
"SOME WEALTHY WOMEN IN ANCIENT ROME WERE ABLE TO LEAD THEIR LIVES FREE OF ALL BUT CURSORY MALE SUPERVISION. THEY MIGHT BE MARRIED IN NAME ONLY, WERE EDUCATED, AND A FEW WERE EVEN WELL-TRAVELED.

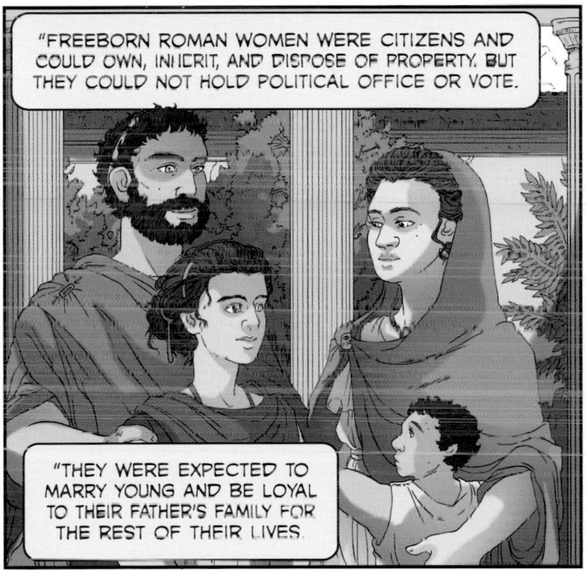
"FREEBORN ROMAN WOMEN WERE CITIZENS AND COULD OWN, INHERIT, AND DISPOSE OF PROPERTY. BUT THEY COULD NOT HOLD POLITICAL OFFICE OR VOTE.
"THEY WERE EXPECTED TO MARRY YOUNG AND BE LOYAL TO THEIR FATHER'S FAMILY FOR THE REST OF THEIR LIVES.

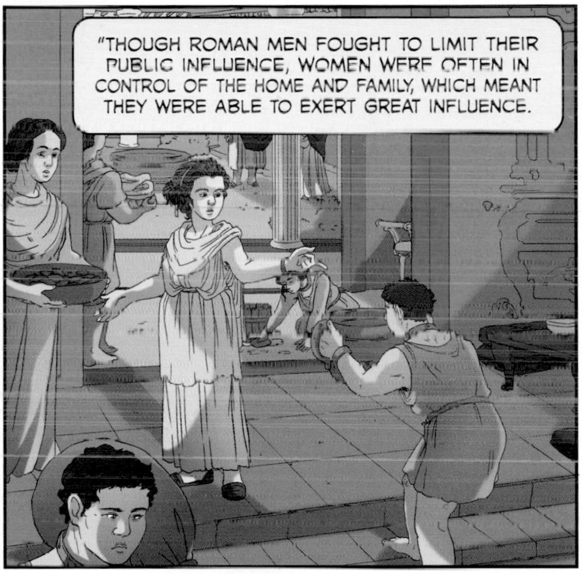
"THOUGH ROMAN MEN FOUGHT TO LIMIT THEIR PUBLIC INFLUENCE, WOMEN WERE OFTEN IN CONTROL OF THE HOME AND FAMILY, WHICH MEANT THEY WERE ABLE TO EXERT GREAT INFLUENCE.

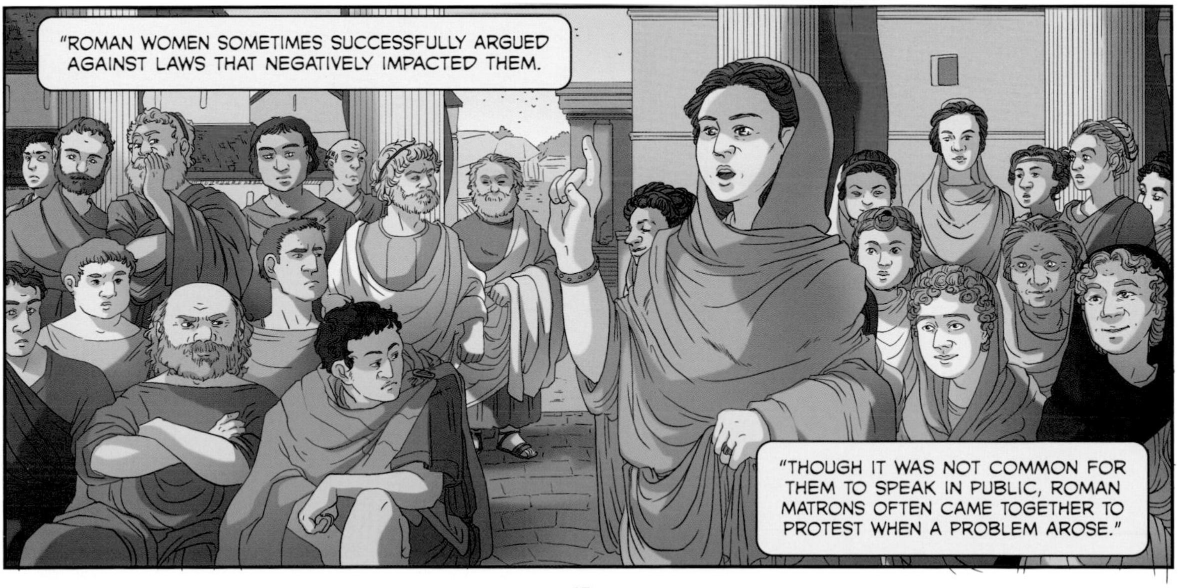
"ROMAN WOMEN SOMETIMES SUCCESSFULLY ARGUED AGAINST LAWS THAT NEGATIVELY IMPACTED THEM.
"THOUGH IT WAS NOT COMMON FOR THEM TO SPEAK IN PUBLIC, ROMAN MATRONS OFTEN CAME TOGETHER TO PROTEST WHEN A PROBLEM AROSE."

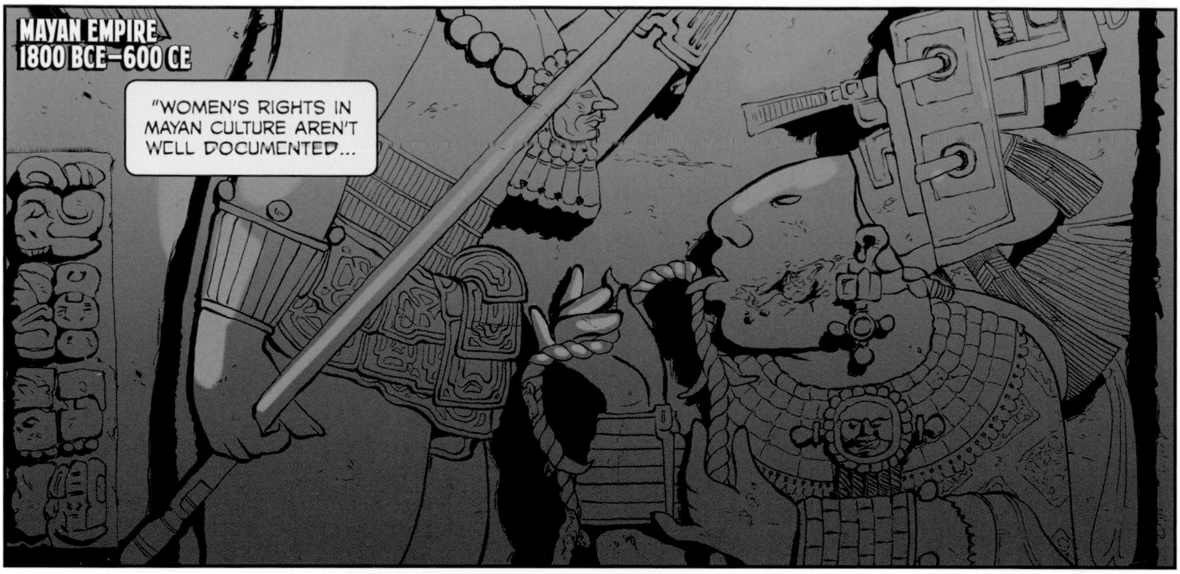
MAYAN EMPIRE
1800 BCE–600 CE
"WOMEN'S RIGHTS IN MAYAN CULTURE AREN'T WELL DOCUMENTED...

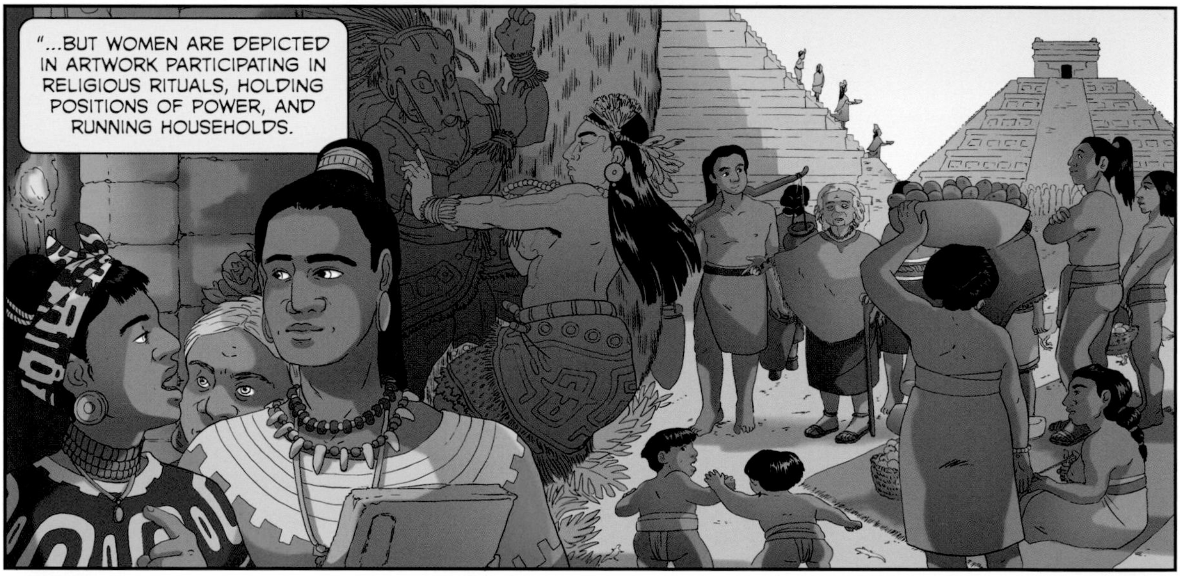
"...BUT WOMEN ARE DEPICTED IN ARTWORK PARTICIPATING IN RELIGIOUS RITUALS, HOLDING POSITIONS OF POWER, AND RUNNING HOUSEHOLDS.

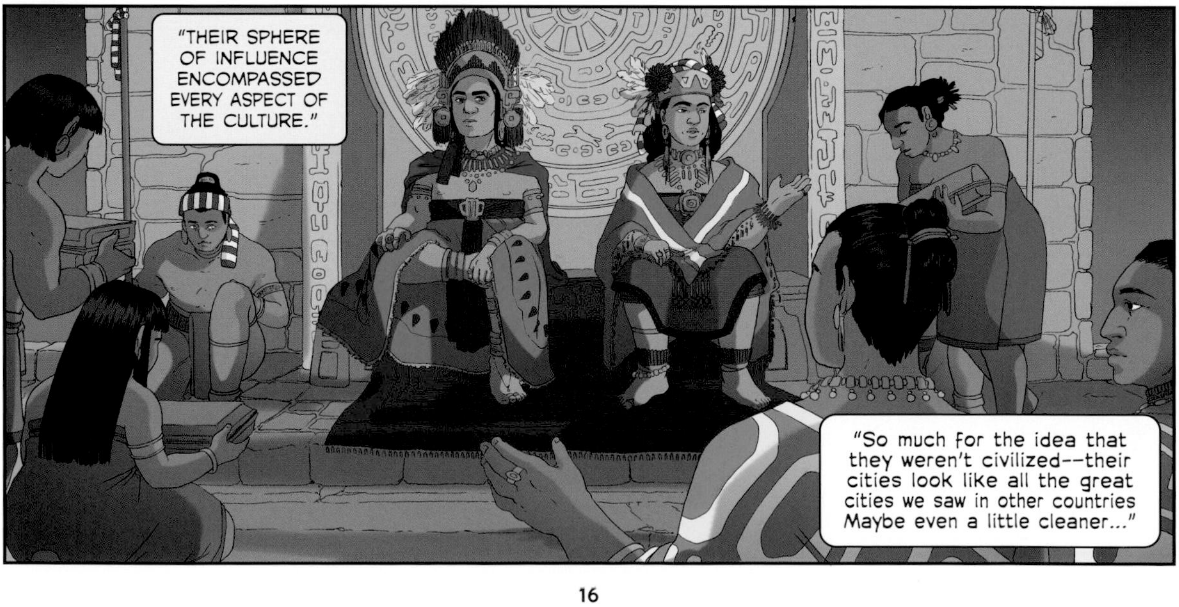
"THEIR SPHERE OF INFLUENCE ENCOMPASSED EVERY ASPECT OF THE CULTURE."
"So much for the idea that they weren't civilized--their cities look like all the great cities we saw in other countries Maybe even a little cleaner..."

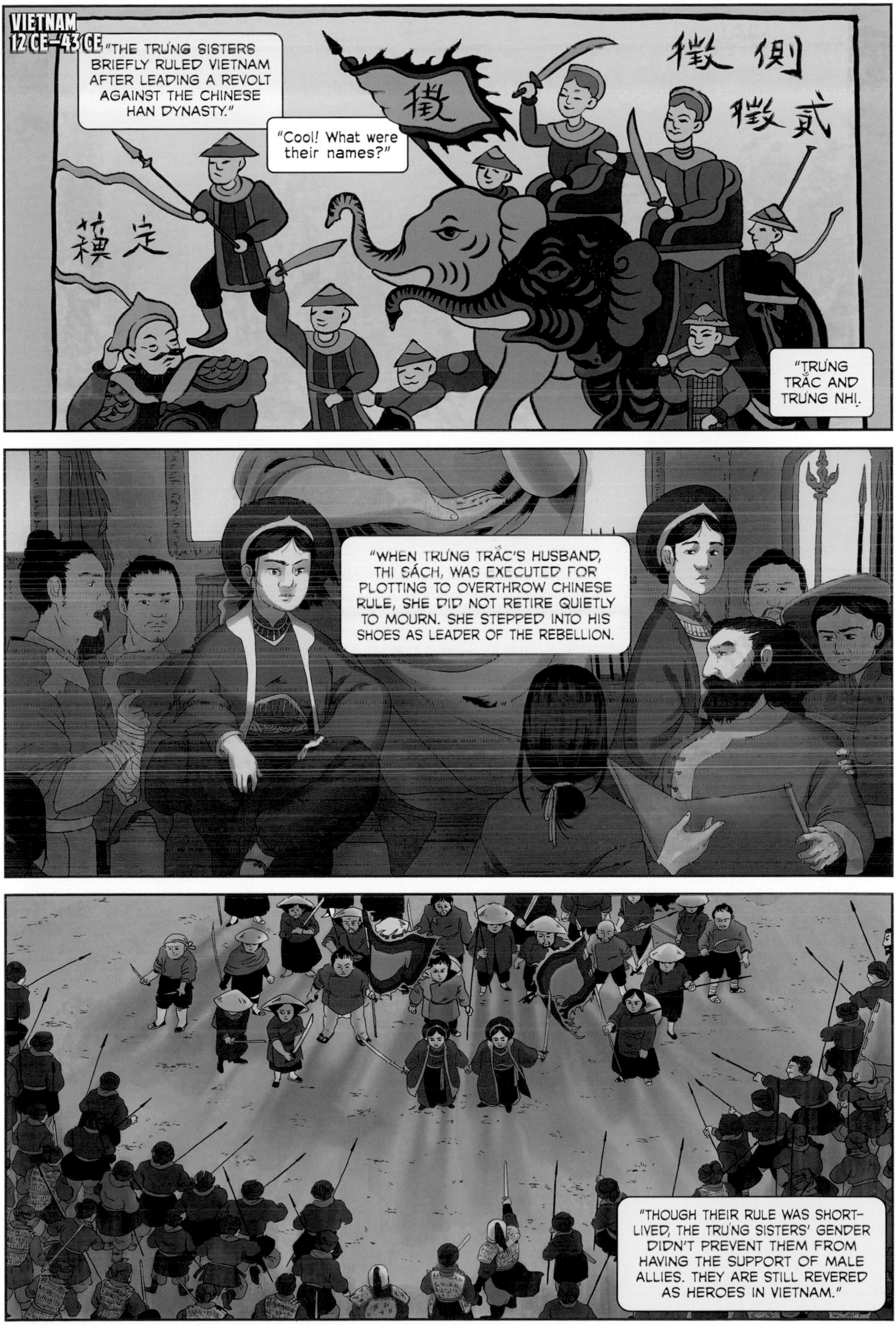
VIETNAM
12 CE–43 CE
"THE TRƯNG SISTERS BRIEFLY RULED VIETNAM AFTER LEADING A REVOLT AGAINST THE CHINESE HAN DYNASTY."
"Cool! What were their names?"
"TRƯNG TRẮC AND TRƯNG NHỊ.
"WHEN TRƯNG TRẮC'S HUSBAND, THI SÁCH, WAS EXECUTED FOR PLOTTING TO OVERTHROW CHINESE RULE, SHE DID NOT RETIRE QUIETLY TO MOURN. SHE STEPPED INTO HIS SHOES AS LEADER OF THE REBELLION.
"THOUGH THEIR RULE WAS SHORT-LIVED, THE TRƯNG SISTERS' GENDER DIDN'T PREVENT THEM FROM HAVING THE SUPPORT OF MALE ALLIES. THEY ARE STILL REVERED AS HEROES IN VIETNAM."

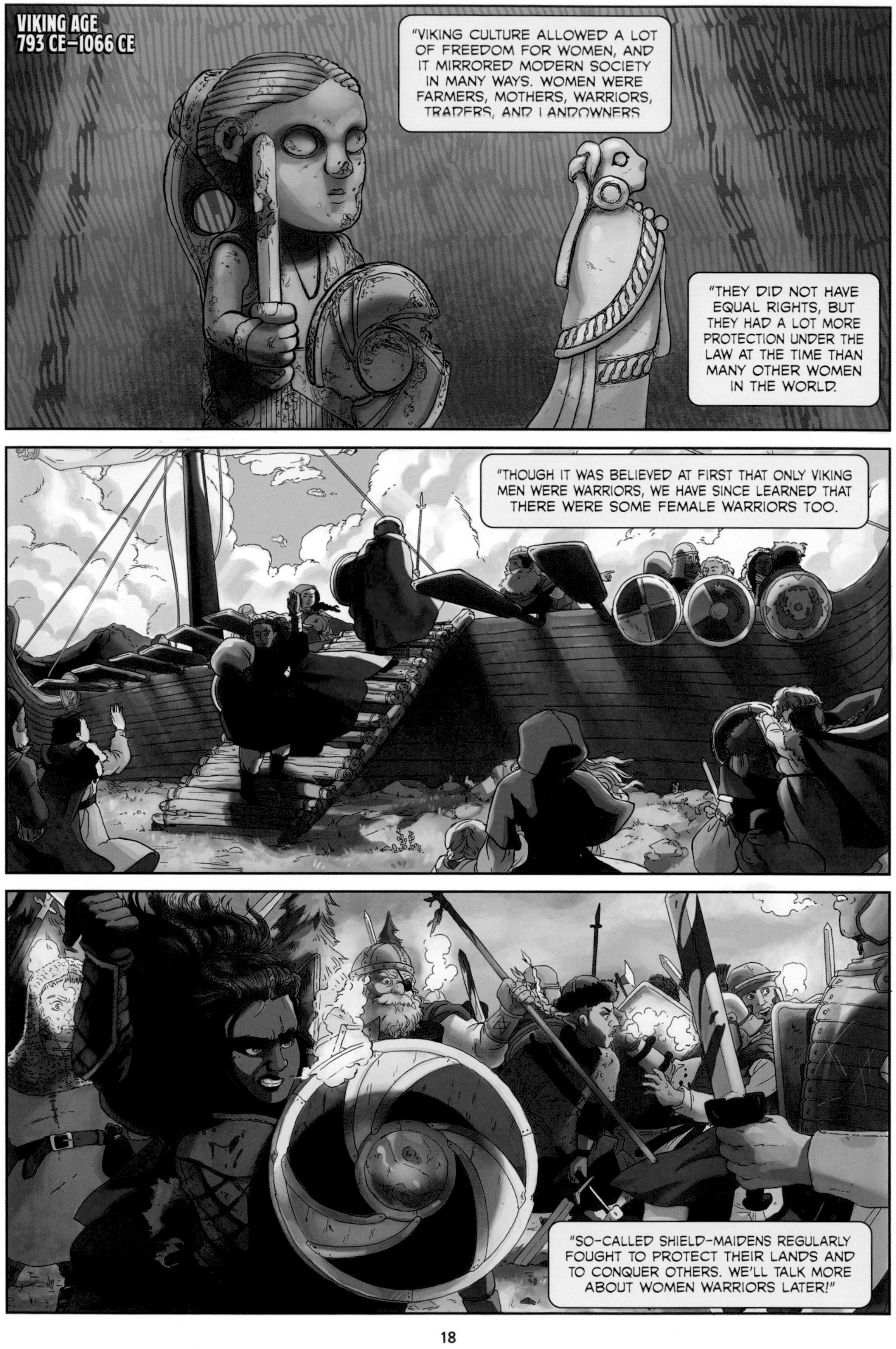
VIKING AGE
793 CE–1066 CE
"VIKING CULTURE ALLOWED A LOT OF FREEDOM FOR WOMEN, AND IT MIRRORED MODERN SOCIETY IN MANY WAYS. WOMEN WERE FARMERS, MOTHERS, WARRIORS, TRADERS, AND LANDOWNERS
"THEY DID NOT HAVE EQUAL RIGHTS, BUT THEY HAD A LOT MORE PROTECTION UNDER THE LAW AT THE TIME THAN MANY OTHER WOMEN IN THE WORLD.
"THOUGH IT WAS BELIEVED AT FIRST THAT ONLY VIKING MEN WERE WARRIORS, WE HAVE SINCE LEARNED THAT THERE WERE SOME FEMALE WARRIORS TOO.
"SO-CALLED SHIELD-MAIDENS REGULARLY FOUGHT TO PROTECT THEIR LANDS AND TO CONQUER OTHERS. WE'LL TALK MORE ABOUT WOMEN WARRIORS LATER!"

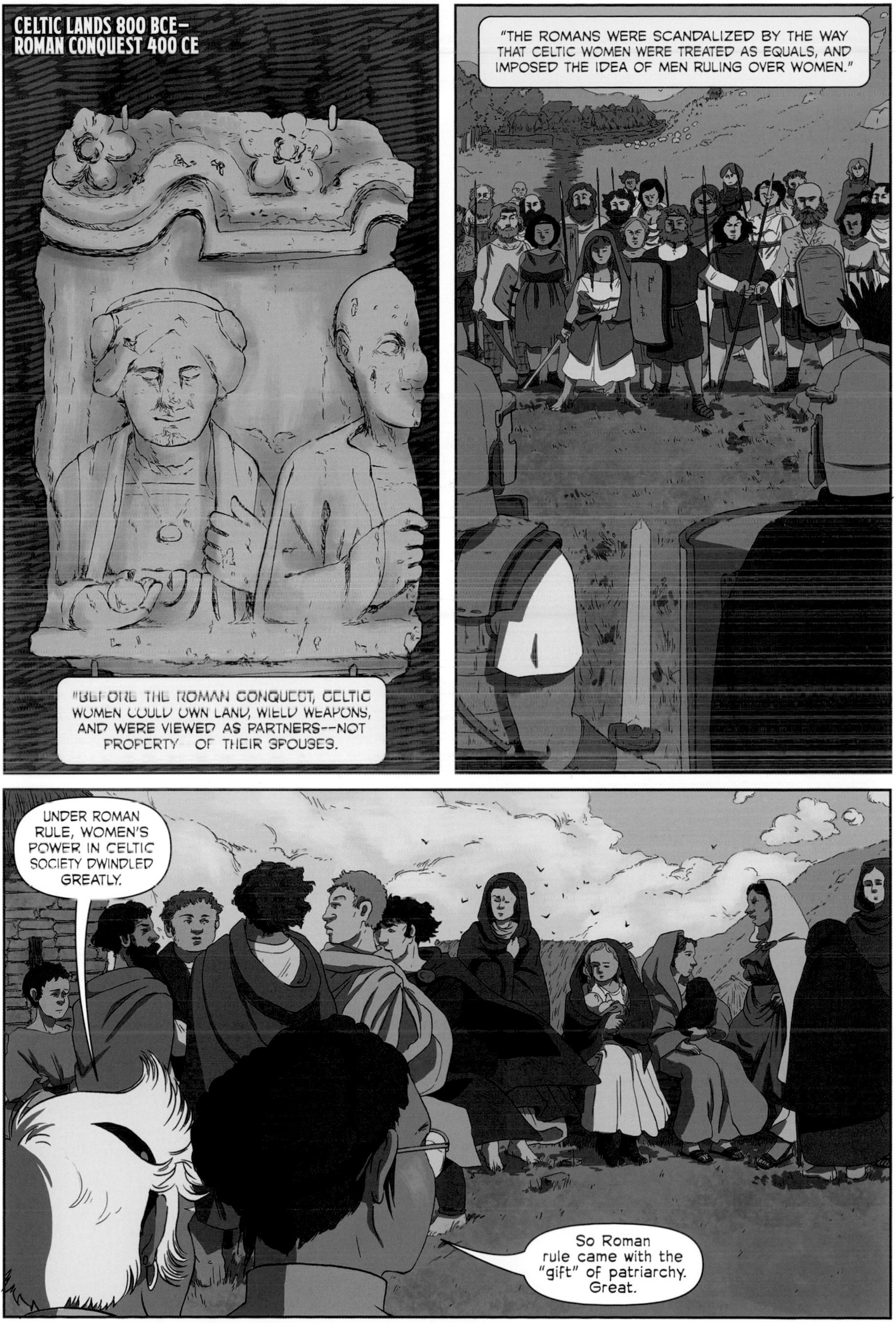
CELTIC LANDS 800 BCE–ROMAN CONQUEST 400 CE
"BEFORE THE ROMAN CONQUEST, CELTIC WOMEN COULD OWN LAND, WIELD WEAPONS, AND WERE VIEWED AS PARTNERS--NOT PROPERTY OF THEIR SPOUSES.
"THE ROMANS WERE SCANDALIZED BY THE WAY THAT CELTIC WOMEN WERE TREATED AS EQUALS, AND IMPOSED THE IDEA OF MEN RULING OVER WOMEN."
UNDER ROMAN RULE, WOMEN'S POWER IN CELTIC SOCIETY DWINDLED GREATLY.
So Roman rule came with the "gift" of patriarchy. Great.

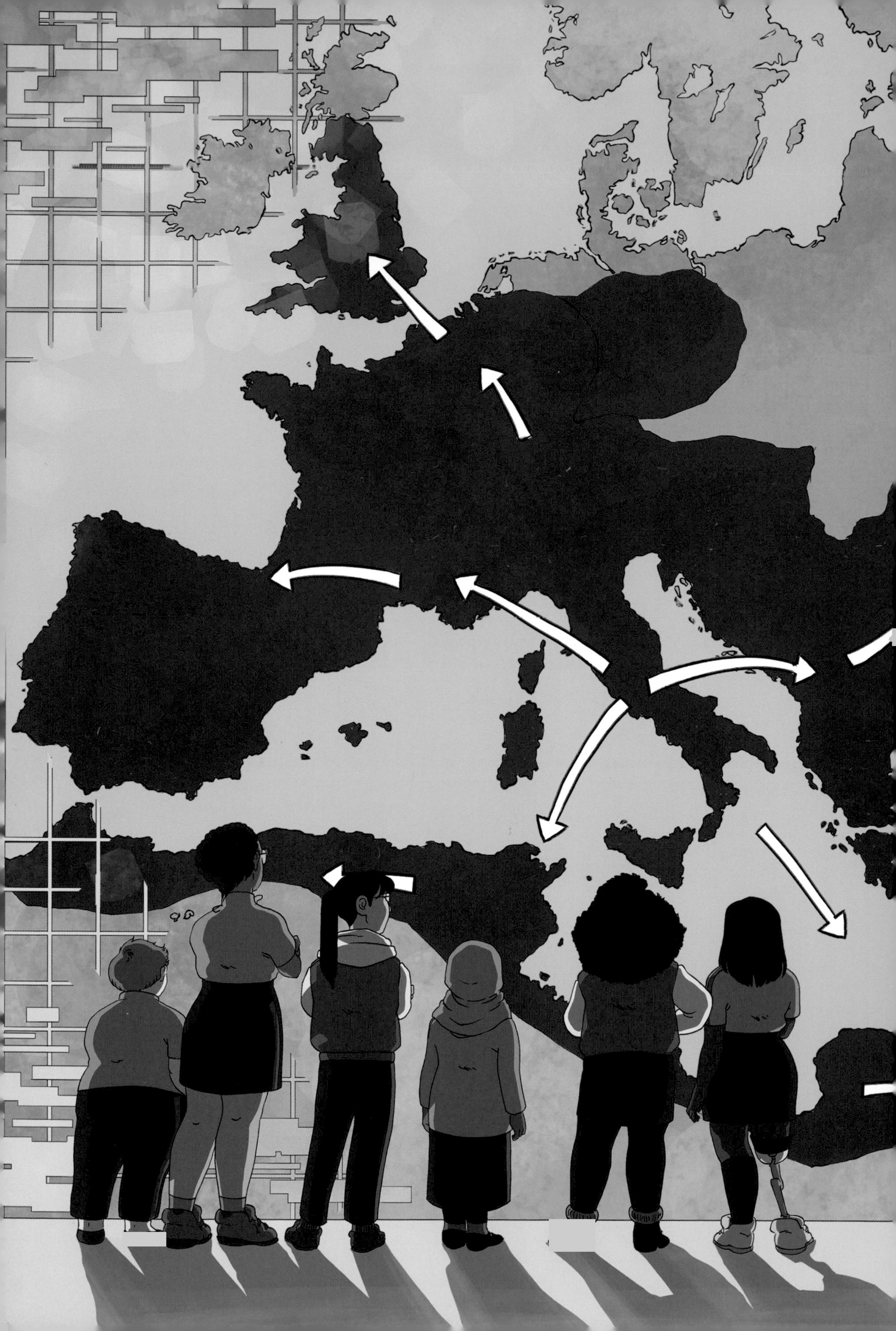

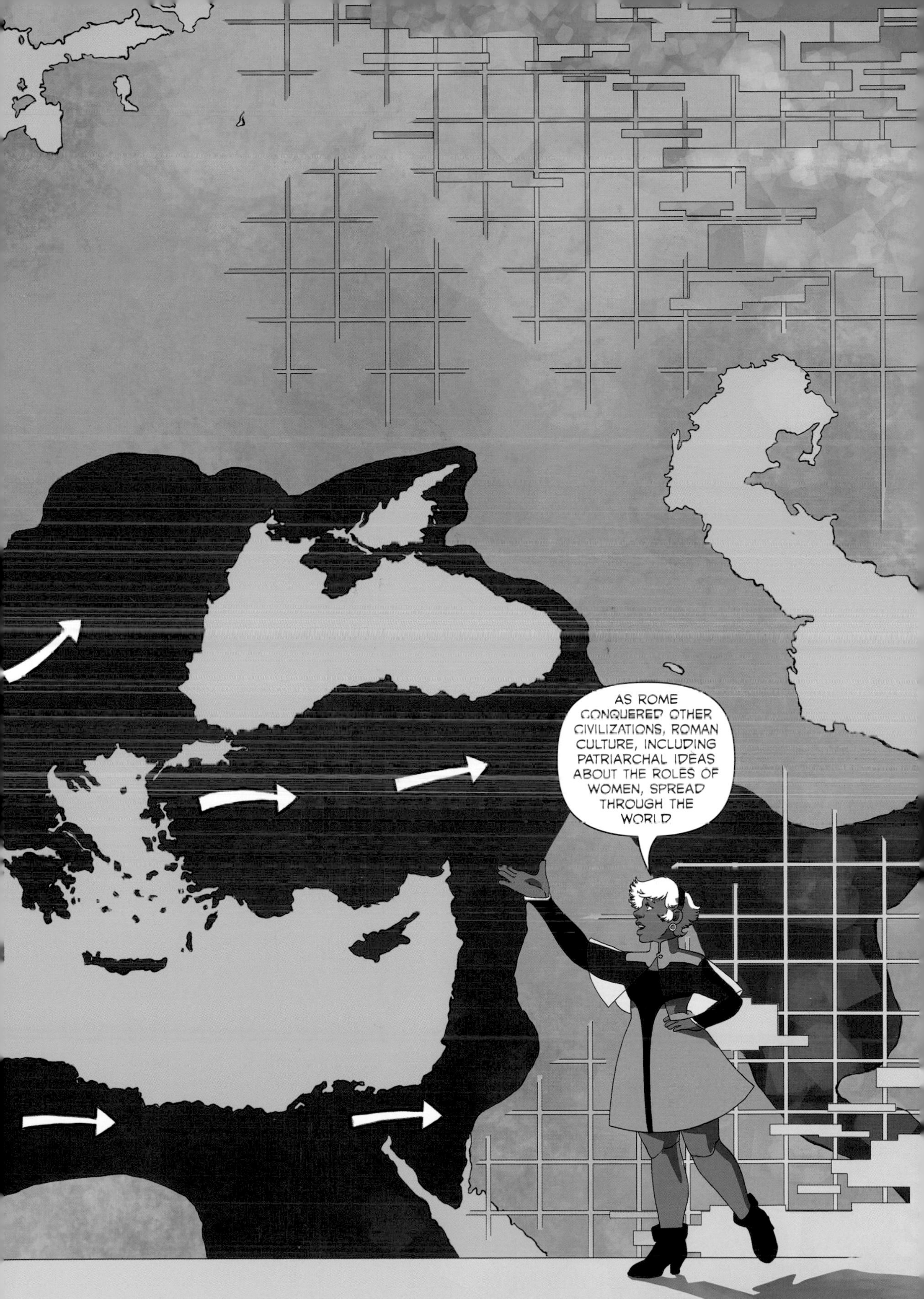
AS ROME CONQUERED OTHER CIVILIZATIONS, ROMAN CULTURE, INCLUDING PATRIARCHAL IDEAS ABOUT THE ROLES OF WOMEN, SPREAD THROUGH THE WORLD

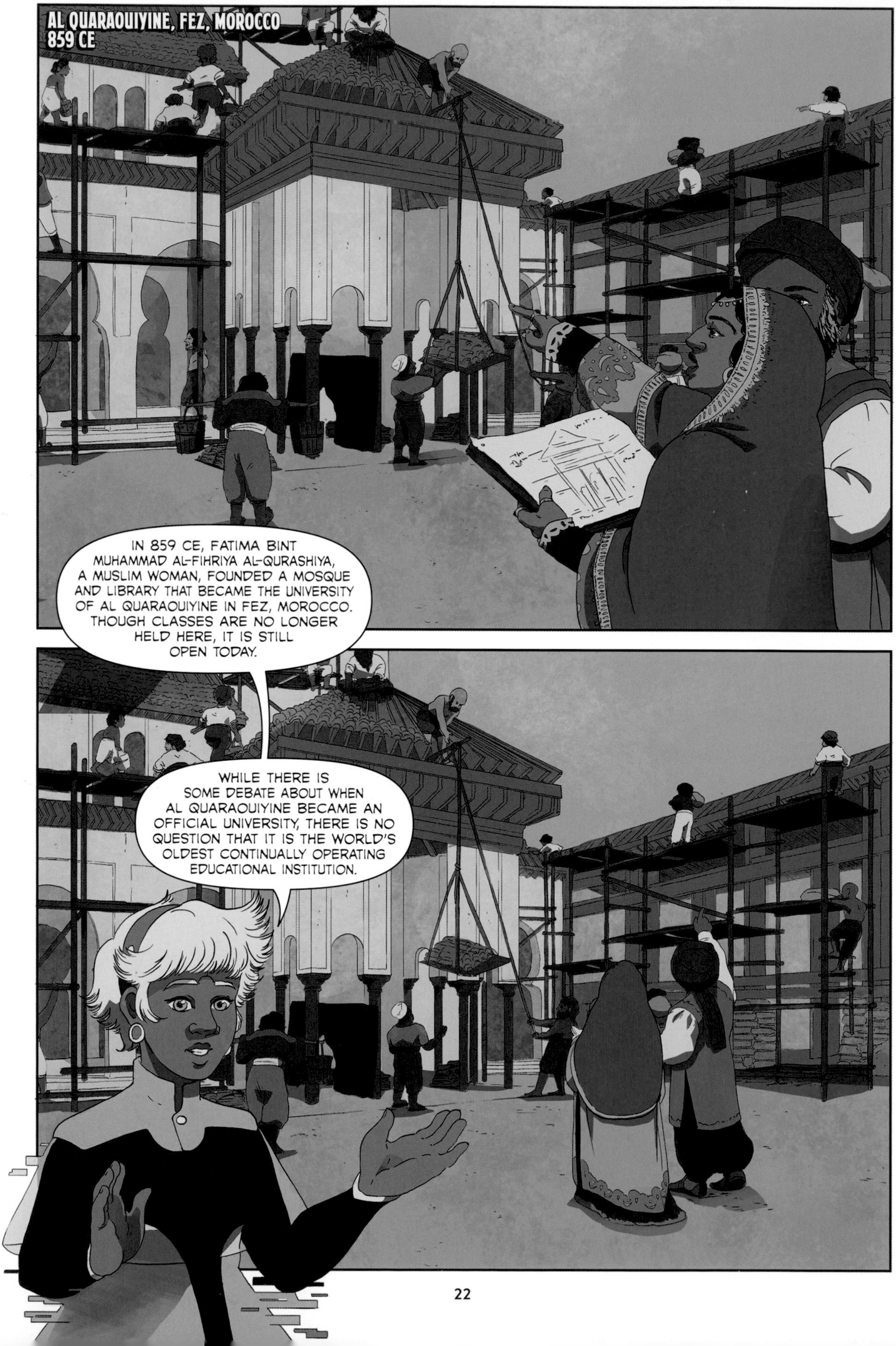
AL QUARAOUIYINE, FEZ, MOROCCO
859 CE
IN 859 CE, FATIMA BINT MUHAMMAD AL-FIHRIYA AL-QURASHIYA, A MUSLIM WOMAN, FOUNDED A MOSQUE AND LIBRARY THAT BECAME THE UNIVERSITY OF AL QUARAOUIYINE IN FEZ, MOROCCO. THOUGH CLASSES ARE NO LONGER HELD HERE, IT IS STILL OPEN TODAY.
WHILE THERE IS SOME DEBATE ABOUT WHEN AL QUARAOUIYINE BECAME AN OFFICIAL UNIVERSITY, THERE IS NO QUESTION THAT IT IS THE WORLD'S OLDEST CONTINUALLY OPERATING EDUCATIONAL INSTITUTION.

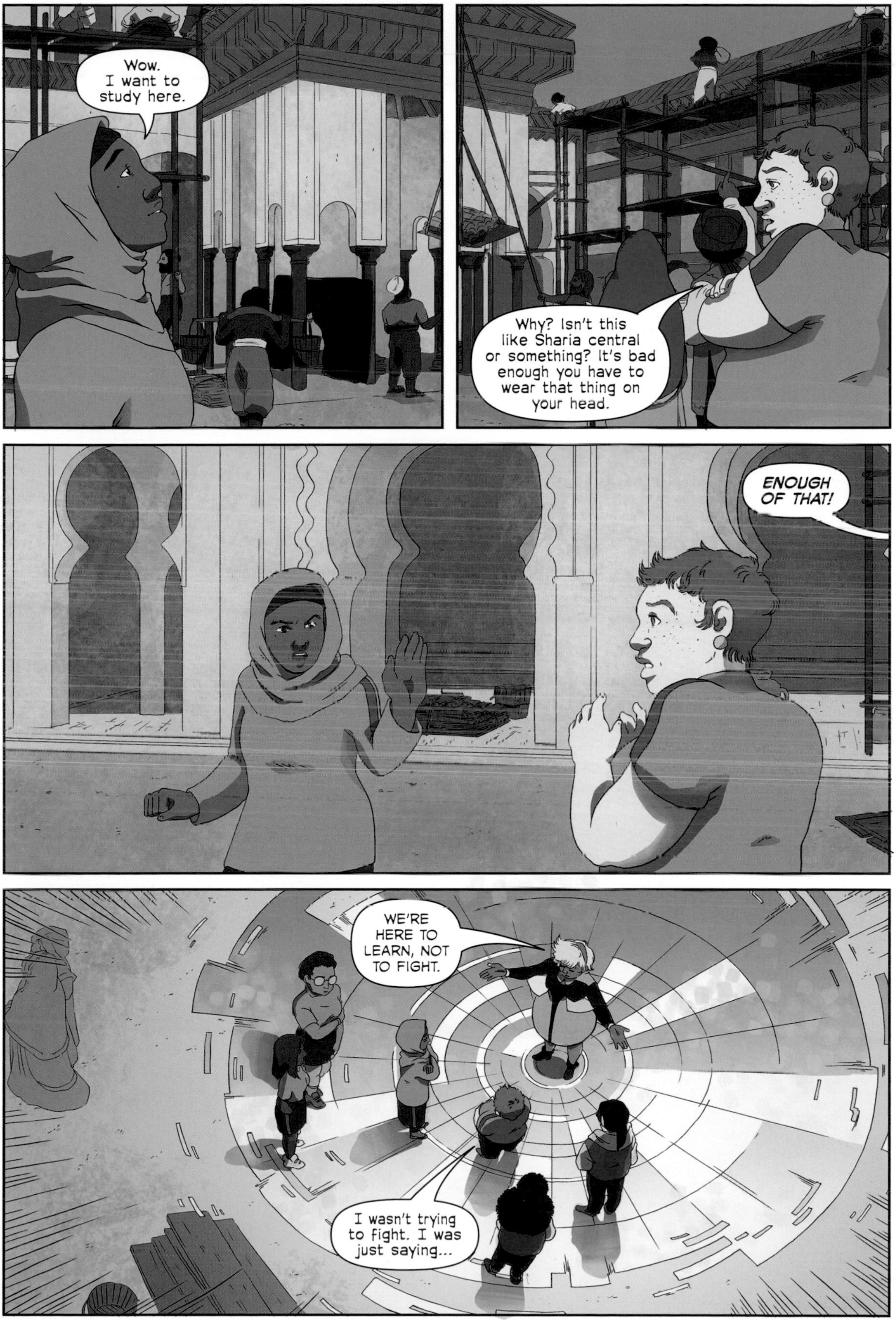
Wow. I want to study here.
Why? Isn't this like Sharia central or something? It's bad enough you have to wear that thing on your head.
ENOUGH OF THAT!
WE'RE HERE TO LEARN, NOT TO FIGHT.
I wasn't trying to fight. I was just saying...

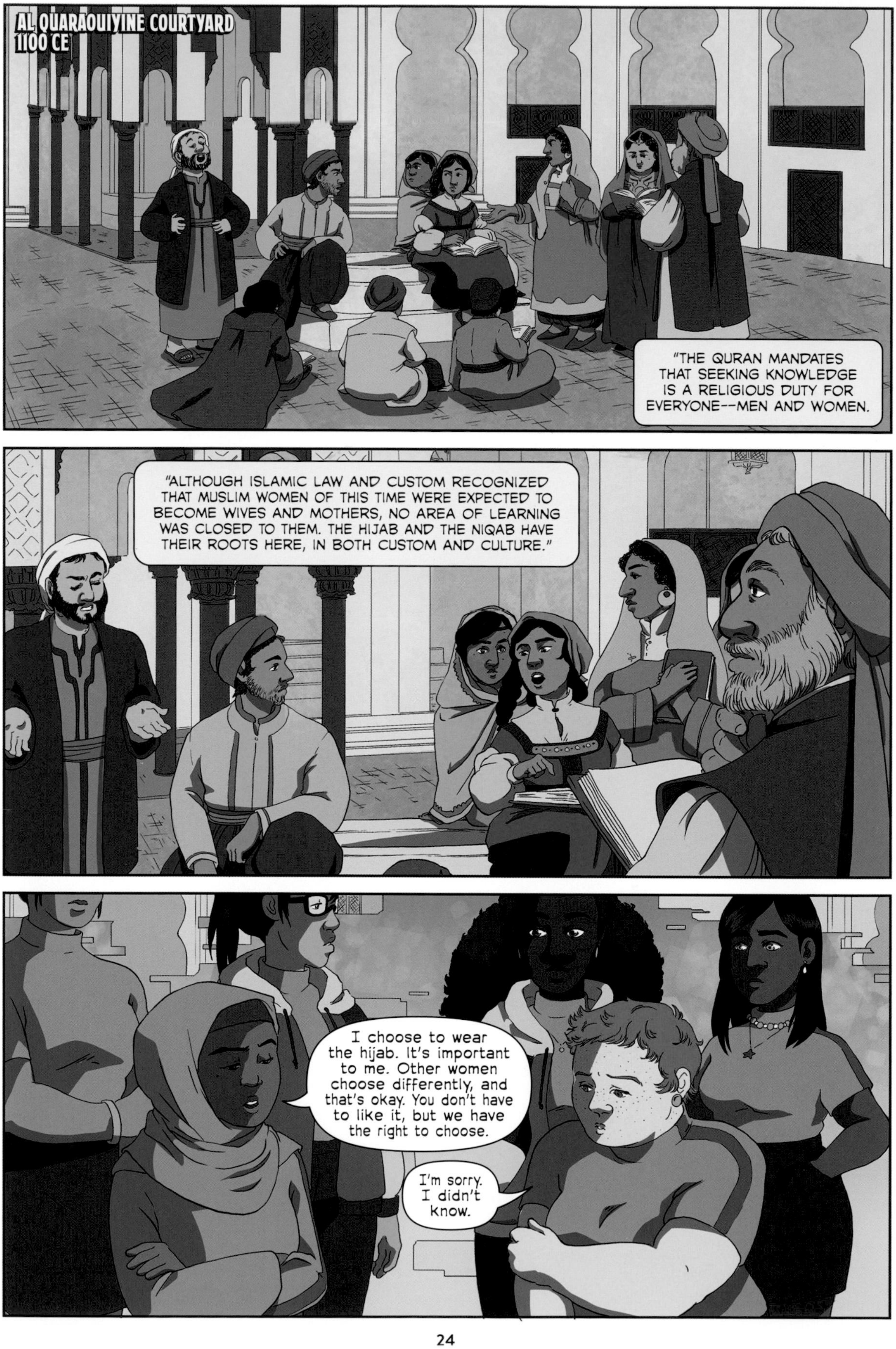
AL QUARAOUIYINE COURTYARD
1100 CE
"THE QURAN MANDATES THAT SEEKING KNOWLEDGE IS A RELIGIOUS DUTY FOR EVERYONE--MEN AND WOMEN.
"ALTHOUGH ISLAMIC LAW AND CUSTOM RECOGNIZED THAT MUSLIM WOMEN OF THIS TIME WERE EXPECTED TO BECOME WIVES AND MOTHERS, NO AREA OF LEARNING WAS CLOSED TO THEM. THE HIJAB AND THE NIQAB HAVE THEIR ROOTS HERE, IN BOTH CUSTOM AND CULTURE."
I choose to wear the hijab. It's important to me. Other women choose differently, and that's okay. You don't have to like it, but we have the right to choose.
I'm sorry. I didn't know.

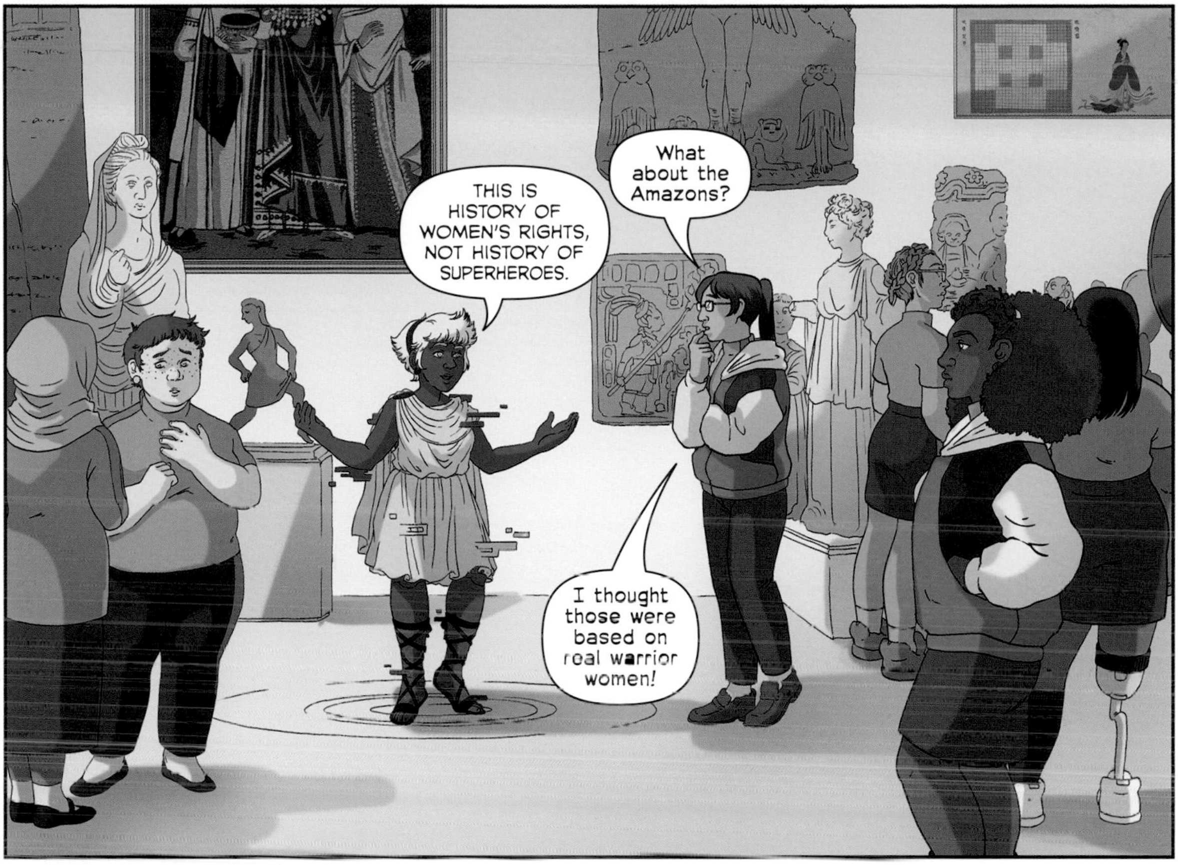
THIS IS HISTORY OF WOMEN'S RIGHTS, NOT HISTORY OF SUPERHEROES.
What about the Amazons?
I thought those were based on real warrior women!

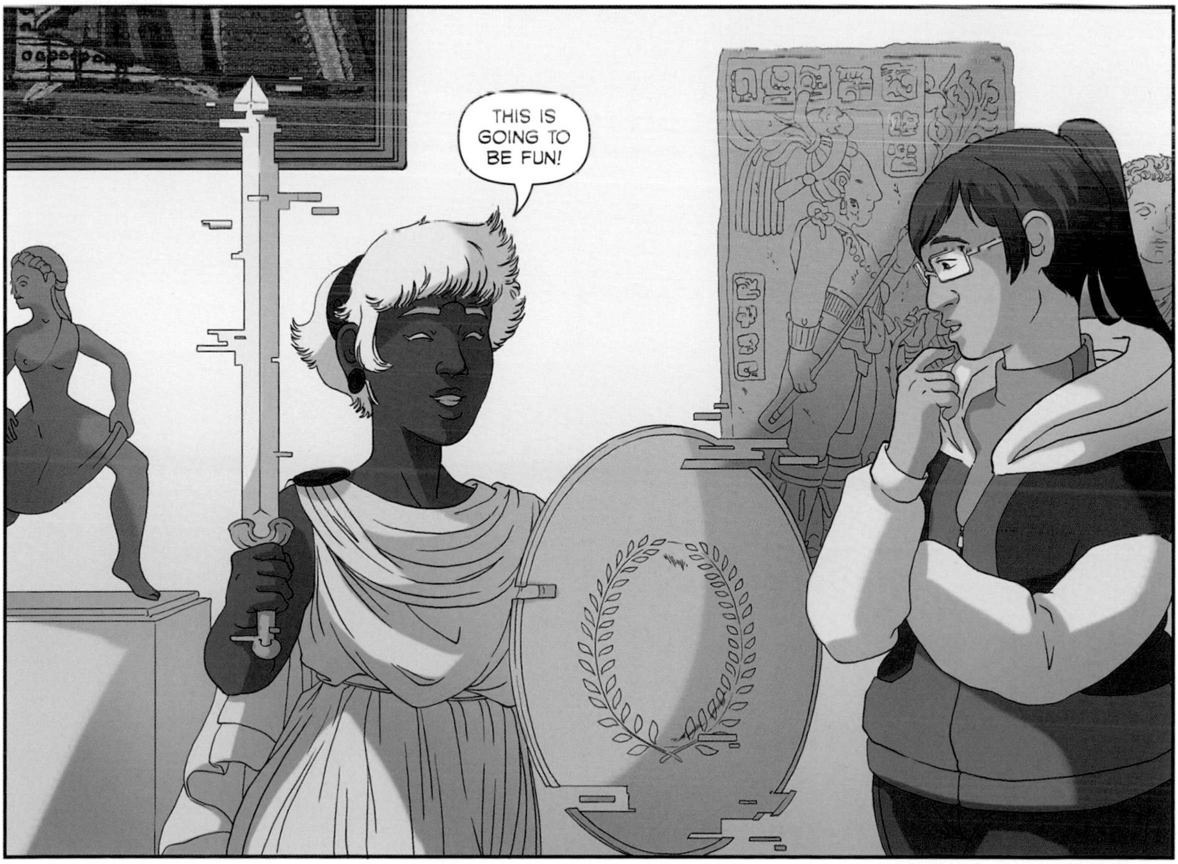
THIS IS GOING TO BE FUN!

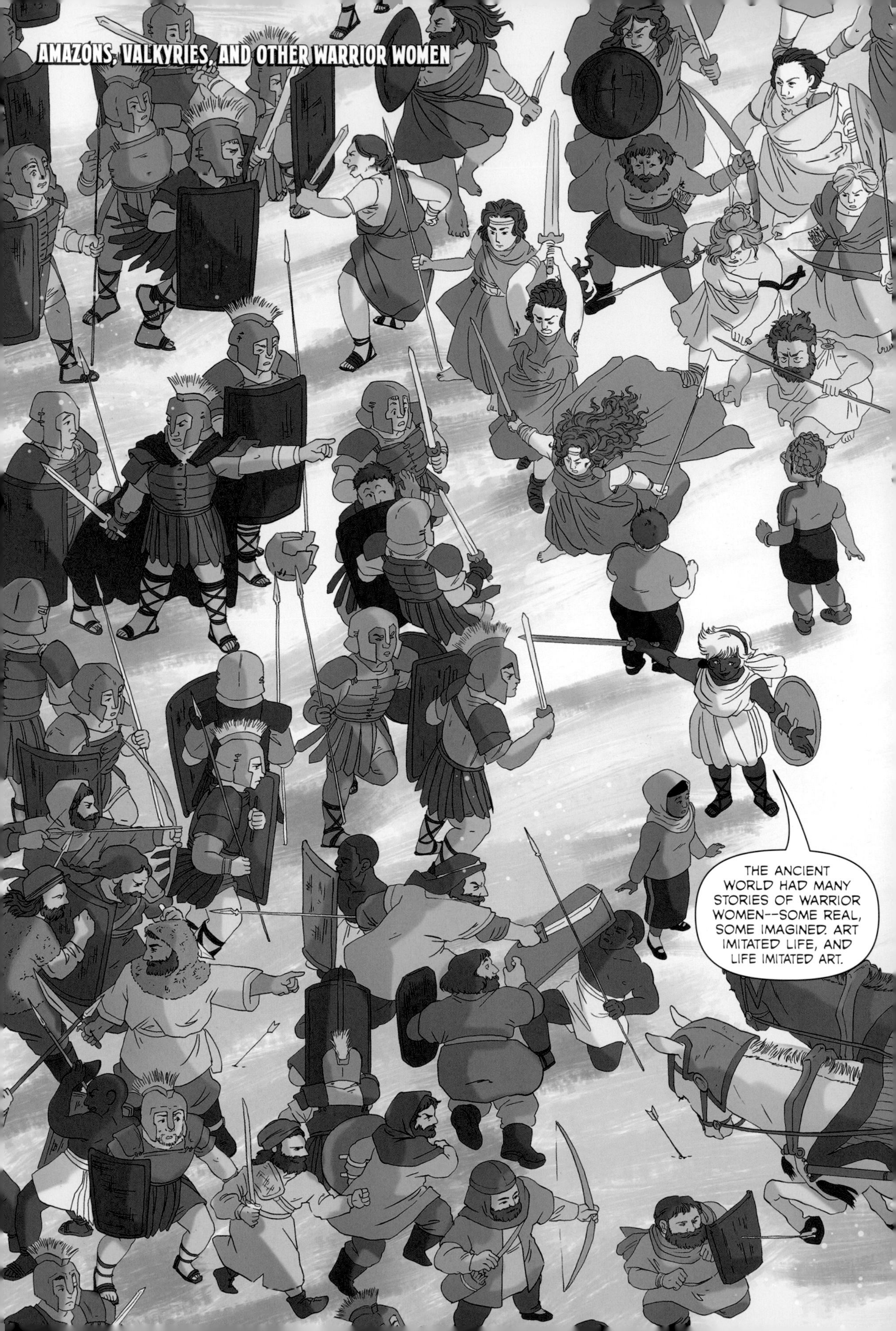
THE ANCIENT WORLD HAD MANY STORIES OF WARRIOR WOMEN--SOME REAL, SOME IMAGINED. ART IMITATED LIFE, AND LIFE IMITATED ART.

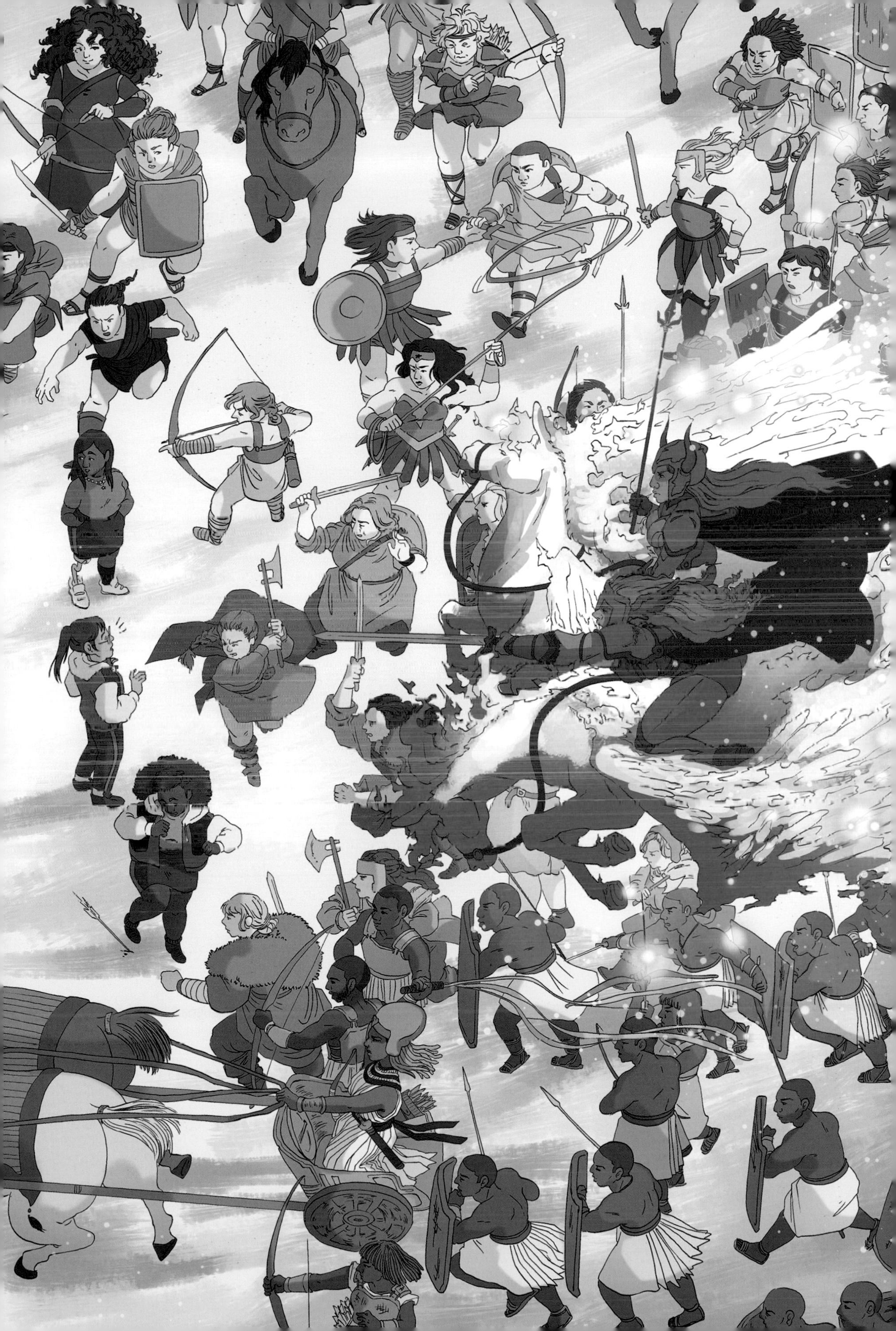

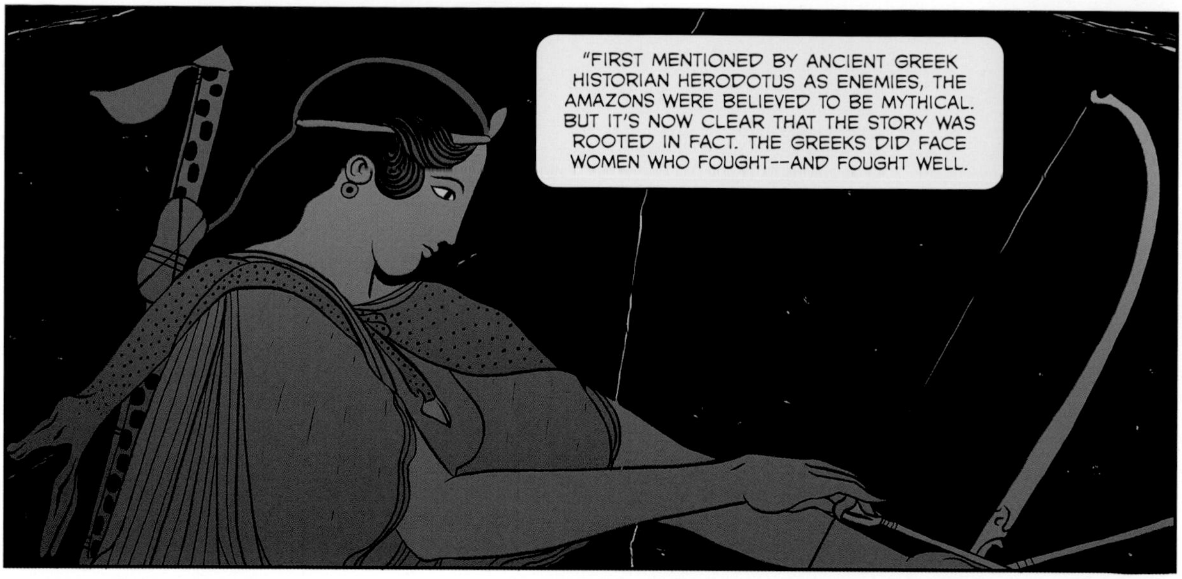
"FIRST MENTIONED BY ANCIENT GREEK HISTORIAN HERODOTUS AS ENEMIES, THE AMAZONS WERE BELIEVED TO BE MYTHICAL. BUT IT'S NOW CLEAR THAT THE STORY WAS ROOTED IN FACT. THE GREEKS DID FACE WOMEN WHO FOUGHT--AND FOUGHT WELL.

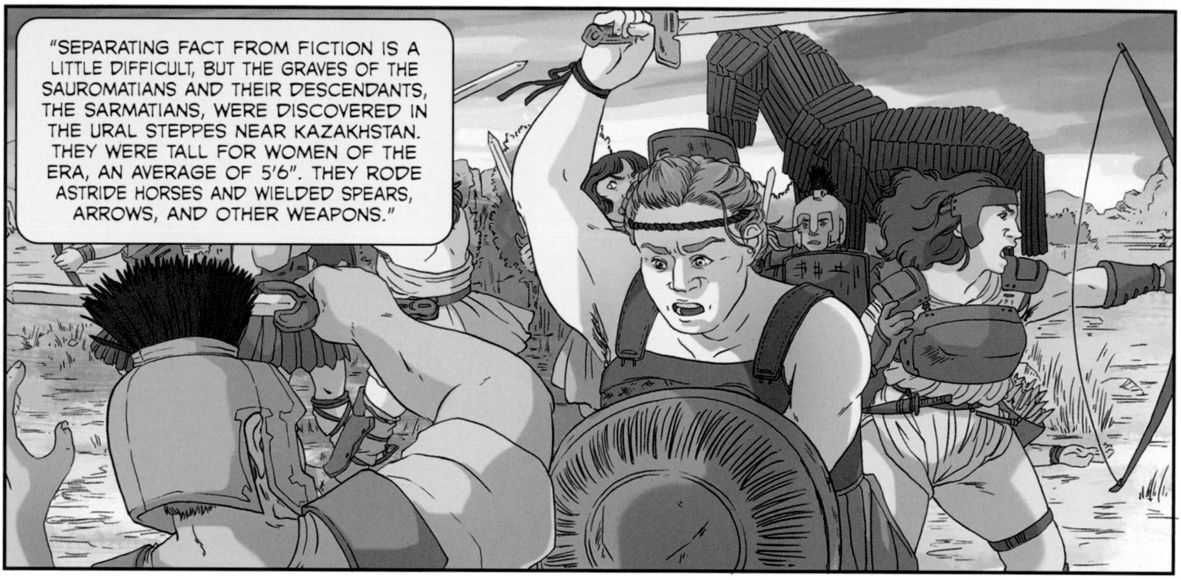
"SEPARATING FACT FROM FICTION IS A LITTLE DIFFICULT, BUT THE GRAVES OF THE SAUROMATIANS AND THEIR DESCENDANTS, THE SARMATIANS, WERE DISCOVERED IN THE URAL STEPPES NEAR KAZAKHSTAN. THEY WERE TALL FOR WOMEN OF THE ERA, AN AVERAGE OF 5'6". THEY RODE ASTRIDE HORSES AND WIELDED SPEARS, ARROWS, AND OTHER WEAPONS."

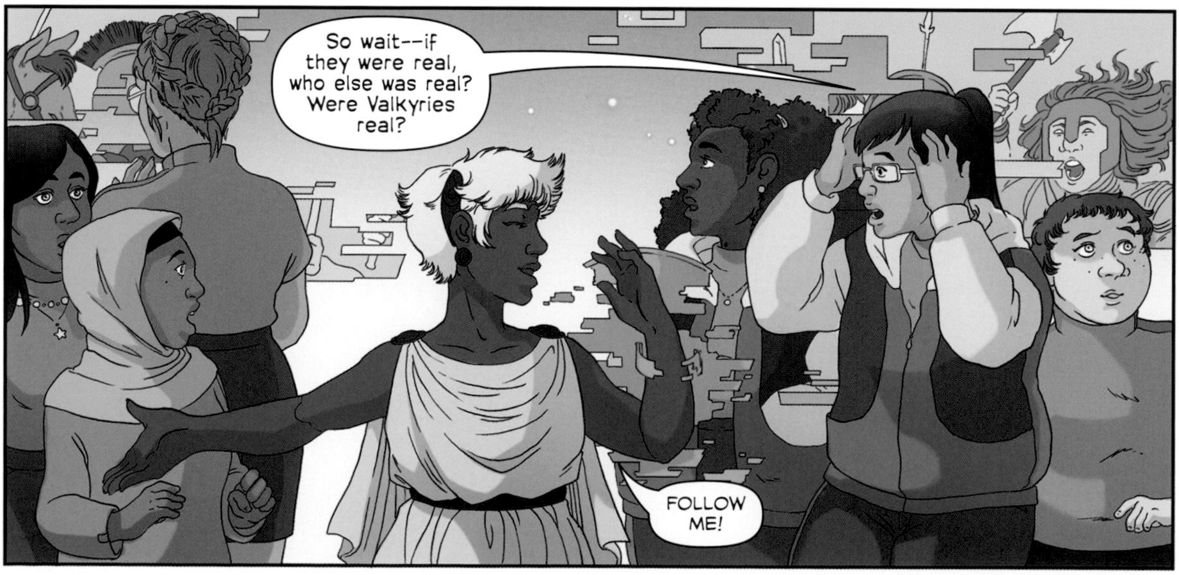
So wait--if they were real, who else was real? Were Valkyries real?
FOLLOW ME!

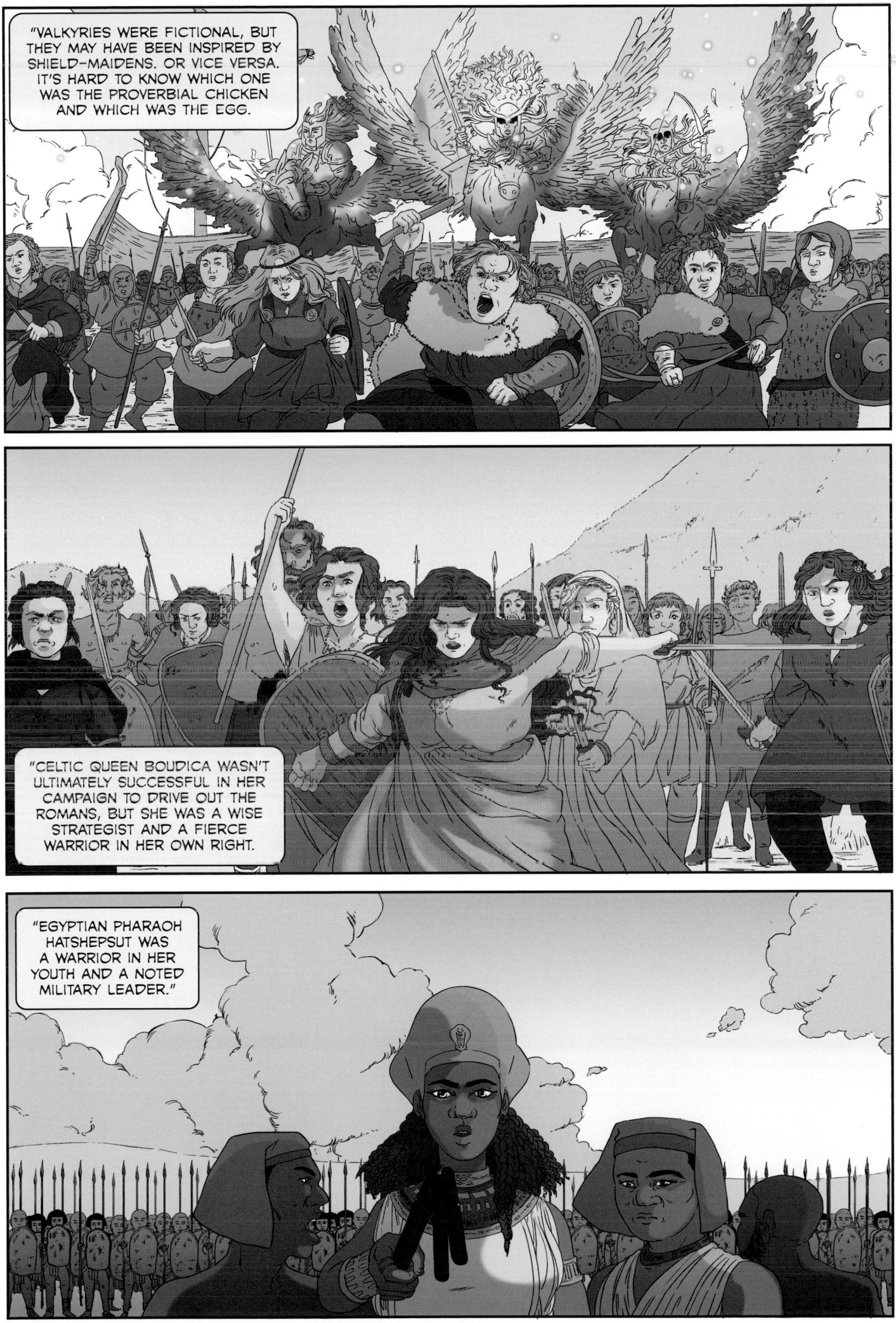
"VALKYRIES WERE FICTIONAL, BUT THEY MAY HAVE BEEN INSPIRED BY SHIELD-MAIDENS. OR VICE VERSA. IT'S HARD TO KNOW WHICH ONE WAS THE PROVERBIAL CHICKEN AND WHICH WAS THE EGG.
"CELTIC QUEEN BOUDICA WASN'T ULTIMATELY SUCCESSFUL IN HER CAMPAIGN TO DRIVE OUT THE ROMANS, BUT SHE WAS A WISE STRATEGIST AND A FIERCE WARRIOR IN HER OWN RIGHT.
"EGYPTIAN PHARAOH HATSHEPSUT WAS A WARRIOR IN HER YOUTH AND A NOTED MILITARY LEADER."

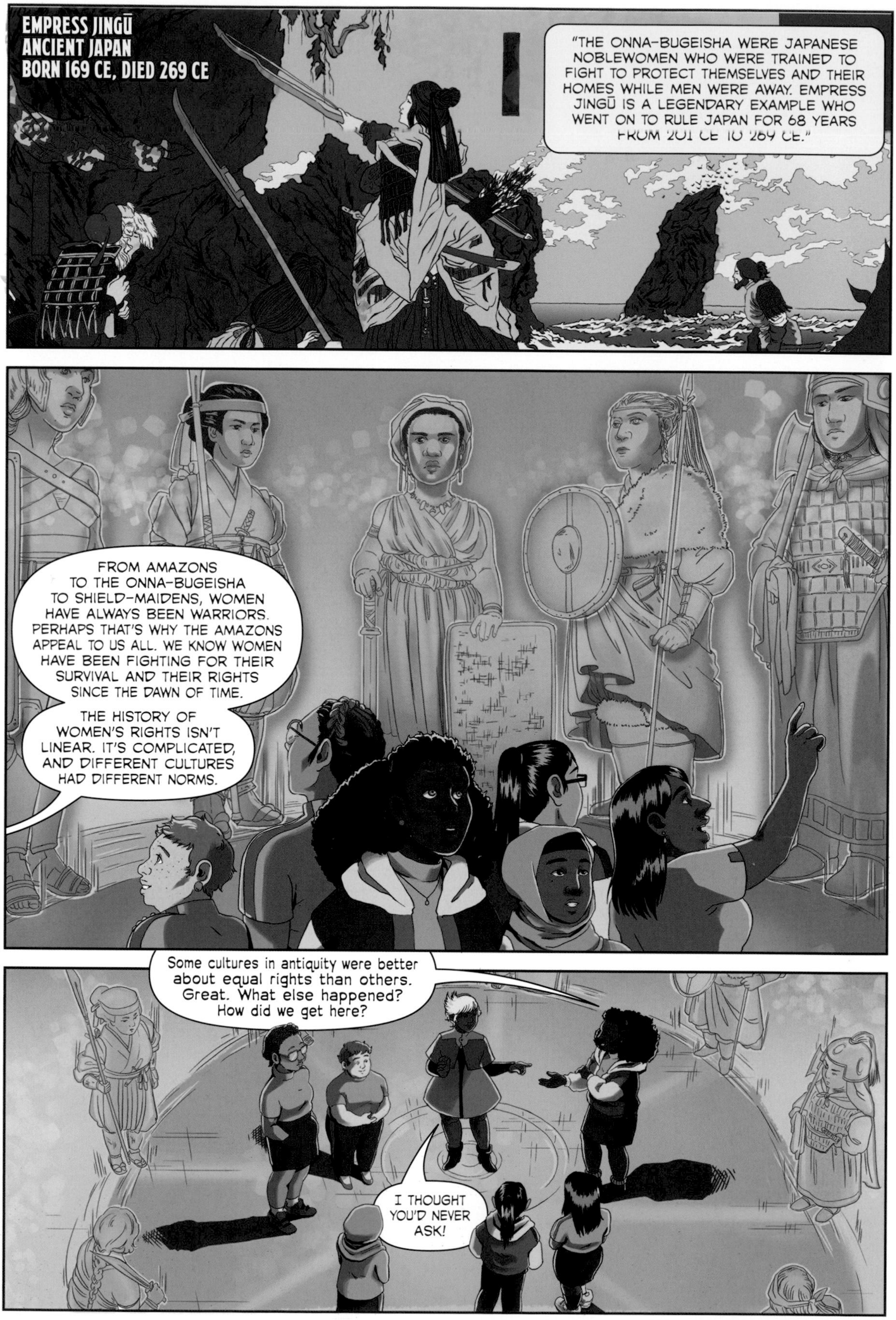
EMPRESS JINGŪ
ANCIENT JAPAN
BORN 169 CE, DIED 269 CE
"THE ONNA-BUGEISHA WERE JAPANESE NOBLEWOMEN WHO WERE TRAINED TO FIGHT TO PROTECT THEMSELVES AND THEIR HOMES WHILE MEN WERE AWAY. EMPRESS JINGŪ IS A LEGENDARY EXAMPLE WHO WENT ON TO RULE JAPAN FOR 68 YEARS FROM 201 CE TO 269 CE."
FROM AMAZONS TO THE ONNA-BUGEISHA TO SHIELD-MAIDENS, WOMEN HAVE ALWAYS BEEN WARRIORS. PERHAPS THAT'S WHY THE AMAZONS APPEAL TO US ALL. WE KNOW WOMEN HAVE BEEN FIGHTING FOR THEIR SURVIVAL AND THEIR RIGHTS SINCE THE DAWN OF TIME.
THE HISTORY OF WOMEN'S RIGHTS ISN'T LINEAR. IT'S COMPLICATED, AND DIFFERENT CULTURES HAD DIFFERENT NORMS.
Some cultures in antiquity were better about equal rights than others. Great. What else happened? How did we get here?
I THOUGHT YOU'D NEVER ASK!

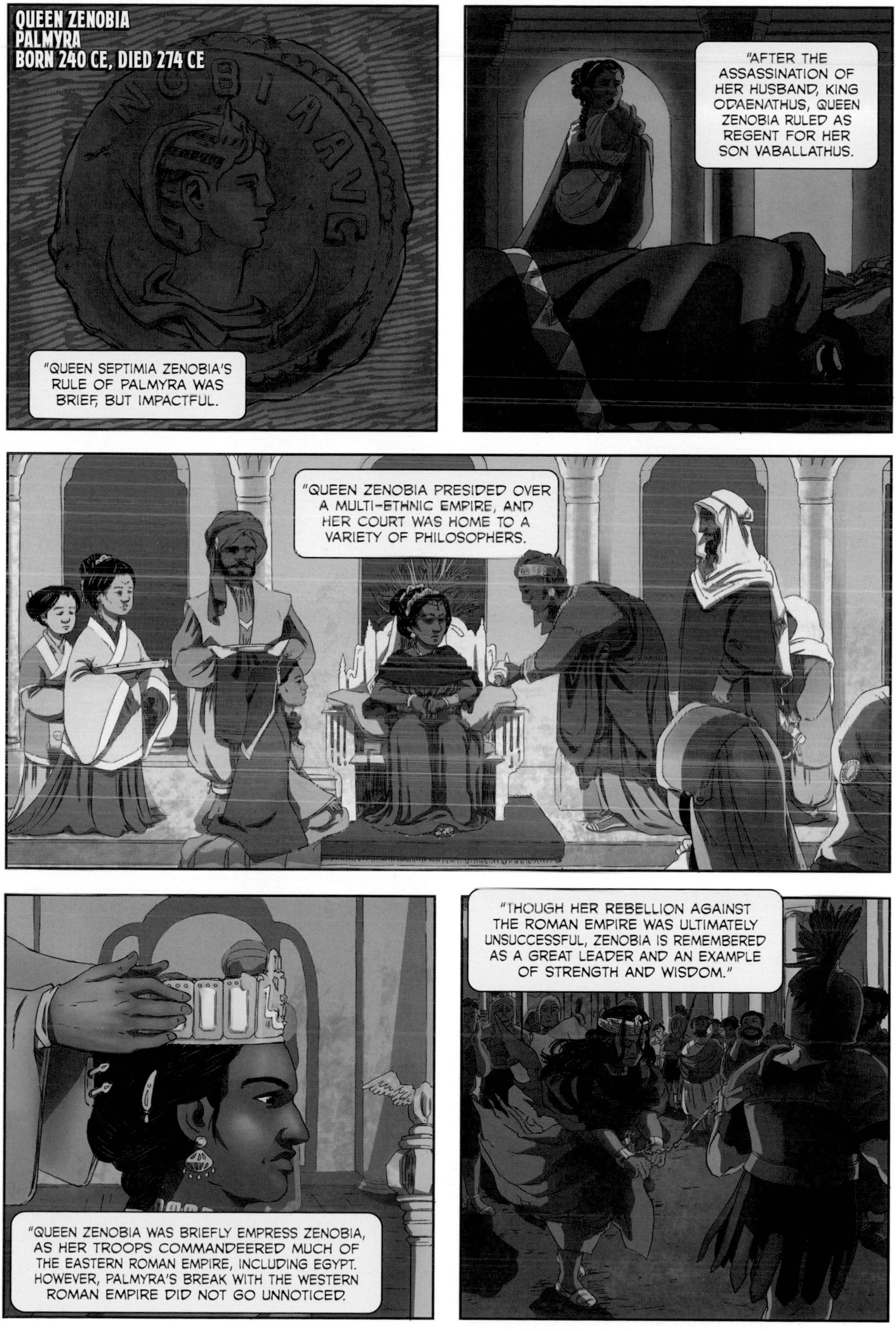
QUEEN ZENOBIA
PALMYRA
BORN 240 CE, DIED 274 CE
"QUEEN SEPTIMIA ZENOBIA'S RULE OF PALMYRA WAS BRIEF, BUT IMPACTFUL.
"AFTER THE ASSASSINATION OF HER HUSBAND, KING ODAENATHUS, QUEEN ZENOBIA RULED AS REGENT FOR HER SON VABALLATHUS.
"QUEEN ZENOBIA PRESIDED OVER A MULTI-ETHNIC EMPIRE, AND HER COURT WAS HOME TO A VARIETY OF PHILOSOPHERS.
"QUEEN ZENOBIA WAS BRIEFLY EMPRESS ZENOBIA, AS HER TROOPS COMMANDEERED MUCH OF THE EASTERN ROMAN EMPIRE, INCLUDING EGYPT. HOWEVER, PALMYRA'S BREAK WITH THE WESTERN ROMAN EMPIRE DID NOT GO UNNOTICED.
"THOUGH HER REBELLION AGAINST THE ROMAN EMPIRE WAS ULTIMATELY UNSUCCESSFUL, ZENOBIA IS REMEMBERED AS A GREAT LEADER AND AN EXAMPLE OF STRENGTH AND WISDOM."

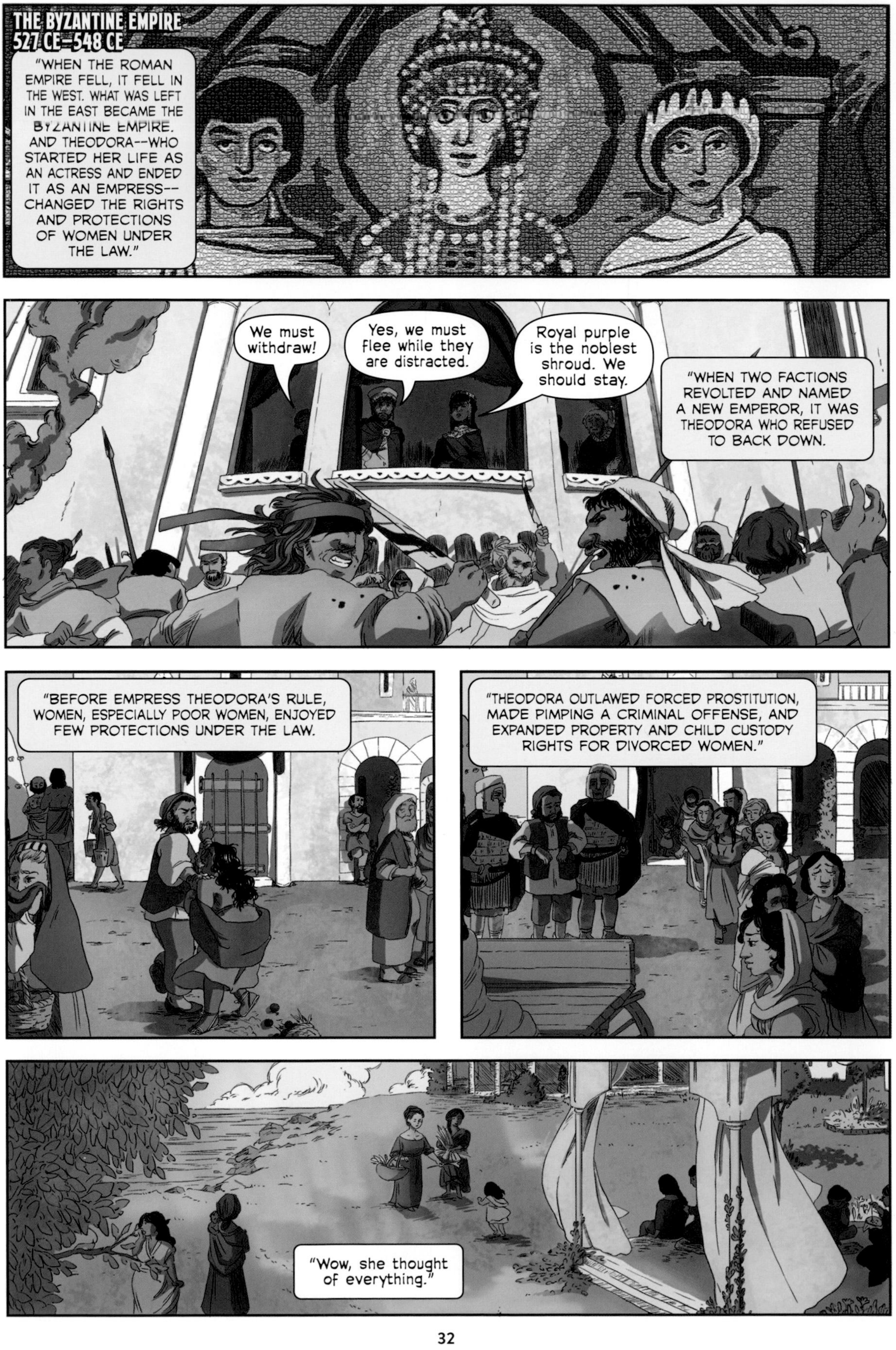
THE BYZANTINE EMPIRE
527 CE–548 CE
"WHEN THE ROMAN EMPIRE FELL, IT FELL IN THE WEST. WHAT WAS LEFT IN THE EAST BECAME THE BYZANTINE EMPIRE. AND THEODORA--WHO STARTED HER LIFE AS AN ACTRESS AND ENDED IT AS AN EMPRESS--CHANGED THE RIGHTS AND PROTECTIONS OF WOMEN UNDER THE LAW."
We must withdraw!
Yes, we must flee while they are distracted.
Royal purple is the noblest shroud. We should stay.
"WHEN TWO FACTIONS REVOLTED AND NAMED A NEW EMPEROR, IT WAS THEODORA WHO REFUSED TO BACK DOWN.
"BEFORE EMPRESS THEODORA'S RULE, WOMEN, ESPECIALLY POOR WOMEN, ENJOYED FEW PROTECTIONS UNDER THE LAW.
"THEODORA OUTLAWED FORCED PROSTITUTION, MADE PIMPING A CRIMINAL OFFENSE, AND EXPANDED PROPERTY AND CHILD CUSTODY RIGHTS FOR DIVORCED WOMEN."
"Wow, she thought of everything."

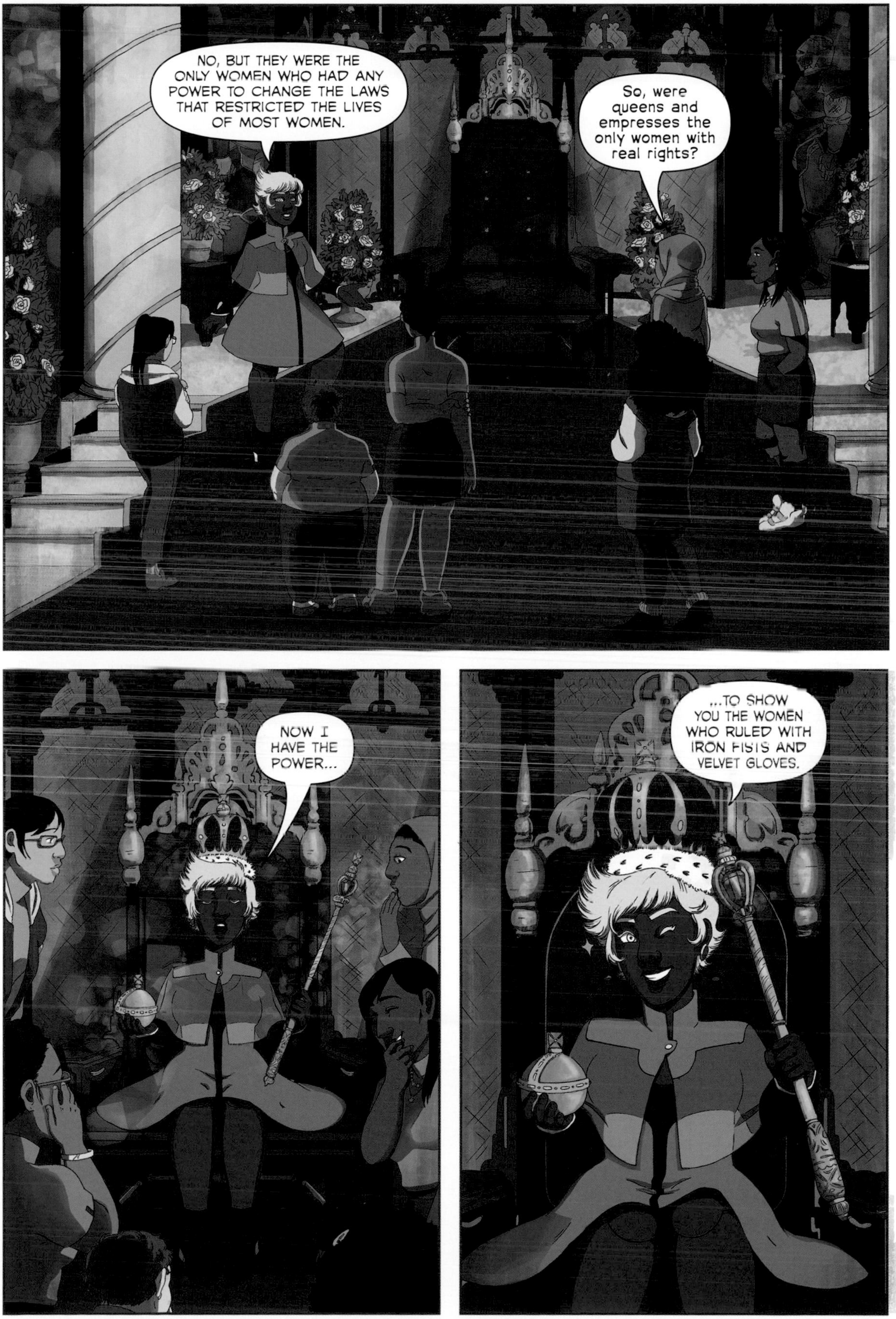
NO, BUT THEY WERE THE ONLY WOMEN WHO HAD ANY POWER TO CHANGE THE LAWS THAT RESTRICTED THE LIVES OF MOST WOMEN.
So, were queens and empresses the only women with real rights?
NOW I HAVE THE POWER...
...TO SHOW YOU THE WOMEN WHO RULED WITH IRON FISTS AND VELVET GLOVES.

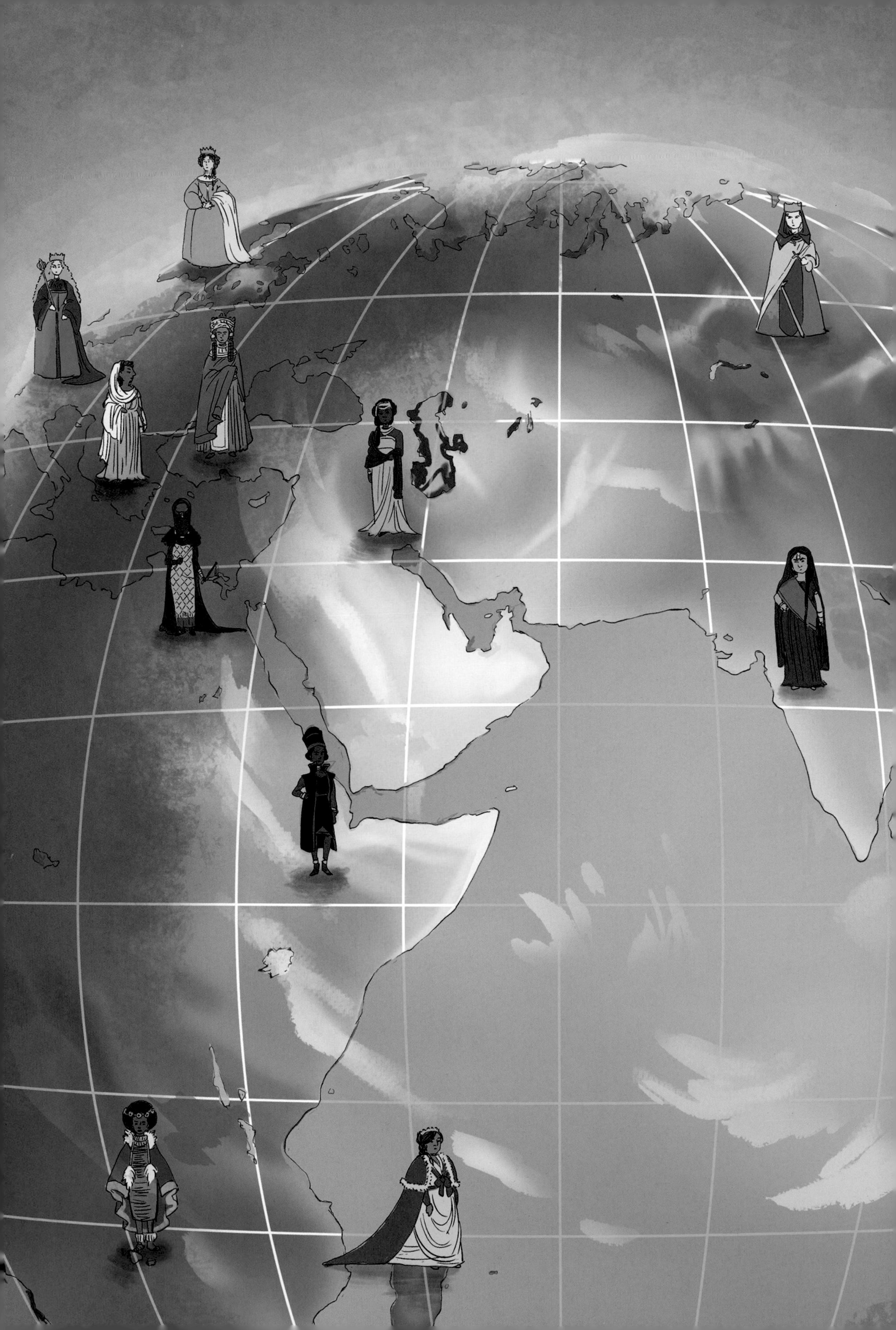

CHAPTER 2
EMPRESSES, QUEENS, AND PRINCESSES: THE POWER ON THE THRONE AND BEHIND IT
GIRLS RULE THE WORLD (KINDA)!

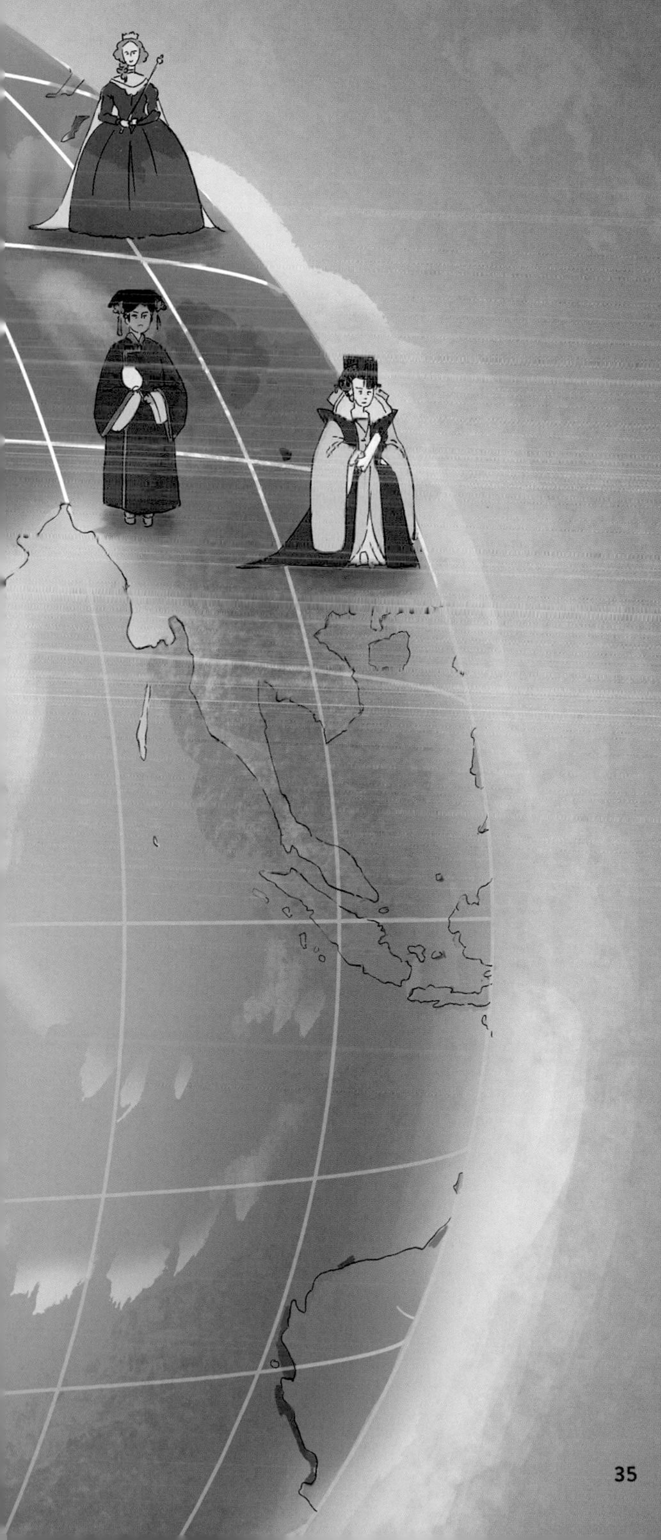

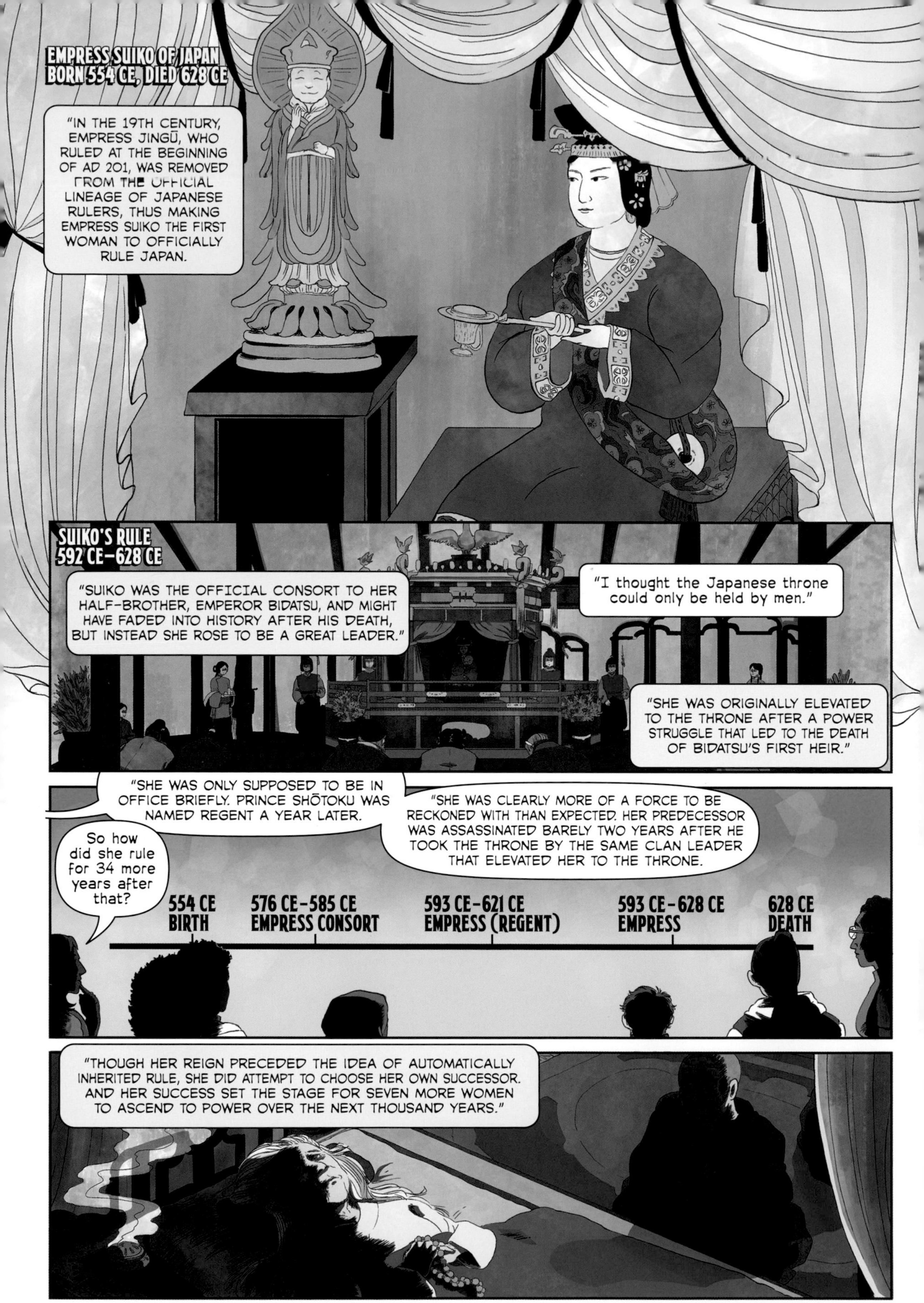
EMPRESS SUIKO OF JAPAN
BORN 554 CE, DIED 628 CE
"IN THE 19TH CENTURY, EMPRESS JINGŪ, WHO RULED AT THE BEGINNING OF AD 201, WAS REMOVED FROM THE OFFICIAL LINEAGE OF JAPANESE RULERS, THUS MAKING EMPRESS SUIKO THE FIRST WOMAN TO OFFICIALLY RULE JAPAN.
SUIKO'S RULE
592 CE–628 CE
"SUIKO WAS THE OFFICIAL CONSORT TO HER HALF-BROTHER, EMPEROR BIDATSU, AND MIGHT HAVE FADED INTO HISTORY AFTER HIS DEATH, BUT INSTEAD SHE ROSE TO BE A GREAT LEADER."
"I thought the Japanese throne could only be held by men."
"SHE WAS ORIGINALLY ELEVATED TO THE THRONE AFTER A POWER STRUGGLE THAT LED TO THE DEATH OF BIDATSU'S FIRST HEIR."
"SHE WAS ONLY SUPPOSED TO BE IN OFFICE BRIEFLY. PRINCE SHŌTOKU WAS NAMED REGENT A YEAR LATER.
So how did she rule for 34 more years after that?
"SHE WAS CLEARLY MORE OF A FORCE TO BE RECKONED WITH THAN EXPECTED. HER PREDECESSOR WAS ASSASSINATED BARELY TWO YEARS AFTER HE TOOK THE THRONE BY THE SAME CLAN LEADER THAT ELEVATED HER TO THE THRONE.
554 CE BIRTH
576 CE–585 CE EMPRESS CONSORT
593 CE–621 CE EMPRESS (REGENT)
593 CE–628 CE EMPRESS
628 CE DEATH
"THOUGH HER REIGN PRECEDED THE IDEA OF AUTOMATICALLY INHERITED RULE, SHE DID ATTEMPT TO CHOOSE HER OWN SUCCESSOR. AND HER SUCCESS SET THE STAGE FOR SEVEN MORE WOMEN TO ASCEND TO POWER OVER THE NEXT THOUSAND YEARS."

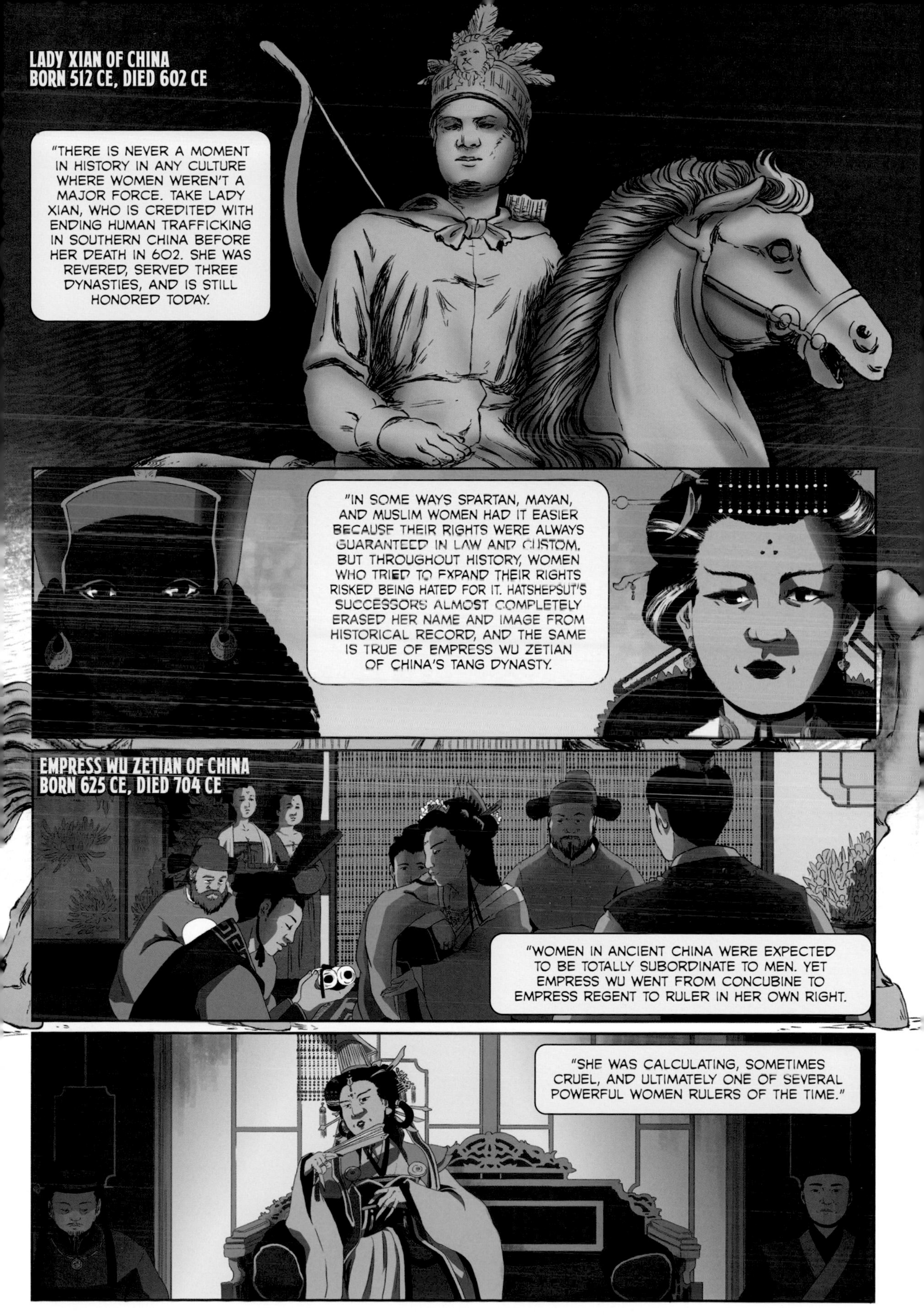
LADY XIAN OF CHINA
BORN 512 CE, DIED 602 CE
"THERE IS NEVER A MOMENT IN HISTORY IN ANY CULTURE WHERE WOMEN WEREN'T A MAJOR FORCE. TAKE LADY XIAN, WHO IS CREDITED WITH ENDING HUMAN TRAFFICKING IN SOUTHERN CHINA BEFORE HER DEATH IN 602. SHE WAS REVERED, SERVED THREE DYNASTIES, AND IS STILL HONORED TODAY.
"IN SOME WAYS SPARTAN, MAYAN, AND MUSLIM WOMEN HAD IT EASIER BECAUSE THEIR RIGHTS WERE ALWAYS GUARANTEED IN LAW AND CUSTOM. BUT THROUGHOUT HISTORY, WOMEN WHO TRIED TO EXPAND THEIR RIGHTS RISKED BEING HATED FOR IT. HATSHEPSUT'S SUCCESSORS ALMOST COMPLETELY ERASED HER NAME AND IMAGE FROM HISTORICAL RECORD, AND THE SAME IS TRUE OF EMPRESS WU ZETIAN OF CHINA'S TANG DYNASTY.
EMPRESS WU ZETIAN OF CHINA
BORN 625 CE, DIED 704 CE
"WOMEN IN ANCIENT CHINA WERE EXPECTED TO BE TOTALLY SUBORDINATE TO MEN. YET EMPRESS WU WENT FROM CONCUBINE TO EMPRESS REGENT TO RULER IN HER OWN RIGHT.
"SHE WAS CALCULATING, SOMETIMES CRUEL, AND ULTIMATELY ONE OF SEVERAL POWERFUL WOMEN RULERS OF THE TIME."

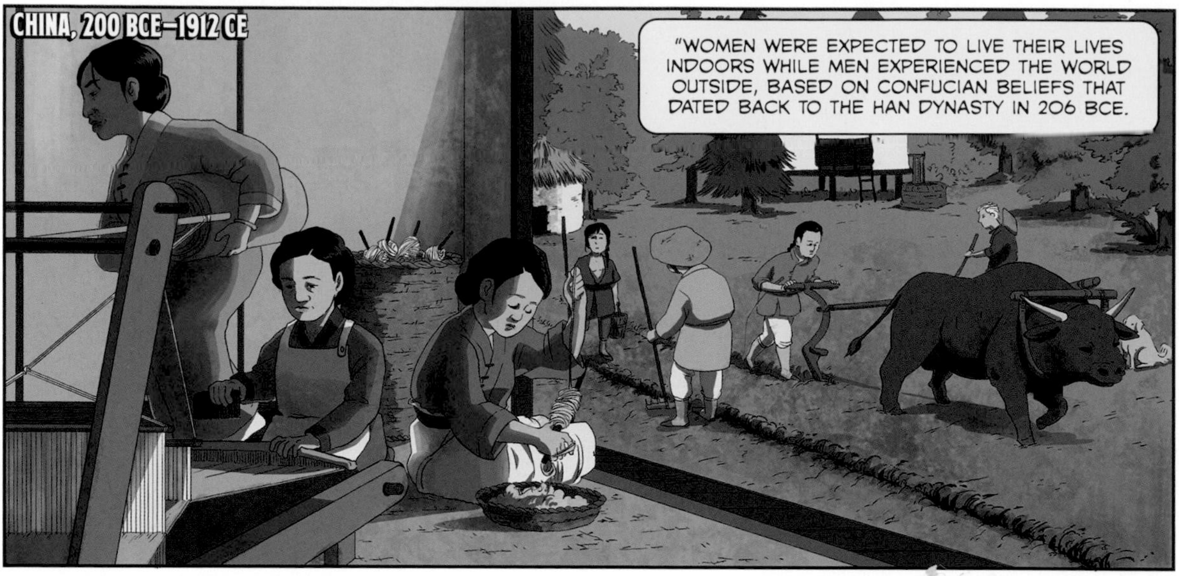
CHINA, 200 BCE–1912 CE
"WOMEN WERE EXPECTED TO LIVE THEIR LIVES INDOORS WHILE MEN EXPERIENCED THE WORLD OUTSIDE, BASED ON CONFUCIAN BELIEFS THAT DATED BACK TO THE HAN DYNASTY IN 206 BCE.

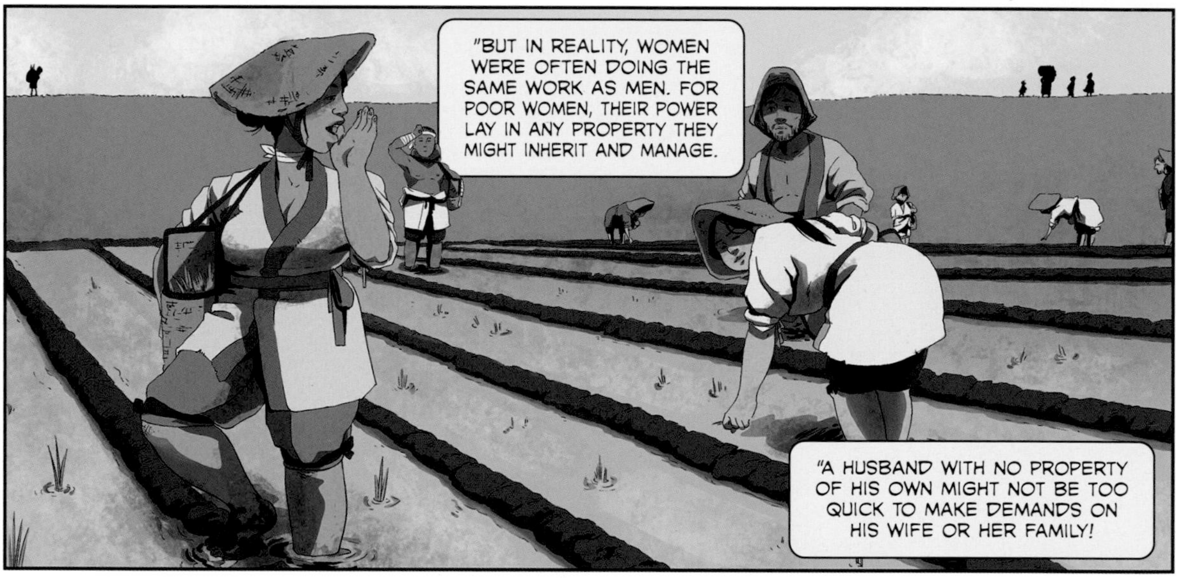
"BUT IN REALITY, WOMEN WERE OFTEN DOING THE SAME WORK AS MEN. FOR POOR WOMEN, THEIR POWER LAY IN ANY PROPERTY THEY MIGHT INHERIT AND MANAGE.
"A HUSBAND WITH NO PROPERTY OF HIS OWN MIGHT NOT BE TOO QUICK TO MAKE DEMANDS ON HIS WIFE OR HER FAMILY!

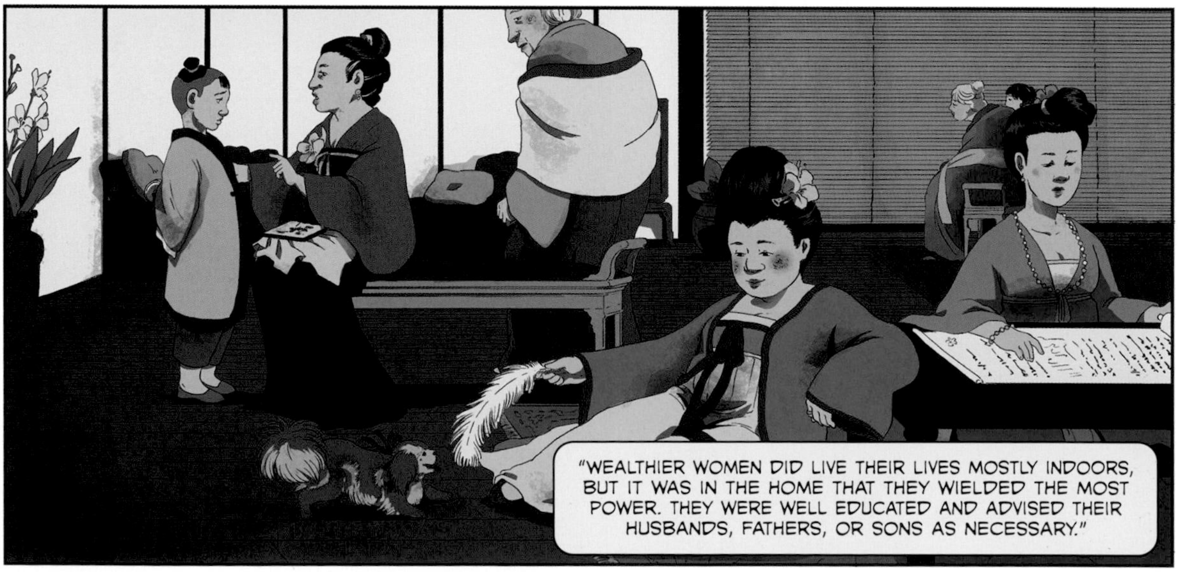
"WEALTHIER WOMEN DID LIVE THEIR LIVES MOSTLY INDOORS, BUT IT WAS IN THE HOME THAT THEY WIELDED THE MOST POWER. THEY WERE WELL EDUCATED AND ADVISED THEIR HUSBANDS, FATHERS, OR SONS AS NECESSARY."

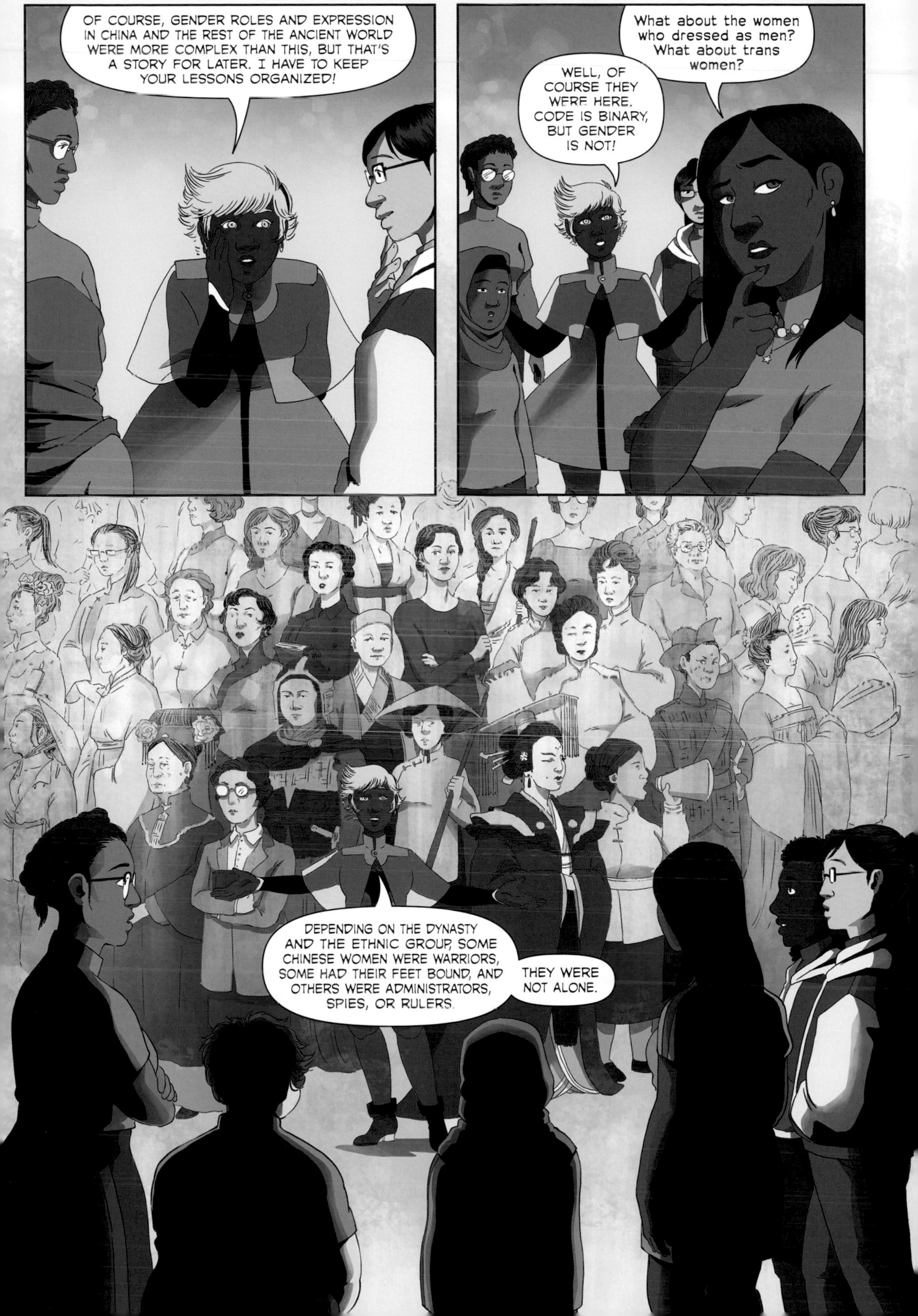
OF COURSE, GENDER ROLES AND EXPRESSION IN CHINA AND THE REST OF THE ANCIENT WORLD WERE MORE COMPLEX THAN THIS, BUT THAT'S A STORY FOR LATER. I HAVE TO KEEP YOUR LESSONS ORGANIZED!
What about the women who dressed as men? What about trans women?
WELL, OF COURSE THEY WERE HERE. CODE IS BINARY, BUT GENDER IS NOT!
DEPENDING ON THE DYNASTY AND THE ETHNIC GROUP, SOME CHINESE WOMEN WERE WARRIORS, SOME HAD THEIR FEET BOUND, AND OTHERS WERE ADMINISTRATORS, SPIES, OR RULERS.
THEY WERE NOT ALONE.

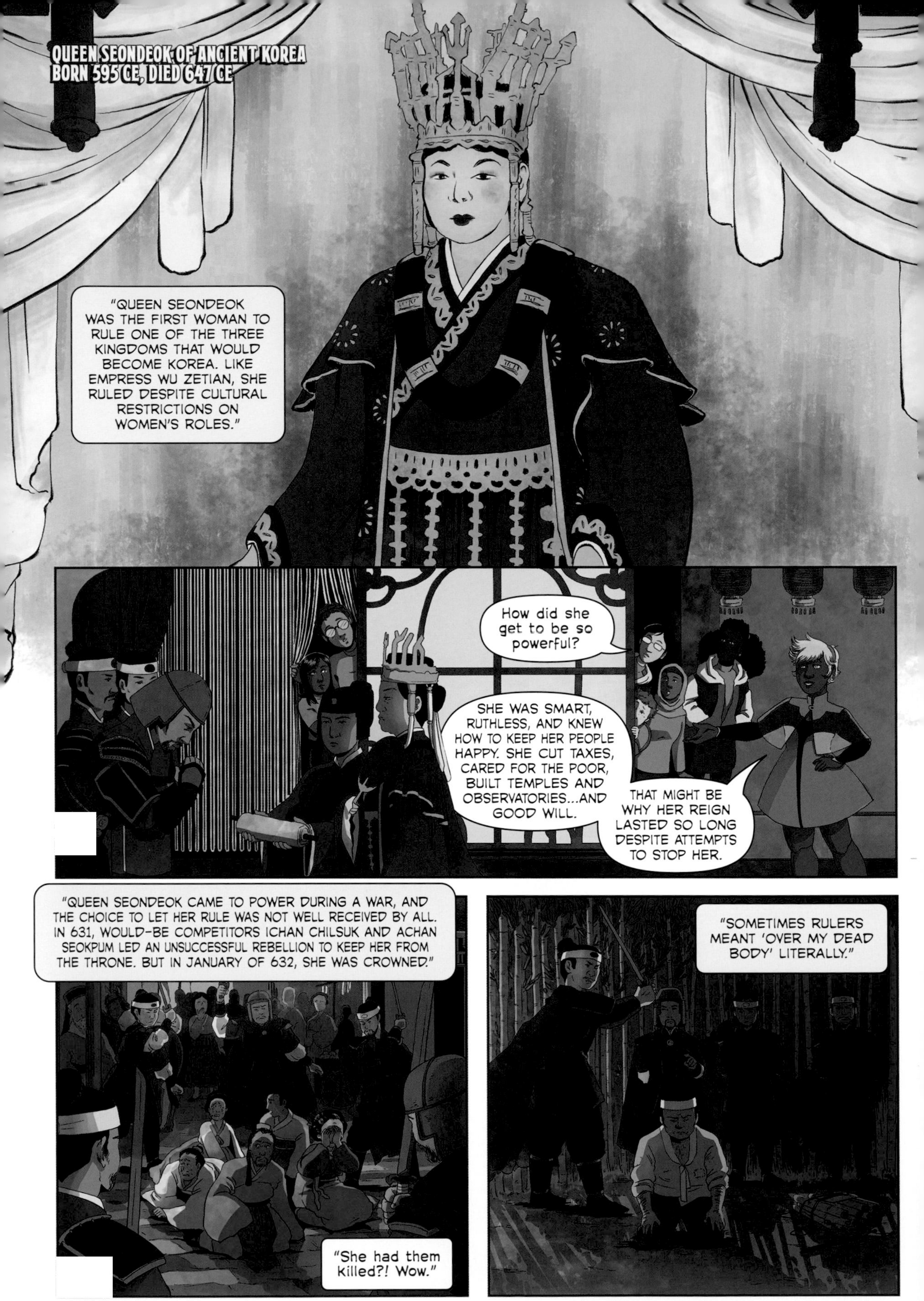
QUEEN SEONDEOK OF ANCIENT KOREA
BORN 595 CE, DIED 647 CE
"QUEEN SEONDEOK WAS THE FIRST WOMAN TO RULE ONE OF THE THREE KINGDOMS THAT WOULD BECOME KOREA. LIKE EMPRESS WU ZETIAN, SHE RULED DESPITE CULTURAL RESTRICTIONS ON WOMEN'S ROLES."
How did she get to be so powerful?
SHE WAS SMART, RUTHLESS, AND KNEW HOW TO KEEP HER PEOPLE HAPPY. SHE CUT TAXES, CARED FOR THE POOR, BUILT TEMPLES AND OBSERVATORIES...AND GOOD WILL.
THAT MIGHT BE WHY HER REIGN LASTED SO LONG DESPITE ATTEMPTS TO STOP HER.
"QUEEN SEONDEOK CAME TO POWER DURING A WAR, AND THE CHOICE TO LET HER RULE WAS NOT WELL RECEIVED BY ALL. IN 631, WOULD-BE COMPETITORS ICHAN CHILSUK AND ACHAN SEOKPUM LED AN UNSUCCESSFUL REBELLION TO KEEP HER FROM THE THRONE. BUT IN JANUARY OF 632, SHE WAS CROWNED."
"She had them killed?! Wow."
"SOMETIMES RULERS MEANT 'OVER MY DEAD BODY' LITERALLY."

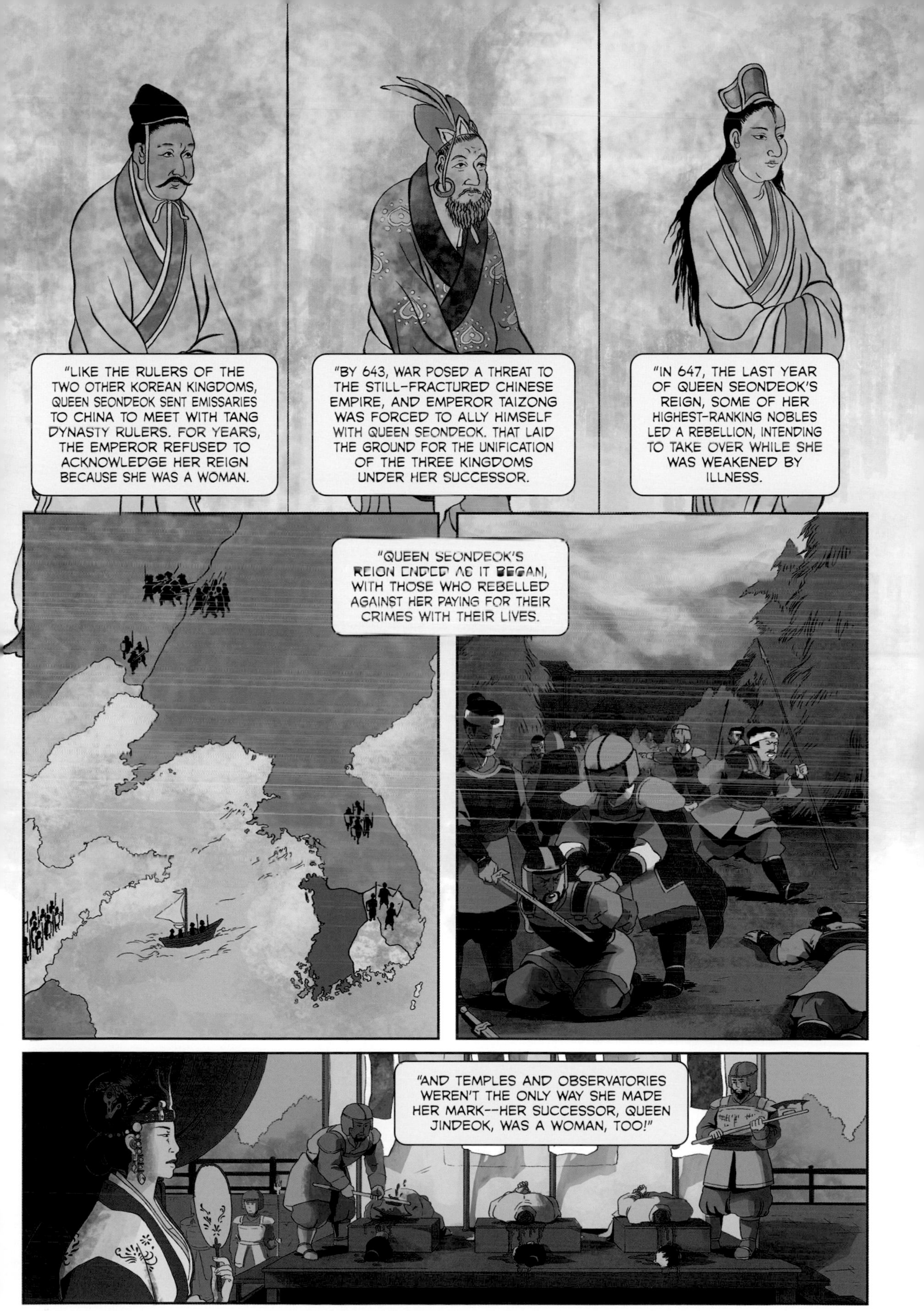
"LIKE THE RULERS OF THE TWO OTHER KOREAN KINGDOMS, QUEEN SEONDEOK SENT EMISSARIES TO CHINA TO MEET WITH TANG DYNASTY RULERS. FOR YEARS, THE EMPEROR REFUSED TO ACKNOWLEDGE HER REIGN BECAUSE SHE WAS A WOMAN.
"BY 643, WAR POSED A THREAT TO THE STILL-FRACTURED CHINESE EMPIRE, AND EMPEROR TAIZONG WAS FORCED TO ALLY HIMSELF WITH QUEEN SEONDEOK. THAT LAID THE GROUND FOR THE UNIFICATION OF THE THREE KINGDOMS UNDER HER SUCCESSOR.
"IN 647, THE LAST YEAR OF QUEEN SEONDEOK'S REIGN, SOME OF HER HIGHEST-RANKING NOBLES LED A REBELLION, INTENDING TO TAKE OVER WHILE SHE WAS WEAKENED BY ILLNESS.
"QUEEN SEONDEOK'S REIGN ENDED AS IT BEGAN, WITH THOSE WHO REBELLED AGAINST HER PAYING FOR THEIR CRIMES WITH THEIR LIVES.
"AND TEMPLES AND OBSERVATORIES WEREN'T THE ONLY WAY SHE MADE HER MARK--HER SUCCESSOR, QUEEN JINDEOK, WAS A WOMAN, TOO!"

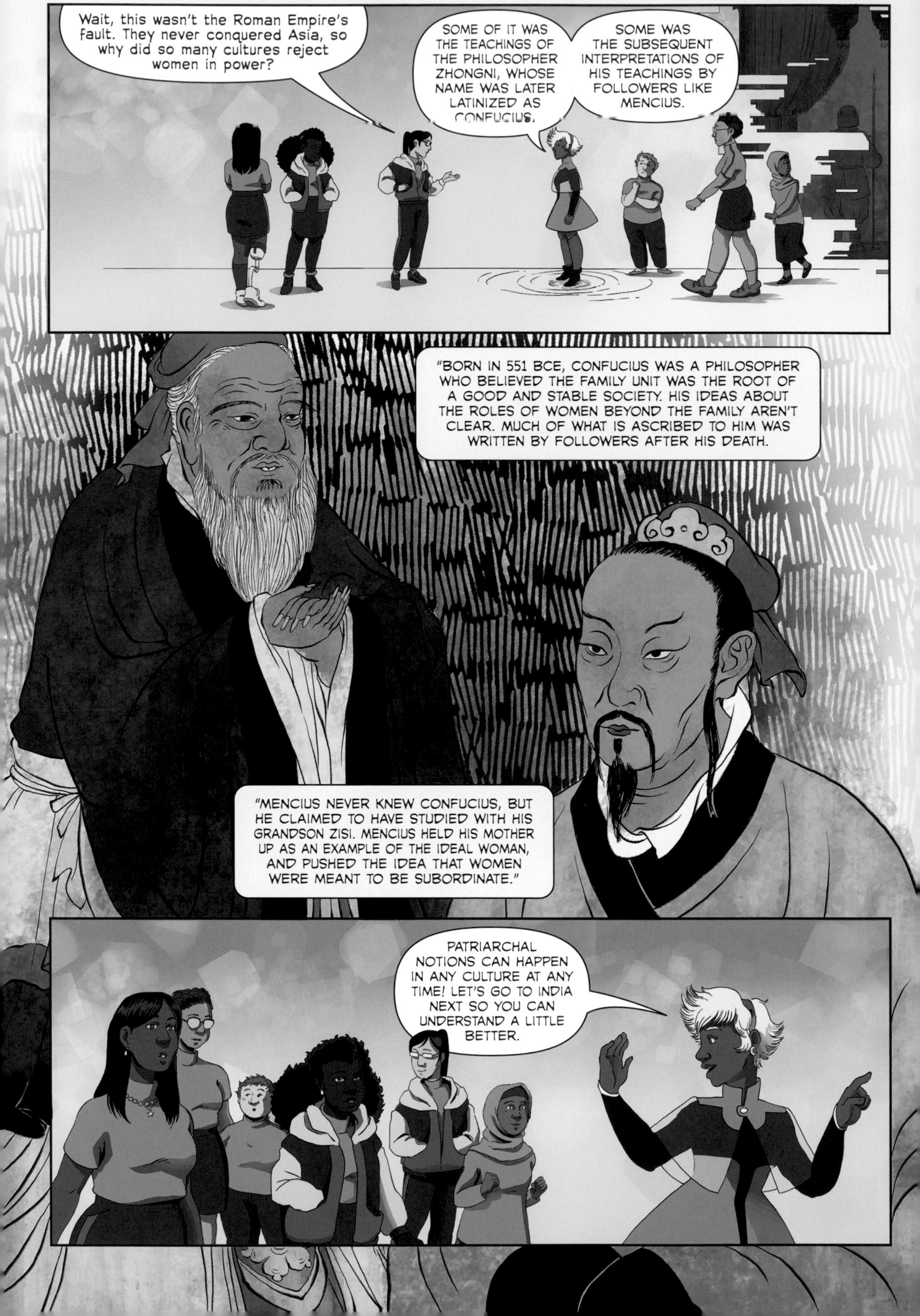
Wait, this wasn't the Roman Empire's fault. They never conquered Asia, so why did so many cultures reject women in power?
SOME OF IT WAS THE TEACHINGS OF THE PHILOSOPHER ZHONGNI, WHOSE NAME WAS LATER LATINIZED AS CONFUCIUS.
SOME WAS THE SUBSEQUENT INTERPRETATIONS OF HIS TEACHINGS BY FOLLOWERS LIKE MENCIUS.
"BORN IN 551 BCE, CONFUCIUS WAS A PHILOSOPHER WHO BELIEVED THE FAMILY UNIT WAS THE ROOT OF A GOOD AND STABLE SOCIETY. HIS IDEAS ABOUT THE ROLES OF WOMEN BEYOND THE FAMILY AREN'T CLEAR. MUCH OF WHAT IS ASCRIBED TO HIM WAS WRITTEN BY FOLLOWERS AFTER HIS DEATH.
"MENCIUS NEVER KNEW CONFUCIUS, BUT HE CLAIMED TO HAVE STUDIED WITH HIS GRANDSON ZISI. MENCIUS HELD HIS MOTHER UP AS AN EXAMPLE OF THE IDEAL WOMAN, AND PUSHED THE IDEA THAT WOMEN WERE MEANT TO BE SUBORDINATE."
PATRIARCHAL NOTIONS CAN HAPPEN IN ANY CULTURE AT ANY TIME! LET'S GO TO INDIA NEXT SO YOU CAN UNDERSTAND A LITTLE BETTER.

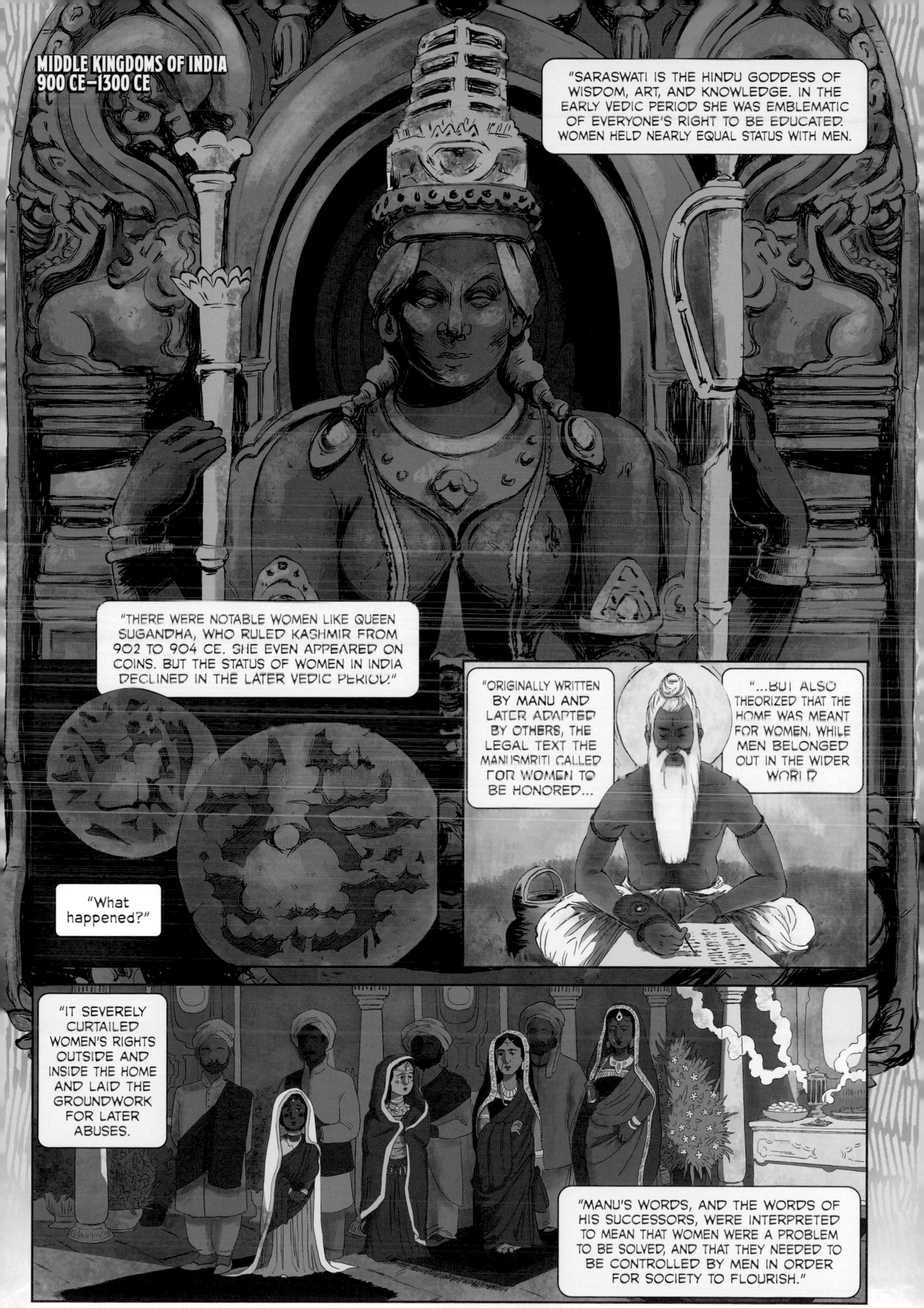
MIDDLE KINGDOMS OF INDIA 900 CE–1300 CE
"SARASWATI IS THE HINDU GODDESS OF WISDOM, ART, AND KNOWLEDGE. IN THE EARLY VEDIC PERIOD SHE WAS EMBLEMATIC OF EVERYONE'S RIGHT TO BE EDUCATED. WOMEN HELD NEARLY EQUAL STATUS WITH MEN.
"THERE WERE NOTABLE WOMEN LIKE QUEEN SUGANDHA, WHO RULED KASHMIR FROM 902 TO 904 CE. SHE EVEN APPEARED ON COINS. BUT THE STATUS OF WOMEN IN INDIA DECLINED IN THE LATER VEDIC PERIOD."
"What happened?"
"ORIGINALLY WRITTEN BY MANU AND LATER ADAPTED BY OTHERS, THE LEGAL TEXT THE MANUSMRITI CALLED FOR WOMEN TO BE HONORED...
"...BUT ALSO THEORIZED THAT THE HOME WAS MEANT FOR WOMEN, WHILE MEN BELONGED OUT IN THE WIDER WORLD.
"IT SEVERELY CURTAILED WOMEN'S RIGHTS OUTSIDE AND INSIDE THE HOME AND LAID THE GROUNDWORK FOR LATER ABUSES.
"MANU'S WORDS, AND THE WORDS OF HIS SUCCESSORS, WERE INTERPRETED TO MEAN THAT WOMEN WERE A PROBLEM TO BE SOLVED, AND THAT THEY NEEDED TO BE CONTROLLED BY MEN IN ORDER FOR SOCIETY TO FLOURISH."

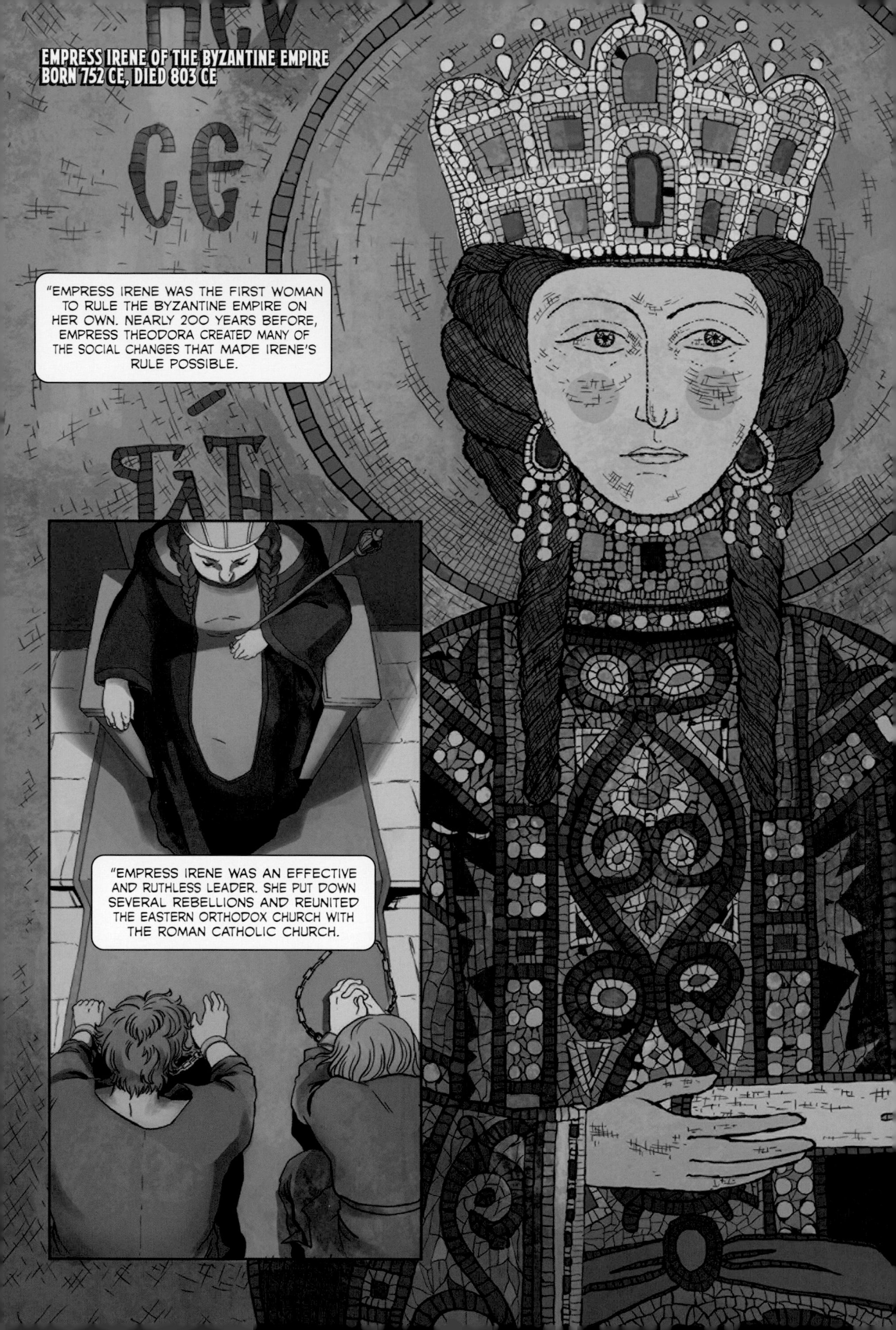
EMPRESS IRENE OF THE BYZANTINE EMPIRE
BORN 752 CE, DIED 803 CE
"EMPRESS IRENE WAS THE FIRST WOMAN TO RULE THE BYZANTINE EMPIRE ON HER OWN. NEARLY 200 YEARS BEFORE, EMPRESS THEODORA CREATED MANY OF THE SOCIAL CHANGES THAT MADE IRENE'S RULE POSSIBLE.
"EMPRESS IRENE WAS AN EFFECTIVE AND RUTHLESS LEADER. SHE PUT DOWN SEVERAL REBELLIONS AND REUNITED THE EASTERN ORTHODOX CHURCH WITH THE ROMAN CATHOLIC CHURCH.

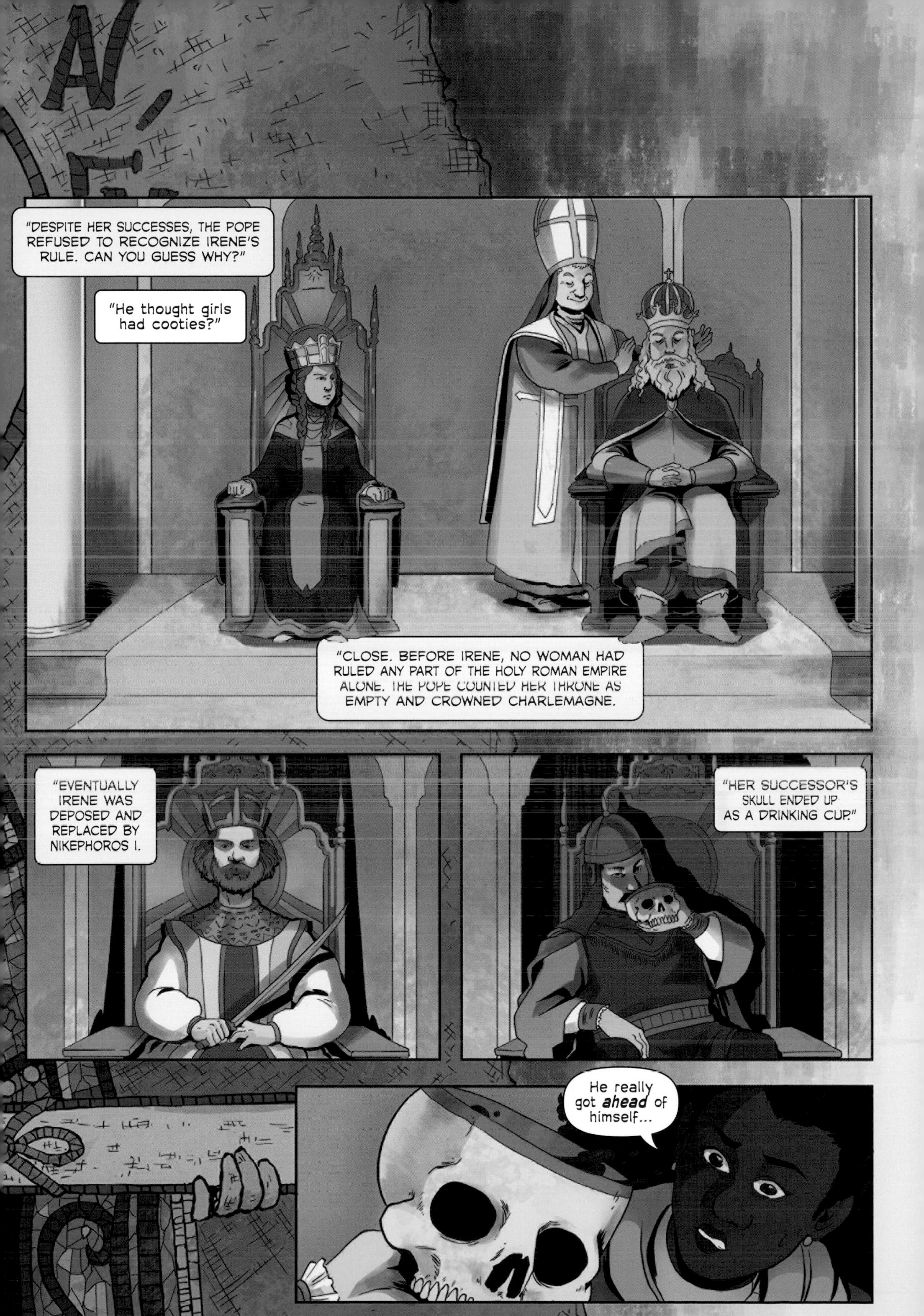
"DESPITE HER SUCCESSES, THE POPE REFUSED TO RECOGNIZE IRENE'S RULE. CAN YOU GUESS WHY?"
"He thought girls had cooties?"
"CLOSE. BEFORE IRENE, NO WOMAN HAD RULED ANY PART OF THE HOLY ROMAN EMPIRE ALONE. THE POPE COUNTED HER THRONE AS EMPTY AND CROWNED CHARLEMAGNE.
"EVENTUALLY IRENE WAS DEPOSED AND REPLACED BY NIKEPHOROS I.
"HER SUCCESSOR'S SKULL ENDED UP AS A DRINKING CUP."
He really got ***ahead*** of himself...

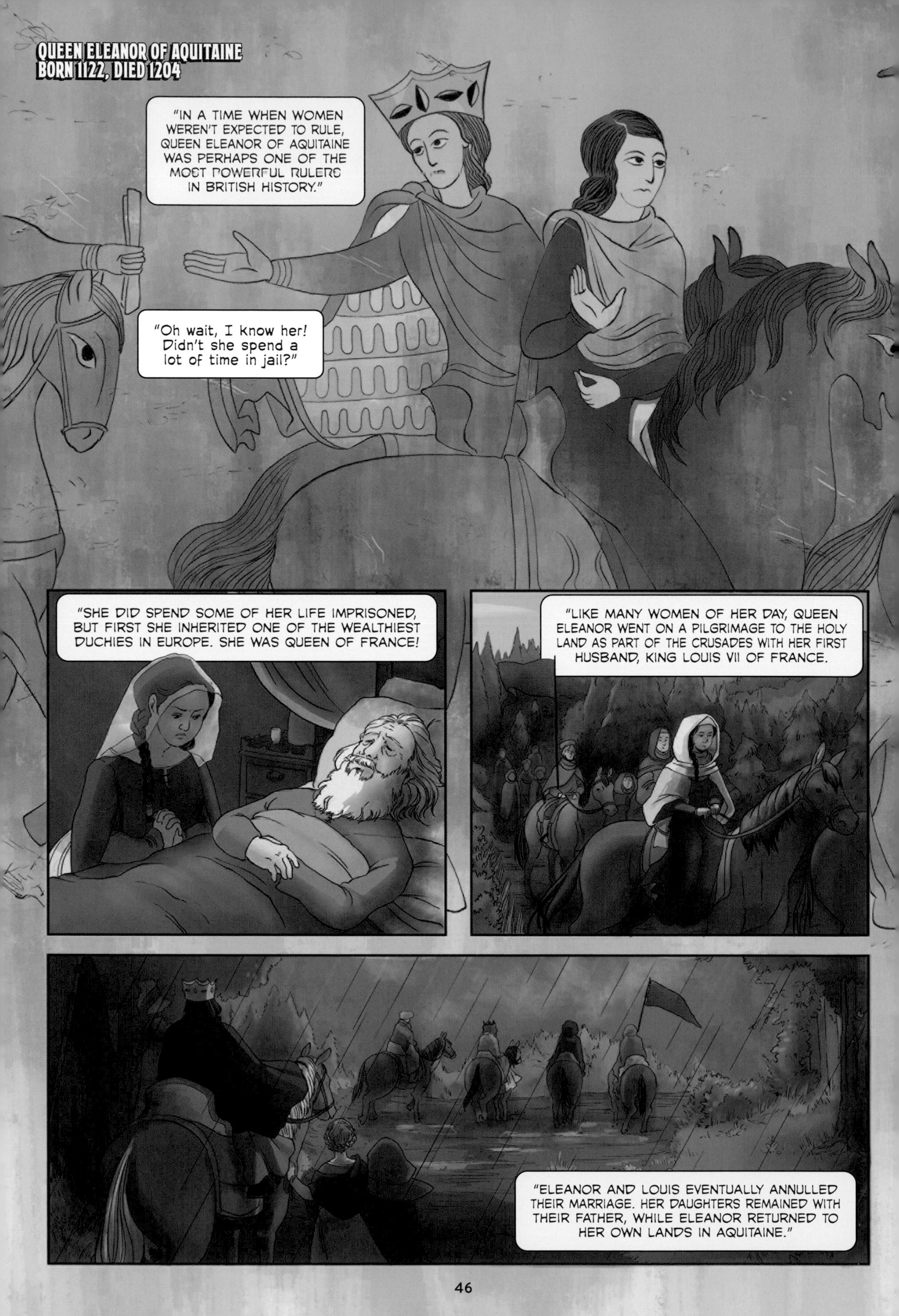
QUEEN ELEANOR OF AQUITAINE
BORN 1122, DIED 1204
"IN A TIME WHEN WOMEN WEREN'T EXPECTED TO RULE, QUEEN ELEANOR OF AQUITAINE WAS PERHAPS ONE OF THE MOST POWERFUL RULERS IN BRITISH HISTORY."
"Oh wait, I know her! Didn't she spend a lot of time in jail?"
"SHE DID SPEND SOME OF HER LIFE IMPRISONED, BUT FIRST SHE INHERITED ONE OF THE WEALTHIEST DUCHIES IN EUROPE. SHE WAS QUEEN OF FRANCE!
"LIKE MANY WOMEN OF HER DAY, QUEEN ELEANOR WENT ON A PILGRIMAGE TO THE HOLY LAND AS PART OF THE CRUSADES WITH HER FIRST HUSBAND, KING LOUIS VII OF FRANCE.
"ELEANOR AND LOUIS EVENTUALLY ANNULLED THEIR MARRIAGE. HER DAUGHTERS REMAINED WITH THEIR FATHER, WHILE ELEANOR RETURNED TO HER OWN LANDS IN AQUITAINE."

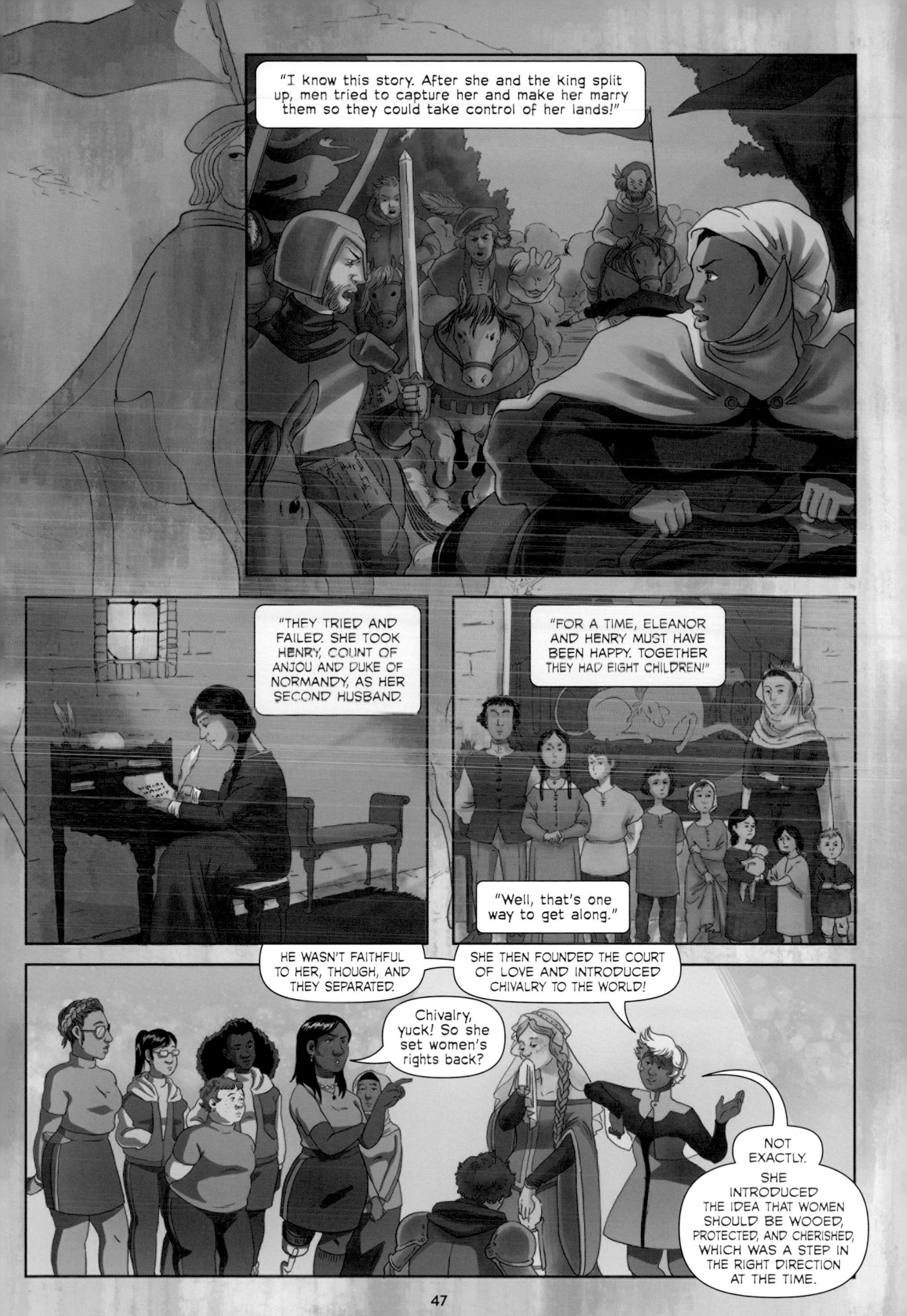
"I know this story. After she and the king split up, men tried to capture her and make her marry them so they could take control of her lands!"
"THEY TRIED AND FAILED. SHE TOOK HENRY, COUNT OF ANJOU AND DUKE OF NORMANDY, AS HER SECOND HUSBAND.
"FOR A TIME, ELEANOR AND HENRY MUST HAVE BEEN HAPPY. TOGETHER THEY HAD EIGHT CHILDREN!"
"Well, that's one way to get along."
HE WASN'T FAITHFUL TO HER, THOUGH, AND THEY SEPARATED.
SHE THEN FOUNDED THE COURT OF LOVE AND INTRODUCED CHIVALRY TO THE WORLD!
Chivalry, yuck! So she set women's rights back?
NOT EXACTLY.
SHE INTRODUCED THE IDEA THAT WOMEN SHOULD BE WOOED, PROTECTED, AND CHERISHED, WHICH WAS A STEP IN THE RIGHT DIRECTION AT THE TIME.

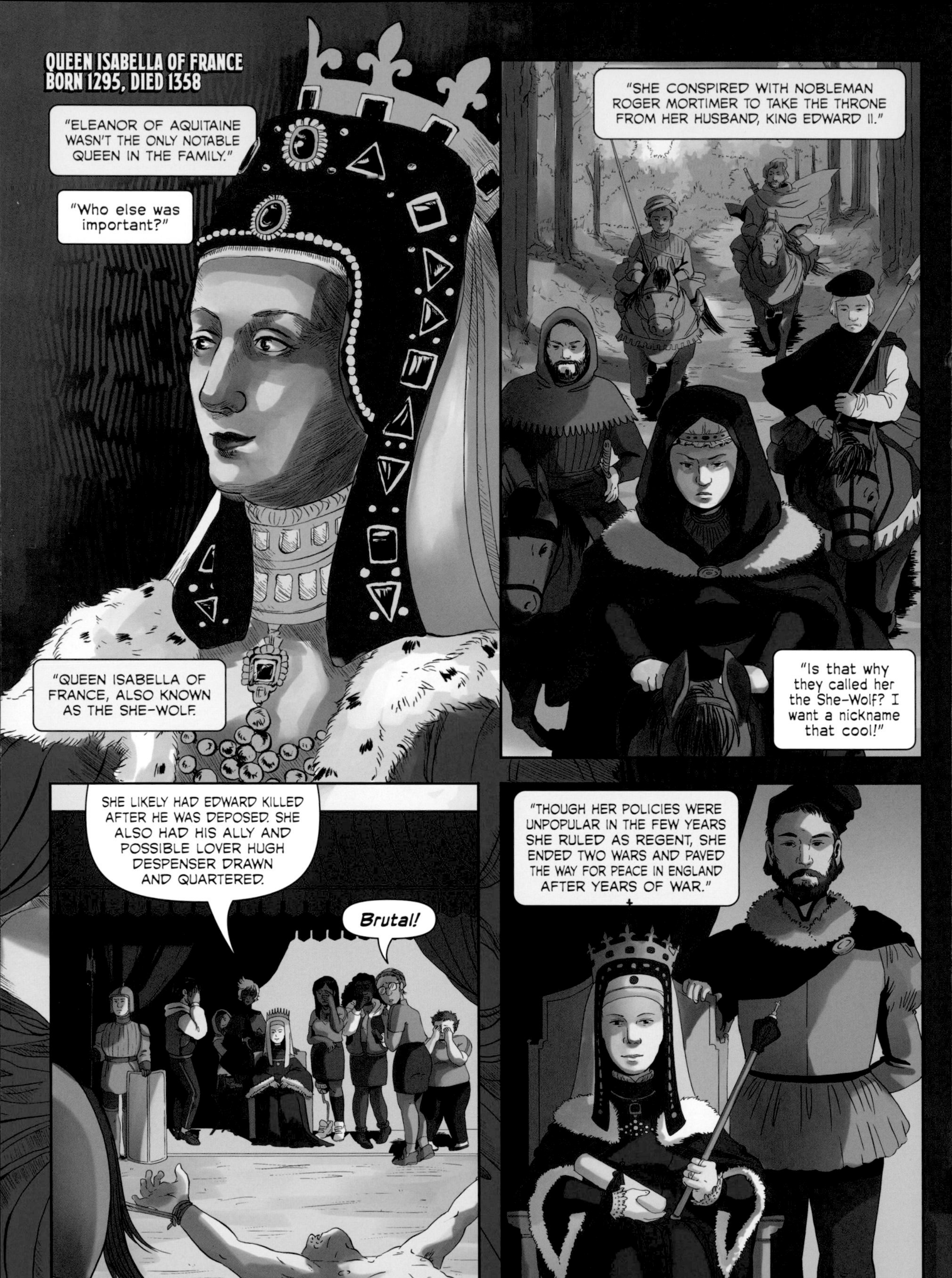
QUEEN ISABELLA OF FRANCE
BORN 1295, DIED 1358
"ELEANOR OF AQUITAINE WASN'T THE ONLY NOTABLE QUEEN IN THE FAMILY."
"Who else was important?"
"QUEEN ISABELLA OF FRANCE, ALSO KNOWN AS THE SHE-WOLF.
"SHE CONSPIRED WITH NOBLEMAN ROGER MORTIMER TO TAKE THE THRONE FROM HER HUSBAND, KING EDWARD II."
"Is that why they called her the She-Wolf? I want a nickname that cool!"
SHE LIKELY HAD EDWARD KILLED AFTER HE WAS DEPOSED. SHE ALSO HAD HIS ALLY AND POSSIBLE LOVER HUGH DESPENSER DRAWN AND QUARTERED.
Brutal!
"THOUGH HER POLICIES WERE UNPOPULAR IN THE FEW YEARS SHE RULED AS REGENT, SHE ENDED TWO WARS AND PAVED THE WAY FOR PEACE IN ENGLAND AFTER YEARS OF WAR."

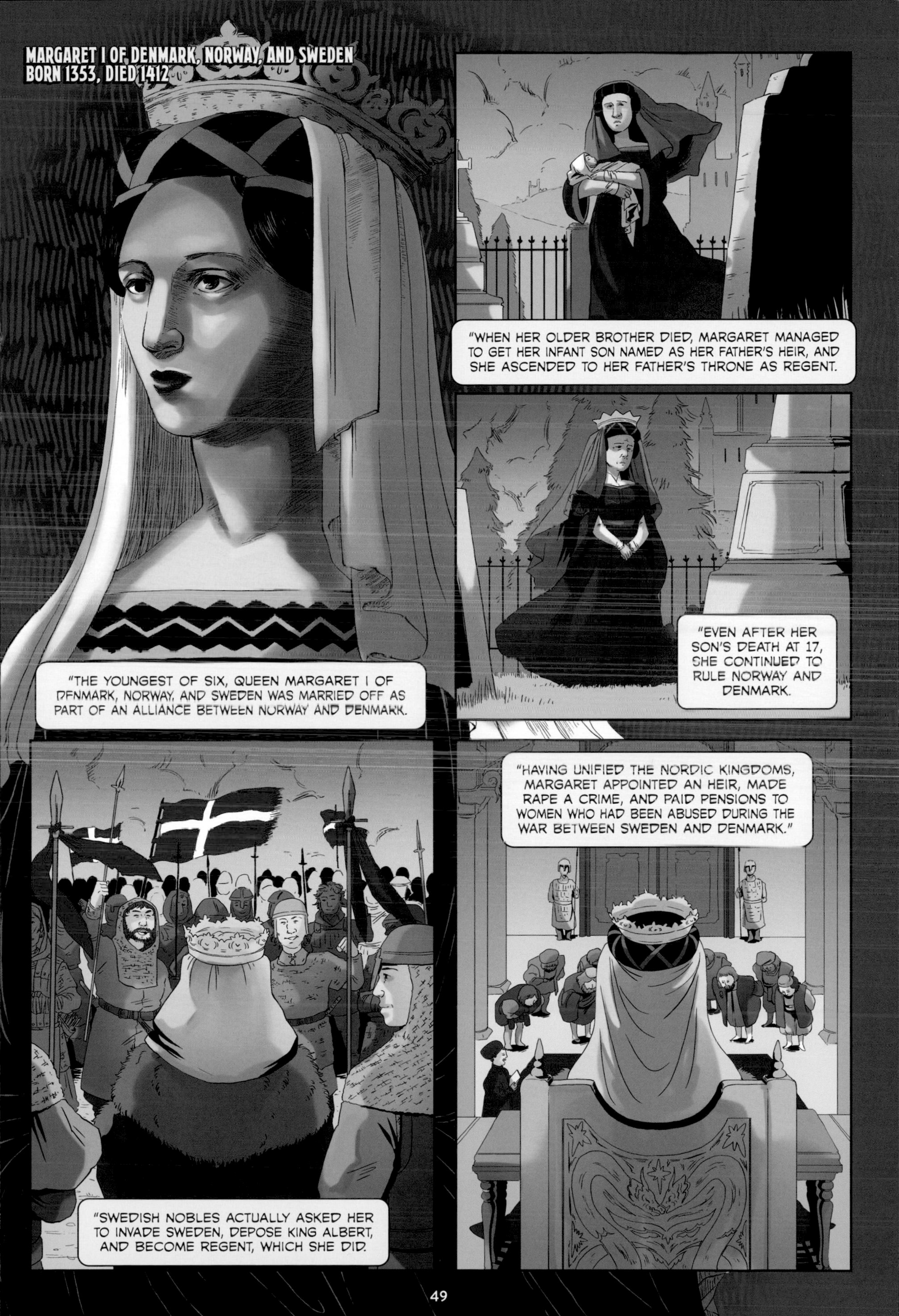
MARGARET I OF DENMARK, NORWAY, AND SWEDEN
BORN 1353, DIED 1412
"THE YOUNGEST OF SIX, QUEEN MARGARET I OF DENMARK, NORWAY, AND SWEDEN WAS MARRIED OFF AS PART OF AN ALLIANCE BETWEEN NORWAY AND DENMARK.
"WHEN HER OLDER BROTHER DIED, MARGARET MANAGED TO GET HER INFANT SON NAMED AS HER FATHER'S HEIR, AND SHE ASCENDED TO HER FATHER'S THRONE AS REGENT.
"EVEN AFTER HER SON'S DEATH AT 17, SHE CONTINUED TO RULE NORWAY AND DENMARK.
"SWEDISH NOBLES ACTUALLY ASKED HER TO INVADE SWEDEN, DEPOSE KING ALBERT, AND BECOME REGENT, WHICH SHE DID.
"HAVING UNIFIED THE NORDIC KINGDOMS, MARGARET APPOINTED AN HEIR, MADE RAPE A CRIME, AND PAID PENSIONS TO WOMEN WHO HAD BEEN ABUSED DURING THE WAR BETWEEN SWEDEN AND DENMARK."

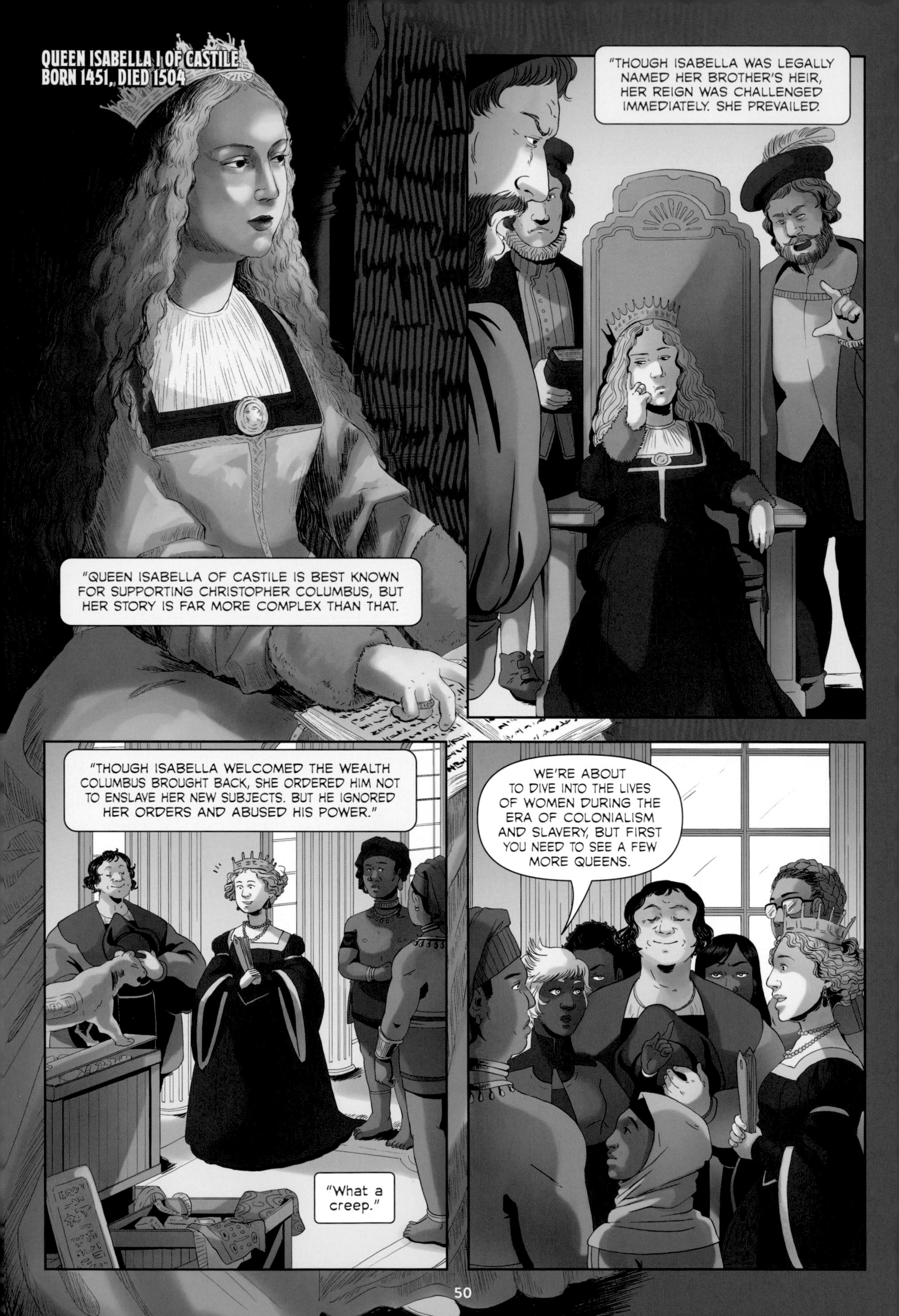

QUEEN ISABELLA I OF CASTILE
BORN 1451, DIED 1504
"QUEEN ISABELLA OF CASTILE IS BEST KNOWN FOR SUPPORTING CHRISTOPHER COLUMBUS, BUT HER STORY IS FAR MORE COMPLEX THAN THAT.
"THOUGH ISABELLA WAS LEGALLY NAMED HER BROTHER'S HEIR, HER REIGN WAS CHALLENGED IMMEDIATELY. SHE PREVAILED.
"THOUGH ISABELLA WELCOMED THE WEALTH COLUMBUS BROUGHT BACK, SHE ORDERED HIM NOT TO ENSLAVE HER NEW SUBJECTS. BUT HE IGNORED HER ORDERS AND ABUSED HIS POWER."
"What a creep."
WE'RE ABOUT TO DIVE INTO THE LIVES OF WOMEN DURING THE ERA OF COLONIALISM AND SLAVERY, BUT FIRST YOU NEED TO SEE A FEW MORE QUEENS.

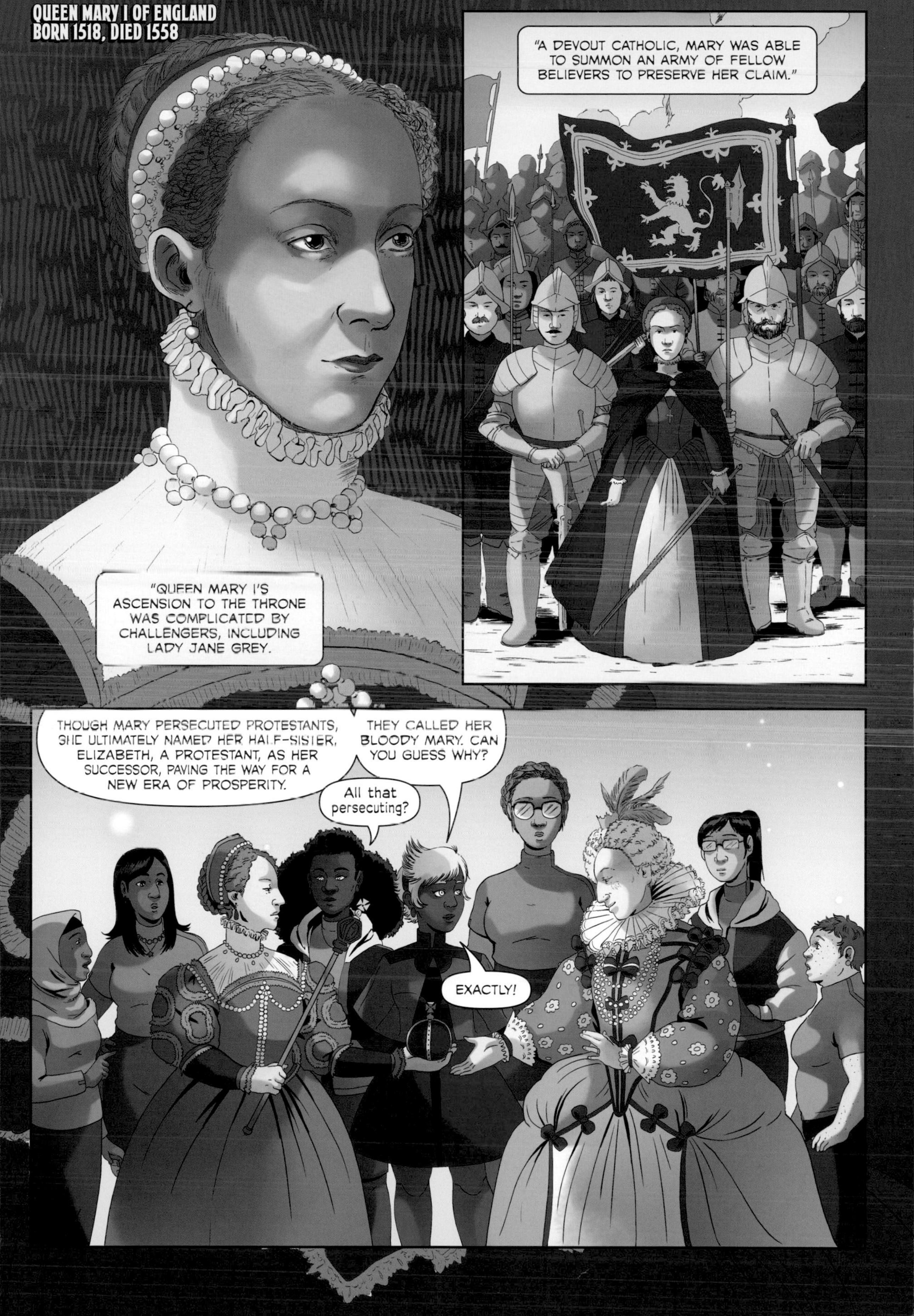
QUEEN MARY I OF ENGLAND
BORN 1518, DIED 1558
"A DEVOUT CATHOLIC, MARY WAS ABLE TO SUMMON AN ARMY OF FELLOW BELIEVERS TO PRESERVE HER CLAIM."
"QUEEN MARY I'S ASCENSION TO THE THRONE WAS COMPLICATED BY CHALLENGERS, INCLUDING LADY JANE GREY.
THOUGH MARY PERSECUTED PROTESTANTS, SHE ULTIMATELY NAMED HER HALF-SISTER, ELIZABETH, A PROTESTANT, AS HER SUCCESSOR, PAVING THE WAY FOR A NEW ERA OF PROSPERITY.
THEY CALLED HER BLOODY MARY. CAN YOU GUESS WHY?
All that persecuting?
EXACTLY!

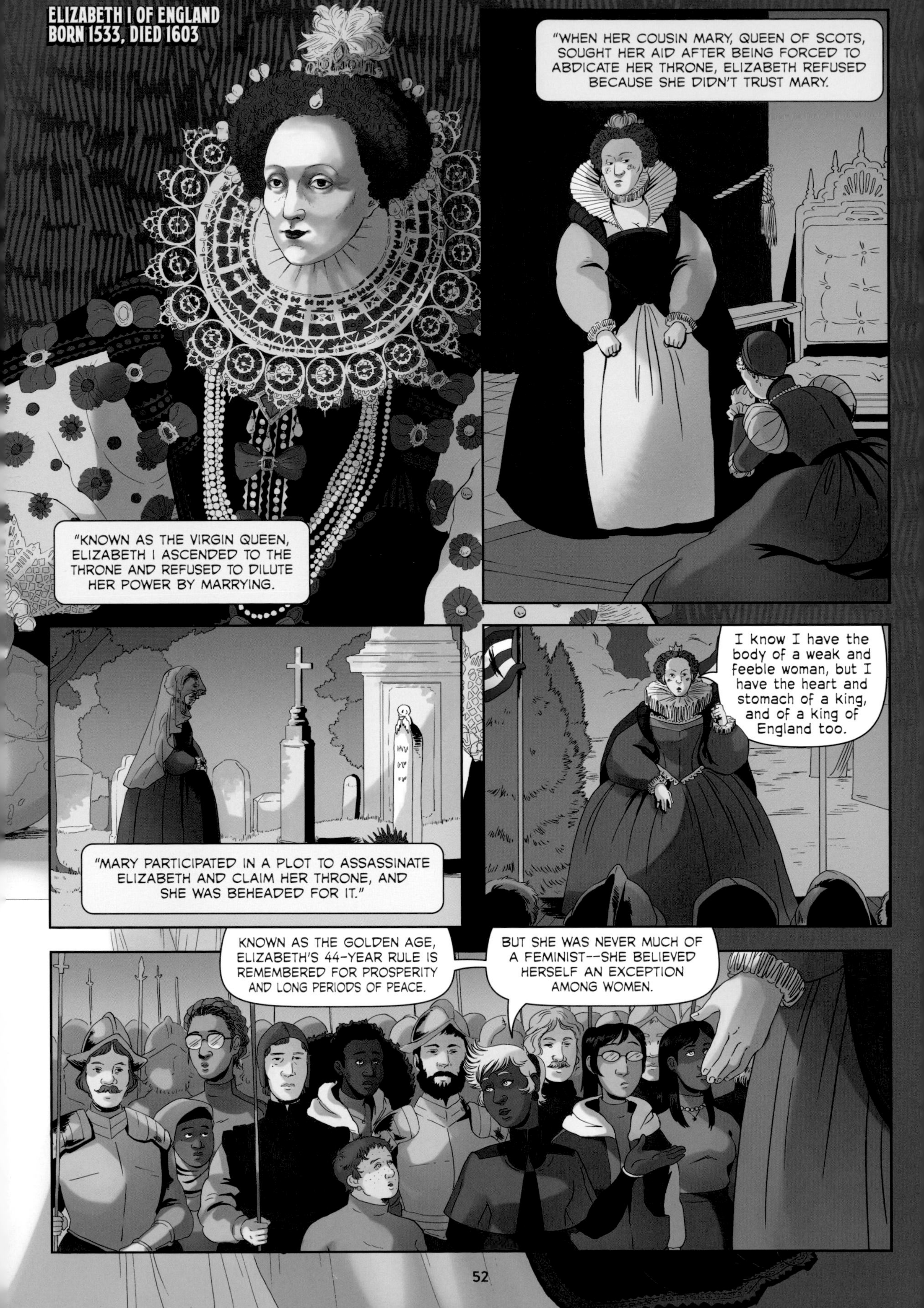
ELIZABETH I OF ENGLAND
BORN 1533, DIED 1603
"KNOWN AS THE VIRGIN QUEEN, ELIZABETH I ASCENDED TO THE THRONE AND REFUSED TO DILUTE HER POWER BY MARRYING.
"WHEN HER COUSIN MARY, QUEEN OF SCOTS, SOUGHT HER AID AFTER BEING FORCED TO ABDICATE HER THRONE, ELIZABETH REFUSED BECAUSE SHE DIDN'T TRUST MARY.
"MARY PARTICIPATED IN A PLOT TO ASSASSINATE ELIZABETH AND CLAIM HER THRONE, AND SHE WAS BEHEADED FOR IT."
I know I have the body of a weak and feeble woman, but I have the heart and stomach of a king, and of a king of England too.
KNOWN AS THE GOLDEN AGE, ELIZABETH'S 44-YEAR RULE IS REMEMBERED FOR PROSPERITY AND LONG PERIODS OF PEACE.
BUT SHE WAS NEVER MUCH OF A FEMINIST--SHE BELIEVED HERSELF AN EXCEPTION AMONG WOMEN.

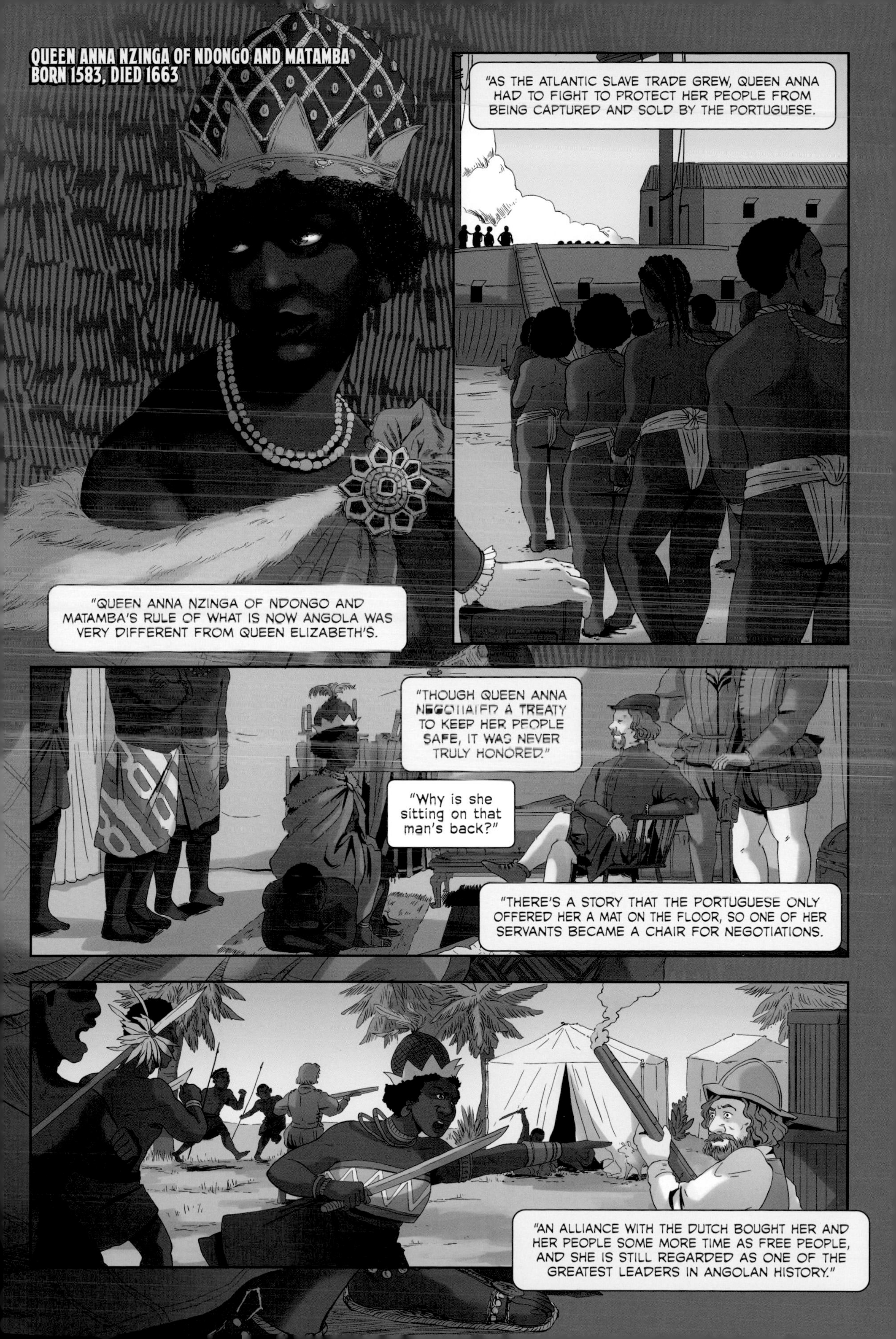
QUEEN ANNA NZINGA OF NDONGO AND MATAMBA
BORN 1583, DIED 1663
"QUEEN ANNA NZINGA OF NDONGO AND MATAMBA'S RULE OF WHAT IS NOW ANGOLA WAS VERY DIFFERENT FROM QUEEN ELIZABETH'S.
"AS THE ATLANTIC SLAVE TRADE GREW, QUEEN ANNA HAD TO FIGHT TO PROTECT HER PEOPLE FROM BEING CAPTURED AND SOLD BY THE PORTUGUESE.
"THOUGH QUEEN ANNA NEGOTIATED A TREATY TO KEEP HER PEOPLE SAFE, IT WAS NEVER TRULY HONORED."
"Why is she sitting on that man's back?"
"THERE'S A STORY THAT THE PORTUGUESE ONLY OFFERED HER A MAT ON THE FLOOR, SO ONE OF HER SERVANTS BECAME A CHAIR FOR NEGOTIATIONS.
"AN ALLIANCE WITH THE DUTCH BOUGHT HER AND HER PEOPLE SOME MORE TIME AS FREE PEOPLE, AND SHE IS STILL REGARDED AS ONE OF THE GREATEST LEADERS IN ANGOLAN HISTORY."

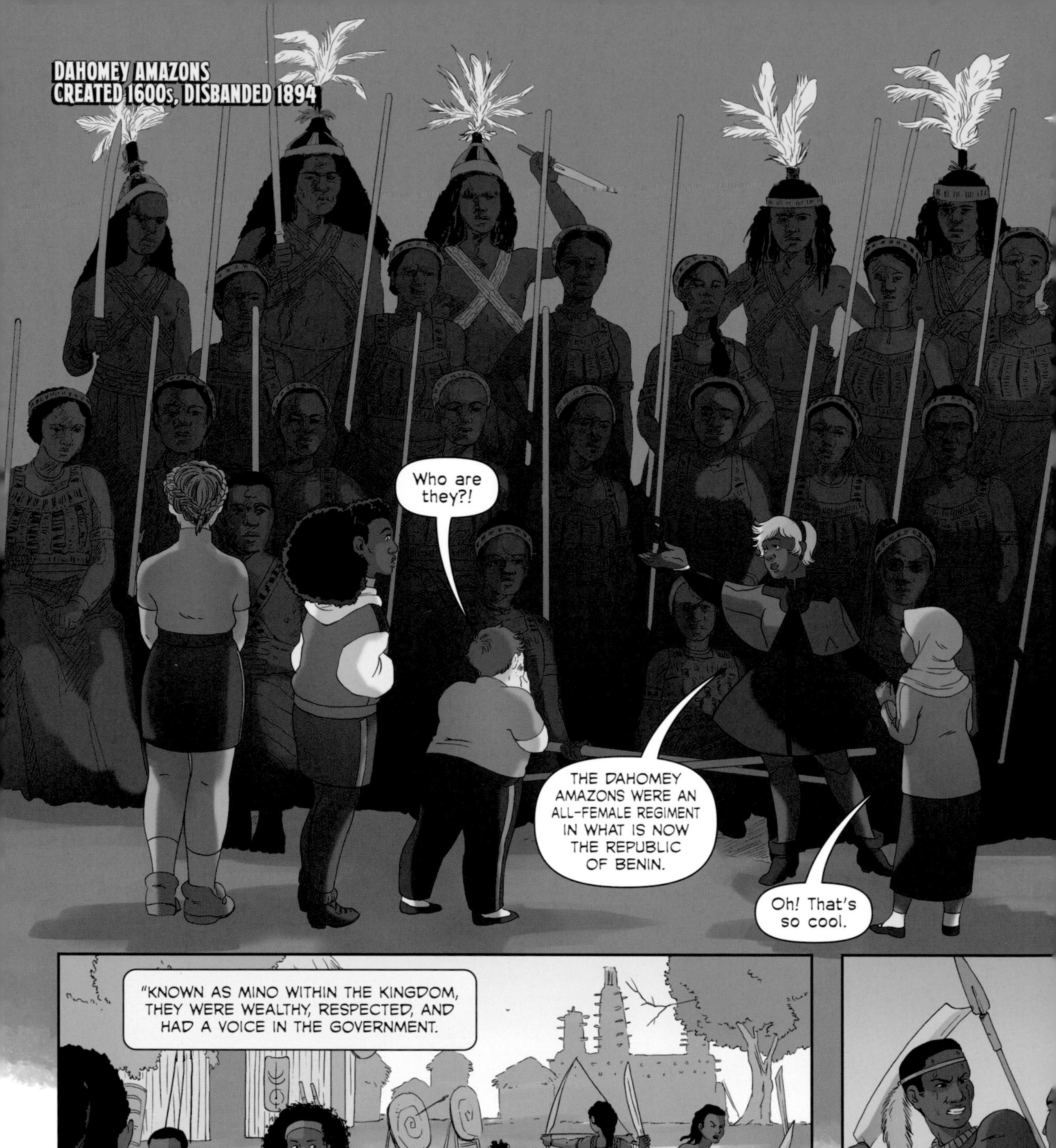
DAHOMEY AMAZONS
CREATED 1600s, DISBANDED 1894
Who are they?!
THE DAHOMEY AMAZONS WERE AN ALL-FEMALE REGIMENT IN WHAT IS NOW THE REPUBLIC OF BENIN.
Oh! That's so cool.

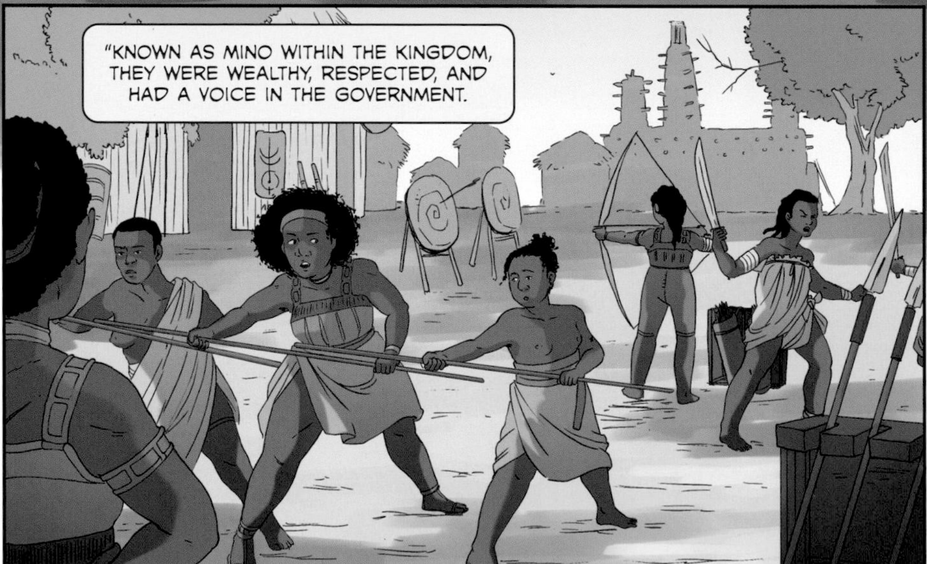
"KNOWN AS MINO WITHIN THE KINGDOM, THEY WERE WEALTHY, RESPECTED, AND HAD A VOICE IN THE GOVERNMENT.

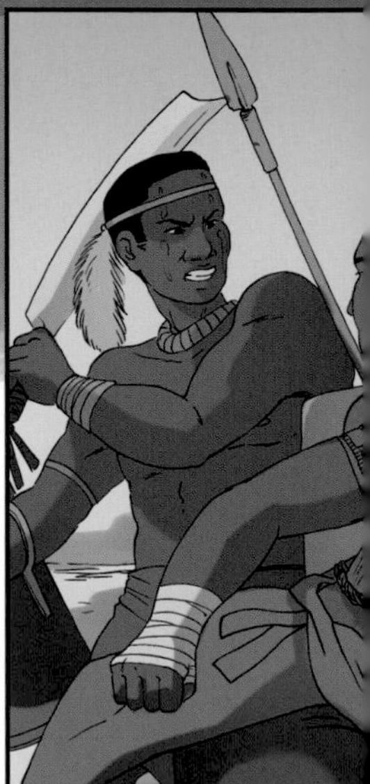

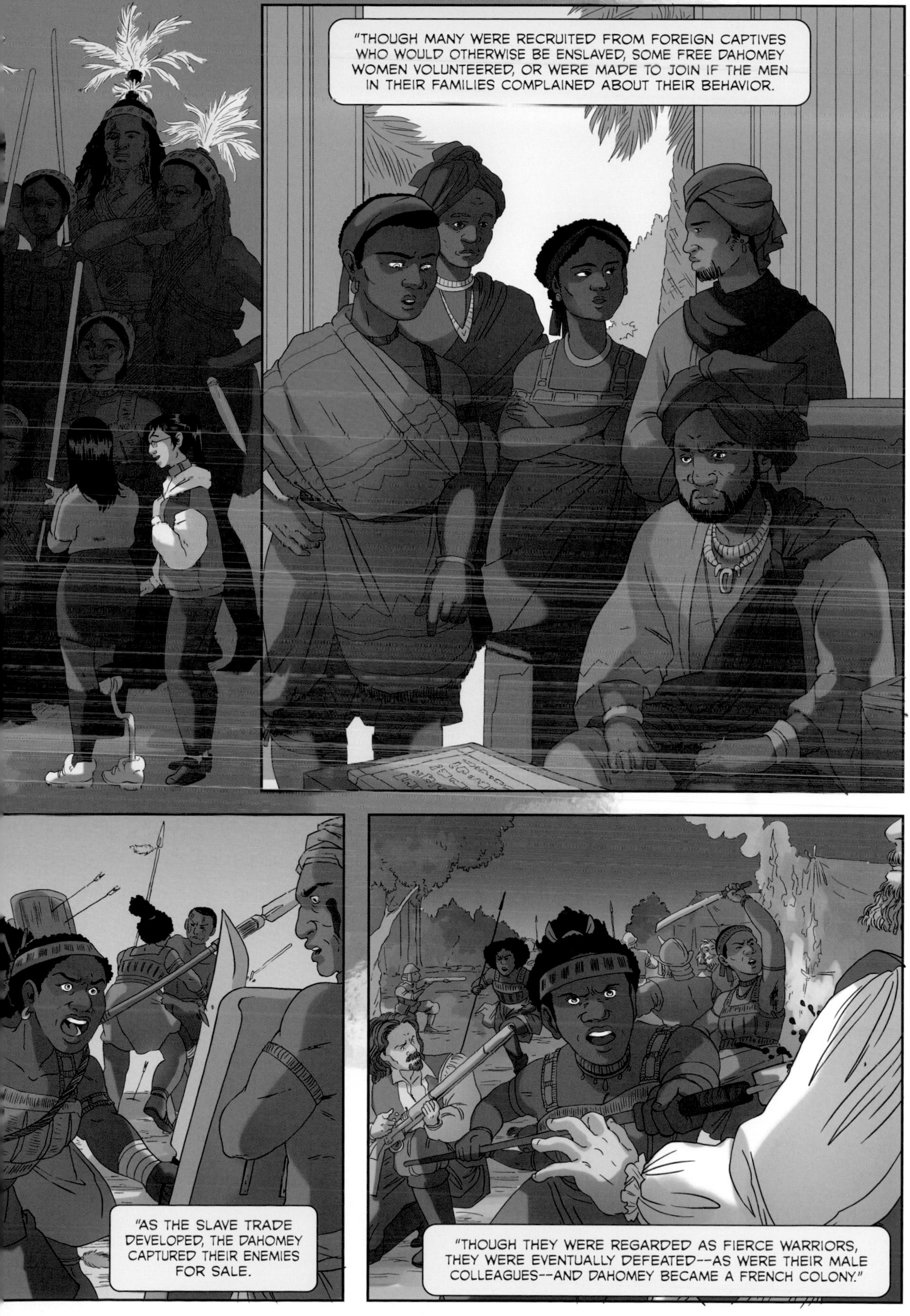
"THOUGH MANY WERE RECRUITED FROM FOREIGN CAPTIVES WHO WOULD OTHERWISE BE ENSLAVED, SOME FREE DAHOMEY WOMEN VOLUNTEERED, OR WERE MADE TO JOIN IF THE MEN IN THEIR FAMILIES COMPLAINED ABOUT THEIR BEHAVIOR.
"AS THE SLAVE TRADE DEVELOPED, THE DAHOMEY CAPTURED THEIR ENEMIES FOR SALE.
"THOUGH THEY WERE REGARDED AS FIERCE WARRIORS, THEY WERE EVENTUALLY DEFEATED--AS WERE THEIR MALE COLLEAGUES--AND DAHOMEY BECAME A FRENCH COLONY."

CHAPTER 3
SLAVERY, COLONIALISM, AND IMPERIALISM: THE RIGHTS OF WOMEN UNDER SIEGE

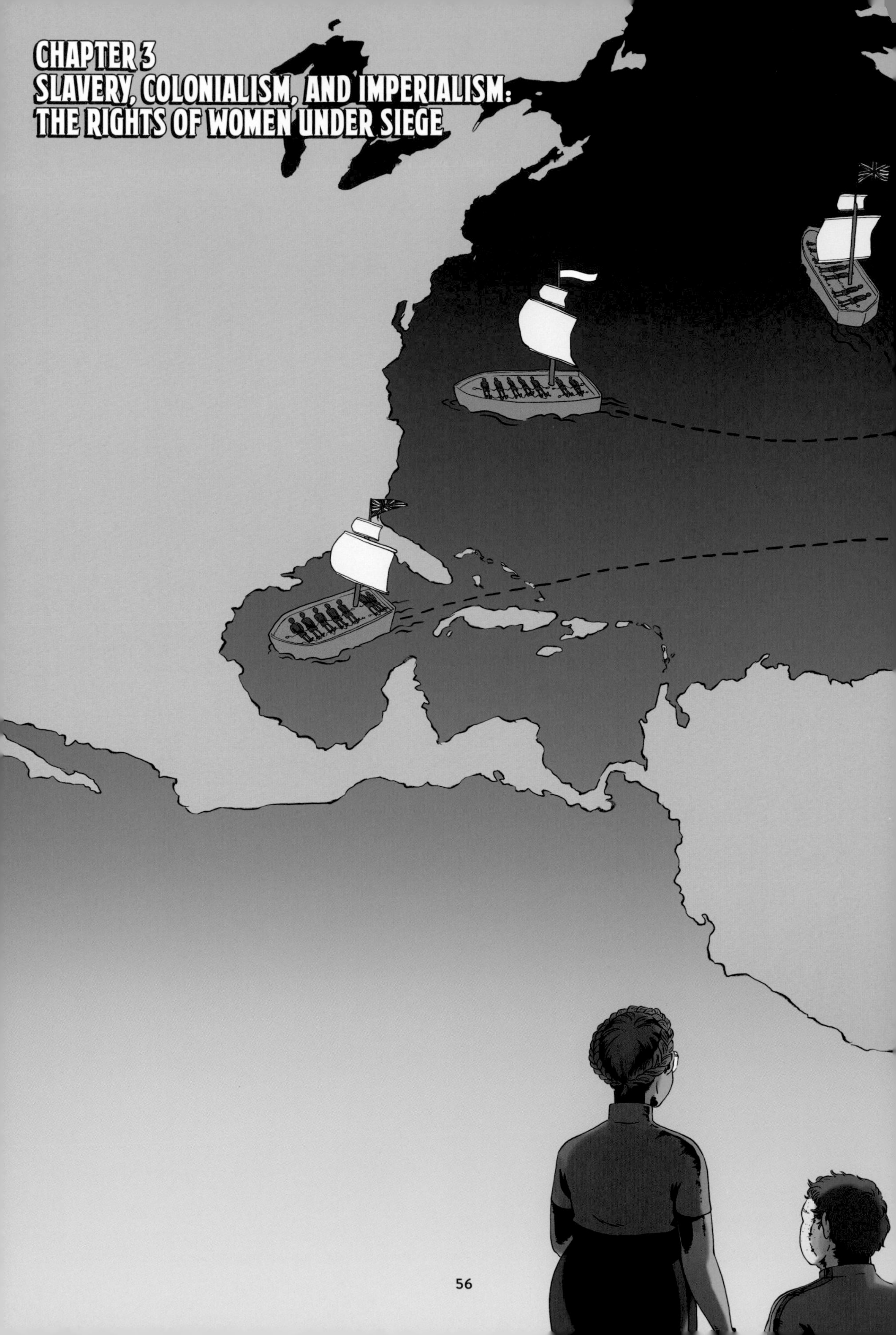

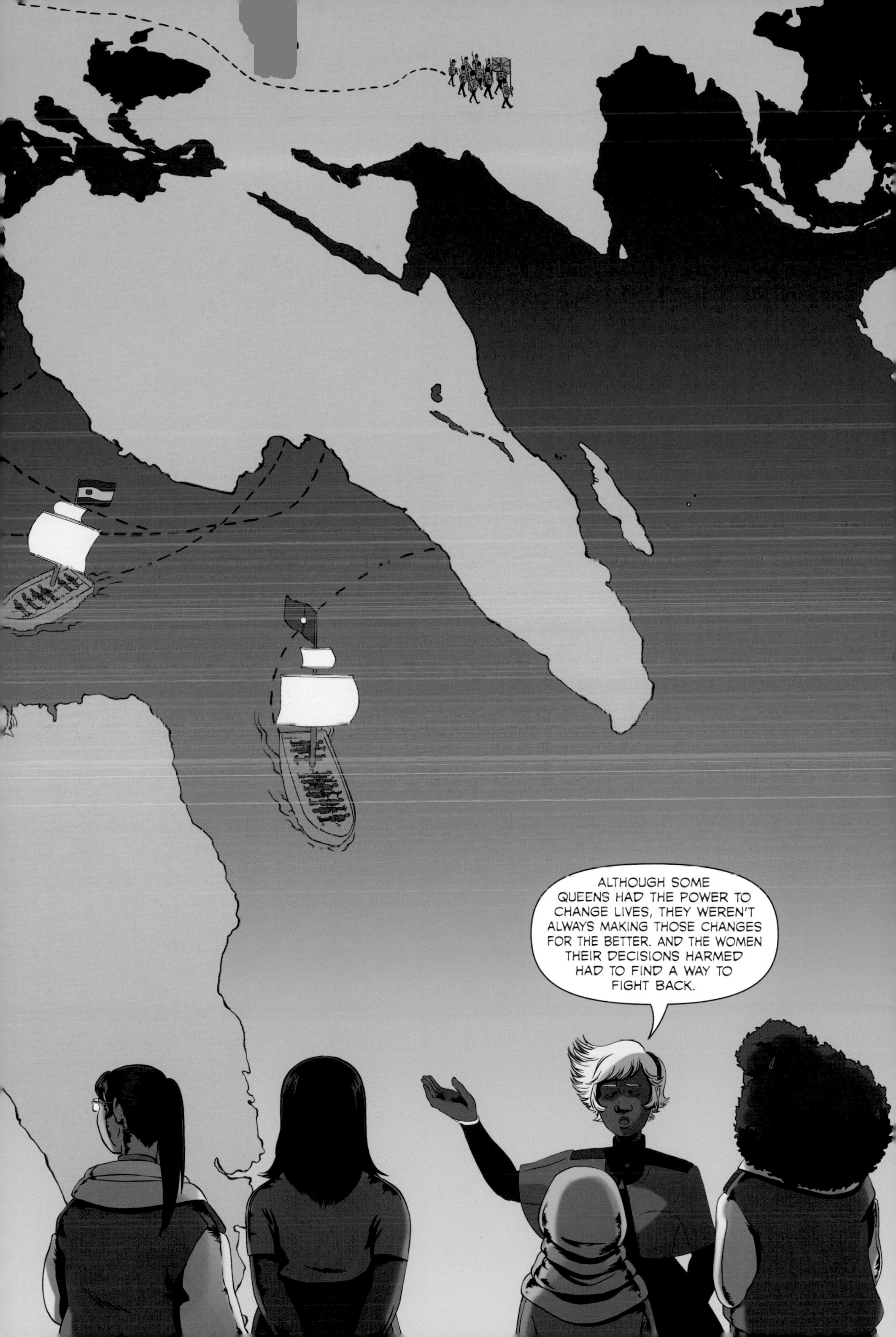
ALTHOUGH SOME QUEENS HAD THE POWER TO CHANGE LIVES, THEY WEREN'T ALWAYS MAKING THOSE CHANGES FOR THE BETTER. AND THE WOMEN THEIR DECISIONS HARMED HAD TO FIND A WAY TO FIGHT BACK.

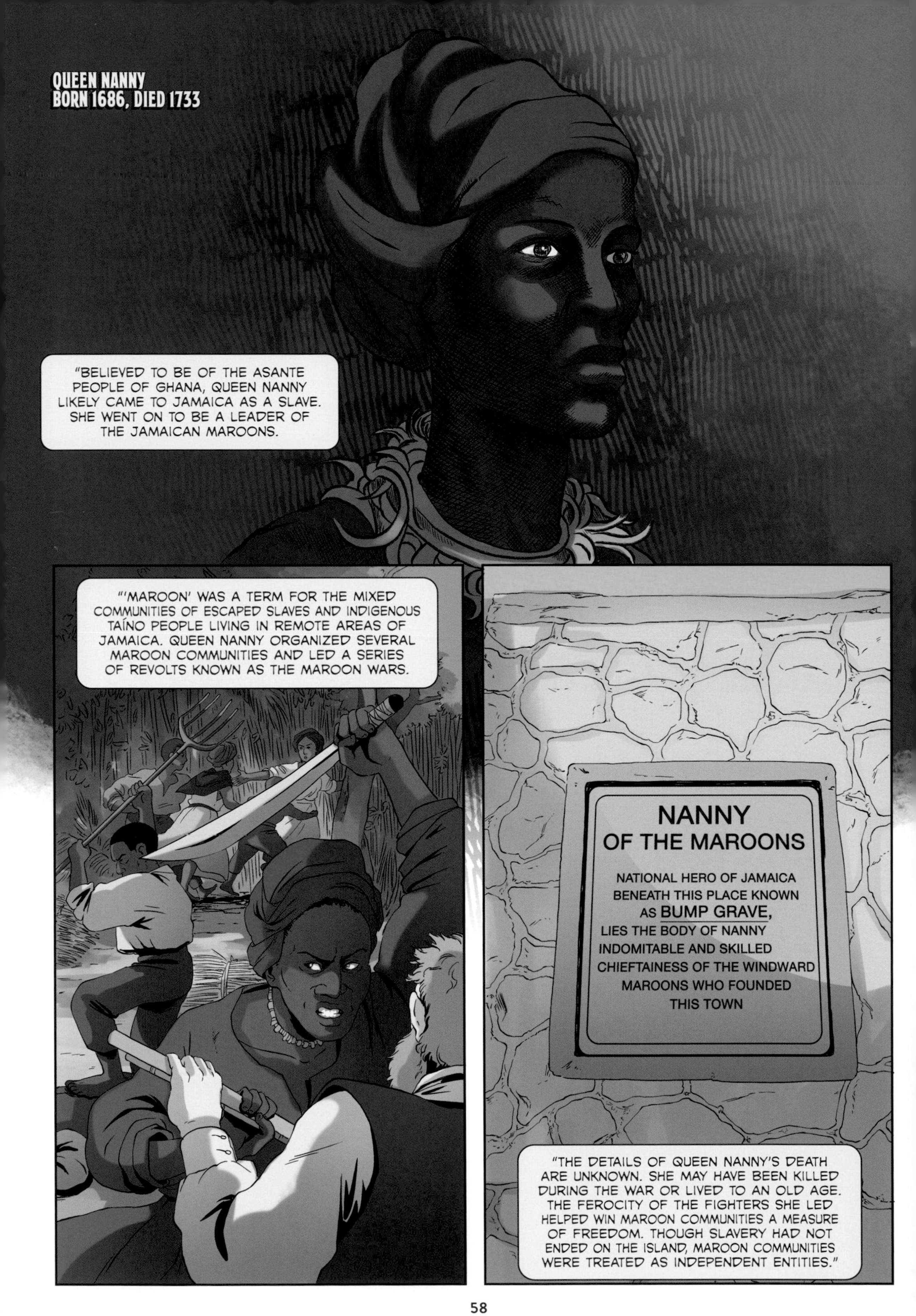
QUEEN NANNY
BORN 1686, DIED 1733
"BELIEVED TO BE OF THE ASANTE PEOPLE OF GHANA, QUEEN NANNY LIKELY CAME TO JAMAICA AS A SLAVE. SHE WENT ON TO BE A LEADER OF THE JAMAICAN MAROONS.
"'MAROON' WAS A TERM FOR THE MIXED COMMUNITIES OF ESCAPED SLAVES AND INDIGENOUS TAÍNO PEOPLE LIVING IN REMOTE AREAS OF JAMAICA. QUEEN NANNY ORGANIZED SEVERAL MAROON COMMUNITIES AND LED A SERIES OF REVOLTS KNOWN AS THE MAROON WARS.
NANNY OF THE MAROONS
NATIONAL HERO OF JAMAICA BENEATH THIS PLACE KNOWN AS BUMP GRAVE, LIES THE BODY OF NANNY INDOMITABLE AND SKILLED CHIEFTAINESS OF THE WINDWARD MAROONS WHO FOUNDED THIS TOWN
"THE DETAILS OF QUEEN NANNY'S DEATH ARE UNKNOWN. SHE MAY HAVE BEEN KILLED DURING THE WAR OR LIVED TO AN OLD AGE. THE FEROCITY OF THE FIGHTERS SHE LED HELPED WIN MAROON COMMUNITIES A MEASURE OF FREEDOM. THOUGH SLAVERY HAD NOT ENDED ON THE ISLAND, MAROON COMMUNITIES WERE TREATED AS INDEPENDENT ENTITIES."

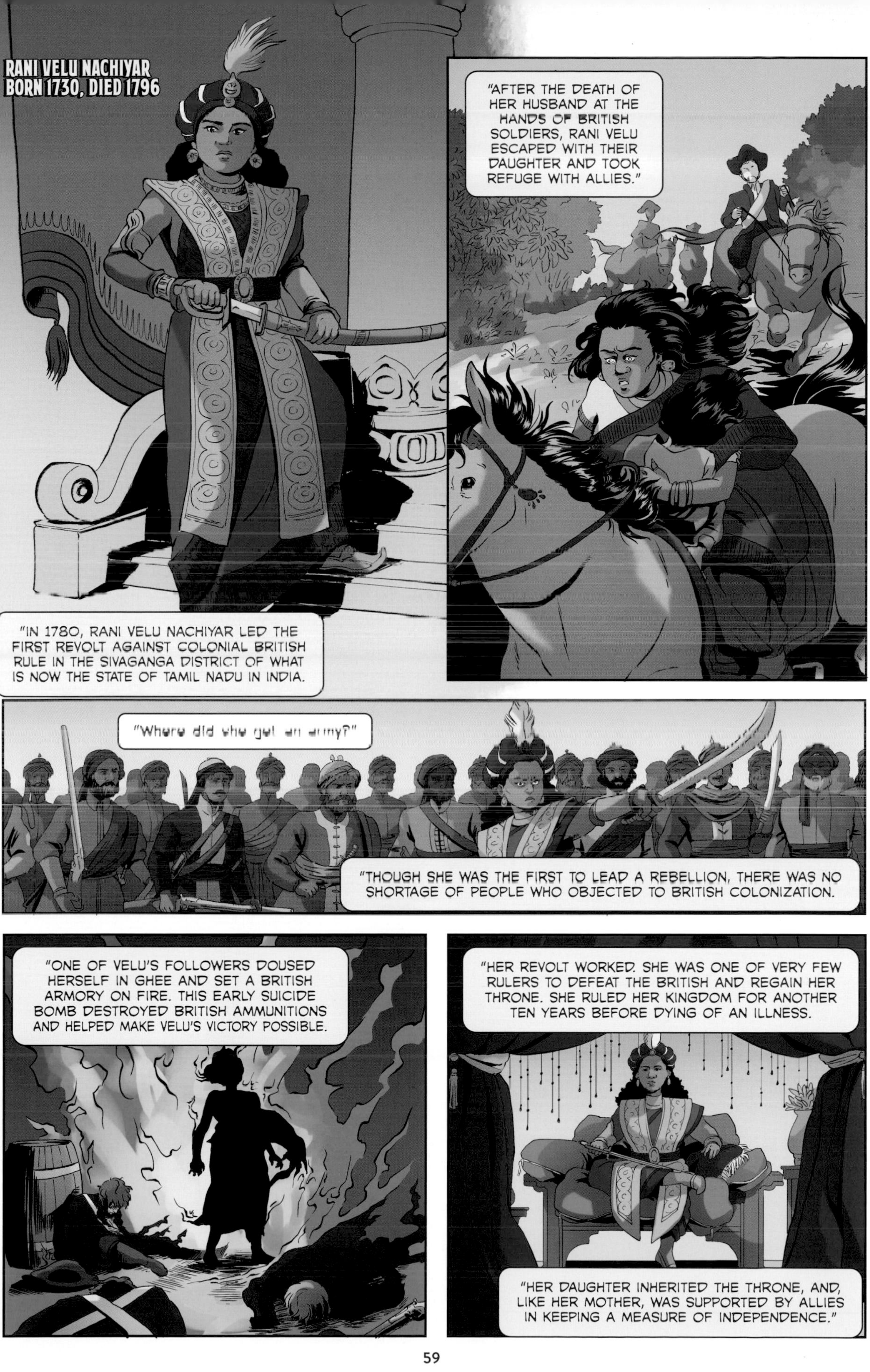
RANI VELU NACHIYAR
BORN 1730, DIED 1796
"IN 1780, RANI VELU NACHIYAR LED THE FIRST REVOLT AGAINST COLONIAL BRITISH RULE IN THE SIVAGANGA DISTRICT OF WHAT IS NOW THE STATE OF TAMIL NADU IN INDIA.
"AFTER THE DEATH OF HER HUSBAND AT THE HANDS OF BRITISH SOLDIERS, RANI VELU ESCAPED WITH THEIR DAUGHTER AND TOOK REFUGE WITH ALLIES."
"Where did she get an army?"
"THOUGH SHE WAS THE FIRST TO LEAD A REBELLION, THERE WAS NO SHORTAGE OF PEOPLE WHO OBJECTED TO BRITISH COLONIZATION.
"ONE OF VELU'S FOLLOWERS DOUSED HERSELF IN GHEE AND SET A BRITISH ARMORY ON FIRE. THIS EARLY SUICIDE BOMB DESTROYED BRITISH AMMUNITIONS AND HELPED MAKE VELU'S VICTORY POSSIBLE.
"HER REVOLT WORKED. SHE WAS ONE OF VERY FEW RULERS TO DEFEAT THE BRITISH AND REGAIN HER THRONE. SHE RULED HER KINGDOM FOR ANOTHER TEN YEARS BEFORE DYING OF AN ILLNESS.
"HER DAUGHTER INHERITED THE THRONE, AND, LIKE HER MOTHER, WAS SUPPORTED BY ALLIES IN KEEPING A MEASURE OF INDEPENDENCE."

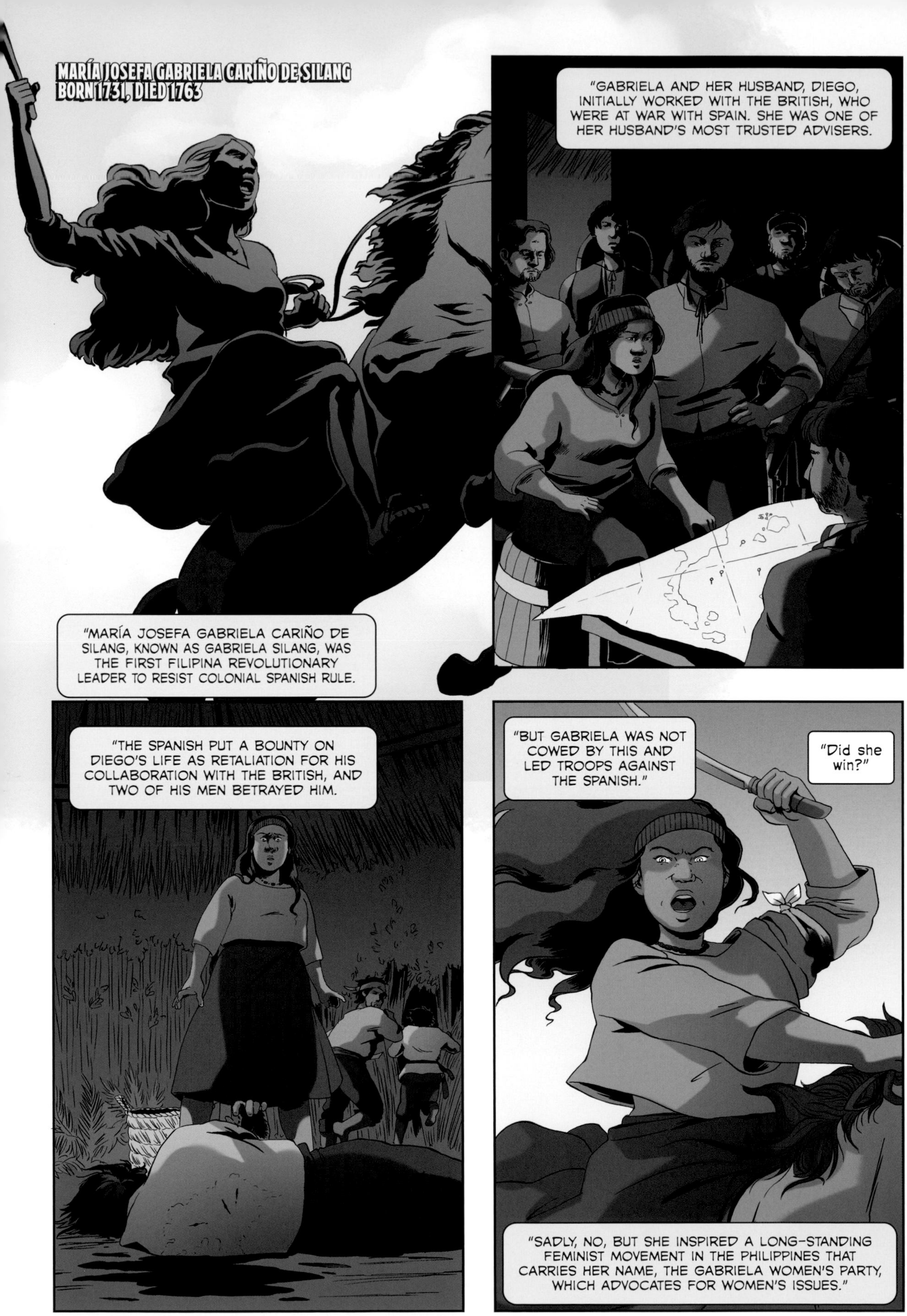
MARÍA JOSEFA GABRIELA CARIÑO DE SILANG
BORN 1731, DIED 1763
"MARÍA JOSEFA GABRIELA CARIÑO DE SILANG, KNOWN AS GABRIELA SILANG, WAS THE FIRST FILIPINA REVOLUTIONARY LEADER TO RESIST COLONIAL SPANISH RULE.
"GABRIELA AND HER HUSBAND, DIEGO, INITIALLY WORKED WITH THE BRITISH, WHO WERE AT WAR WITH SPAIN. SHE WAS ONE OF HER HUSBAND'S MOST TRUSTED ADVISERS.
"THE SPANISH PUT A BOUNTY ON DIEGO'S LIFE AS RETALIATION FOR HIS COLLABORATION WITH THE BRITISH, AND TWO OF HIS MEN BETRAYED HIM.
"BUT GABRIELA WAS NOT COWED BY THIS AND LED TROOPS AGAINST THE SPANISH."
"Did she win?"
"SADLY, NO, BUT SHE INSPIRED A LONG-STANDING FEMINIST MOVEMENT IN THE PHILIPPINES THAT CARRIES HER NAME, THE GABRIELA WOMEN'S PARTY, WHICH ADVOCATES FOR WOMEN'S ISSUES."

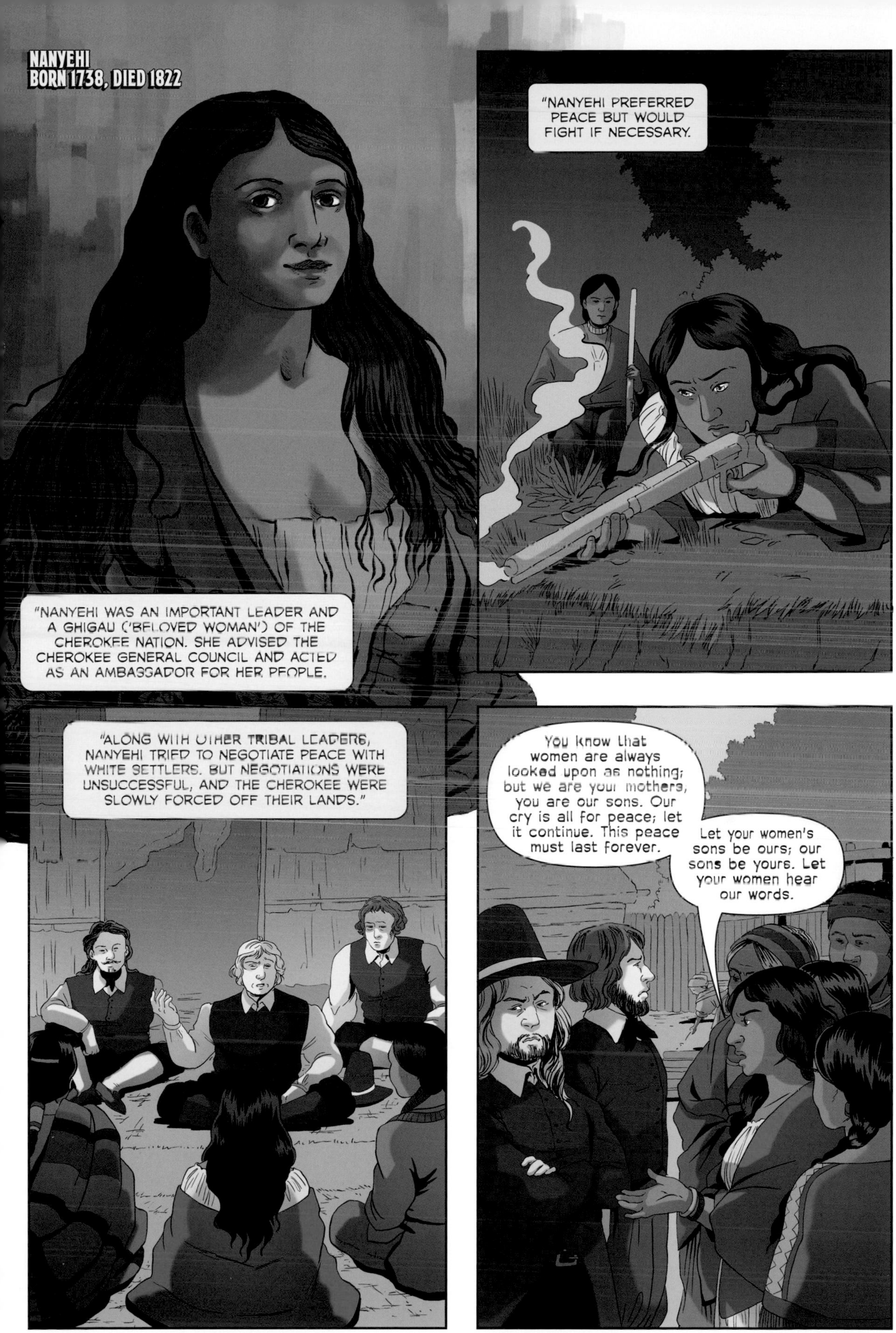
NANYEHI
BORN 1738, DIED 1822
"NANYEHI WAS AN IMPORTANT LEADER AND A GHIGAU ('BELOVED WOMAN') OF THE CHEROKEE NATION. SHE ADVISED THE CHEROKEE GENERAL COUNCIL AND ACTED AS AN AMBASSADOR FOR HER PEOPLE.
"NANYEHI PREFERRED PEACE BUT WOULD FIGHT IF NECESSARY.
"ALONG WITH OTHER TRIBAL LEADERS, NANYEHI TRIED TO NEGOTIATE PEACE WITH WHITE SETTLERS. BUT NEGOTIATIONS WERE UNSUCCESSFUL, AND THE CHEROKEE WERE SLOWLY FORCED OFF THEIR LANDS."
You know that women are always looked upon as nothing; but we are your mothers, you are our sons. Our cry is all for peace; let it continue. This peace must last forever.
Let your women's sons be ours; our sons be yours. Let your women hear our words.

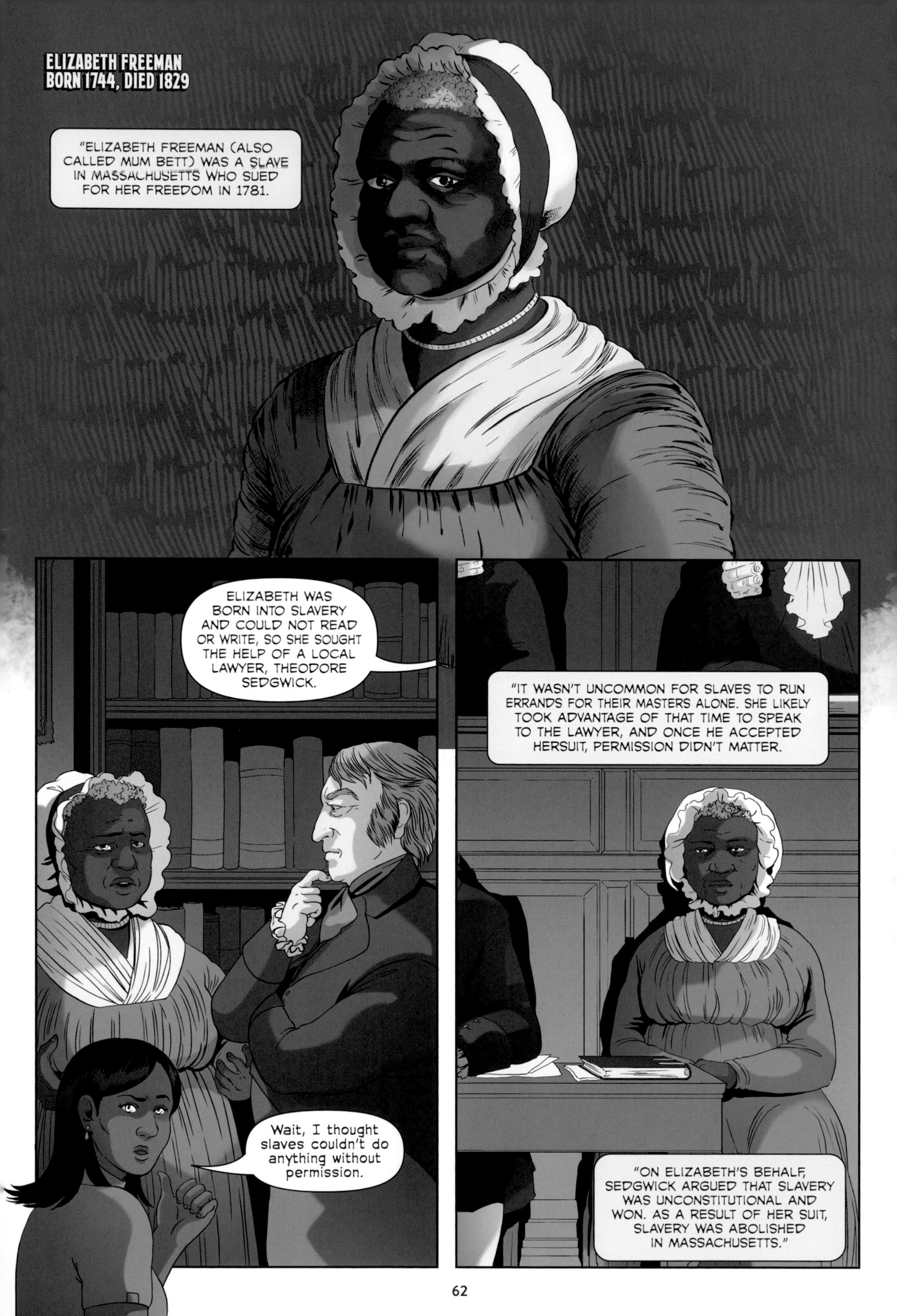
ELIZABETH FREEMAN
BORN 1744, DIED 1829
"ELIZABETH FREEMAN (ALSO CALLED MUM BETT) WAS A SLAVE IN MASSACHUSETTS WHO SUED FOR HER FREEDOM IN 1781.
ELIZABETH WAS BORN INTO SLAVERY AND COULD NOT READ OR WRITE, SO SHE SOUGHT THE HELP OF A LOCAL LAWYER, THEODORE SEDGWICK.
Wait, I thought slaves couldn't do anything without permission.
"IT WASN'T UNCOMMON FOR SLAVES TO RUN ERRANDS FOR THEIR MASTERS ALONE. SHE LIKELY TOOK ADVANTAGE OF THAT TIME TO SPEAK TO THE LAWYER, AND ONCE HE ACCEPTED HERSUIT, PERMISSION DIDN'T MATTER.
"ON ELIZABETH'S BEHALF, SEDGWICK ARGUED THAT SLAVERY WAS UNCONSTITUTIONAL AND WON. AS A RESULT OF HER SUIT, SLAVERY WAS ABOLISHED IN MASSACHUSETTS."

LUCRETIA MOTT
BORN 1793, DIED 1880

"LUCRETIA MOTT WAS AN ABOLITIONIST AND WOMEN'S RIGHTS ACTIVIST.

"ABOLITION WAS ALREADY AN UNPOPULAR TOPIC IN THE UNITED STATES BEFORE THE CIVIL WAR, AND THE IDEA OF WOMEN ENGAGING IN PUBLIC LIFE INSPIRED RAGE AND SOMETIMES VIOLENCE.

"IN 1840, LUCRETIA TRAVELED TO LONDON TO ATTEND AN ANTI-SLAVERY CONVENTION, BUT SHE AND ALL OTHER WOMEN WERE EXCLUDED FROM THE CONFERENCE.

World Anti-Slavery Convention

"IN 1848, LUCRETIA VISITED SENECA FALLS AND SAW THAT THE WOMEN IN THE HAUDENOSAUNEE CONFEDERACY WERE TREATED AS EQUALS. MODERN FEMINISM OWES A LOT TO THEM."

"I thought they were called the Iroquois?"

"HAUDENOSAUNEE IS THE SAME NATION, BUT 'IROQUOIS' WAS A DEROGATORY TERM FROM THE FRENCH."

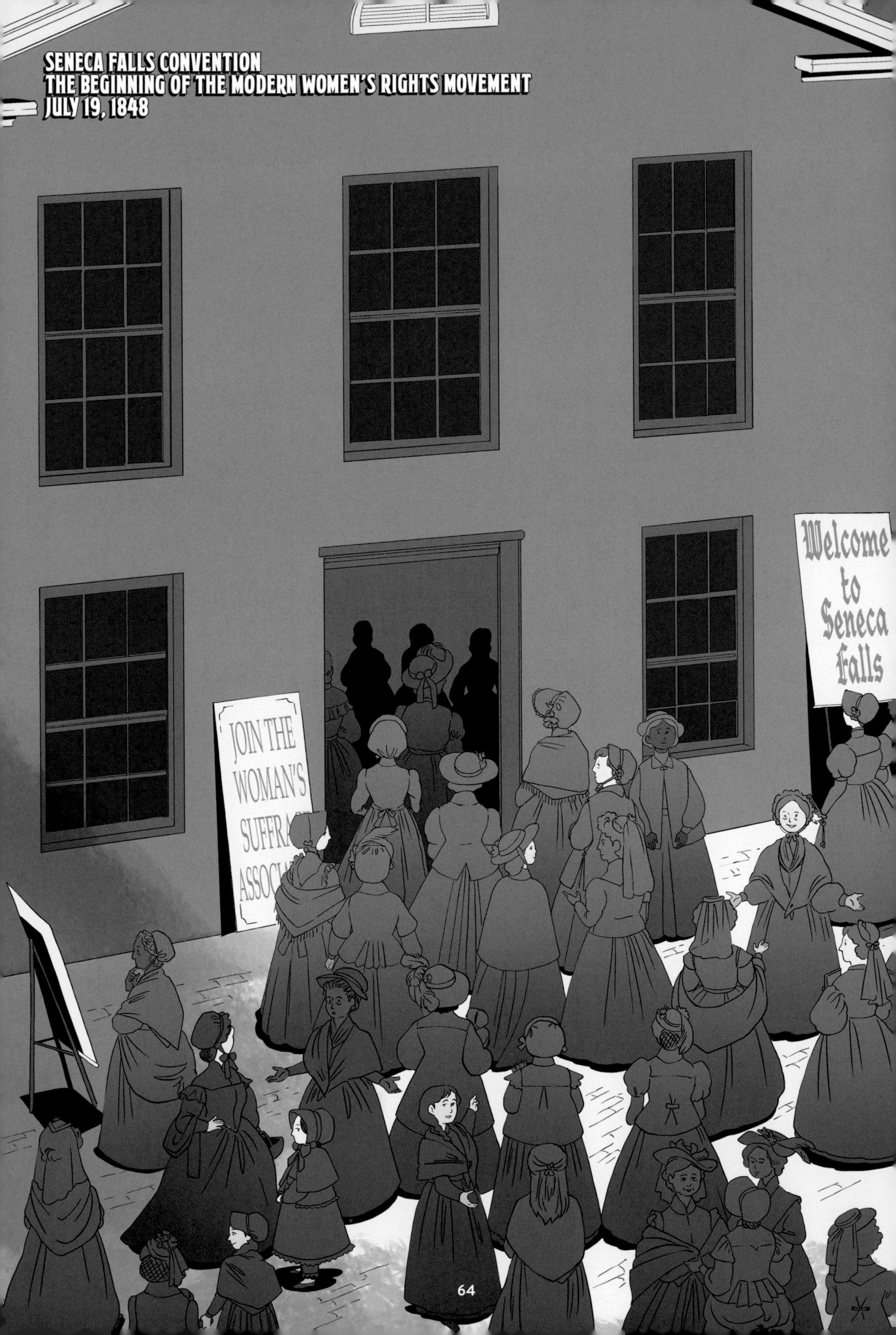
SENECA FALLS CONVENTION
THE BEGINNING OF THE MODERN WOMEN'S RIGHTS MOVEMENT
JULY 19, 1848
Welcome to Seneca Falls
JOIN THE
WOMAN'S

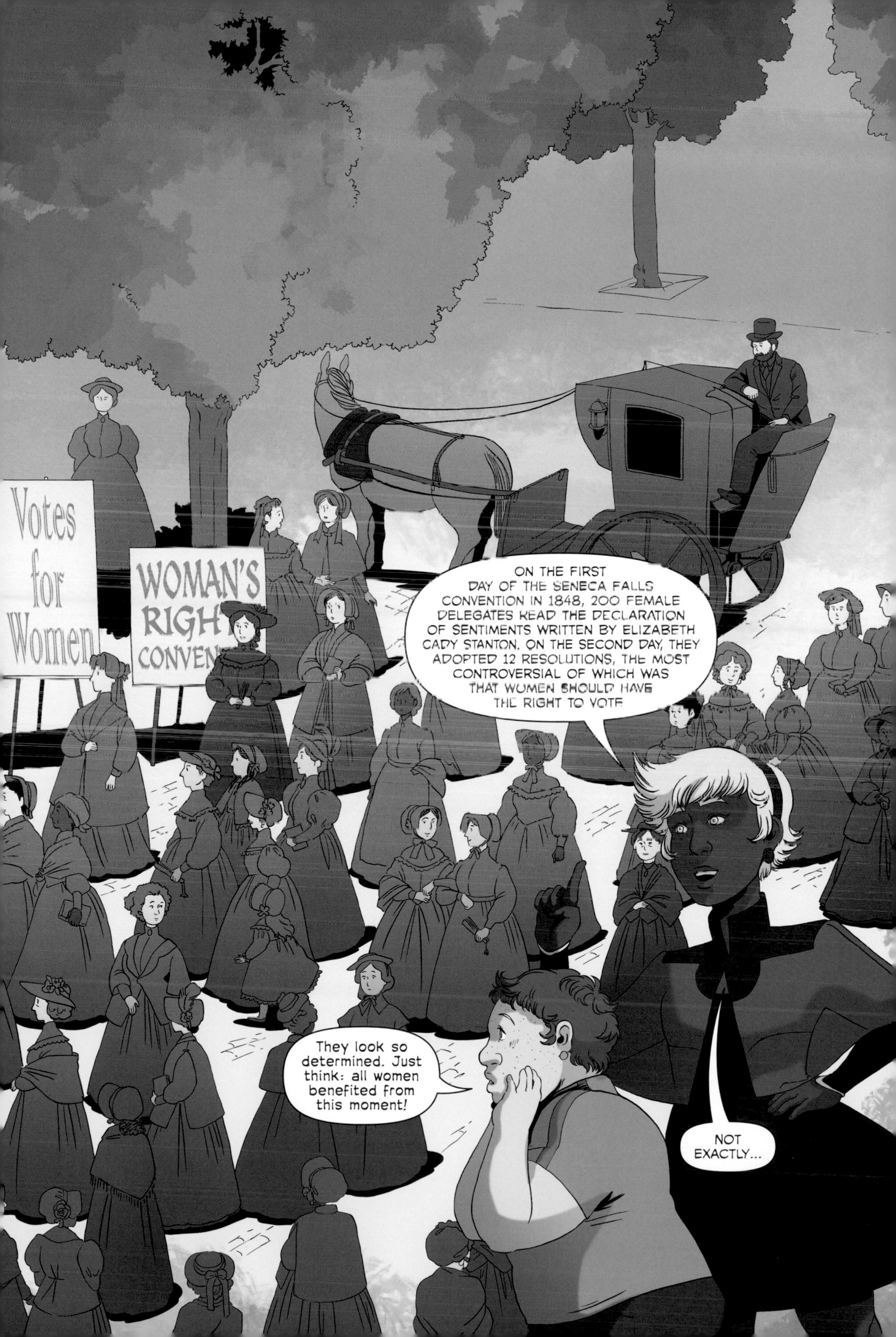
Votes for Women
WOMAN'S RIGH CONVEN
ON THE FIRST DAY OF THE SENECA FALLS CONVENTION IN 1848, 200 FEMALE DELEGATES READ THE DECLARATION OF SENTIMENTS WRITTEN BY ELIZABETH CADY STANTON. ON THE SECOND DAY, THEY ADOPTED 12 RESOLUTIONS, THE MOST CONTROVERSIAL OF WHICH WAS THAT WOMEN SHOULD HAVE THE RIGHT TO VOTE
They look so determined. Just think: all women benefited from this moment!
NOT EXACTLY...

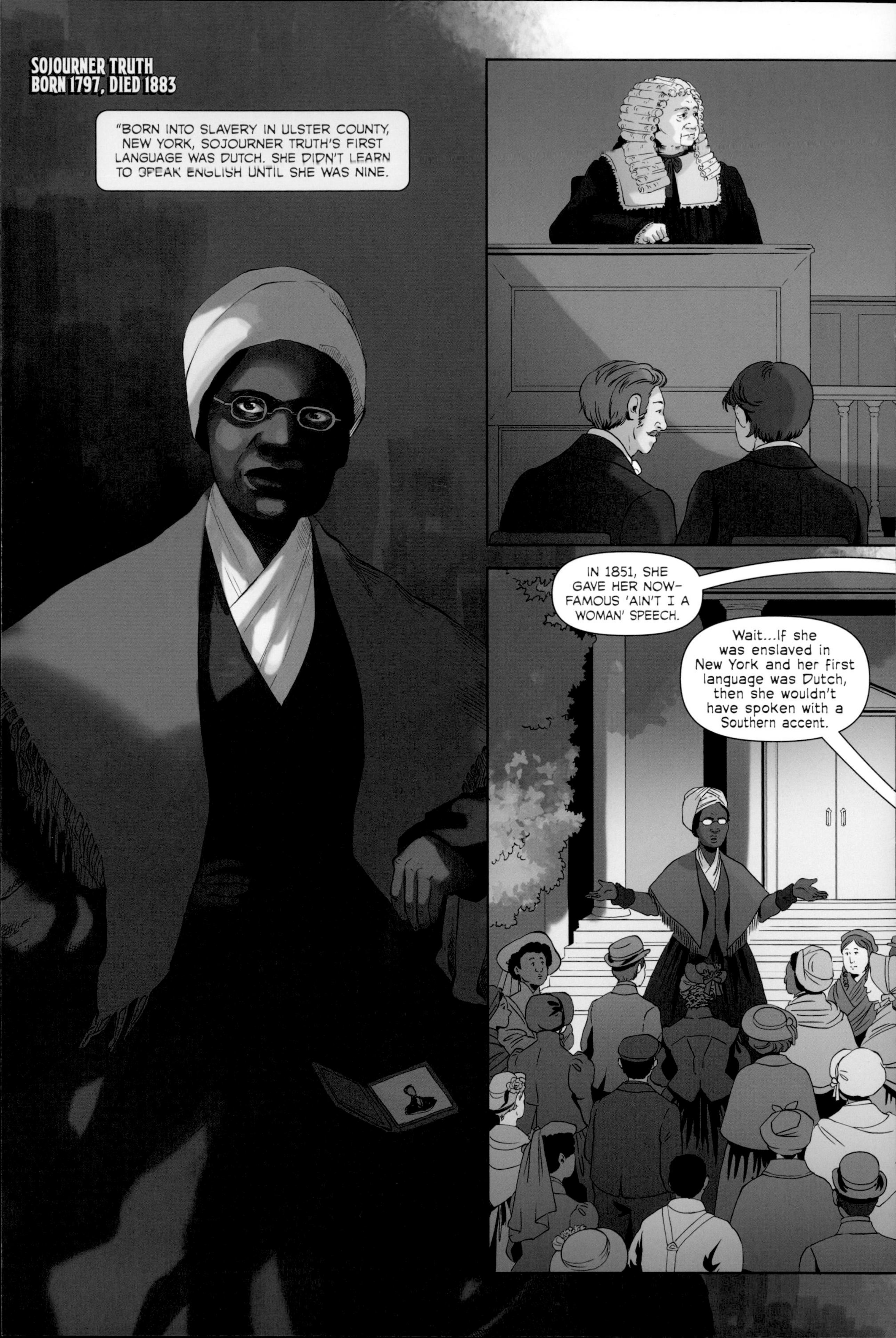
SOJOURNER TRUTH
BORN 1797, DIED 1883
"BORN INTO SLAVERY IN ULSTER COUNTY, NEW YORK, SOJOURNER TRUTH'S FIRST LANGUAGE WAS DUTCH. SHE DIDN'T LEARN TO SPEAK ENGLISH UNTIL SHE WAS NINE.
IN 1851, SHE GAVE HER NOW-FAMOUS 'AIN'T I A WOMAN' SPEECH.
Wait...If she was enslaved in New York and her first language was Dutch, then she wouldn't have spoken with a Southern accent.

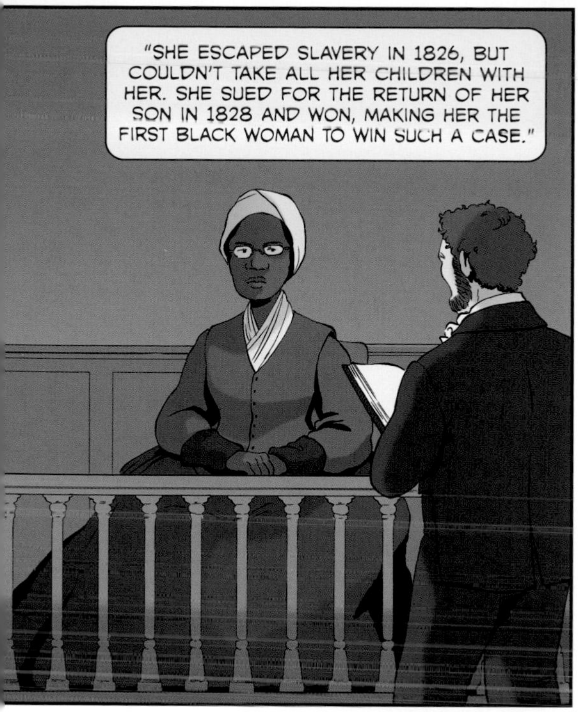
"SHE ESCAPED SLAVERY IN 1826, BUT COULDN'T TAKE ALL HER CHILDREN WITH HER. SHE SUED FOR THE RETURN OF HER SON IN 1828 AND WON, MAKING HER THE FIRST BLACK WOMAN TO WIN SUCH A CASE."

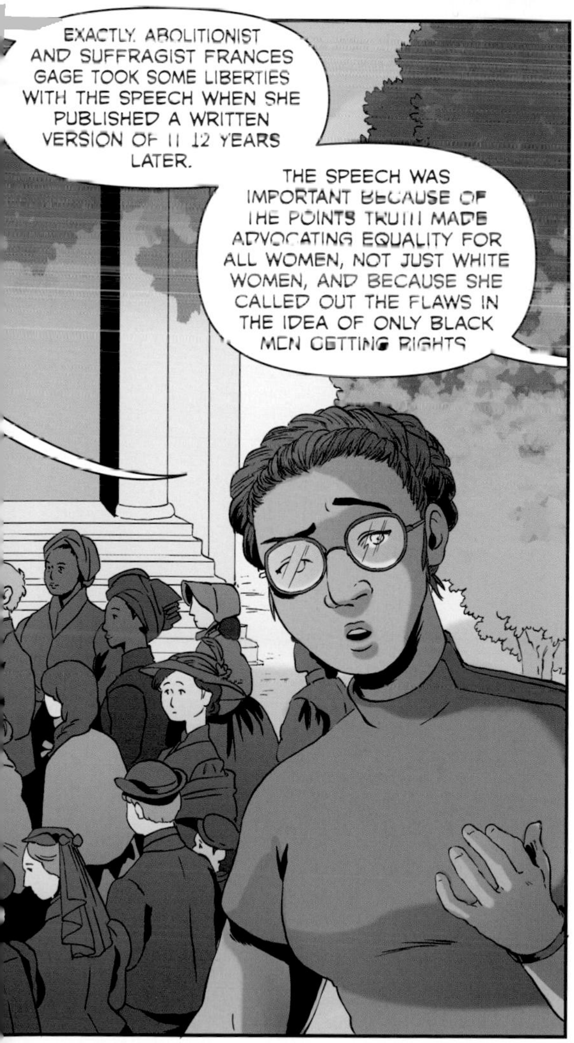
EXACTLY. ABOLITIONIST AND SUFFRAGIST FRANCES GAGE TOOK SOME LIBERTIES WITH THE SPEECH WHEN SHE PUBLISHED A WRITTEN VERSION OF IT 12 YEARS LATER.
THE SPEECH WAS IMPORTANT BECAUSE OF THE POINTS TRUTH MADE ADVOCATING EQUALITY FOR ALL WOMEN, NOT JUST WHITE WOMEN, AND BECAUSE SHE CALLED OUT THE FLAWS IN THE IDEA OF ONLY BLACK MEN GETTING RIGHTS.

I want to say a few words about this matter. I am a woman's rights. I have as much muscle as any man, and can do as much work as any man. I have plowed and reaped and husked and chopped and mowed, and can any man do more than that? I have heard much about the sexes being equal; I can carry as much as any man, and can eat as much too, if I can get it. I am as strong as any man that is now. As for intellect, all I can say is, if woman have a pint, and a man a quart—why can't she have her little pint full? You need not be afraid to give us our rights for fear we will take too much,—for we can't take more than our pint'll hold. The poor men seem to be all in confusion and don't know what to do. Why children, if you have woman's rights give it to her and you will feel better. You will have your own rights, and they won't be so much trouble. I can't read, but I can hear. I have heard the bible and have learned that Eve caused man to sin. Well if woman upset the world, do give her a chance to set it right side up again. The Lady has spoken about Jesus, how he never spurned woman from him, and she was right. When Lazarus died, Mary and Martha came to him with faith and love and besought him to raise their brother. And Jesus wept—and Lazarus came forth. And how came Jesus into the world? Through God who created him and woman who bore him. Man, where is your part? But the women are coming up blessed be God and a few of the men are coming up with them. But man is in a tight place, the poor slave is on him, woman is coming on him, and he is surely between a hawk and a buzzard.

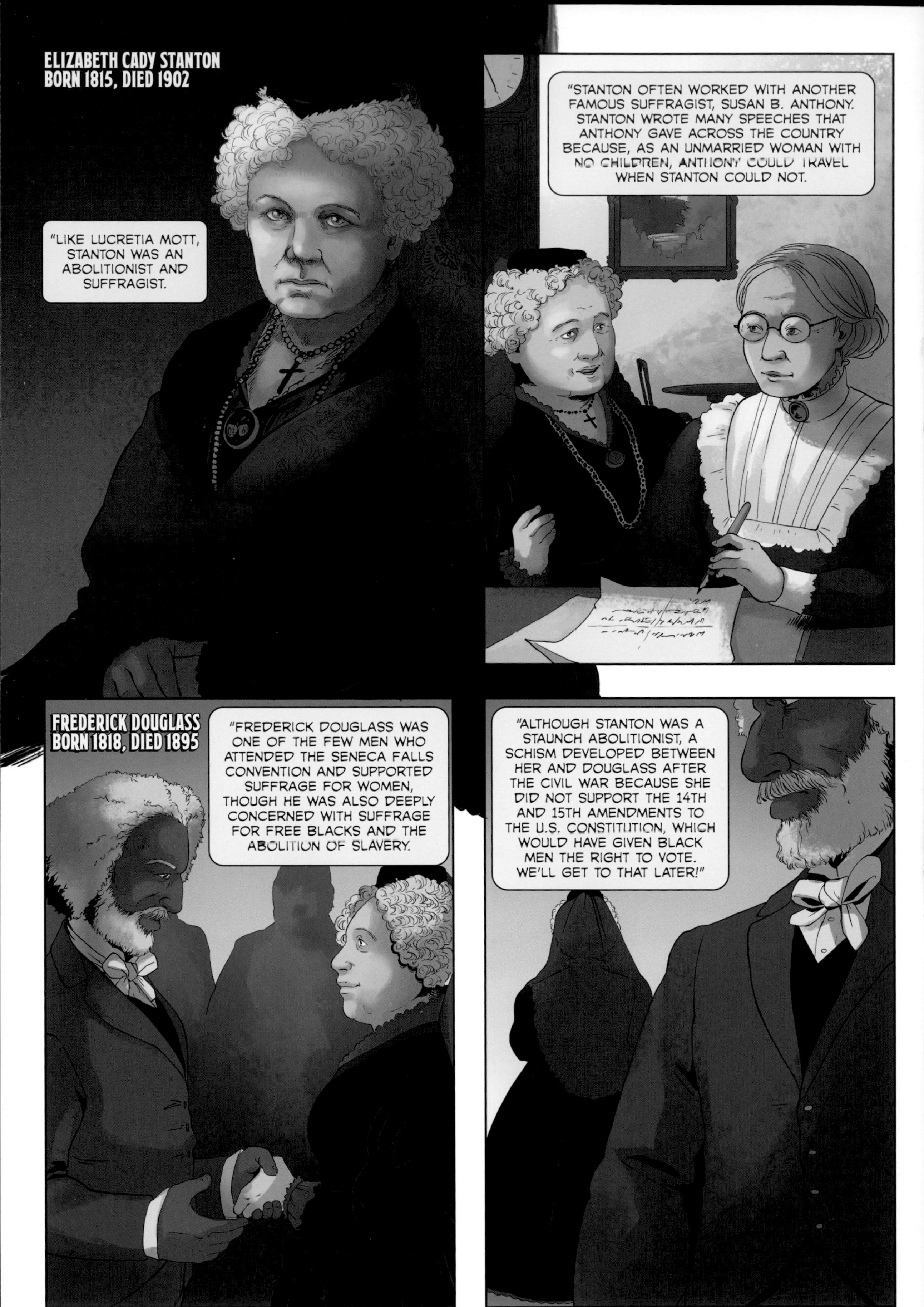
ELIZABETH CADY STANTON
BORN 1815, DIED 1902
"LIKE LUCRETIA MOTT, STANTON WAS AN ABOLITIONIST AND SUFFRAGIST.
"STANTON OFTEN WORKED WITH ANOTHER FAMOUS SUFFRAGIST, SUSAN B. ANTHONY. STANTON WROTE MANY SPEECHES THAT ANTHONY GAVE ACROSS THE COUNTRY BECAUSE, AS AN UNMARRIED WOMAN WITH NO CHILDREN, ANTHONY COULD TRAVEL WHEN STANTON COULD NOT.
FREDERICK DOUGLASS
BORN 1818, DIED 1895
"FREDERICK DOUGLASS WAS ONE OF THE FEW MEN WHO ATTENDED THE SENECA FALLS CONVENTION AND SUPPORTED SUFFRAGE FOR WOMEN, THOUGH HE WAS ALSO DEEPLY CONCERNED WITH SUFFRAGE FOR FREE BLACKS AND THE ABOLITION OF SLAVERY.
"ALTHOUGH STANTON WAS A STAUNCH ABOLITIONIST, A SCHISM DEVELOPED BETWEEN HER AND DOUGLASS AFTER THE CIVIL WAR BECAUSE SHE DID NOT SUPPORT THE 14TH AND 15TH AMENDMENTS TO THE U.S. CONSTITUTION, WHICH WOULD HAVE GIVEN BLACK MEN THE RIGHT TO VOTE. WE'LL GET TO THAT LATER!"

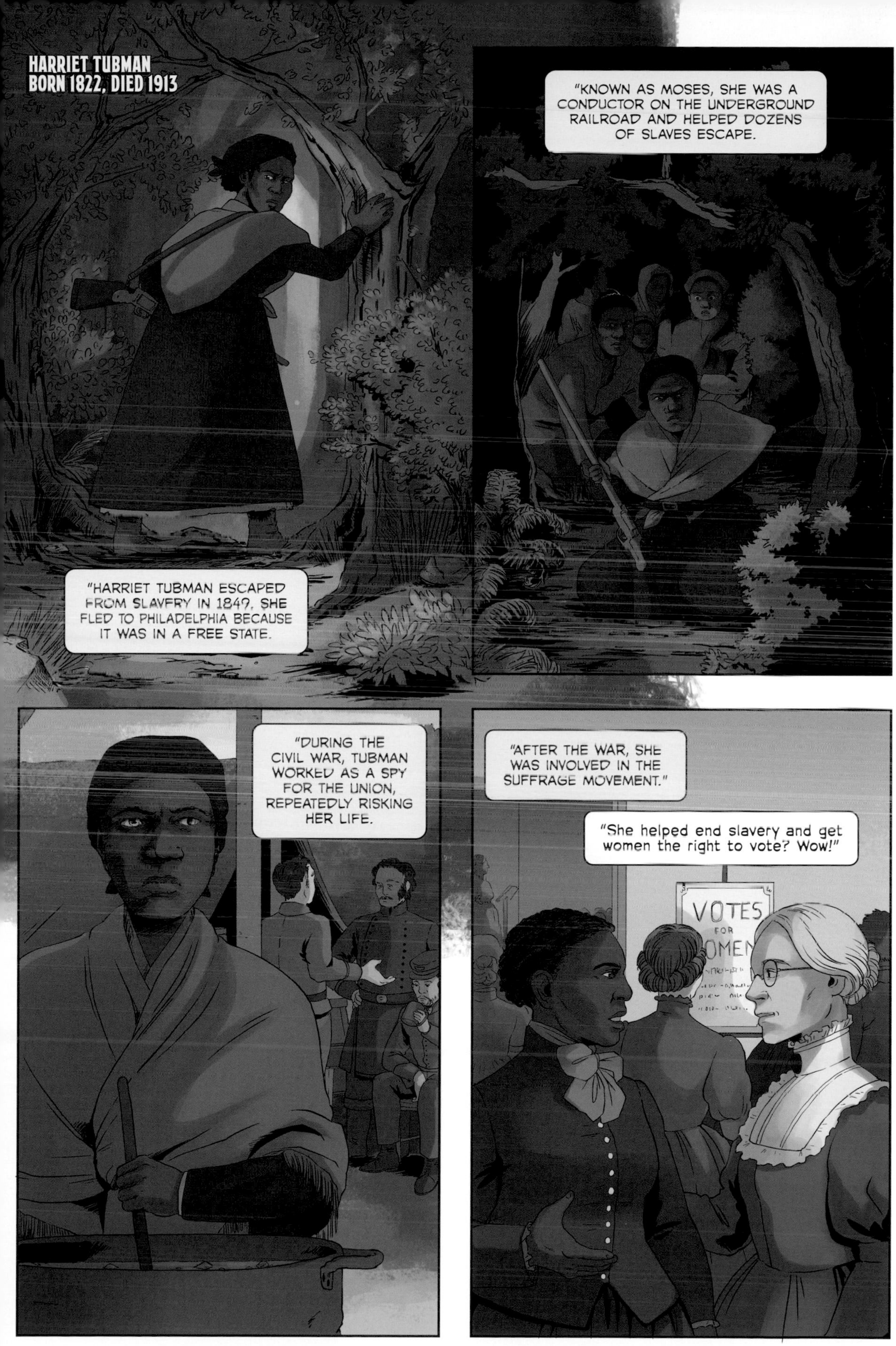
HARRIET TUBMAN
BORN 1822, DIED 1913
"HARRIET TUBMAN ESCAPED FROM SLAVERY IN 1849. SHE FLED TO PHILADELPHIA BECAUSE IT WAS IN A FREE STATE.
"KNOWN AS MOSES, SHE WAS A CONDUCTOR ON THE UNDERGROUND RAILROAD AND HELPED DOZENS OF SLAVES ESCAPE.
"DURING THE CIVIL WAR, TUBMAN WORKED AS A SPY FOR THE UNION, REPEATEDLY RISKING HER LIFE.
"AFTER THE WAR, SHE WAS INVOLVED IN THE SUFFRAGE MOVEMENT."
"She helped end slavery and get women the right to vote? Wow!"
VOTES
FOR

CHAPTER 4
SUFFRAGE AND SUFFERING: WOMEN FIGHT FOR FREEDOM

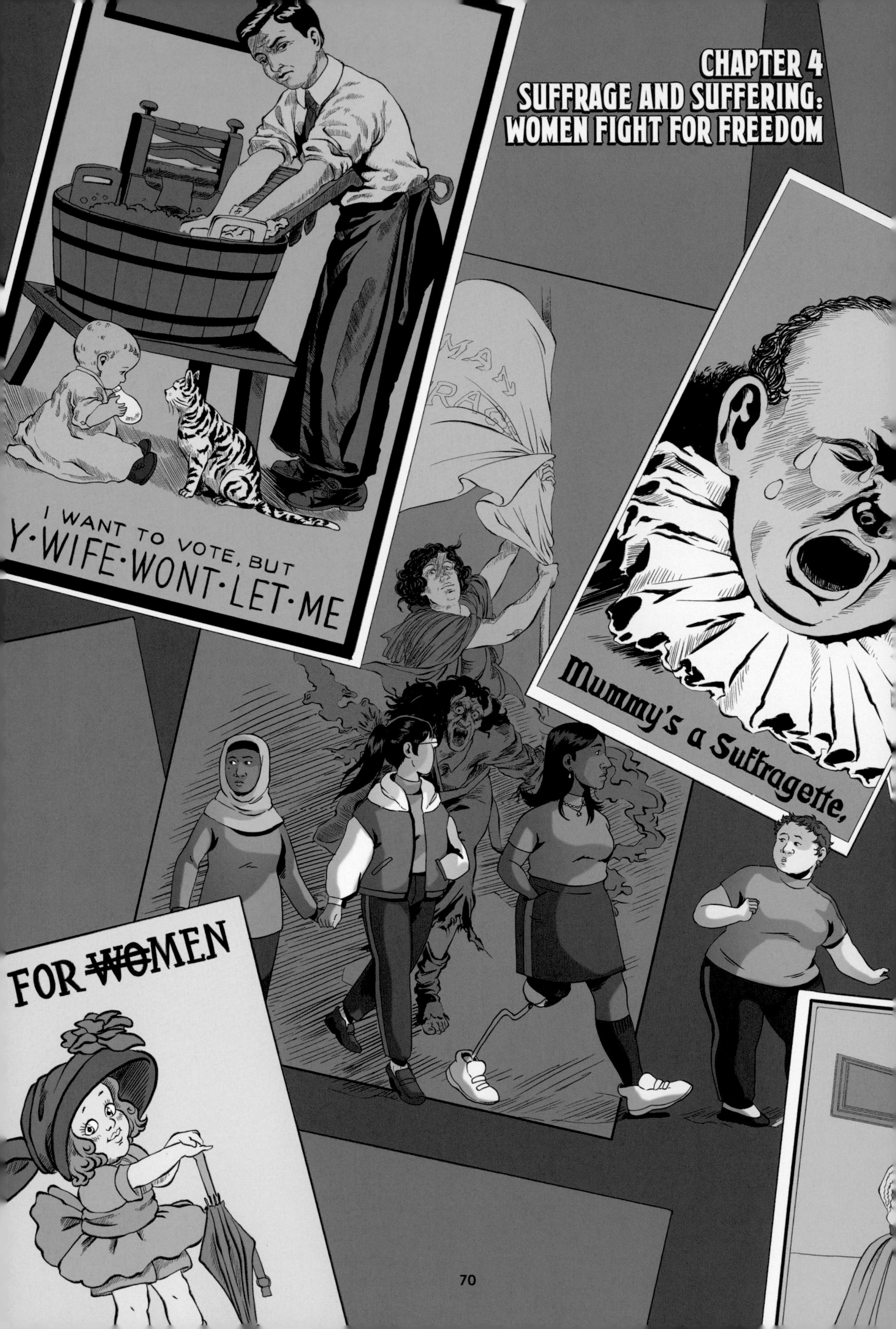
I WANT TO VOTE, BUT
Y·WIFE·WONT·LET·ME
Mummy's a Suffragette,
FOR ~~WO~~MEN

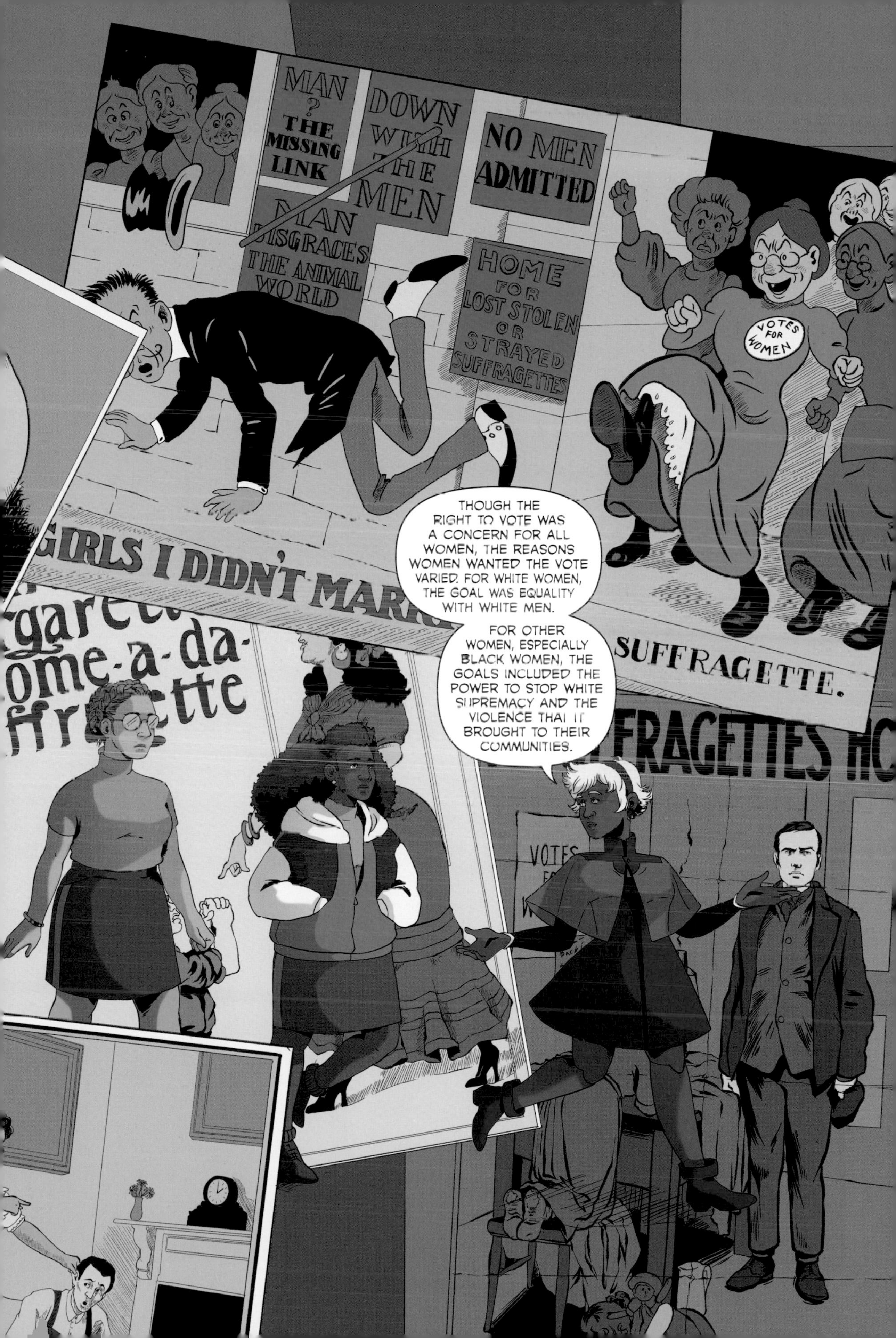
MAN ? THE MISSING LINK
DOWN WITH THE MEN
NO MEN ADMITTED
MAN DISGRACES THE ANIMAL WORLD
HOME FOR LOST STOLEN OR STRAYED SUFFRAGETTES
VOTES FOR WOMEN
SUFFRAGETTE.
THOUGH THE RIGHT TO VOTE WAS A CONCERN FOR ALL WOMEN, THE REASONS WOMEN WANTED THE VOTE VARIED. FOR WHITE WOMEN, THE GOAL WAS EQUALITY WITH WHITE MEN.
FOR OTHER WOMEN, ESPECIALLY BLACK WOMEN, THE GOALS INCLUDED THE POWER TO STOP WHITE SUPREMACY AND THE VIOLENCE THAT IT BROUGHT TO THEIR COMMUNITIES.

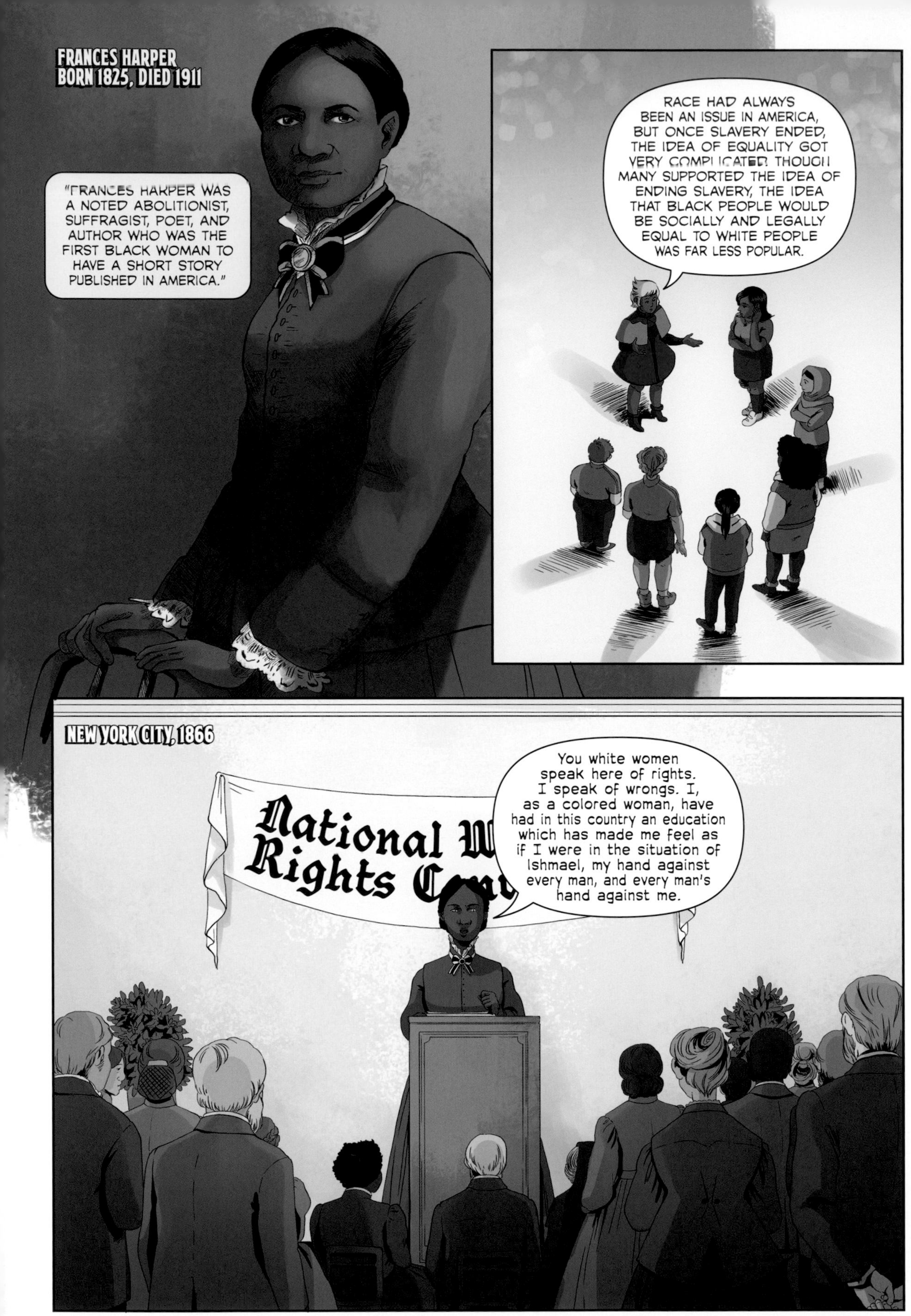
FRANCES HARPER
BORN 1825, DIED 1911
"FRANCES HARPER WAS A NOTED ABOLITIONIST, SUFFRAGIST, POET, AND AUTHOR WHO WAS THE FIRST BLACK WOMAN TO HAVE A SHORT STORY PUBLISHED IN AMERICA."
RACE HAD ALWAYS BEEN AN ISSUE IN AMERICA, BUT ONCE SLAVERY ENDED, THE IDEA OF EQUALITY GOT VERY COMPLICATED. THOUGH MANY SUPPORTED THE IDEA OF ENDING SLAVERY, THE IDEA THAT BLACK PEOPLE WOULD BE SOCIALLY AND LEGALLY EQUAL TO WHITE PEOPLE WAS FAR LESS POPULAR.
NEW YORK CITY, 1866
National
Rights
You white women speak here of rights. I speak of wrongs. I, as a colored woman, have had in this country an education which has made me feel as if I were in the situation of Ishmael, my hand against every man, and every man's hand against me.

NEW YORK CITY, 1867

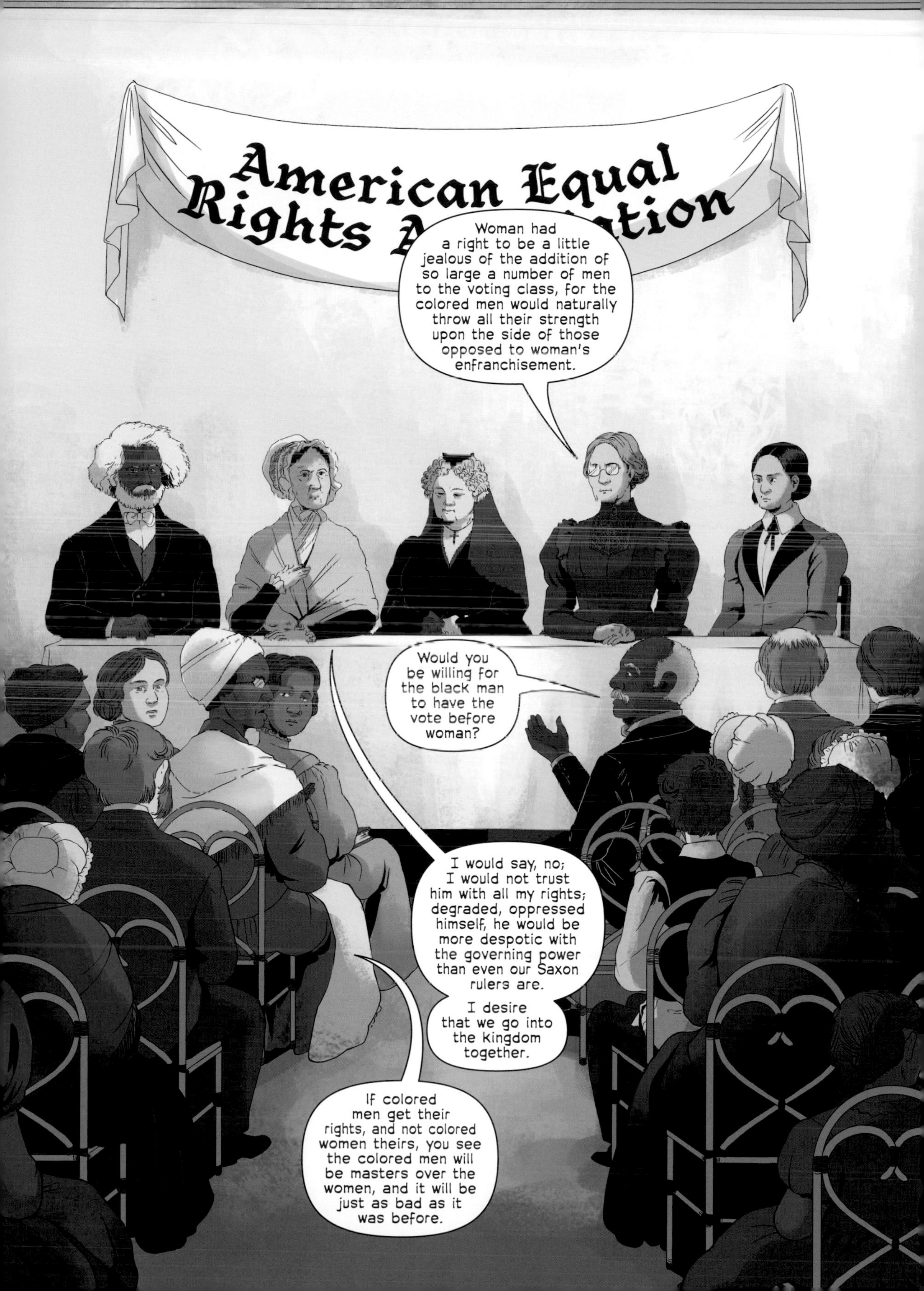
American Equal Rights A
ation
Woman had a right to be a little jealous of the addition of so large a number of men to the voting class, for the colored men would naturally throw all their strength upon the side of those opposed to woman's enfranchisement.
Would you be willing for the black man to have the vote before woman?
I would say, no; I would not trust him with all my rights; degraded, oppressed himself, he would be more despotic with the governing power than even our Saxon rulers are.
I desire that we go into the kingdom together.
If colored men get their rights, and not colored women theirs, you see the colored men will be masters over the women, and it will be just as bad as it was before.

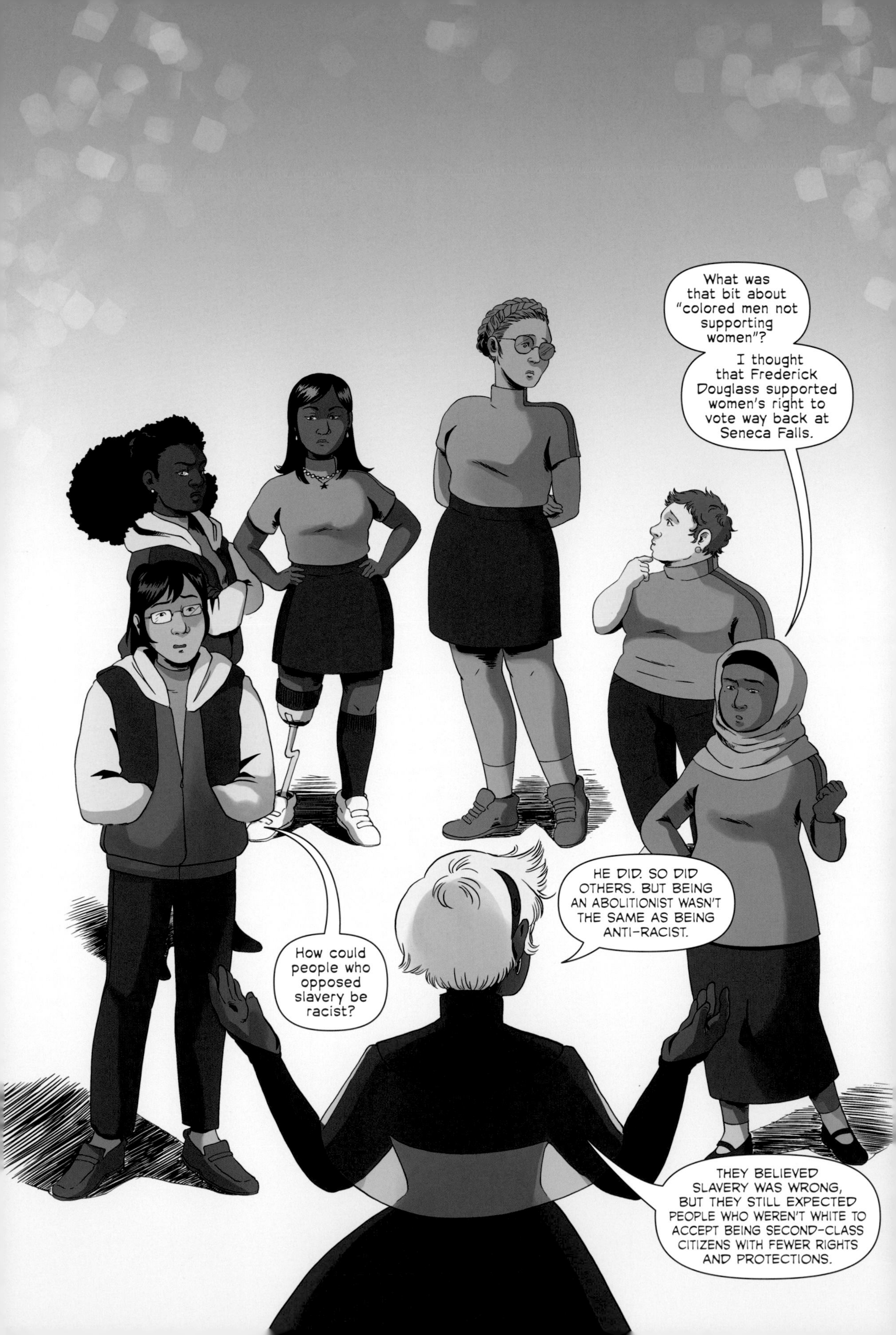
What was that bit about "colored men not supporting women"?
I thought that Frederick Douglass supported women's right to vote way back at Seneca Falls.
How could people who opposed slavery be racist?
HE DID. SO DID OTHERS. BUT BEING AN ABOLITIONIST WASN'T THE SAME AS BEING ANTI-RACIST.
THEY BELIEVED SLAVERY WAS WRONG, BUT THEY STILL EXPECTED PEOPLE WHO WEREN'T WHITE TO ACCEPT BEING SECOND-CLASS CITIZENS WITH FEWER RIGHTS AND PROTECTIONS.

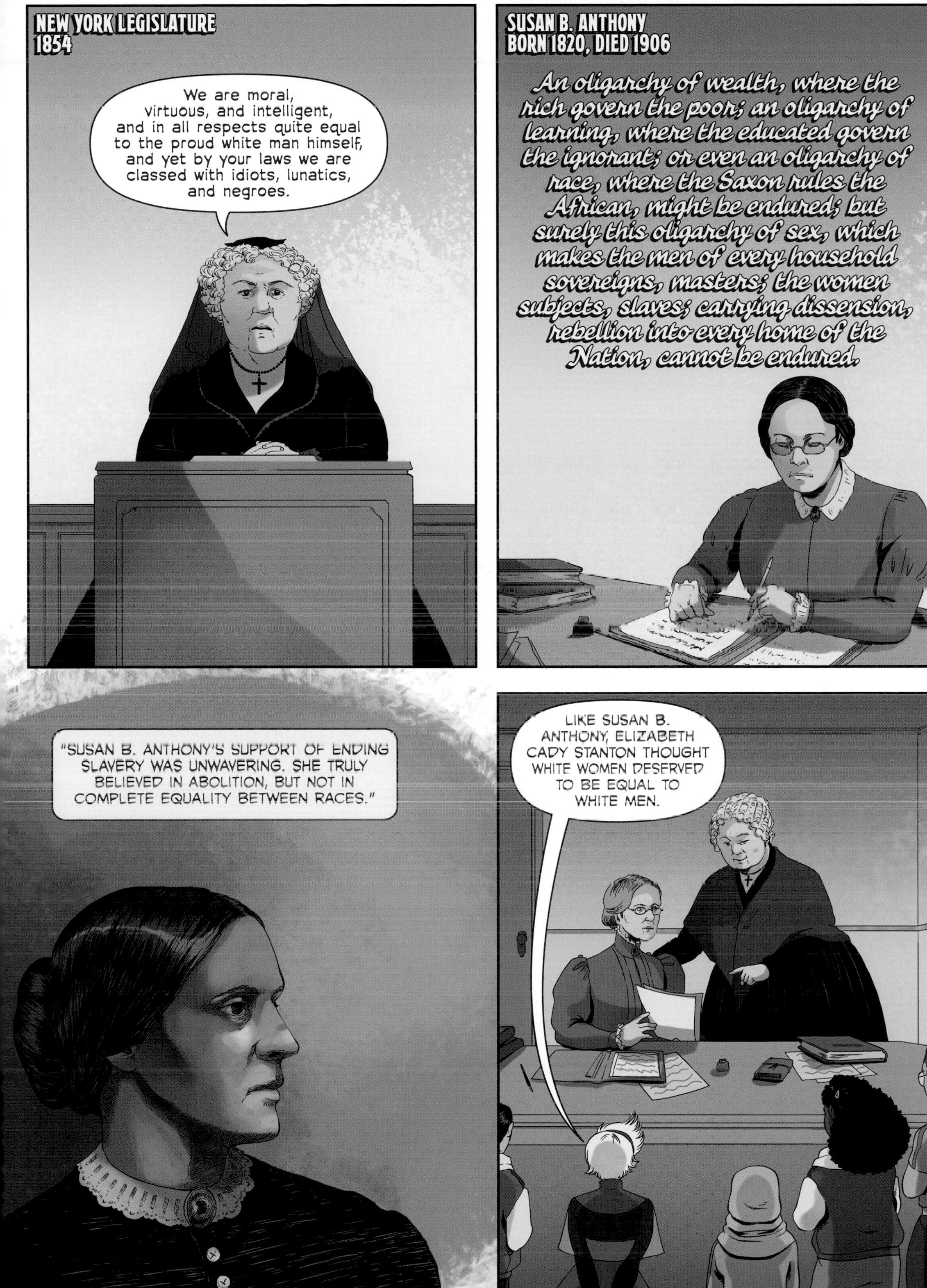
NEW YORK LEGISLATURE
1854
We are moral, virtuous, and intelligent, and in all respects quite equal to the proud white man himself, and yet by your laws we are classed with idiots, lunatics, and negroes.
SUSAN B. ANTHONY
BORN 1820, DIED 1906
An oligarchy of wealth, where the rich govern the poor; an oligarchy of learning, where the educated govern the ignorant; or even an oligarchy of race, where the Saxon rules the African, might be endured; but surely this oligarchy of sex, which makes the men of every household sovereigns, masters; the women subjects, slaves; carrying dissension, rebellion into every home of the Nation, cannot be endured.
"SUSAN B. ANTHONY'S SUPPORT OF ENDING SLAVERY WAS UNWAVERING. SHE TRULY BELIEVED IN ABOLITION, BUT NOT IN COMPLETE EQUALITY BETWEEN RACES."
LIKE SUSAN B. ANTHONY, ELIZABETH CADY STANTON THOUGHT WHITE WOMEN DESERVED TO BE EQUAL TO WHITE MEN.

SARAH WINNEMUCCA
BORN 1840, DIED 1891

"ALTHOUGH THE CIVIL WAR ENDED THE LEGALIZED ENSLAVEMENT OF AFRICAN AMERICANS, CONDITIONS FOR INDIGENOUS PEOPLE DID NOT IMPROVE. SOME, LIKE THE PAIUTE, WERE FORCED AT GUNPOINT BY THE U.S. GOVERNMENT TO RELOCATE TO RESERVATIONS.

"ABOLITION AND SUFFRAGE WEREN'T THE ONLY ISSUES IN AMERICA. LEADERS LIKE SARAH WINNEMUCCA WORKED TIRELESSLY TO HELP THE PAIUTE AND OTHER INDIGENOUS NATIONS, AND EVEN PETITIONED CONGRESS TO FREE HER PEOPLE.

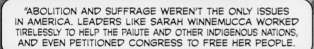

MANKATO, MINNESOTA
DECEMBER 26, 1862

"OTHERS, LIKE THE DAKOTAS, PART OF THE SIOUX NATION, WERE PUNISHED WITH MASS HANGINGS FOR FIGHTING BACK IN AN ONGOING WAR AGAINST THE SETTLERS TAKING THEIR LANDS.

"THE U.S. GOVERNMENT IGNORED TREATIES AND AGREEMENTS WITH MANY INDIGENOUS NATIONS, SO ACTIVISTS LIKE WINNEMUCCA HAD TO BAND TOGETHER TO ADVOCATE FOR ALL INDIGENOUS PEOPLE."

THOUGH WE THINK OF PRESIDENT LINCOLN AS THE MAN WHO ENDED SLAVERY, HE DIDN'T END OPPRESSION IN AMERICA ON ANY LEVEL.

NO INDIVIDUAL PERSON COULD. THAT'S WHY SO MANY MOVEMENTS HAPPENED AT THE SAME TIME.

So, America was a big mess with constant fighting for rights and equality. Was it better in the UK, since they got rid of slavery earlier?

THE ROAD TO SUFFRAGE IN ENGLAND WAS DIFFERENT, BUT IT WASN'T EASIER.

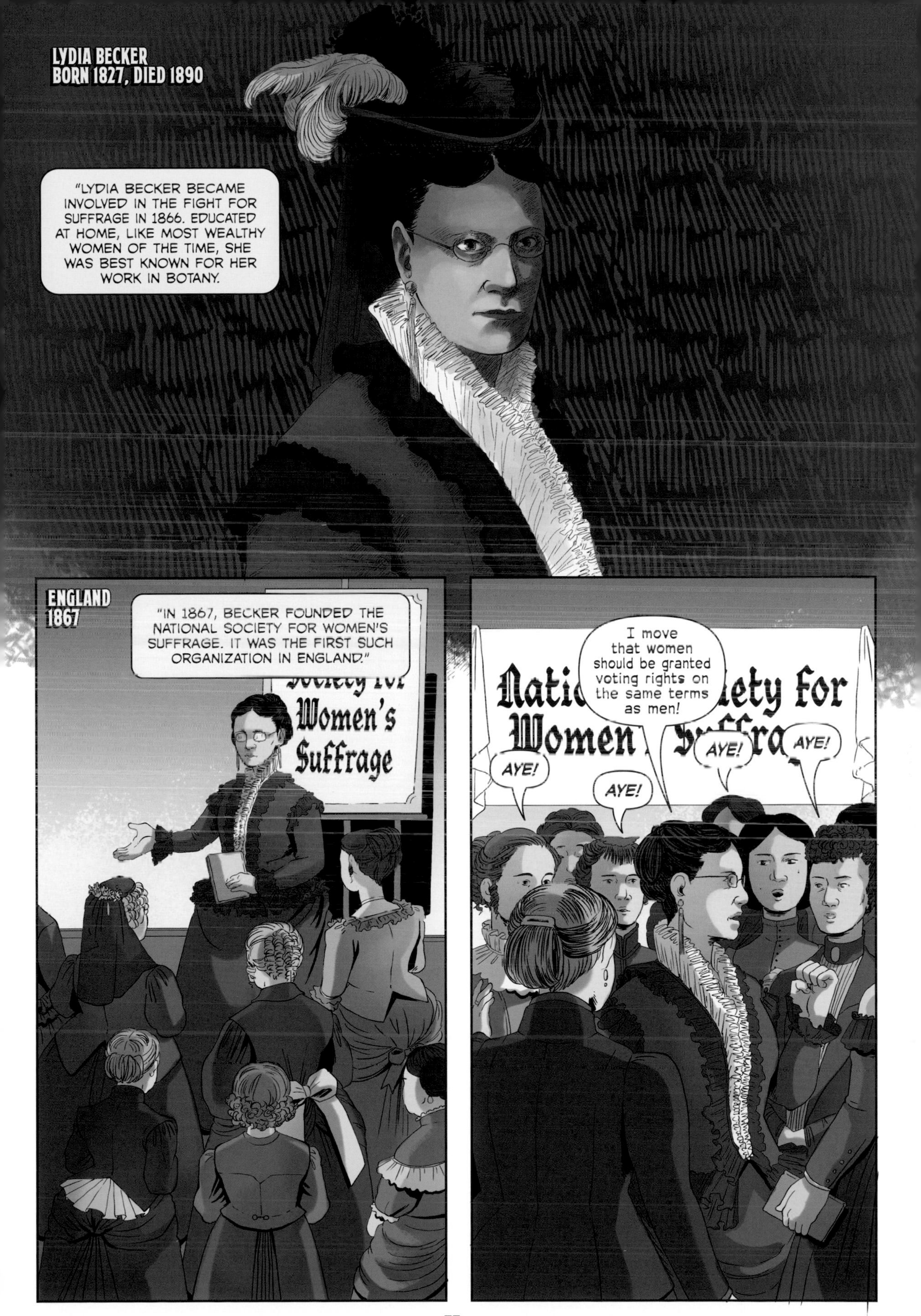
LYDIA BECKER
BORN 1827, DIED 1890
"LYDIA BECKER BECAME INVOLVED IN THE FIGHT FOR SUFFRAGE IN 1866. EDUCATED AT HOME, LIKE MOST WEALTHY WOMEN OF THE TIME, SHE WAS BEST KNOWN FOR HER WORK IN BOTANY.
ENGLAND
1867
"IN 1867, BECKER FOUNDED THE NATIONAL SOCIETY FOR WOMEN'S SUFFRAGE. IT WAS THE FIRST SUCH ORGANIZATION IN ENGLAND."
Society for Women's Suffrage
I move that women should be granted voting rights on the same terms as men!
AYE!
AYE!
AYE!
AYE!

JOSEPHINE BUTLER
BORN 1828, DIED 1906

"ENGLISH SOCIAL REFORMER JOSEPHINE BUTLER FOUGHT FOR WOMEN'S SUFFRAGE, AND FOR ENDING CHILD PROSTITUTION AND HUMAN TRAFFICKING.

"BUTLER'S EFFORTS NOT ONLY BROUGHT ABOUT THE REPEAL OF THE CONTAGIOUS DISEASES ACTS...

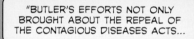

REPORT ON THE

CONTAGIOUS DISEASES A

TO THE

CIVIL POPULATION

BY JOHN SIMON,

"...THEY ALSO PUSHED PARLIAMENT TO LEGALLY PROTECT CHILDREN AND YOUNG WOMEN FROM BEING FORCED INTO PROSTITUTION."

FLORENCE NIGHTINGALE
BORN 1820, DIED 1910

"THOUGH WOMEN OFTEN CARED FOR THE SICK, THE IDEA OF TRAINING WOMEN AND TREATING IT AS PROFESSIONAL WORK WAS NEW.

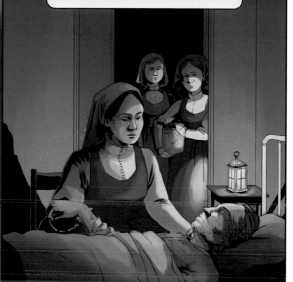

"THOUGH SHE WAS BORN INTO A WEALTHY ENGLISH FAMILY, FLORENCE NIGHTINGALE CHOSE TO WORK AS A NURSE RATHER THAN MARRY AND LIVE A LIFE OF LEISURE.

"FLORENCE MENTORED MANY NURSES, INCLUDING LINDA RICHARDS, WHO WAS THE FIRST PROFESSIONALLY TRAINED AMERICAN NURSE."

Why was training so important?

NIGHTINGALE'S WORK TO STANDARDIZE TRAINING AND MAKE NURSING A PROFESSION MADE HEALTH CARE SAFER FOR NURSES-- AND THEIR PATIENTS.

Since she gave women a better way to work, was she a suffragist?

SHE SUPPORTED SUFFRAGE, BUT VOTING WASN'T AS IMPORTANT TO HER AS SELF-SUFFICIENCY.

SHE WANTED WOMEN TO BE MORE THAN HOUSEHOLD ORNAMENTS. GIVING WOMEN A WAY TO SUPPORT THEMSELVES GAVE THEM GREATER FINANCIAL AND SOCIAL POWER.

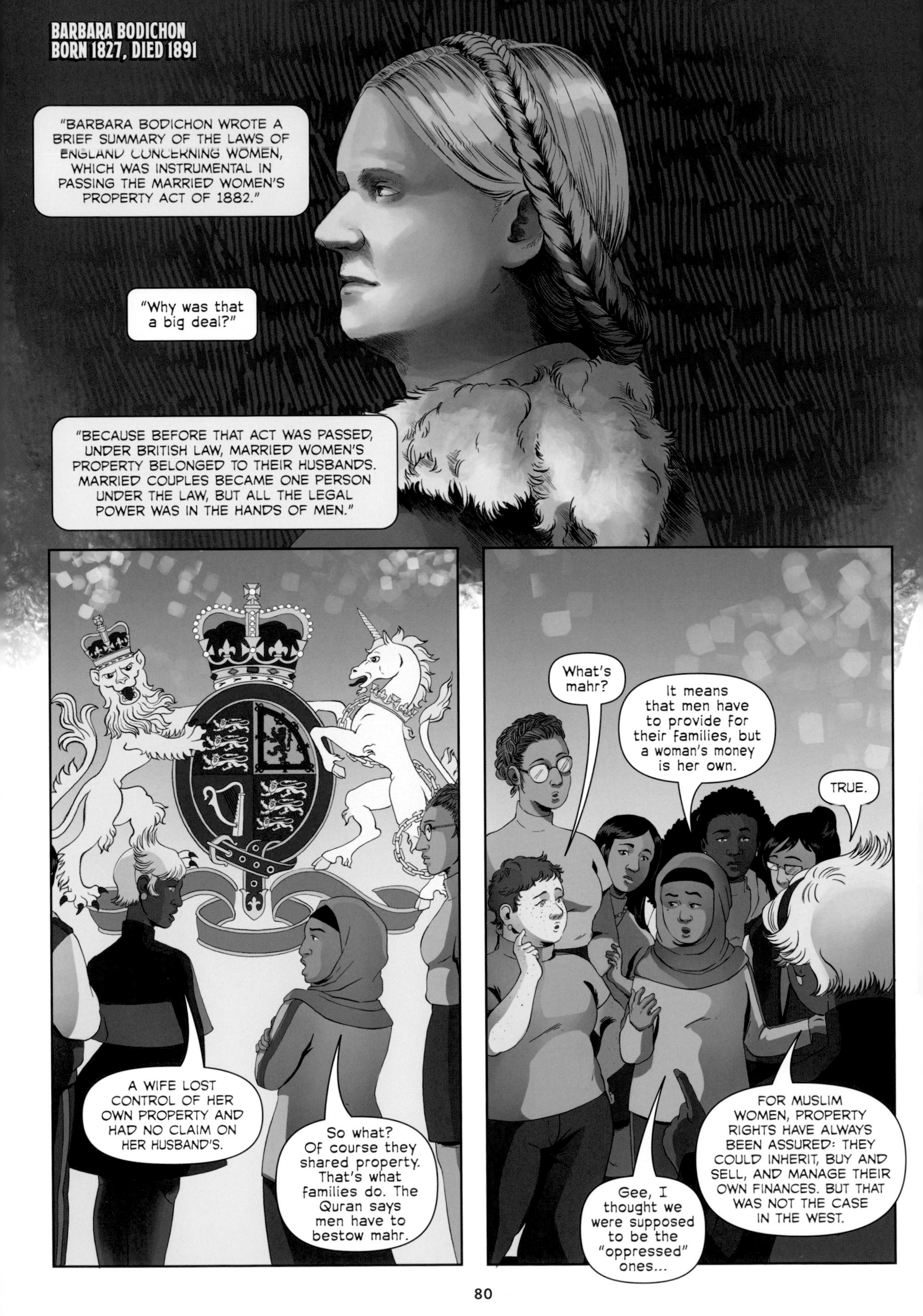
BARBARA BODICHON
BORN 1827, DIED 1891
"BARBARA BODICHON WROTE A BRIEF SUMMARY OF THE LAWS OF ENGLAND CONCERNING WOMEN, WHICH WAS INSTRUMENTAL IN PASSING THE MARRIED WOMEN'S PROPERTY ACT OF 1882."
"Why was that a big deal?"
"BECAUSE BEFORE THAT ACT WAS PASSED, UNDER BRITISH LAW, MARRIED WOMEN'S PROPERTY BELONGED TO THEIR HUSBANDS. MARRIED COUPLES BECAME ONE PERSON UNDER THE LAW, BUT ALL THE LEGAL POWER WAS IN THE HANDS OF MEN."
A WIFE LOST CONTROL OF HER OWN PROPERTY AND HAD NO CLAIM ON HER HUSBAND'S.
So what? Of course they shared property. That's what families do. The Quran says men have to bestow mahr.
What's mahr?
It means that men have to provide for their families, but a woman's money is her own.
TRUE.
FOR MUSLIM WOMEN, PROPERTY RIGHTS HAVE ALWAYS BEEN ASSURED: THEY COULD INHERIT, BUY AND SELL, AND MANAGE THEIR OWN FINANCES. BUT THAT WAS NOT THE CASE IN THE WEST.
Gee, I thought we were supposed to be the "oppressed" ones...

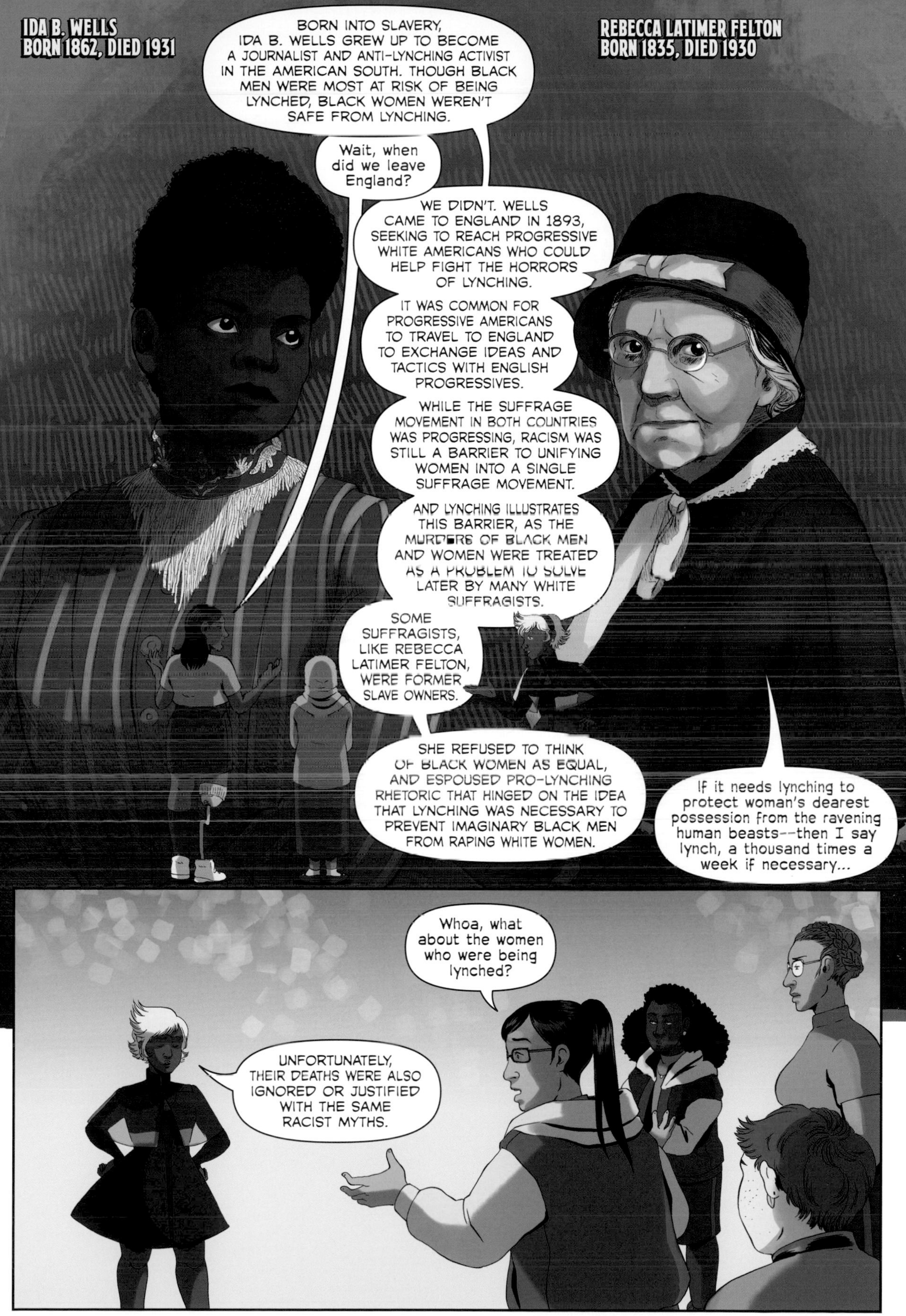
IDA B. WELLS
BORN 1862, DIED 1931
BORN INTO SLAVERY, IDA B. WELLS GREW UP TO BECOME A JOURNALIST AND ANTI-LYNCHING ACTIVIST IN THE AMERICAN SOUTH. THOUGH BLACK MEN WERE MOST AT RISK OF BEING LYNCHED, BLACK WOMEN WEREN'T SAFE FROM LYNCHING.
REBECCA LATIMER FELTON
BORN 1835, DIED 1930
Wait, when did we leave England?
WE DIDN'T. WELLS CAME TO ENGLAND IN 1893, SEEKING TO REACH PROGRESSIVE WHITE AMERICANS WHO COULD HELP FIGHT THE HORRORS OF LYNCHING.
IT WAS COMMON FOR PROGRESSIVE AMERICANS TO TRAVEL TO ENGLAND TO EXCHANGE IDEAS AND TACTICS WITH ENGLISH PROGRESSIVES.
WHILE THE SUFFRAGE MOVEMENT IN BOTH COUNTRIES WAS PROGRESSING, RACISM WAS STILL A BARRIER TO UNIFYING WOMEN INTO A SINGLE SUFFRAGE MOVEMENT.
AND LYNCHING ILLUSTRATES THIS BARRIER, AS THE MURDERS OF BLACK MEN AND WOMEN WERE TREATED AS A PROBLEM TO SOLVE LATER BY MANY WHITE SUFFRAGISTS.
SOME SUFFRAGISTS, LIKE REBECCA LATIMER FELTON, WERE FORMER SLAVE OWNERS.
SHE REFUSED TO THINK OF BLACK WOMEN AS EQUAL, AND ESPOUSED PRO-LYNCHING RHETORIC THAT HINGED ON THE IDEA THAT LYNCHING WAS NECESSARY TO PREVENT IMAGINARY BLACK MEN FROM RAPING WHITE WOMEN.
If it needs lynching to protect woman's dearest possession from the ravening human beasts--then I say lynch, a thousand times a week if necessary...
Whoa, what about the women who were being lynched?
UNFORTUNATELY, THEIR DEATHS WERE ALSO IGNORED OR JUSTIFIED WITH THE SAME RACIST MYTHS.

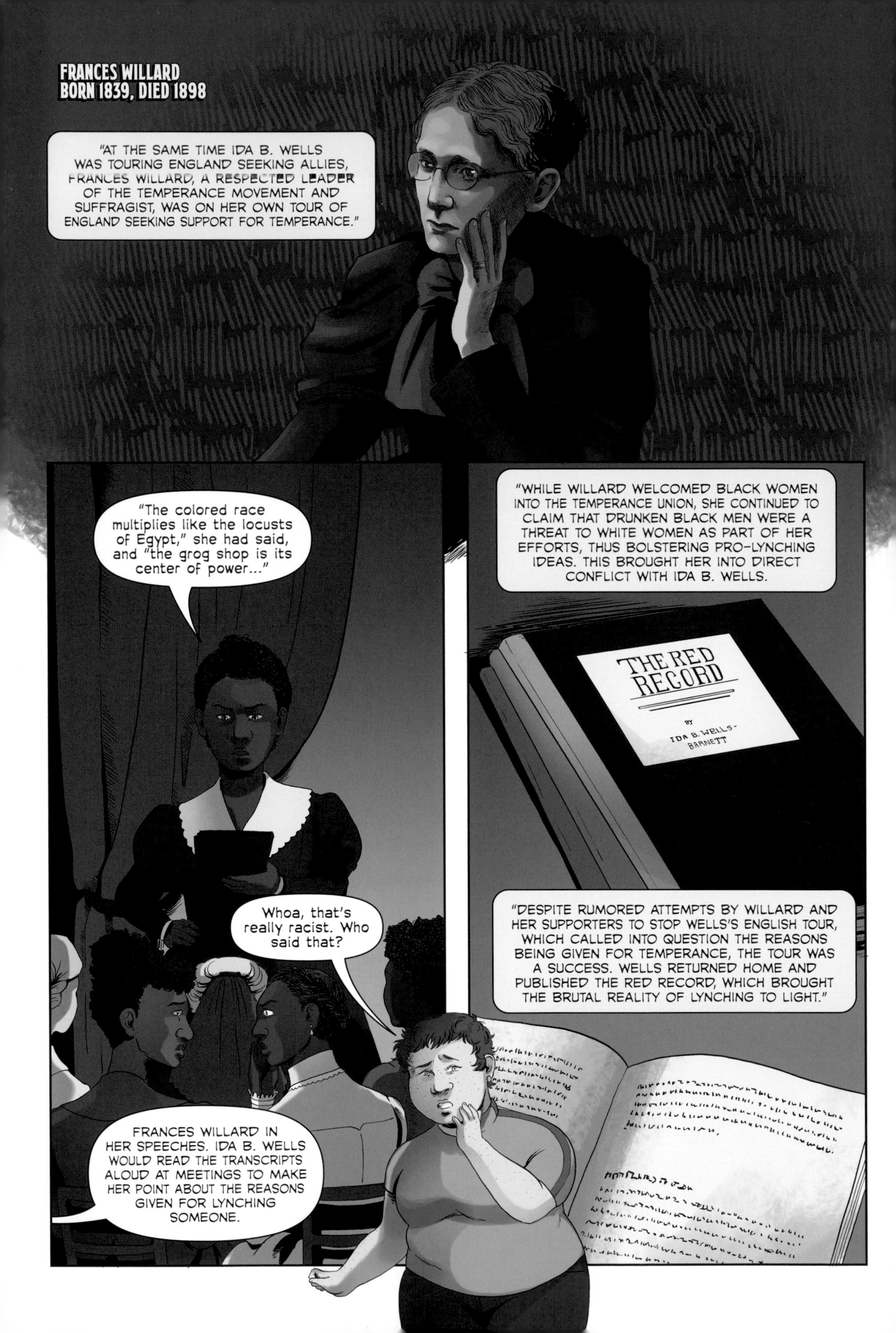
FRANCES WILLARD
BORN 1839, DIED 1898
"AT THE SAME TIME IDA B. WELLS WAS TOURING ENGLAND SEEKING ALLIES, FRANCES WILLARD, A RESPECTED LEADER OF THE TEMPERANCE MOVEMENT AND SUFFRAGIST, WAS ON HER OWN TOUR OF ENGLAND SEEKING SUPPORT FOR TEMPERANCE."
"The colored race multiplies like the locusts of Egypt," she had said, and "the grog shop is its center of power..."
Whoa, that's really racist. Who said that?
FRANCES WILLARD IN HER SPEECHES. IDA B. WELLS WOULD READ THE TRANSCRIPTS ALOUD AT MEETINGS TO MAKE HER POINT ABOUT THE REASONS GIVEN FOR LYNCHING SOMEONE.
"WHILE WILLARD WELCOMED BLACK WOMEN INTO THE TEMPERANCE UNION, SHE CONTINUED TO CLAIM THAT DRUNKEN BLACK MEN WERE A THREAT TO WHITE WOMEN AS PART OF HER EFFORTS, THUS BOLSTERING PRO-LYNCHING IDEAS. THIS BROUGHT HER INTO DIRECT CONFLICT WITH IDA B. WELLS.
THE RED RECORD
BY
IDA B. WELLS-BARNETT
"DESPITE RUMORED ATTEMPTS BY WILLARD AND HER SUPPORTERS TO STOP WELLS'S ENGLISH TOUR, WHICH CALLED INTO QUESTION THE REASONS BEING GIVEN FOR TEMPERANCE, THE TOUR WAS A SUCCESS. WELLS RETURNED HOME AND PUBLISHED THE RED RECORD, WHICH BROUGHT THE BRUTAL REALITY OF LYNCHING TO LIGHT."

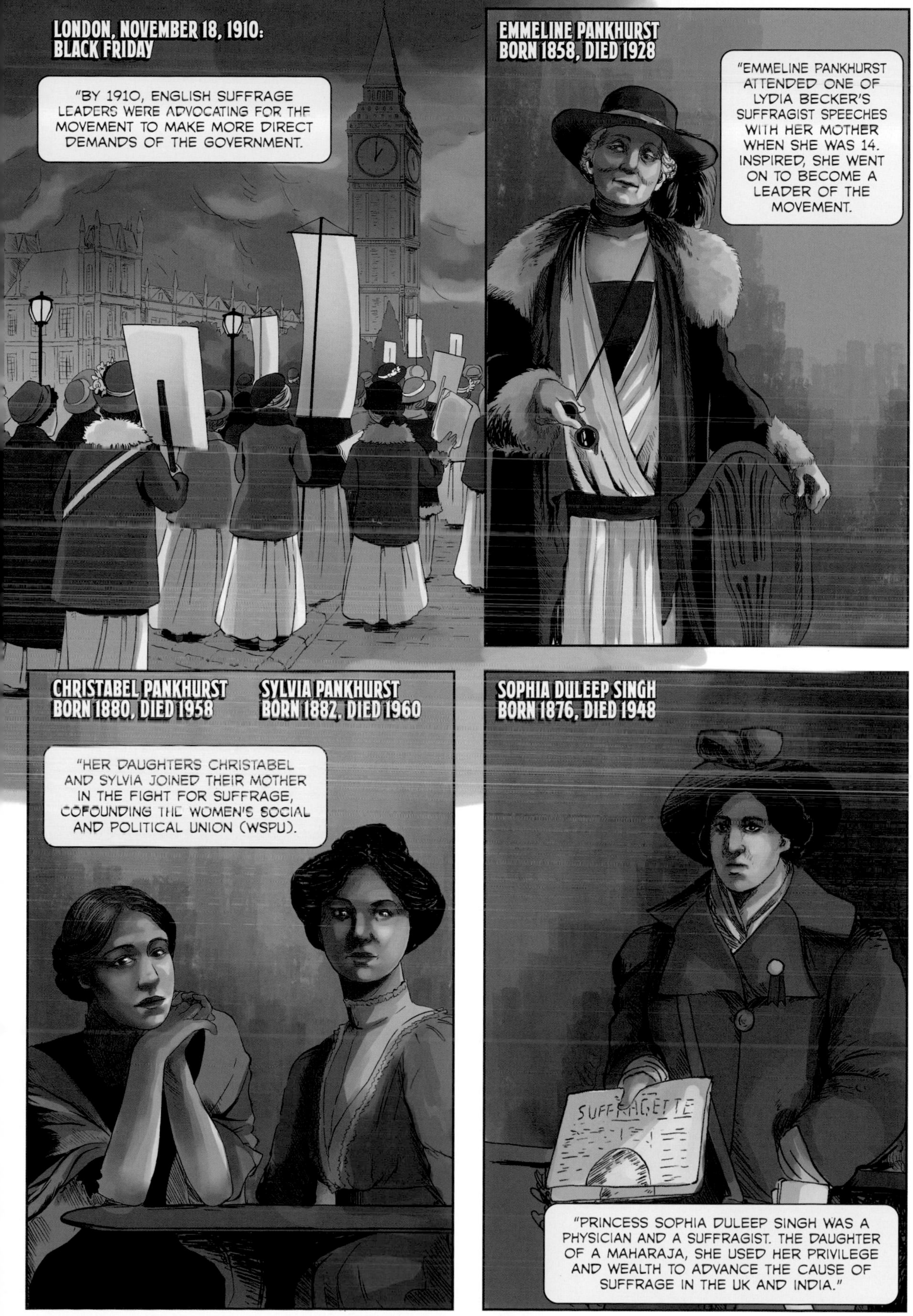
LONDON, NOVEMBER 18, 1910: BLACK FRIDAY
"BY 1910, ENGLISH SUFFRAGE LEADERS WERE ADVOCATING FOR THE MOVEMENT TO MAKE MORE DIRECT DEMANDS OF THE GOVERNMENT.
EMMELINE PANKHURST BORN 1858, DIED 1928
"EMMELINE PANKHURST ATTENDED ONE OF LYDIA BECKER'S SUFFRAGIST SPEECHES WITH HER MOTHER WHEN SHE WAS 14. INSPIRED, SHE WENT ON TO BECOME A LEADER OF THE MOVEMENT.
CHRISTABEL PANKHURST BORN 1880, DIED 1958
SYLVIA PANKHURST BORN 1882, DIED 1960
"HER DAUGHTERS CHRISTABEL AND SYLVIA JOINED THEIR MOTHER IN THE FIGHT FOR SUFFRAGE, COFOUNDING THE WOMEN'S SOCIAL AND POLITICAL UNION (WSPU).
SOPHIA DULEEP SINGH BORN 1876, DIED 1948
SUFFRAGETTE
"PRINCESS SOPHIA DULEEP SINGH WAS A PHYSICIAN AND A SUFFRAGIST. THE DAUGHTER OF A MAHARAJA, SHE USED HER PRIVILEGE AND WEALTH TO ADVANCE THE CAUSE OF SUFFRAGE IN THE UK AND INDIA."

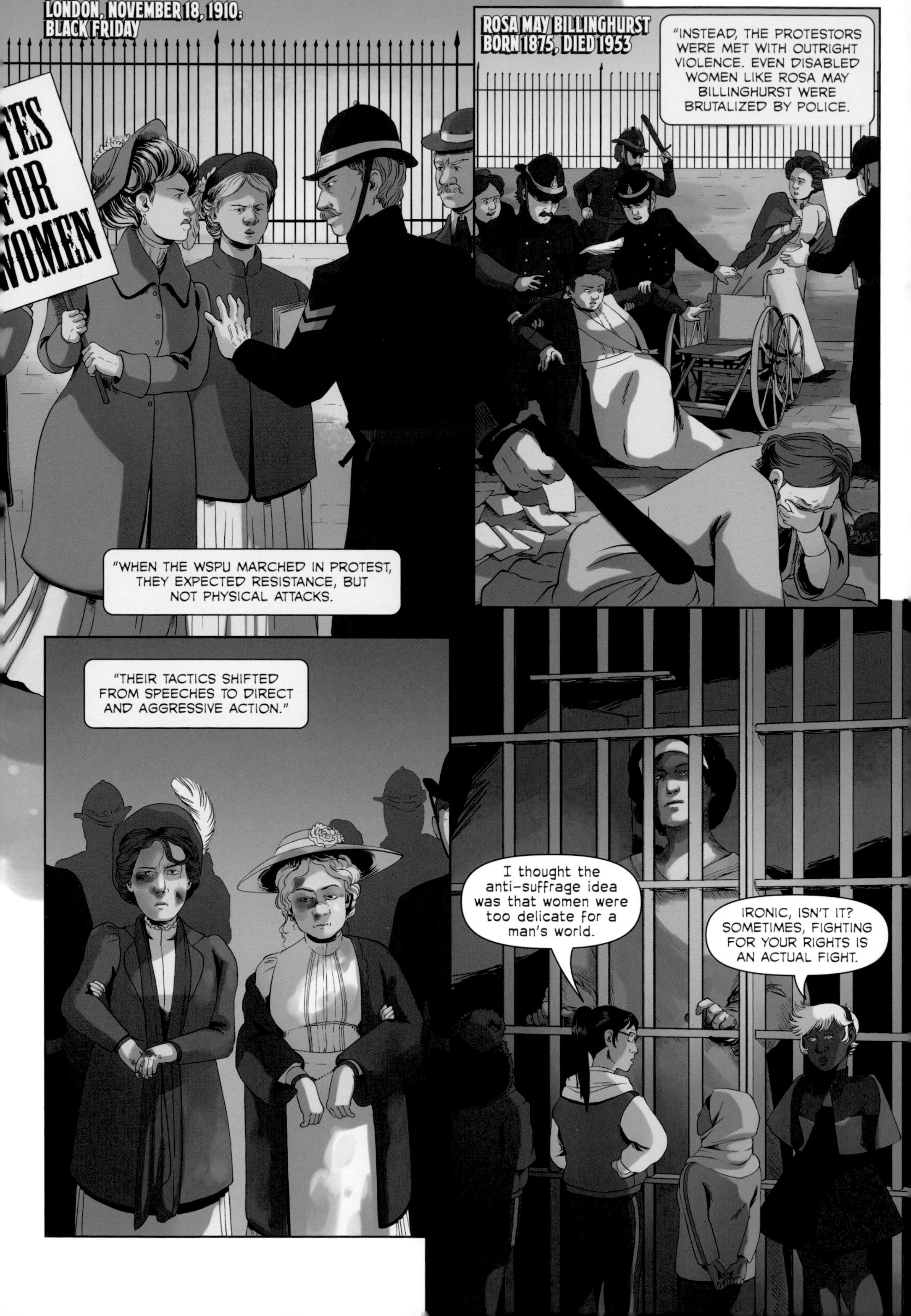
LONDON, NOVEMBER 18, 1910: BLACK FRIDAY
"WHEN THE WSPU MARCHED IN PROTEST, THEY EXPECTED RESISTANCE, BUT NOT PHYSICAL ATTACKS.
ROSA MAY BILLINGHURST BORN 1875, DIED 1953
"INSTEAD, THE PROTESTORS WERE MET WITH OUTRIGHT VIOLENCE. EVEN DISABLED WOMEN LIKE ROSA MAY BILLINGHURST WERE BRUTALIZED BY POLICE.
"THEIR TACTICS SHIFTED FROM SPEECHES TO DIRECT AND AGGRESSIVE ACTION."
I thought the anti-suffrage idea was that women were too delicate for a man's world.
IRONIC, ISN'T IT? SOMETIMES, FIGHTING FOR YOUR RIGHTS IS AN ACTUAL FIGHT.

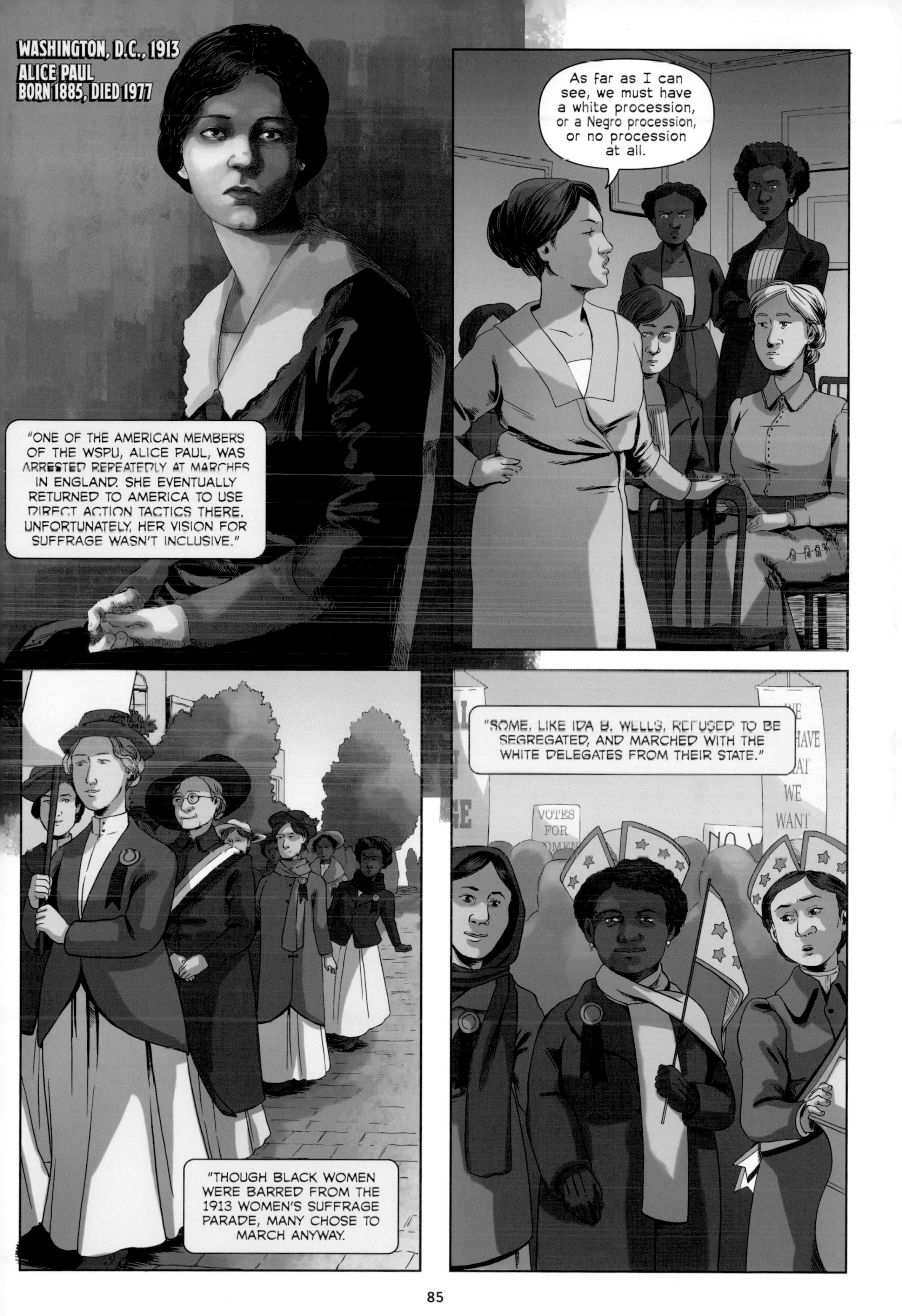
WASHINGTON, D.C., 1913
ALICE PAUL
BORN 1885, DIED 1977
"ONE OF THE AMERICAN MEMBERS OF THE WSPU, ALICE PAUL, WAS ARRESTED REPEATEDLY AT MARCHES IN ENGLAND. SHE EVENTUALLY RETURNED TO AMERICA TO USE DIRECT ACTION TACTICS THERE. UNFORTUNATELY, HER VISION FOR SUFFRAGE WASN'T INCLUSIVE."
As far as I can see, we must have a white procession, or a Negro procession, or no procession at all.
"THOUGH BLACK WOMEN WERE BARRED FROM THE 1913 WOMEN'S SUFFRAGE PARADE, MANY CHOSE TO MARCH ANYWAY.
"SOME, LIKE IDA B. WELLS, REFUSED TO BE SEGREGATED, AND MARCHED WITH THE WHITE DELEGATES FROM THEIR STATE."
VOTES FOR

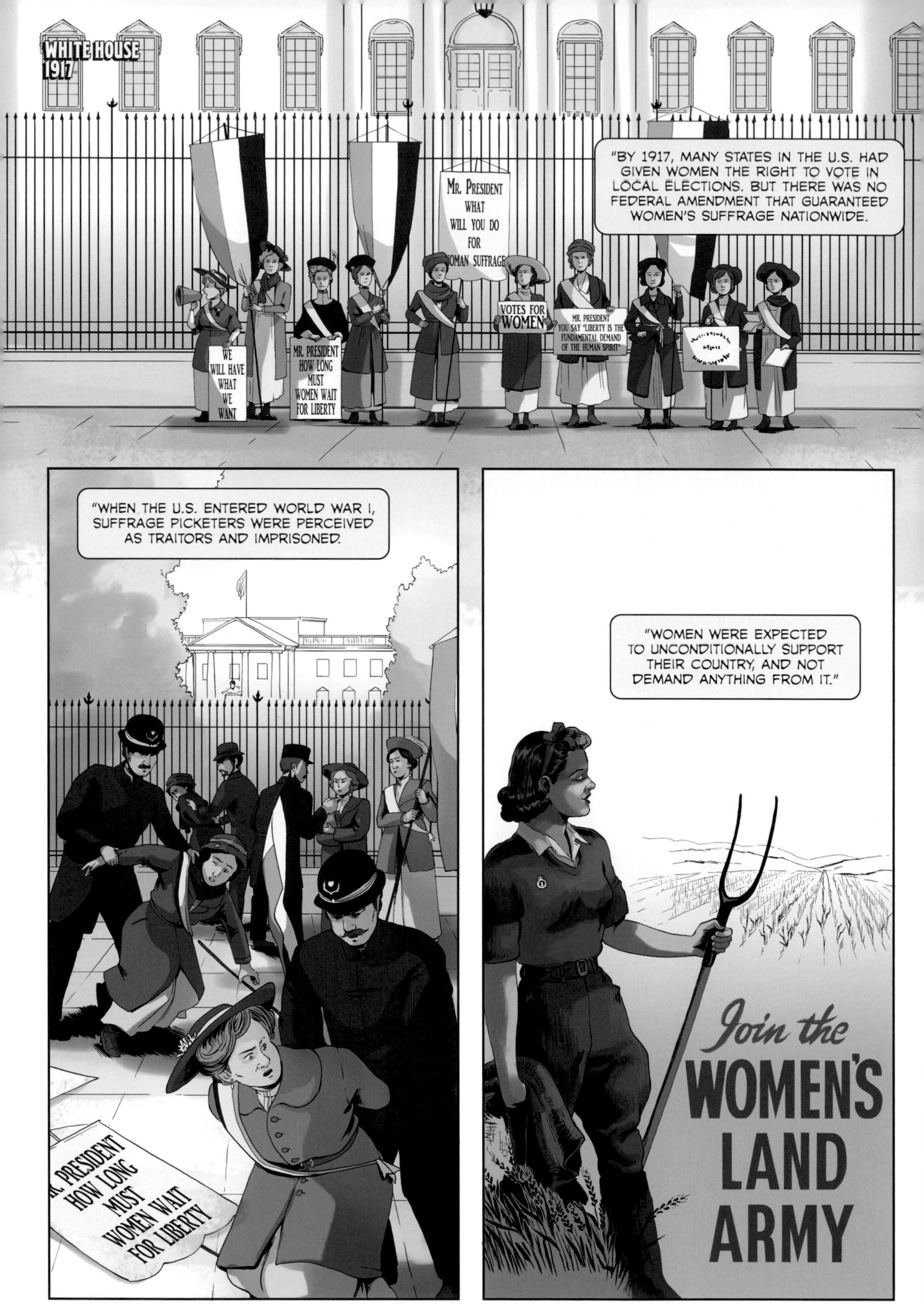
WHITE HOUSE 1917
"BY 1917, MANY STATES IN THE U.S. HAD GIVEN WOMEN THE RIGHT TO VOTE IN LOCAL ELECTIONS. BUT THERE WAS NO FEDERAL AMENDMENT THAT GUARANTEED WOMEN'S SUFFRAGE NATIONWIDE.
WE WILL HAVE WHAT WE WANT
MR. PRESIDENT HOW LONG MUST WOMEN WAIT FOR LIBERTY
MR. PRESIDENT WHAT WILL YOU DO FOR
OMAN SUFFRAGE
VOTES FOR WOMEN
MR. PRESIDENT YOU SAY "LIBERTY IS THE FUNDAMENTAL DEMAND OF THE HUMAN SPIRIT"
"WHEN THE U.S. ENTERED WORLD WAR I, SUFFRAGE PICKETERS WERE PERCEIVED AS TRAITORS AND IMPRISONED.
R. PRESIDENT HOW LONG MUST WOMEN WAIT FOR LIBERTY
"WOMEN WERE EXPECTED TO UNCONDITIONALLY SUPPORT THEIR COUNTRY, AND NOT DEMAND ANYTHING FROM IT."
Join the WOMEN'S LAND ARMY

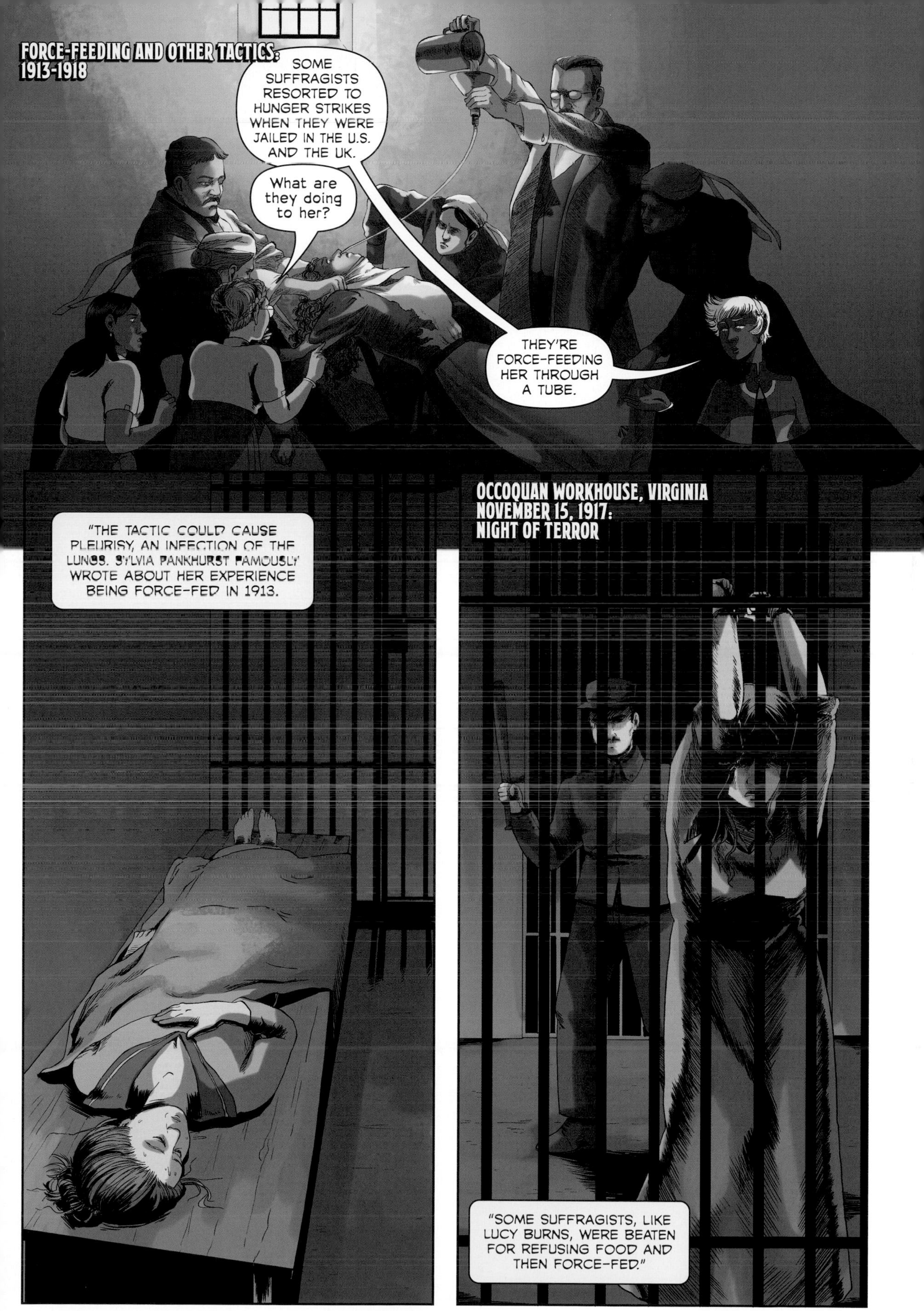
FORCE-FEEDING AND OTHER TACTICS: 1913-1918
SOME SUFFRAGISTS RESORTED TO HUNGER STRIKES WHEN THEY WERE JAILED IN THE U.S. AND THE UK.
What are they doing to her?
THEY'RE FORCE-FEEDING HER THROUGH A TUBE.
"THE TACTIC COULD CAUSE PLEURISY, AN INFECTION OF THE LUNGS. SYLVIA PANKHURST FAMOUSLY WROTE ABOUT HER EXPERIENCE BEING FORCE-FED IN 1913.
OCCOQUAN WORKHOUSE, VIRGINIA NOVEMBER 15, 1917: NIGHT OF TERROR
"SOME SUFFRAGISTS, LIKE LUCY BURNS, WERE BEATEN FOR REFUSING FOOD AND THEN FORCE-FED."

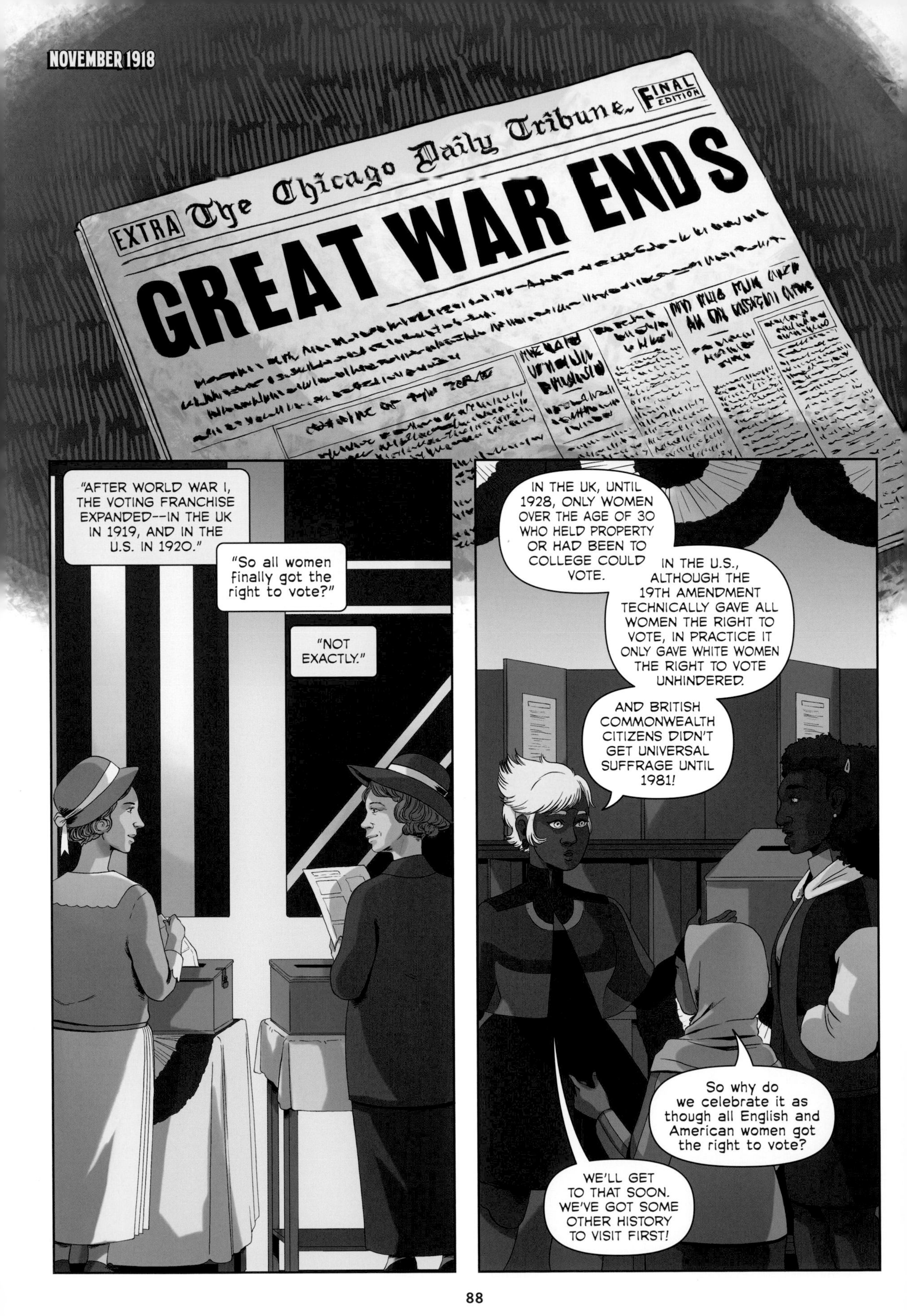
NOVEMBER 1918
EXTRA
The Chicago Daily Tribune
FINAL EDITION
GREAT WAR ENDS
"AFTER WORLD WAR I, THE VOTING FRANCHISE EXPANDED--IN THE UK IN 1919, AND IN THE U.S. IN 1920."
"So all women finally got the right to vote?"
"NOT EXACTLY."
IN THE UK, UNTIL 1928, ONLY WOMEN OVER THE AGE OF 30 WHO HELD PROPERTY OR HAD BEEN TO COLLEGE COULD VOTE.
IN THE U.S., ALTHOUGH THE 19TH AMENDMENT TECHNICALLY GAVE ALL WOMEN THE RIGHT TO VOTE, IN PRACTICE IT ONLY GAVE WHITE WOMEN THE RIGHT TO VOTE UNHINDERED.
AND BRITISH COMMONWEALTH CITIZENS DIDN'T GET UNIVERSAL SUFFRAGE UNTIL 1981!
So why do we celebrate it as though all English and American women got the right to vote?
WE'LL GET TO THAT SOON. WE'VE GOT SOME OTHER HISTORY TO VISIT FIRST!

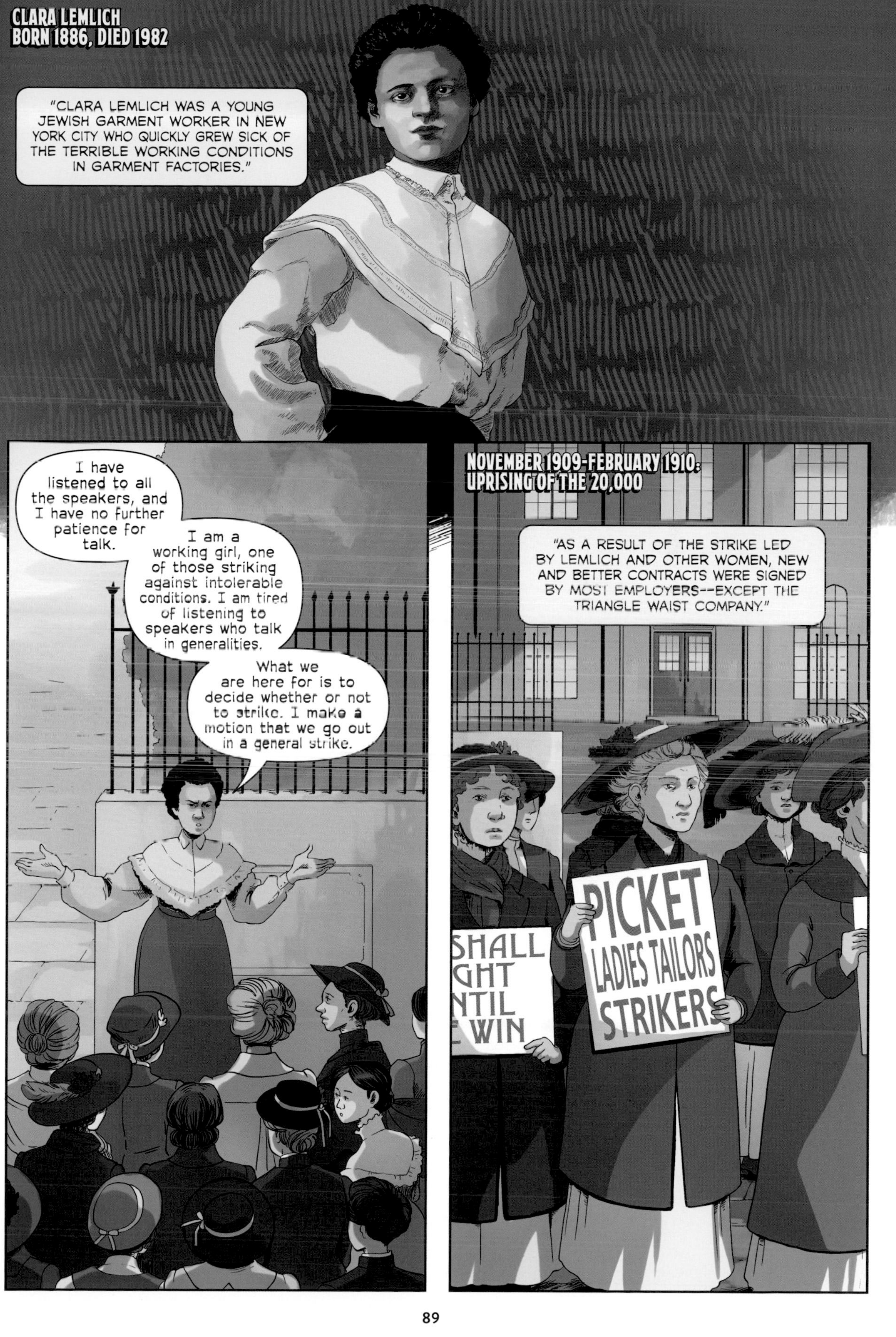
CLARA LEMLICH
BORN 1886, DIED 1982
"CLARA LEMLICH WAS A YOUNG JEWISH GARMENT WORKER IN NEW YORK CITY WHO QUICKLY GREW SICK OF THE TERRIBLE WORKING CONDITIONS IN GARMENT FACTORIES."
I have listened to all the speakers, and I have no further patience for talk.
I am a working girl, one of those striking against intolerable conditions. I am tired of listening to speakers who talk in generalities.
What we are here for is to decide whether or not to strike. I make a motion that we go out in a general strike.
NOVEMBER 1909-FEBRUARY 1910:
UPRISING OF THE 20,000
"AS A RESULT OF THE STRIKE LED BY LEMLICH AND OTHER WOMEN, NEW AND BETTER CONTRACTS WERE SIGNED BY MOST EMPLOYERS--EXCEPT THE TRIANGLE WAIST COMPANY."
SHALL
GHT
NTIL
E WIN
PICKET
LADIES TAILORS
STRIKERS

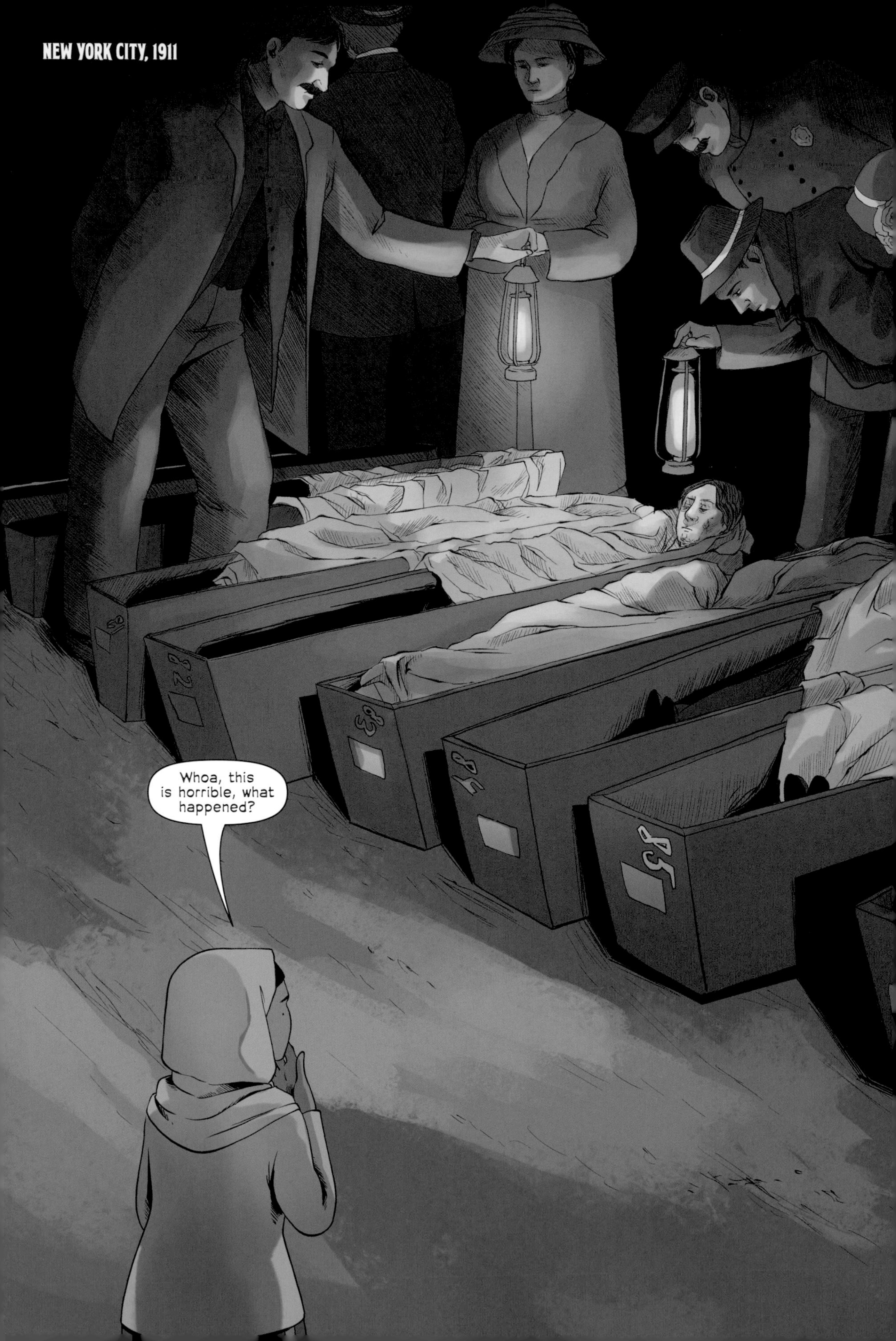
NEW YORK CITY, 1911
Whoa, this is horrible, what happened?

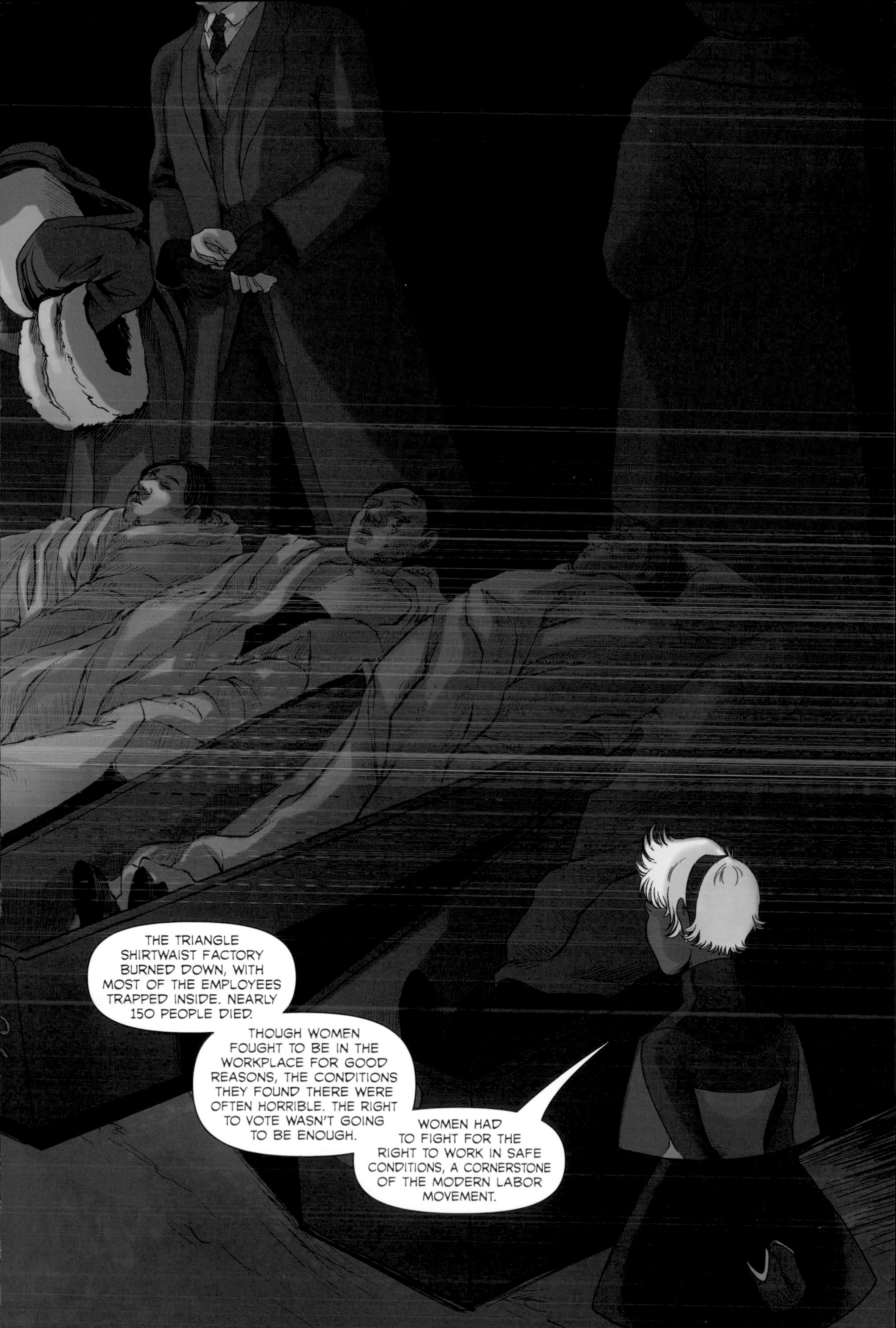
THE TRIANGLE SHIRTWAIST FACTORY BURNED DOWN, WITH MOST OF THE EMPLOYEES TRAPPED INSIDE. NEARLY 150 PEOPLE DIED.
THOUGH WOMEN FOUGHT TO BE IN THE WORKPLACE FOR GOOD REASONS, THE CONDITIONS THEY FOUND THERE WERE OFTEN HORRIBLE. THE RIGHT TO VOTE WASN'T GOING TO BE ENOUGH.
WOMEN HAD TO FIGHT FOR THE RIGHT TO WORK IN SAFE CONDITIONS, A CORNERSTONE OF THE MODERN LABOR MOVEMENT.

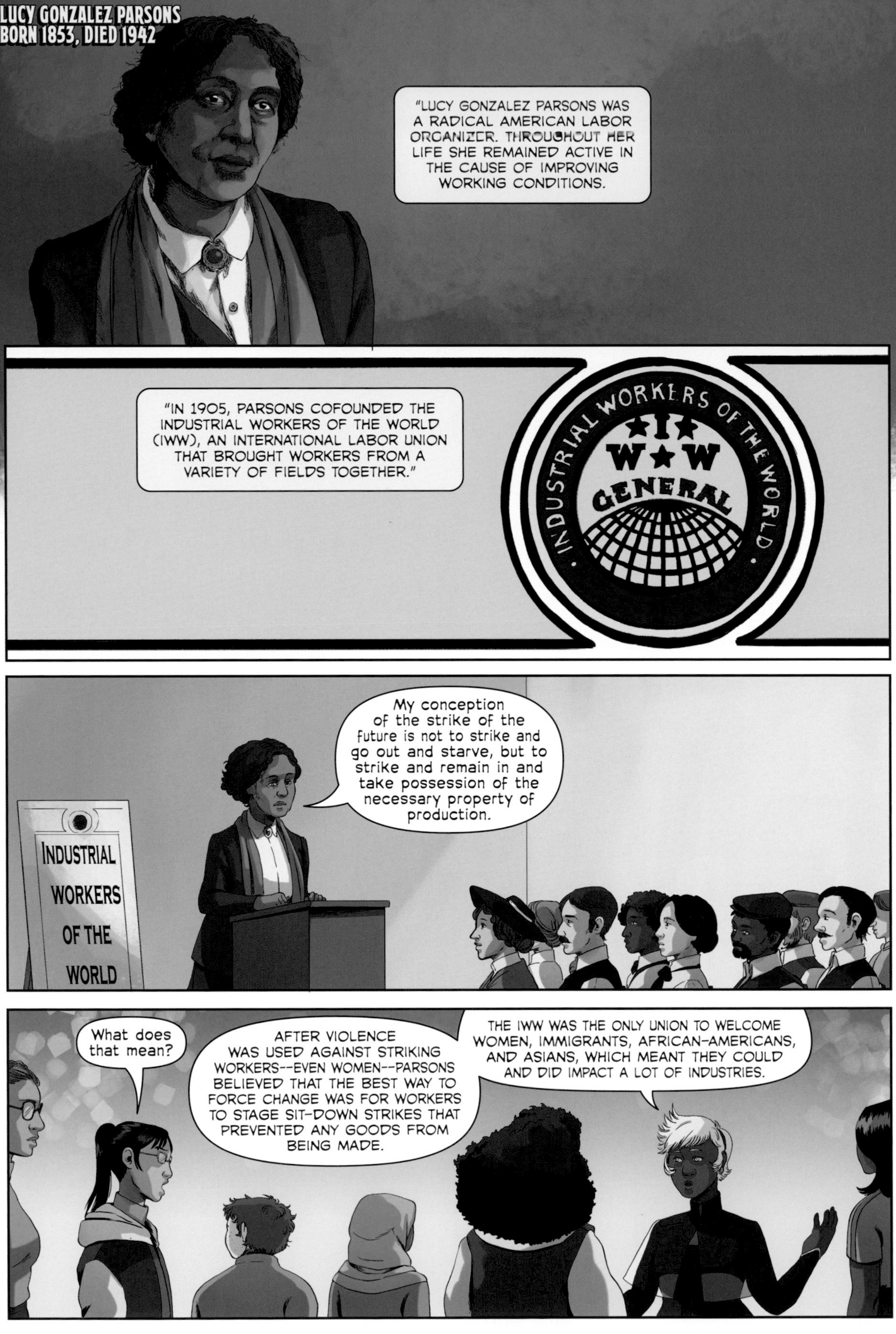
LUCY GONZALEZ PARSONS
BORN 1853, DIED 1942
"LUCY GONZALEZ PARSONS WAS A RADICAL AMERICAN LABOR ORGANIZER. THROUGHOUT HER LIFE SHE REMAINED ACTIVE IN THE CAUSE OF IMPROVING WORKING CONDITIONS.
"IN 1905, PARSONS COFOUNDED THE INDUSTRIAL WORKERS OF THE WORLD (IWW), AN INTERNATIONAL LABOR UNION THAT BROUGHT WORKERS FROM A VARIETY OF FIELDS TOGETHER."
INDUSTRIAL WORKERS OF THE WORLD
I W W
GENERAL
My conception of the strike of the future is not to strike and go out and starve, but to strike and remain in and take possession of the necessary property of production.
INDUSTRIAL WORKERS OF THE WORLD
What does that mean?
AFTER VIOLENCE WAS USED AGAINST STRIKING WORKERS--EVEN WOMEN--PARSONS BELIEVED THAT THE BEST WAY TO FORCE CHANGE WAS FOR WORKERS TO STAGE SIT-DOWN STRIKES THAT PREVENTED ANY GOODS FROM BEING MADE.
THE IWW WAS THE ONLY UNION TO WELCOME WOMEN, IMMIGRANTS, AFRICAN-AMERICANS, AND ASIANS, WHICH MEANT THEY COULD AND DID IMPACT A LOT OF INDUSTRIES.

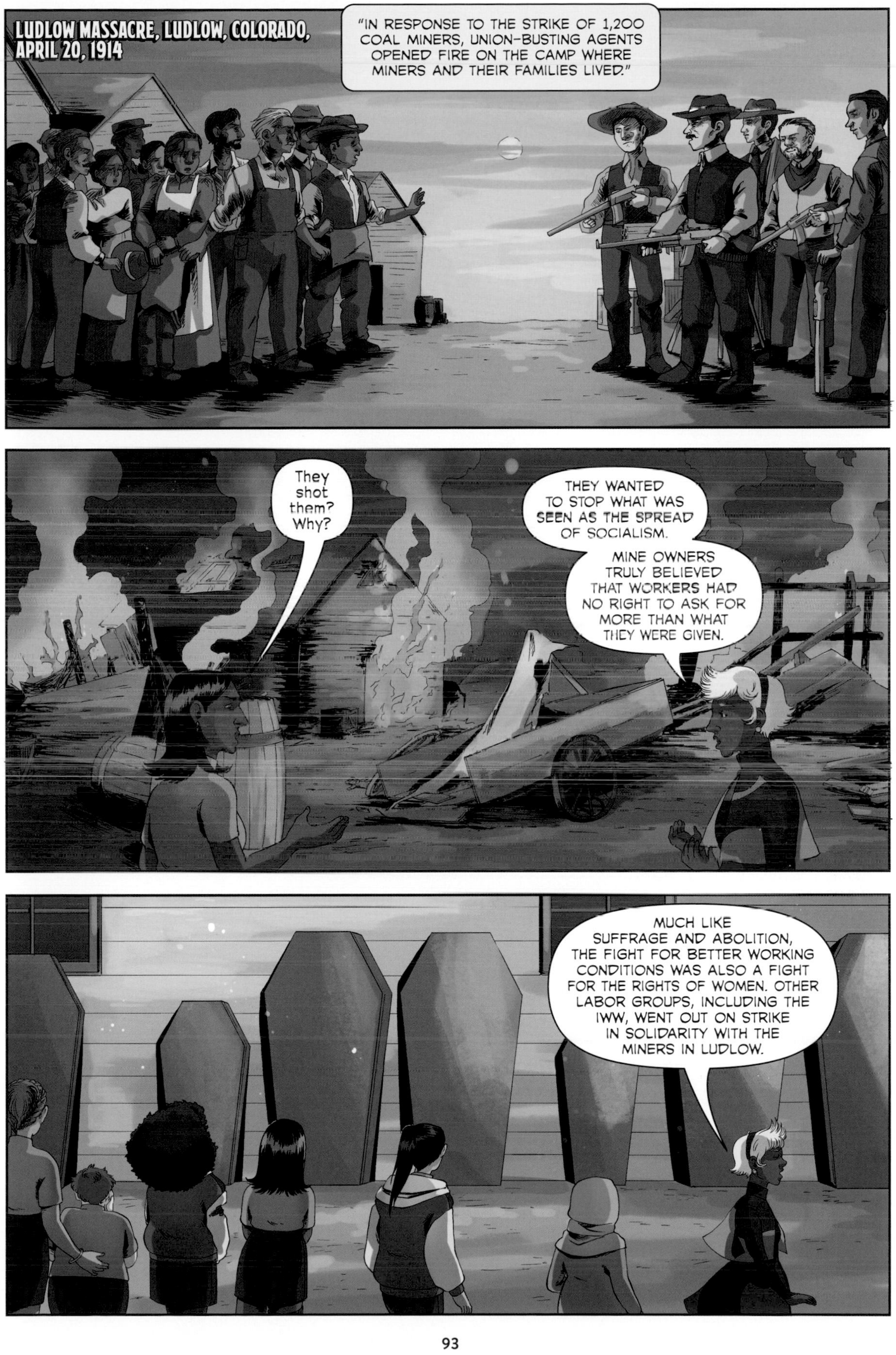
LUDLOW MASSACRE, LUDLOW, COLORADO, APRIL 20, 1914
"IN RESPONSE TO THE STRIKE OF 1,200 COAL MINERS, UNION-BUSTING AGENTS OPENED FIRE ON THE CAMP WHERE MINERS AND THEIR FAMILIES LIVED."
They shot them? Why?
THEY WANTED TO STOP WHAT WAS SEEN AS THE SPREAD OF SOCIALISM.
MINE OWNERS TRULY BELIEVED THAT WORKERS HAD NO RIGHT TO ASK FOR MORE THAN WHAT THEY WERE GIVEN.
MUCH LIKE SUFFRAGE AND ABOLITION, THE FIGHT FOR BETTER WORKING CONDITIONS WAS ALSO A FIGHT FOR THE RIGHTS OF WOMEN. OTHER LABOR GROUPS, INCLUDING THE IWW, WENT OUT ON STRIKE IN SOLIDARITY WITH THE MINERS IN LUDLOW.

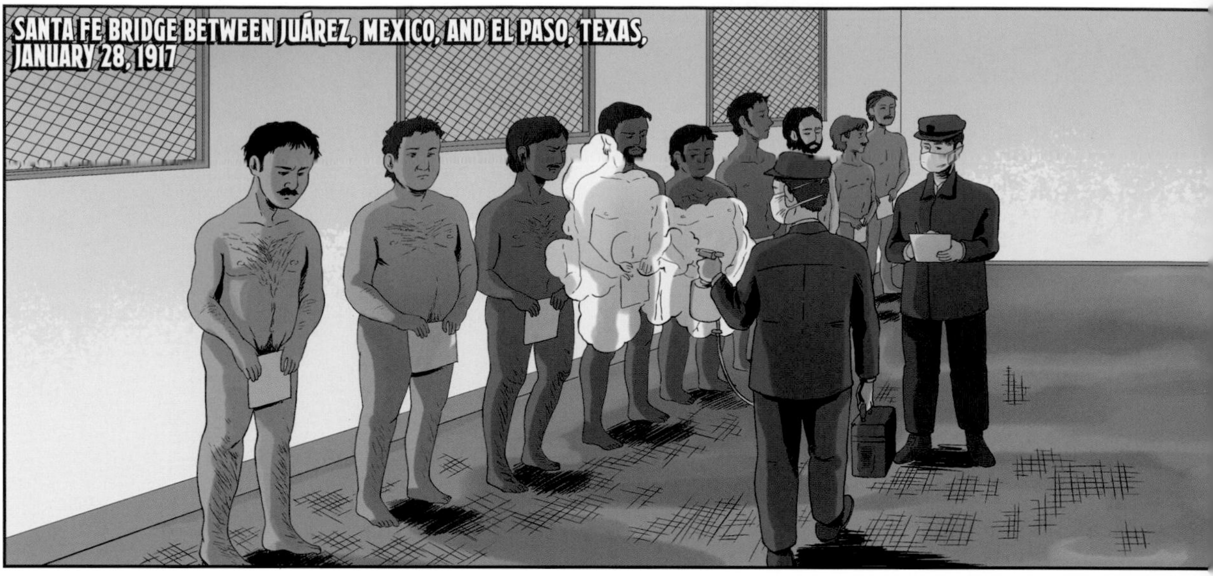
SANTA FE BRIDGE BETWEEN JUÁREZ, MEXICO, AND EL PASO, TEXAS, JANUARY 28, 1917

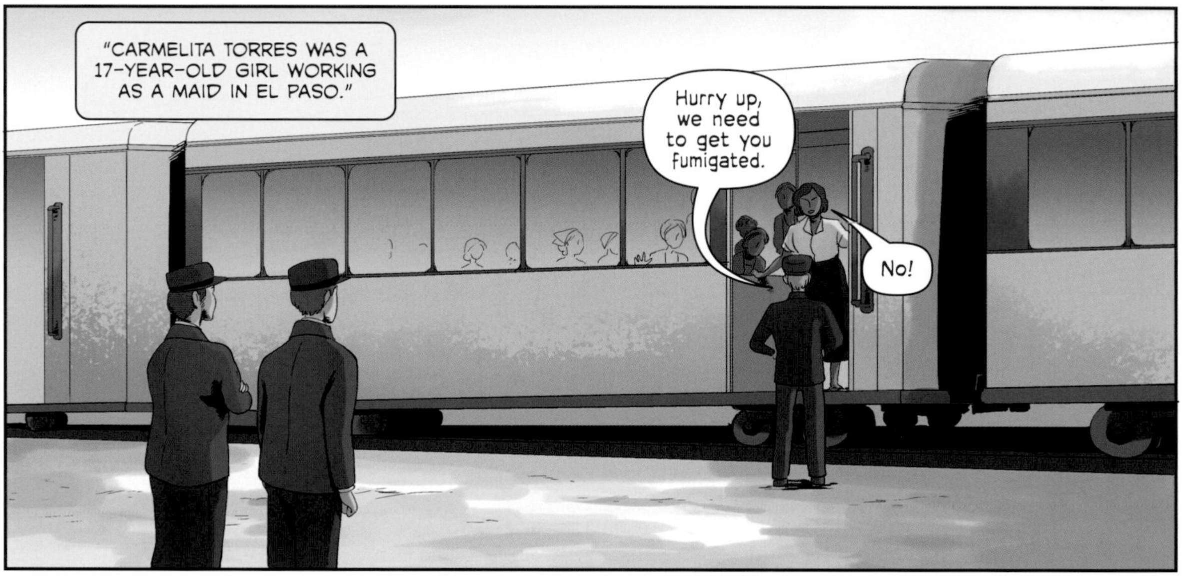
"CARMELITA TORRES WAS A 17-YEAR-OLD GIRL WORKING AS A MAID IN EL PASO."
Hurry up, we need to get you fumigated.
No!

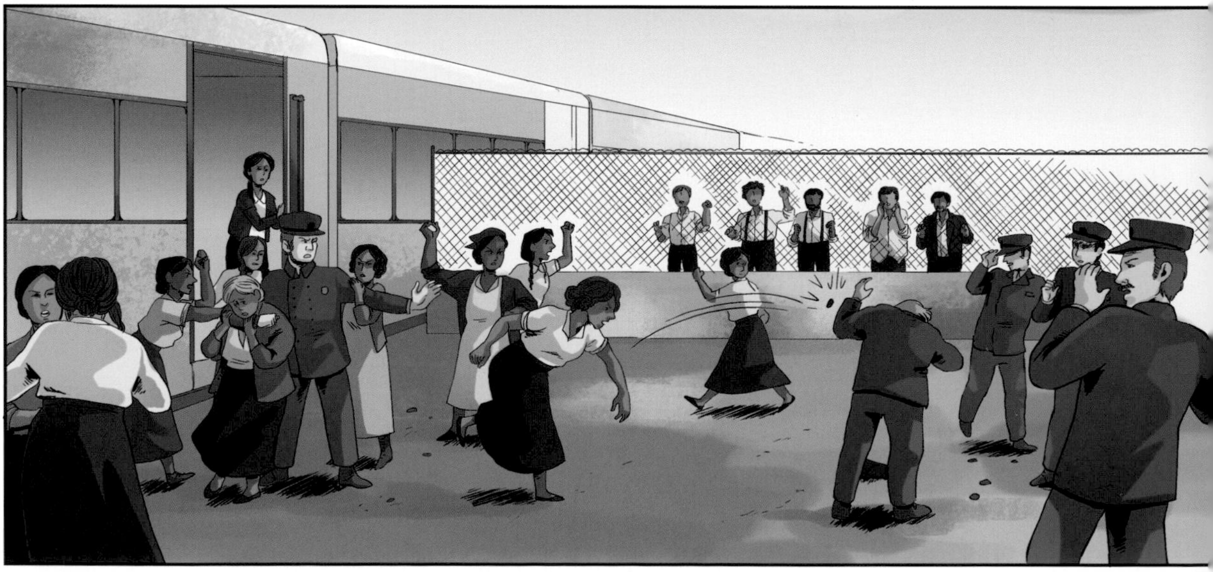

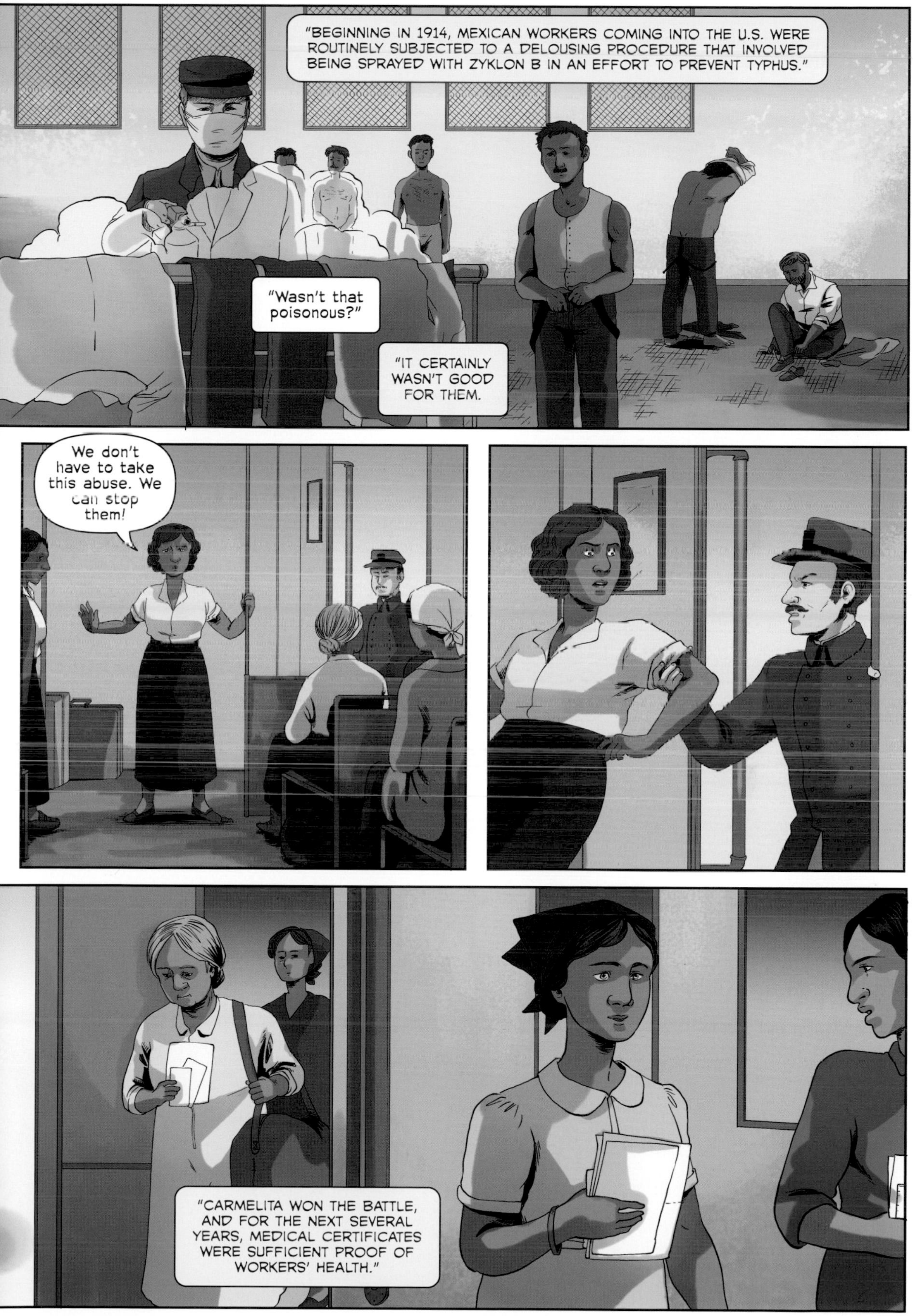
"BEGINNING IN 1914, MEXICAN WORKERS COMING INTO THE U.S. WERE ROUTINELY SUBJECTED TO A DELOUSING PROCEDURE THAT INVOLVED BEING SPRAYED WITH ZYKLON B IN AN EFFORT TO PREVENT TYPHUS."
"Wasn't that poisonous?"
"IT CERTAINLY WASN'T GOOD FOR THEM.
We don't have to take this abuse. We can stop them!
"CARMELITA WON THE BATTLE, AND FOR THE NEXT SEVERAL YEARS, MEDICAL CERTIFICATES WERE SUFFICIENT PROOF OF WORKERS' HEALTH."

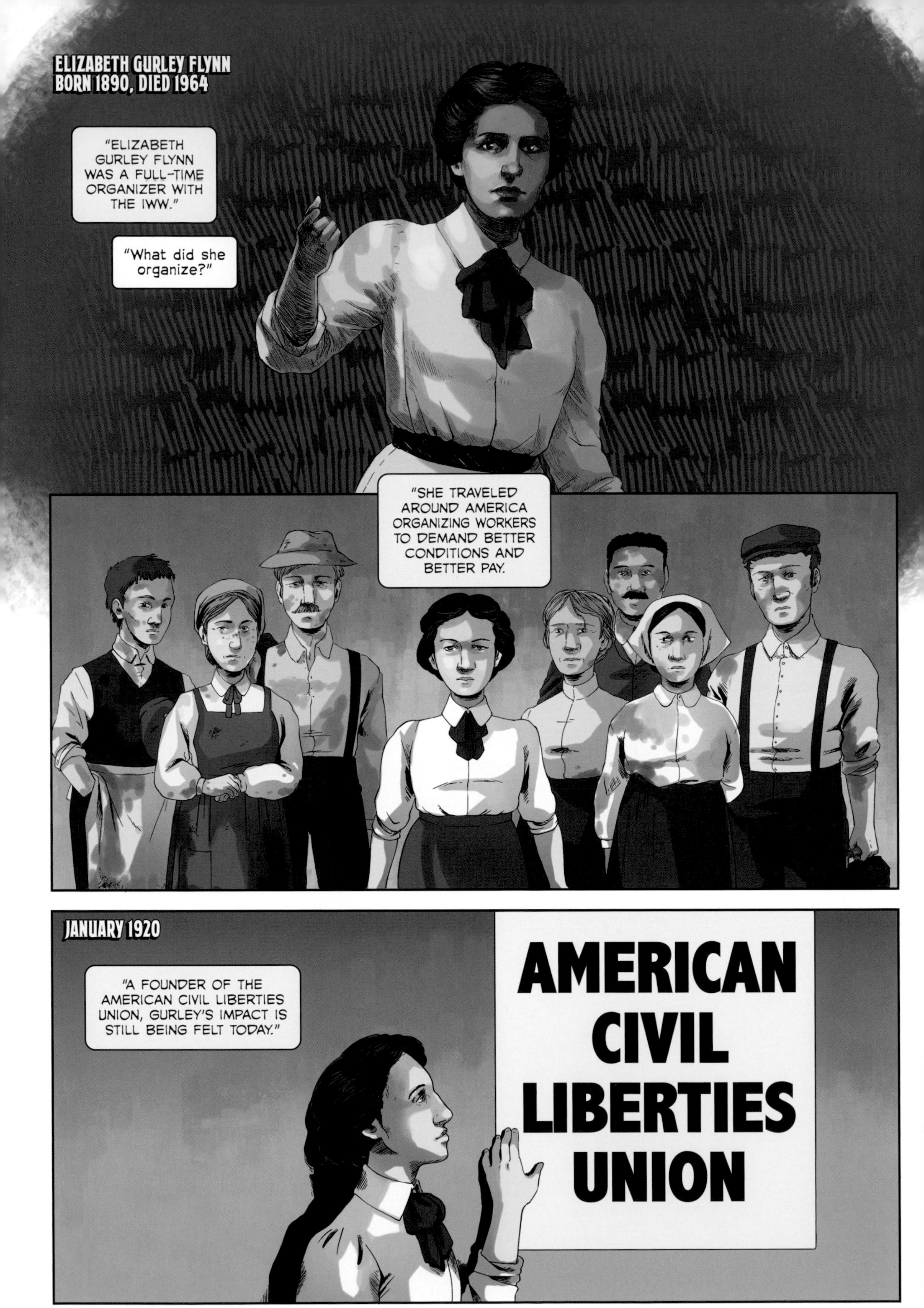
ELIZABETH GURLEY FLYNN
BORN 1890, DIED 1964
"ELIZABETH GURLEY FLYNN WAS A FULL-TIME ORGANIZER WITH THE IWW."
"What did she organize?"
"SHE TRAVELED AROUND AMERICA ORGANIZING WORKERS TO DEMAND BETTER CONDITIONS AND BETTER PAY.
JANUARY 1920
"A FOUNDER OF THE AMERICAN CIVIL LIBERTIES UNION, GURLEY'S IMPACT IS STILL BEING FELT TODAY."
AMERICAN CIVIL LIBERTIES UNION

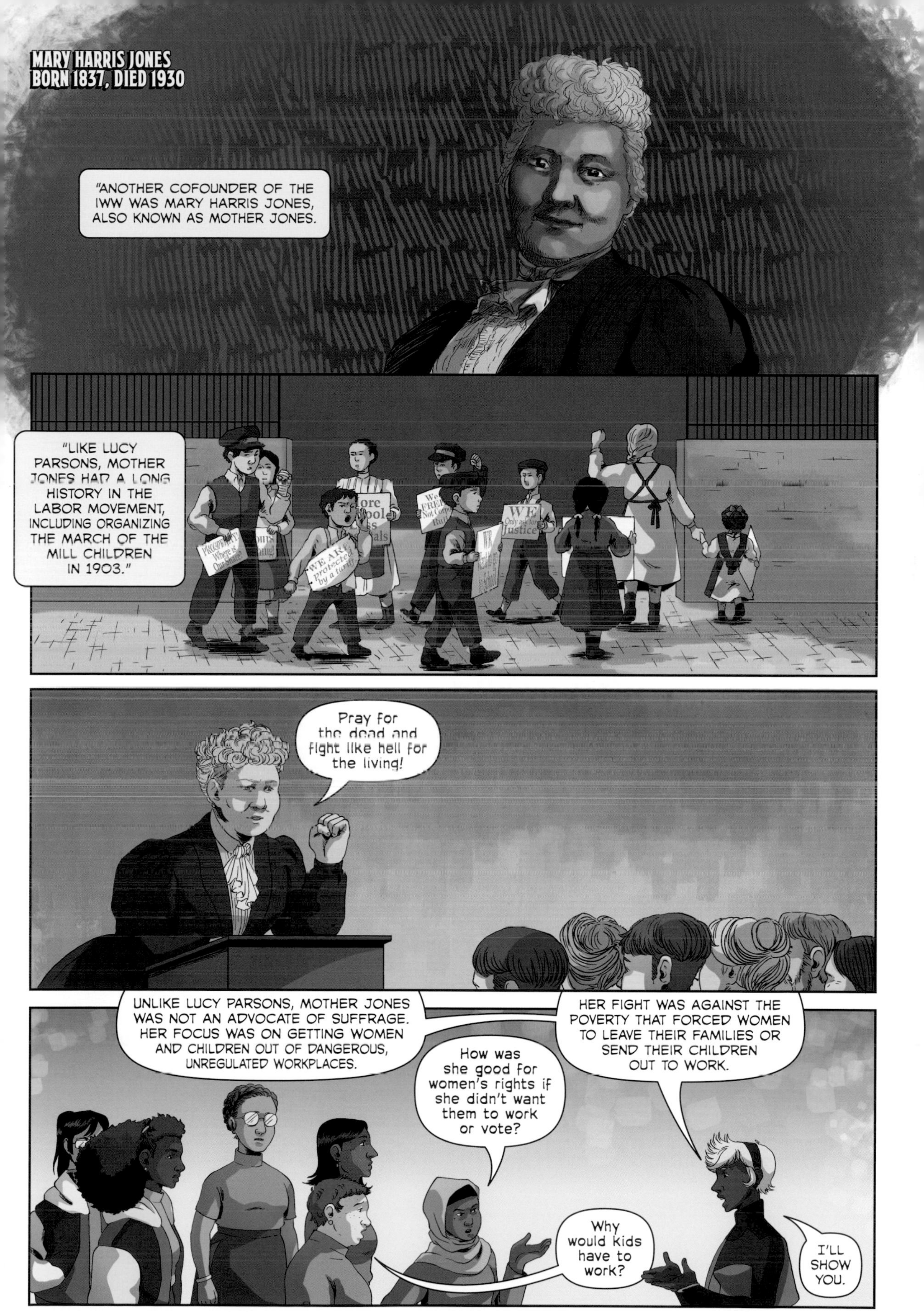
MARY HARRIS JONES
BORN 1837, DIED 1930
"ANOTHER COFOUNDER OF THE IWW WAS MARY HARRIS JONES, ALSO KNOWN AS MOTHER JONES.
"LIKE LUCY PARSONS, MOTHER JONES HAD A LONG HISTORY IN THE LABOR MOVEMENT, INCLUDING ORGANIZING THE MARCH OF THE MILL CHILDREN IN 1903."
Pray for the dead and fight like hell for the living!
UNLIKE LUCY PARSONS, MOTHER JONES WAS NOT AN ADVOCATE OF SUFFRAGE. HER FOCUS WAS ON GETTING WOMEN AND CHILDREN OUT OF DANGEROUS, UNREGULATED WORKPLACES.
How was she good for women's rights if she didn't want them to work or vote?
HER FIGHT WAS AGAINST THE POVERTY THAT FORCED WOMEN TO LEAVE THEIR FAMILIES OR SEND THEIR CHILDREN OUT TO WORK.
Why would kids have to work?
I'LL SHOW YOU.

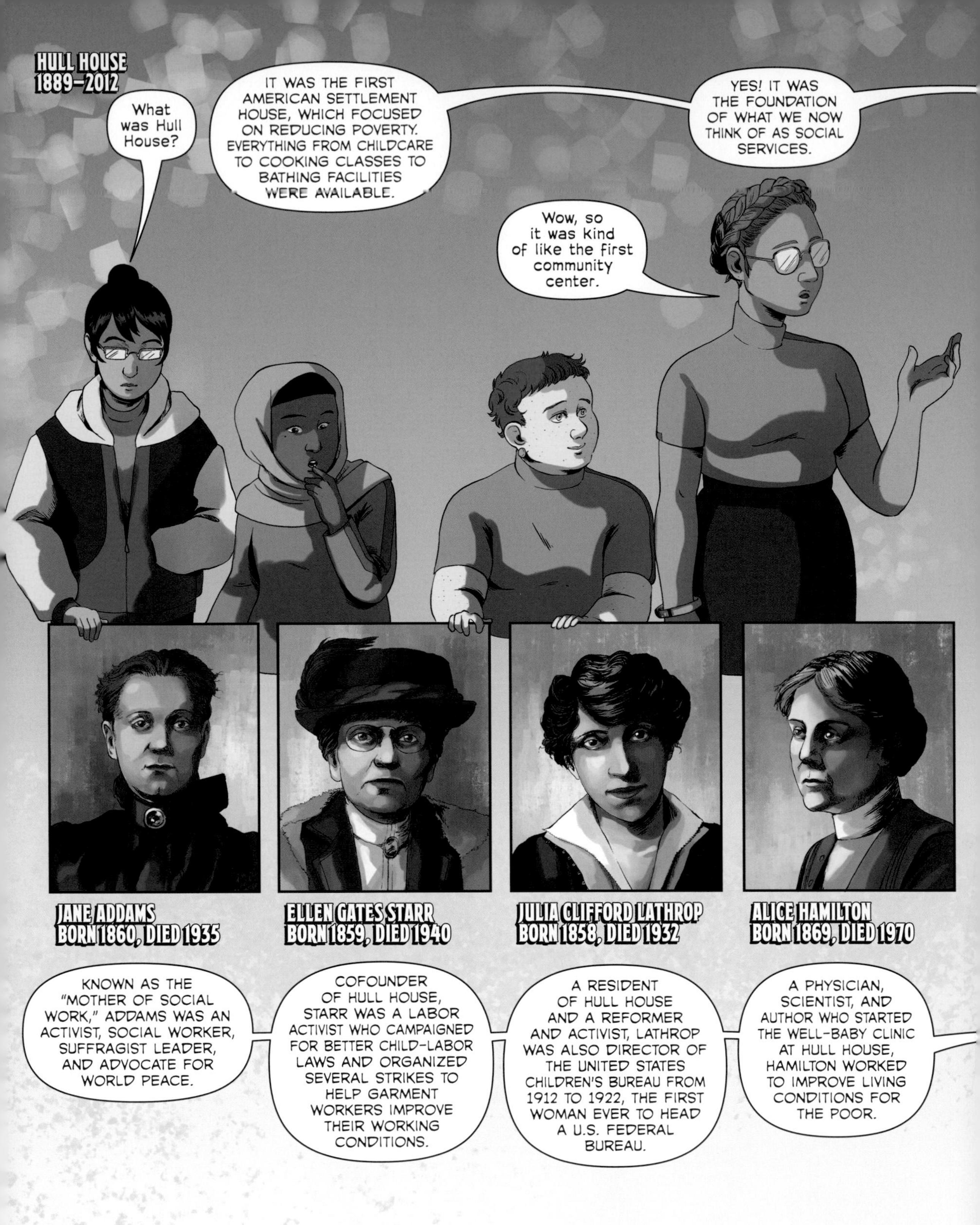
HULL HOUSE
1889–2012
What was Hull House?
IT WAS THE FIRST AMERICAN SETTLEMENT HOUSE, WHICH FOCUSED ON REDUCING POVERTY. EVERYTHING FROM CHILDCARE TO COOKING CLASSES TO BATHING FACILITIES WERE AVAILABLE.
YES! IT WAS THE FOUNDATION OF WHAT WE NOW THINK OF AS SOCIAL SERVICES.
Wow, so it was kind of like the first community center.
JANE ADDAMS
BORN 1860, DIED 1935
ELLEN GATES STARR
BORN 1859, DIED 1940
JULIA CLIFFORD LATHROP
BORN 1858, DIED 1932
ALICE HAMILTON
BORN 1869, DIED 1970
KNOWN AS THE "MOTHER OF SOCIAL WORK," ADDAMS WAS AN ACTIVIST, SOCIAL WORKER, SUFFRAGIST LEADER, AND ADVOCATE FOR WORLD PEACE.
COFOUNDER OF HULL HOUSE, STARR WAS A LABOR ACTIVIST WHO CAMPAIGNED FOR BETTER CHILD-LABOR LAWS AND ORGANIZED SEVERAL STRIKES TO HELP GARMENT WORKERS IMPROVE THEIR WORKING CONDITIONS.
A RESIDENT OF HULL HOUSE AND A REFORMER AND ACTIVIST, LATHROP WAS ALSO DIRECTOR OF THE UNITED STATES CHILDREN'S BUREAU FROM 1912 TO 1922, THE FIRST WOMAN EVER TO HEAD A U.S. FEDERAL BUREAU.
A PHYSICIAN, SCIENTIST, AND AUTHOR WHO STARTED THE WELL-BABY CLINIC AT HULL HOUSE, HAMILTON WORKED TO IMPROVE LIVING CONDITIONS FOR THE POOR.

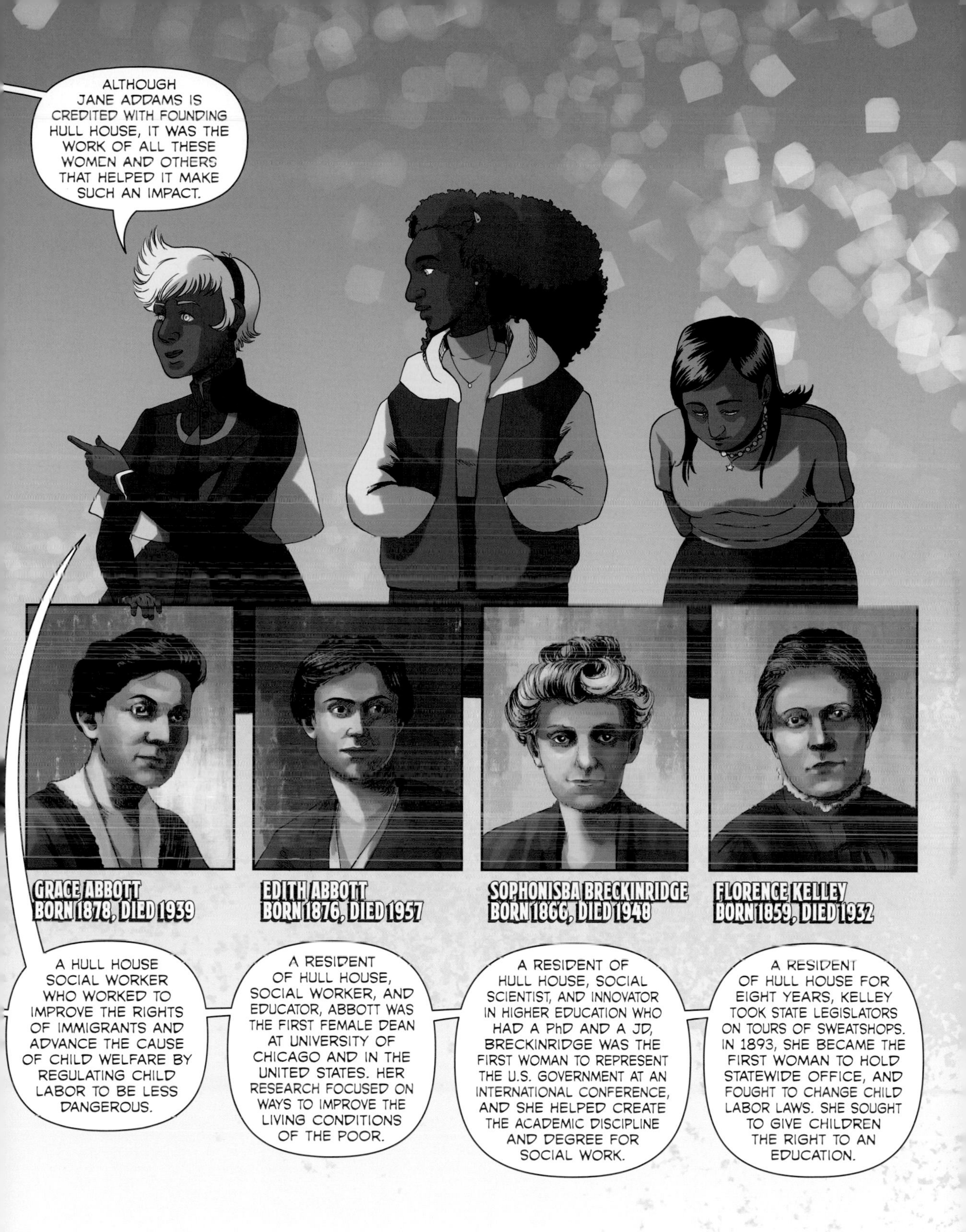

ALTHOUGH JANE ADDAMS IS CREDITED WITH FOUNDING HULL HOUSE, IT WAS THE WORK OF ALL THESE WOMEN AND OTHERS THAT HELPED IT MAKE SUCH AN IMPACT.
GRACE ABBOTT BORN 1878, DIED 1939
EDITH ABBOTT BORN 1876, DIED 1957
SOPHONISBA BRECKINRIDGE BORN 1866, DIED 1948
FLORENCE KELLEY BORN 1859, DIED 1932
A HULL HOUSE SOCIAL WORKER WHO WORKED TO IMPROVE THE RIGHTS OF IMMIGRANTS AND ADVANCE THE CAUSE OF CHILD WELFARE BY REGULATING CHILD LABOR TO BE LESS DANGEROUS.
A RESIDENT OF HULL HOUSE, SOCIAL WORKER, AND EDUCATOR, ABBOTT WAS THE FIRST FEMALE DEAN AT UNIVERSITY OF CHICAGO AND IN THE UNITED STATES. HER RESEARCH FOCUSED ON WAYS TO IMPROVE THE LIVING CONDITIONS OF THE POOR.
A RESIDENT OF HULL HOUSE, SOCIAL SCIENTIST, AND INNOVATOR IN HIGHER EDUCATION WHO HAD A PhD AND A JD, BRECKINRIDGE WAS THE FIRST WOMAN TO REPRESENT THE U.S. GOVERNMENT AT AN INTERNATIONAL CONFERENCE, AND SHE HELPED CREATE THE ACADEMIC DISCIPLINE AND DEGREE FOR SOCIAL WORK.
A RESIDENT OF HULL HOUSE FOR EIGHT YEARS, KELLEY TOOK STATE LEGISLATORS ON TOURS OF SWEATSHOPS. IN 1893, SHE BECAME THE FIRST WOMAN TO HOLD STATEWIDE OFFICE, AND FOUGHT TO CHANGE CHILD LABOR LAWS. SHE SOUGHT TO GIVE CHILDREN THE RIGHT TO AN EDUCATION.

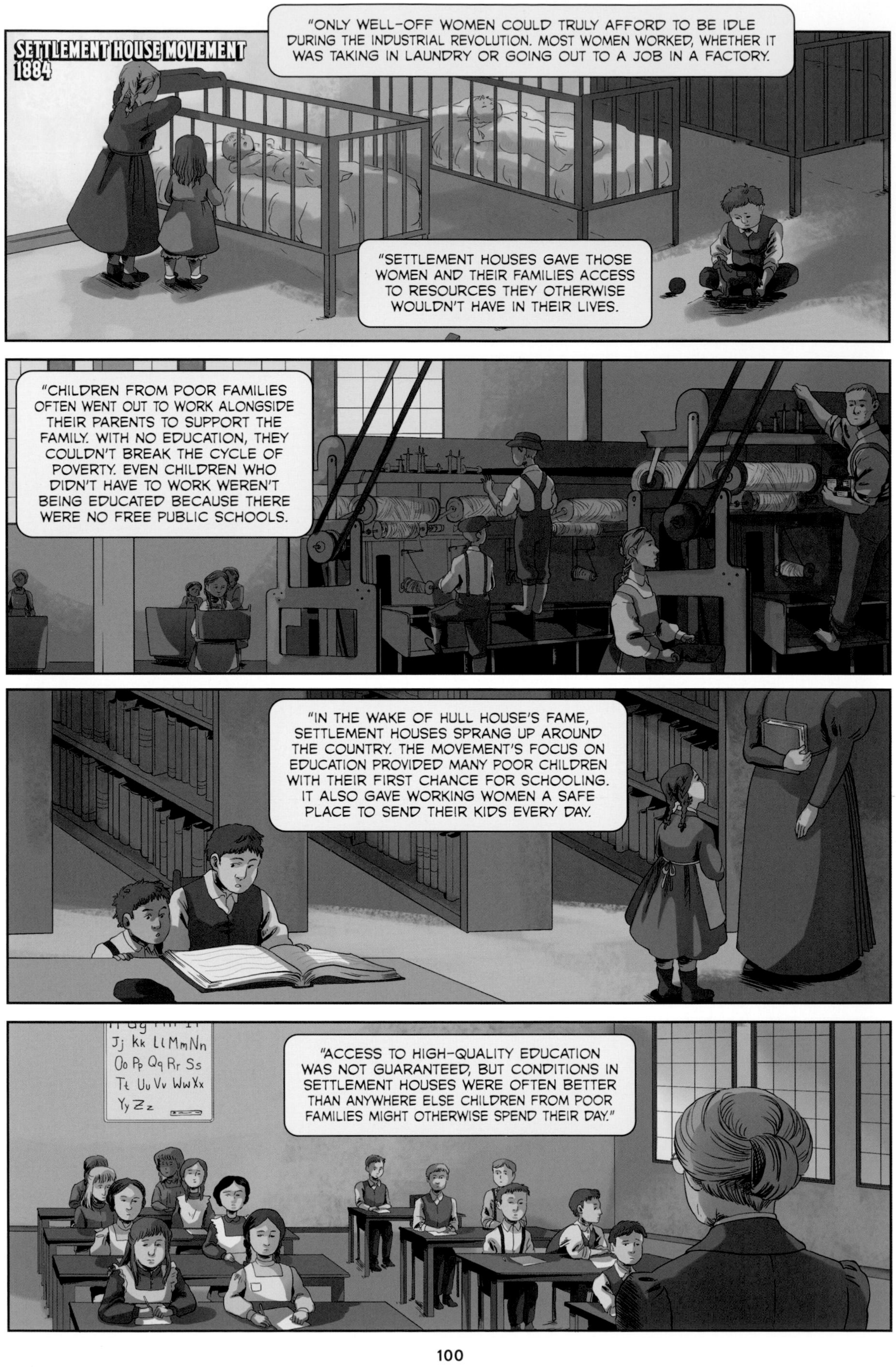
SETTLEMENT HOUSE MOVEMENT 1884
"ONLY WELL-OFF WOMEN COULD TRULY AFFORD TO BE IDLE DURING THE INDUSTRIAL REVOLUTION. MOST WOMEN WORKED, WHETHER IT WAS TAKING IN LAUNDRY OR GOING OUT TO A JOB IN A FACTORY.
"SETTLEMENT HOUSES GAVE THOSE WOMEN AND THEIR FAMILIES ACCESS TO RESOURCES THEY OTHERWISE WOULDN'T HAVE IN THEIR LIVES.
"CHILDREN FROM POOR FAMILIES OFTEN WENT OUT TO WORK ALONGSIDE THEIR PARENTS TO SUPPORT THE FAMILY. WITH NO EDUCATION, THEY COULDN'T BREAK THE CYCLE OF POVERTY. EVEN CHILDREN WHO DIDN'T HAVE TO WORK WEREN'T BEING EDUCATED BECAUSE THERE WERE NO FREE PUBLIC SCHOOLS.
"IN THE WAKE OF HULL HOUSE'S FAME, SETTLEMENT HOUSES SPRANG UP AROUND THE COUNTRY. THE MOVEMENT'S FOCUS ON EDUCATION PROVIDED MANY POOR CHILDREN WITH THEIR FIRST CHANCE FOR SCHOOLING. IT ALSO GAVE WORKING WOMEN A SAFE PLACE TO SEND THEIR KIDS EVERY DAY.
Jj Kk Ll Mm Nn
Oo Pp Qq Rr Ss
Tt Uu Vv Ww Xx
Yy Zz
"ACCESS TO HIGH-QUALITY EDUCATION WAS NOT GUARANTEED, BUT CONDITIONS IN SETTLEMENT HOUSES WERE OFTEN BETTER THAN ANYWHERE ELSE CHILDREN FROM POOR FAMILIES MIGHT OTHERWISE SPEND THEIR DAY."

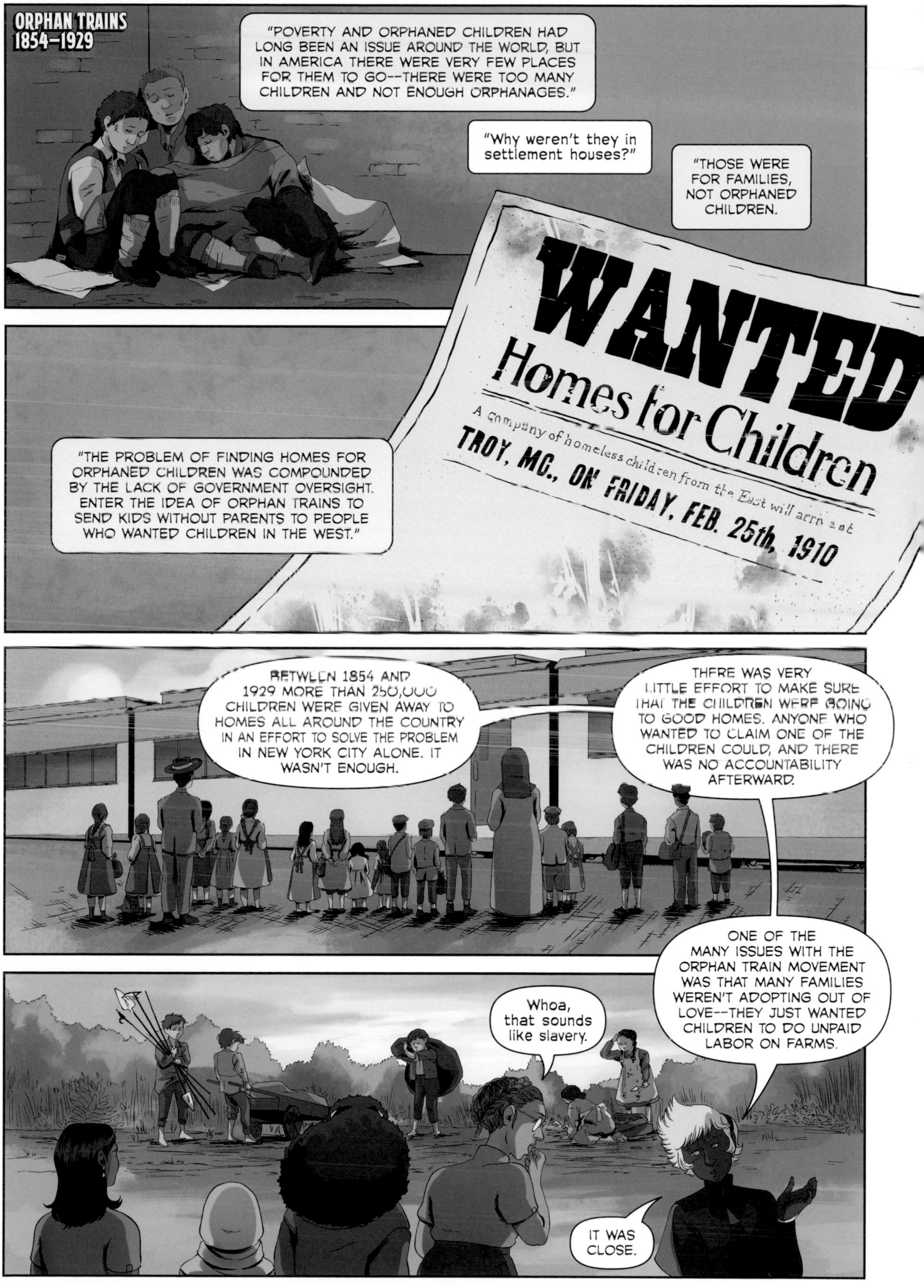
ORPHAN TRAINS 1854–1929
"POVERTY AND ORPHANED CHILDREN HAD LONG BEEN AN ISSUE AROUND THE WORLD, BUT IN AMERICA THERE WERE VERY FEW PLACES FOR THEM TO GO--THERE WERE TOO MANY CHILDREN AND NOT ENOUGH ORPHANAGES."
"Why weren't they in settlement houses?"
"THOSE WERE FOR FAMILIES, NOT ORPHANED CHILDREN.
WANTED
Homes for Children
A company of homeless children from the East will arrive at
TROY, MO., ON FRIDAY, FEB. 25th, 1910
"THE PROBLEM OF FINDING HOMES FOR ORPHANED CHILDREN WAS COMPOUNDED BY THE LACK OF GOVERNMENT OVERSIGHT. ENTER THE IDEA OF ORPHAN TRAINS TO SEND KIDS WITHOUT PARENTS TO PEOPLE WHO WANTED CHILDREN IN THE WEST."
BETWEEN 1854 AND 1929 MORE THAN 250,000 CHILDREN WERE GIVEN AWAY TO HOMES ALL AROUND THE COUNTRY IN AN EFFORT TO SOLVE THE PROBLEM IN NEW YORK CITY ALONE. IT WASN'T ENOUGH.
THERE WAS VERY LITTLE EFFORT TO MAKE SURE THAT THE CHILDREN WERE GOING TO GOOD HOMES. ANYONE WHO WANTED TO CLAIM ONE OF THE CHILDREN COULD, AND THERE WAS NO ACCOUNTABILITY AFTERWARD.
ONE OF THE MANY ISSUES WITH THE ORPHAN TRAIN MOVEMENT WAS THAT MANY FAMILIES WEREN'T ADOPTING OUT OF LOVE--THEY JUST WANTED CHILDREN TO DO UNPAID LABOR ON FARMS.
Whoa, that sounds like slavery.
IT WAS CLOSE.

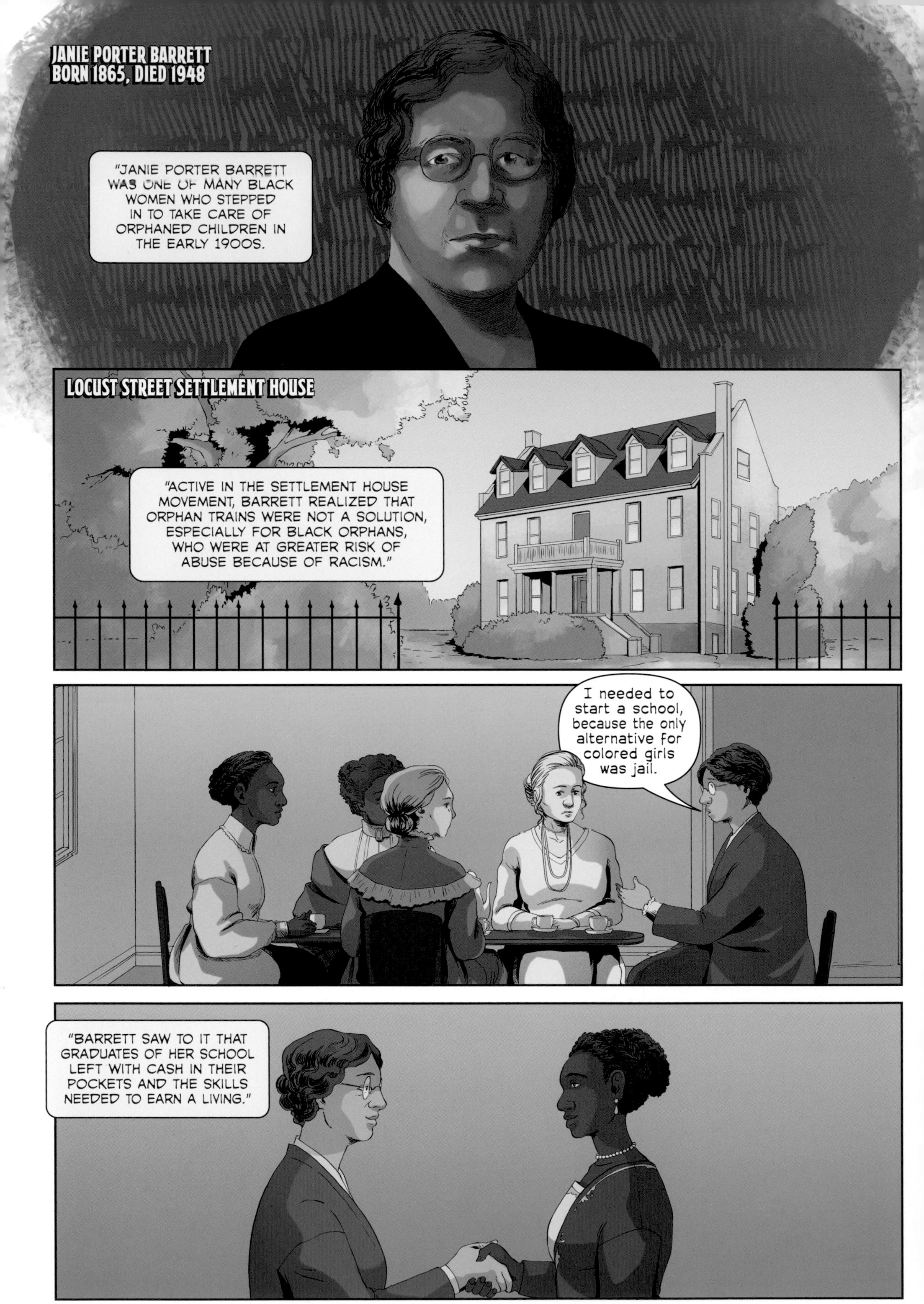
JANIE PORTER BARRETT
BORN 1865, DIED 1948
"JANIE PORTER BARRETT WAS ONE OF MANY BLACK WOMEN WHO STEPPED IN TO TAKE CARE OF ORPHANED CHILDREN IN THE EARLY 1900S.
LOCUST STREET SETTLEMENT HOUSE
"ACTIVE IN THE SETTLEMENT HOUSE MOVEMENT, BARRETT REALIZED THAT ORPHAN TRAINS WERE NOT A SOLUTION, ESPECIALLY FOR BLACK ORPHANS, WHO WERE AT GREATER RISK OF ABUSE BECAUSE OF RACISM."
I needed to start a school, because the only alternative for colored girls was jail.
"BARRETT SAW TO IT THAT GRADUATES OF HER SCHOOL LEFT WITH CASH IN THEIR POCKETS AND THE SKILLS NEEDED TO EARN A LIVING."

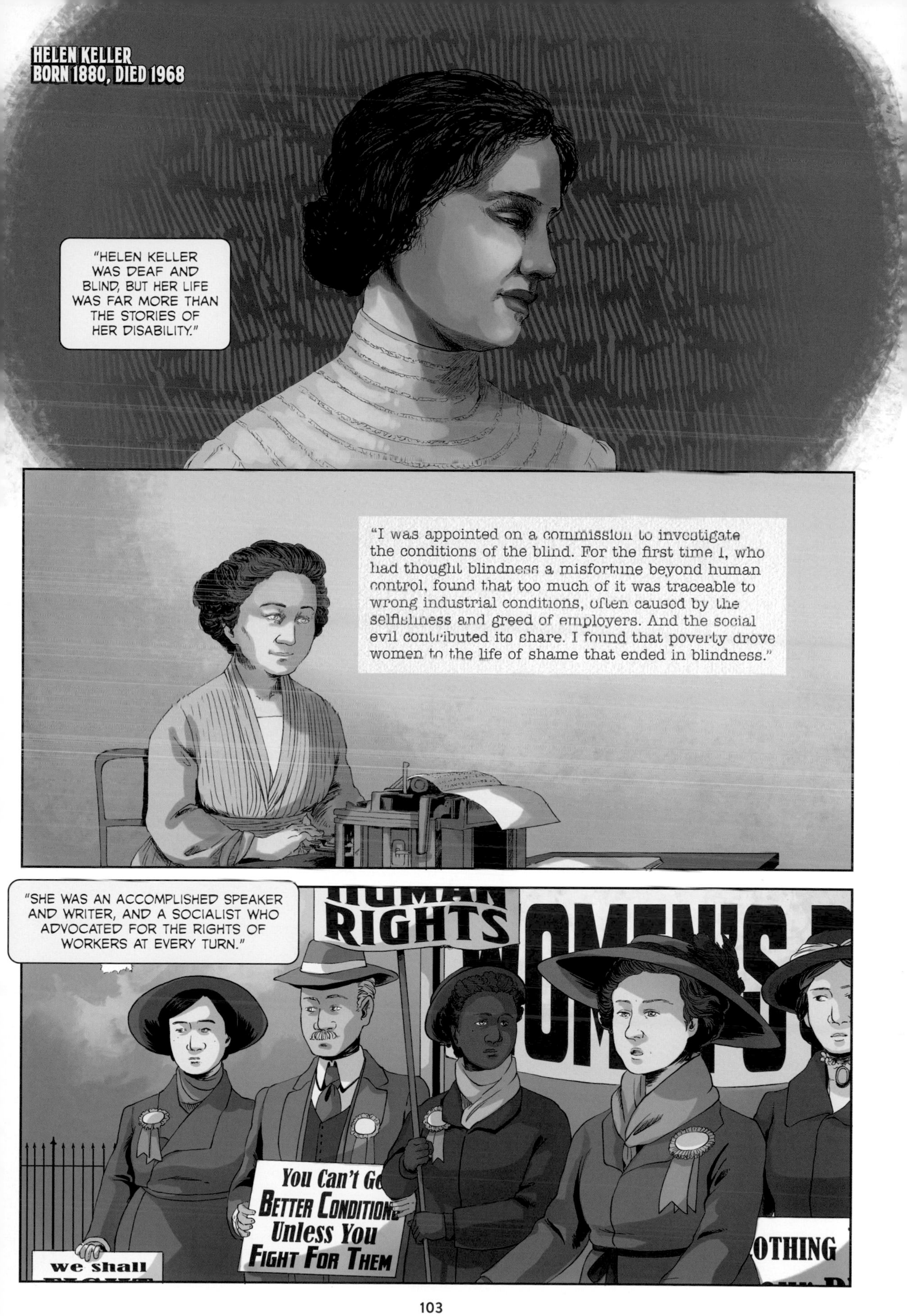
HELEN KELLER
BORN 1880, DIED 1968
"HELEN KELLER WAS DEAF AND BLIND, BUT HER LIFE WAS FAR MORE THAN THE STORIES OF HER DISABILITY."
"I was appointed on a commission to investigate the conditions of the blind. For the first time I, who had thought blindness a misfortune beyond human control, found that too much of it was traceable to wrong industrial conditions, often caused by the selfishness and greed of employers. And the social evil contributed its share. I found that poverty drove women to the life of shame that ended in blindness."
"SHE WAS AN ACCOMPLISHED SPEAKER AND WRITER, AND A SOCIALIST WHO ADVOCATED FOR THE RIGHTS OF WORKERS AT EVERY TURN."
RIGHTS
Unless You
FIGHT FOR THEM
we shall

CHAPTER 5
THE SLOW MARCH TO EQUALITY: CIVIL RIGHTS AND VOTING

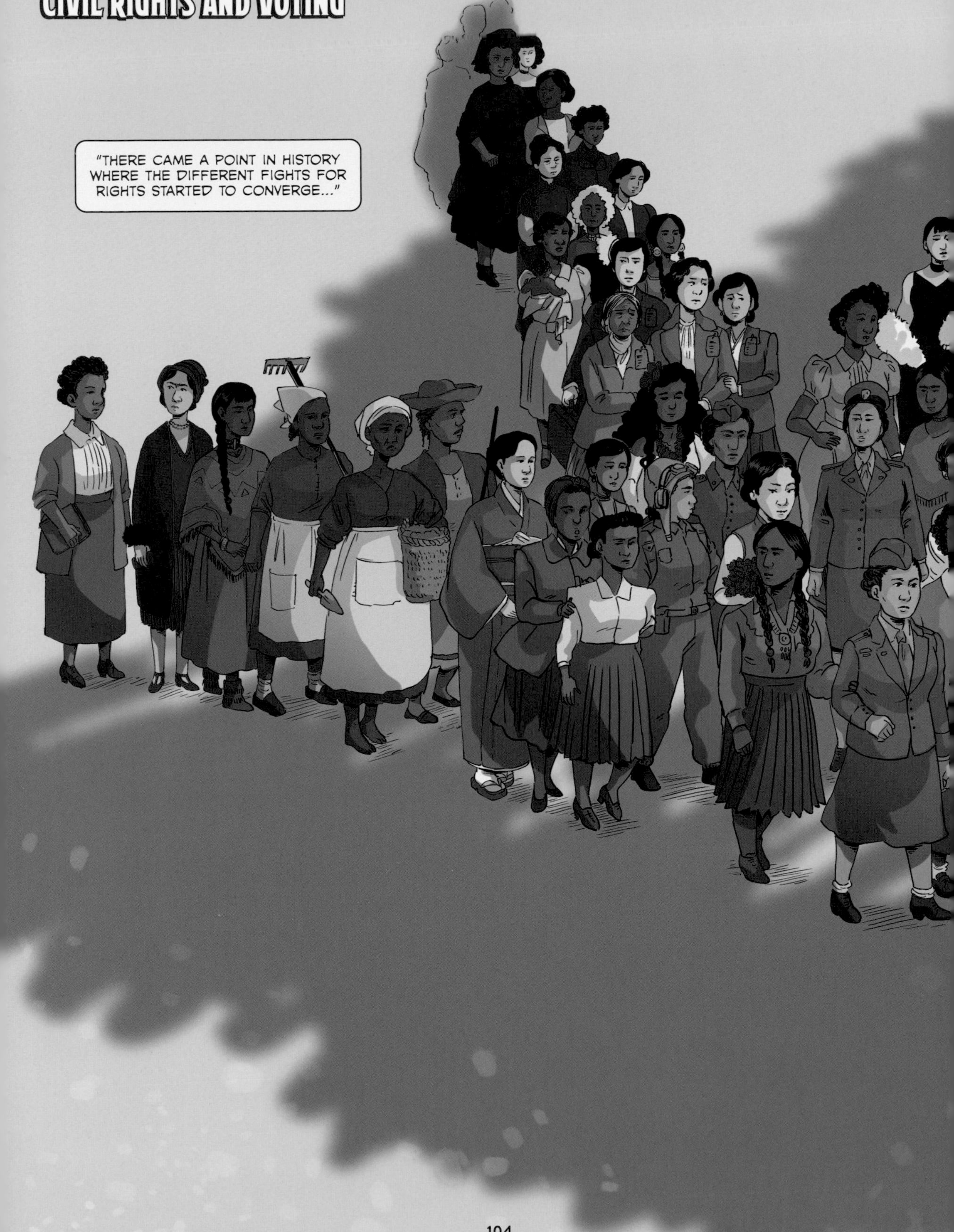
"THERE CAME A POINT IN HISTORY WHERE THE DIFFERENT FIGHTS FOR RIGHTS STARTED TO CONVERGE..."

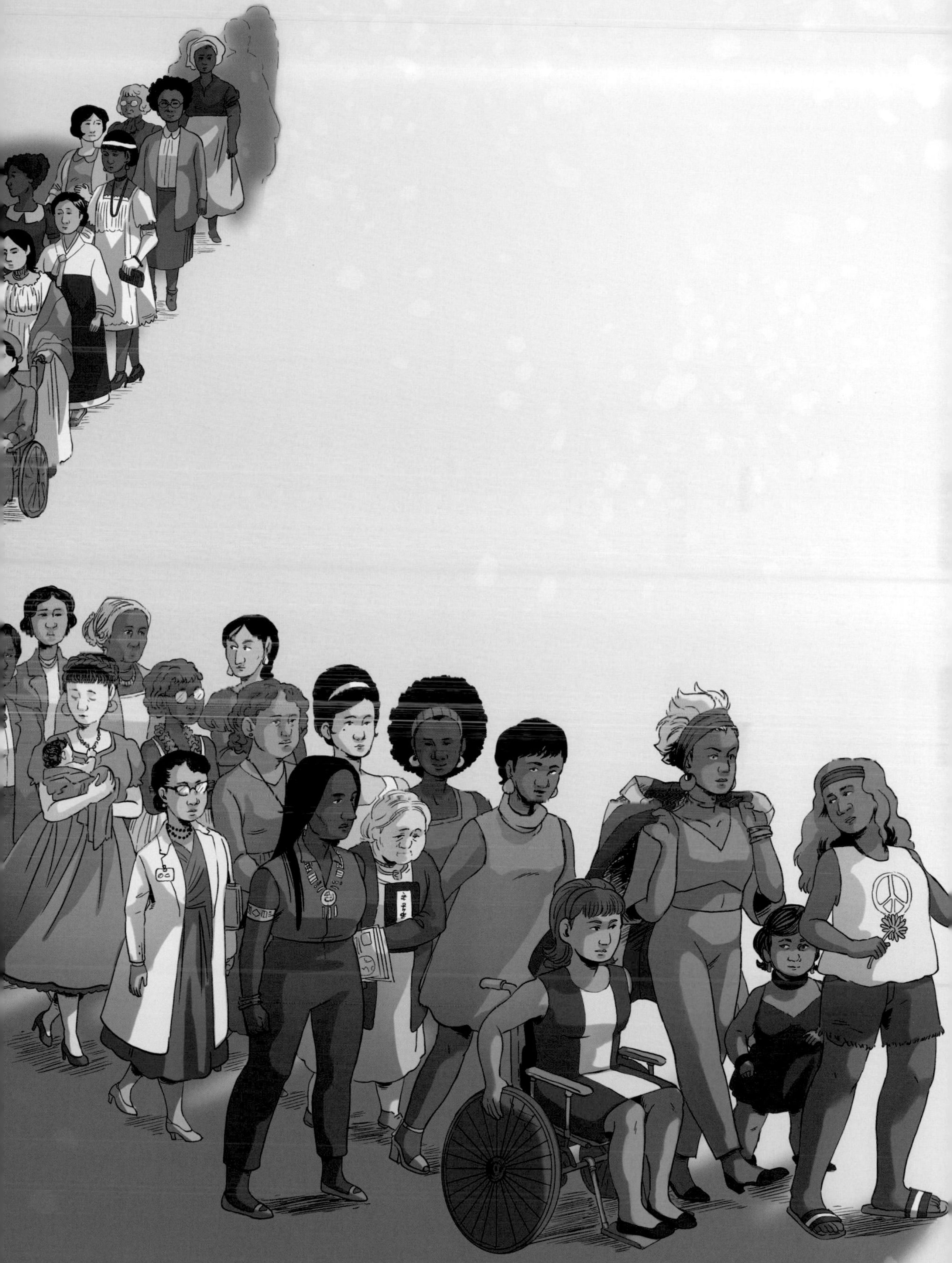

FAMILY PLANNING AND EUGENICS

MARGARET SANGER
BORN 1879, DIED 1966

"IN 1921, MARGARET SANGER FOUNDED THE AMERICAN BIRTH CONTROL LEAGUE. HER GOAL WAS TO GIVE WOMEN CONTROL OVER THEIR OWN FERTILITY.

"BIRTH CONTROL WASN'T THE SAME THING AS EUGENICS, BUT THERE WAS A SIGNIFICANT OVERLAP BETWEEN THE TWO MOVEMENTS. BIRTH CONTROL WAS A WOMAN'S PERSONAL CHOICE, WHILE EUGENICS ADVOCATES THOUGHT THE STATE SHOULD CHOOSE WHO COULD OR COULD NOT CONCEIVE.

"SANGER BELIEVED THAT SMALLER FAMILIES WERE KEY TO ACHIEVING WOMEN'S EQUALITY AND ENDING POVERTY."

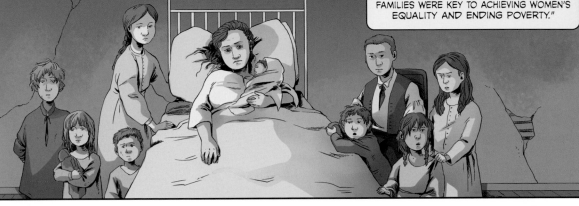

We hold that children should be (1) Conceived in love; (2) Born of the mother's conscious desire; (3) And only begotten under conditions which render possible the heritage of health. Therefore we hold that every woman must possess the power and freedom to prevent conception except when these conditions can be satisfied.

CONTRACEPTION AND ABORTION HAD ALWAYS BEEN CONCERNS OF WOMEN, AND HOME REMEDIES FOR BOTH WERE COMMON BUT TECHNICALLY ILLEGAL IN SANGER'S DAY.

That doesn't make any sense.

You just said there were hundreds of thousands of orphans with no one to take care of them. Wouldn't fewer babies have been a *good* thing?

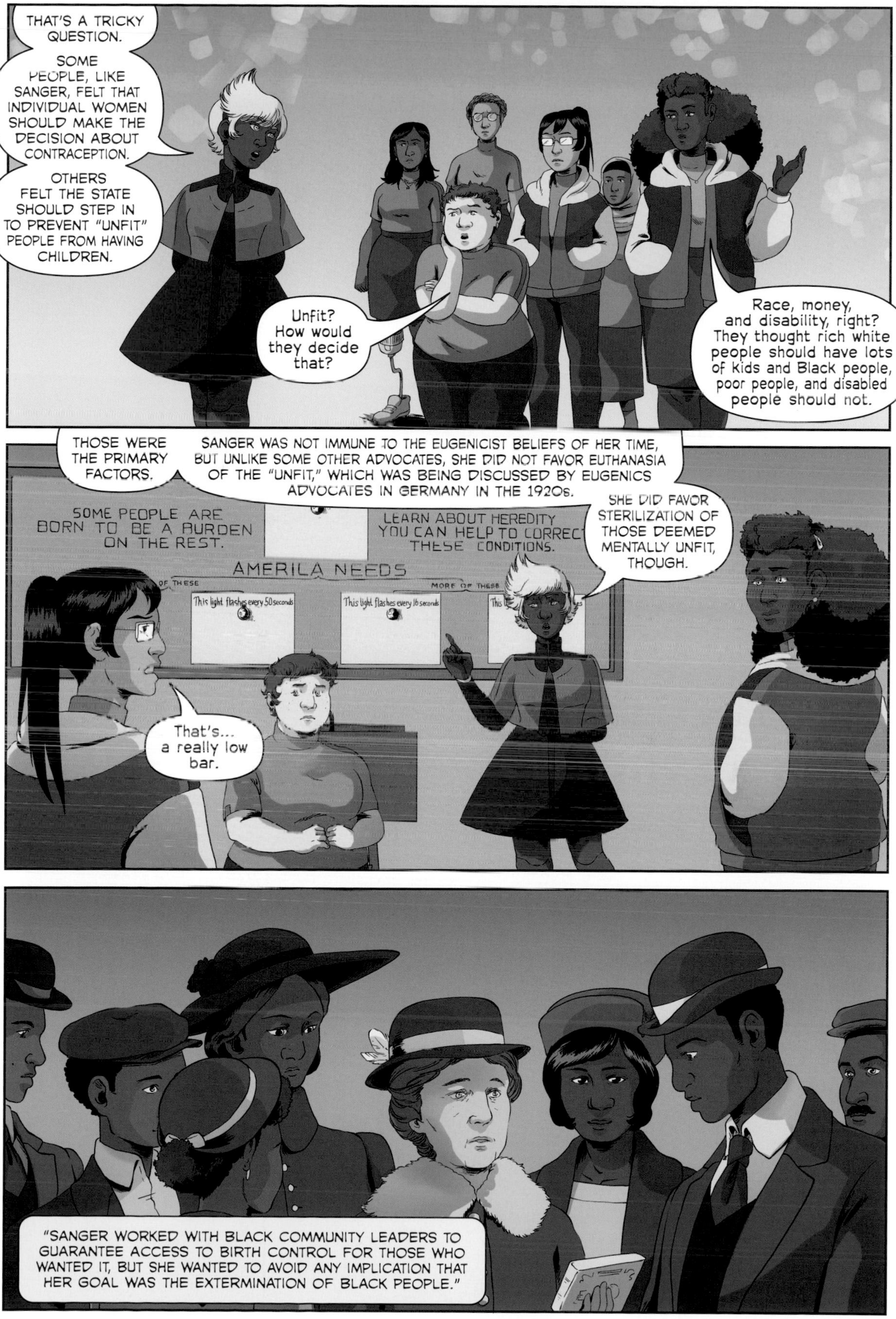
THAT'S A TRICKY QUESTION.
SOME PEOPLE, LIKE SANGER, FELT THAT INDIVIDUAL WOMEN SHOULD MAKE THE DECISION ABOUT CONTRACEPTION.
OTHERS FELT THE STATE SHOULD STEP IN TO PREVENT "UNFIT" PEOPLE FROM HAVING CHILDREN.
Unfit? How would they decide that?
Race, money, and disability, right? They thought rich white people should have lots of kids and Black people, poor people, and disabled people should not.
THOSE WERE THE PRIMARY FACTORS.
SANGER WAS NOT IMMUNE TO THE EUGENICIST BELIEFS OF HER TIME, BUT UNLIKE SOME OTHER ADVOCATES, SHE DID NOT FAVOR EUTHANASIA OF THE "UNFIT," WHICH WAS BEING DISCUSSED BY EUGENICS ADVOCATES IN GERMANY IN THE 1920s.
SOME PEOPLE ARE BORN TO BE A BURDEN ON THE REST.
LEARN ABOUT HEREDITY YOU CAN HELP TO CORRECT THESE CONDITIONS.
AMERILA NEEDS
OF THESE
MORE OF THESE
This light flashes every 50 seconds
This light flashes every 16 seconds
SHE DID FAVOR STERILIZATION OF THOSE DEEMED MENTALLY UNFIT, THOUGH.
That's... a really low bar.
"SANGER WORKED WITH BLACK COMMUNITY LEADERS TO GUARANTEE ACCESS TO BIRTH CONTROL FOR THOSE WHO WANTED IT, BUT SHE WANTED TO AVOID ANY IMPLICATION THAT HER GOAL WAS THE EXTERMINATION OF BLACK PEOPLE."

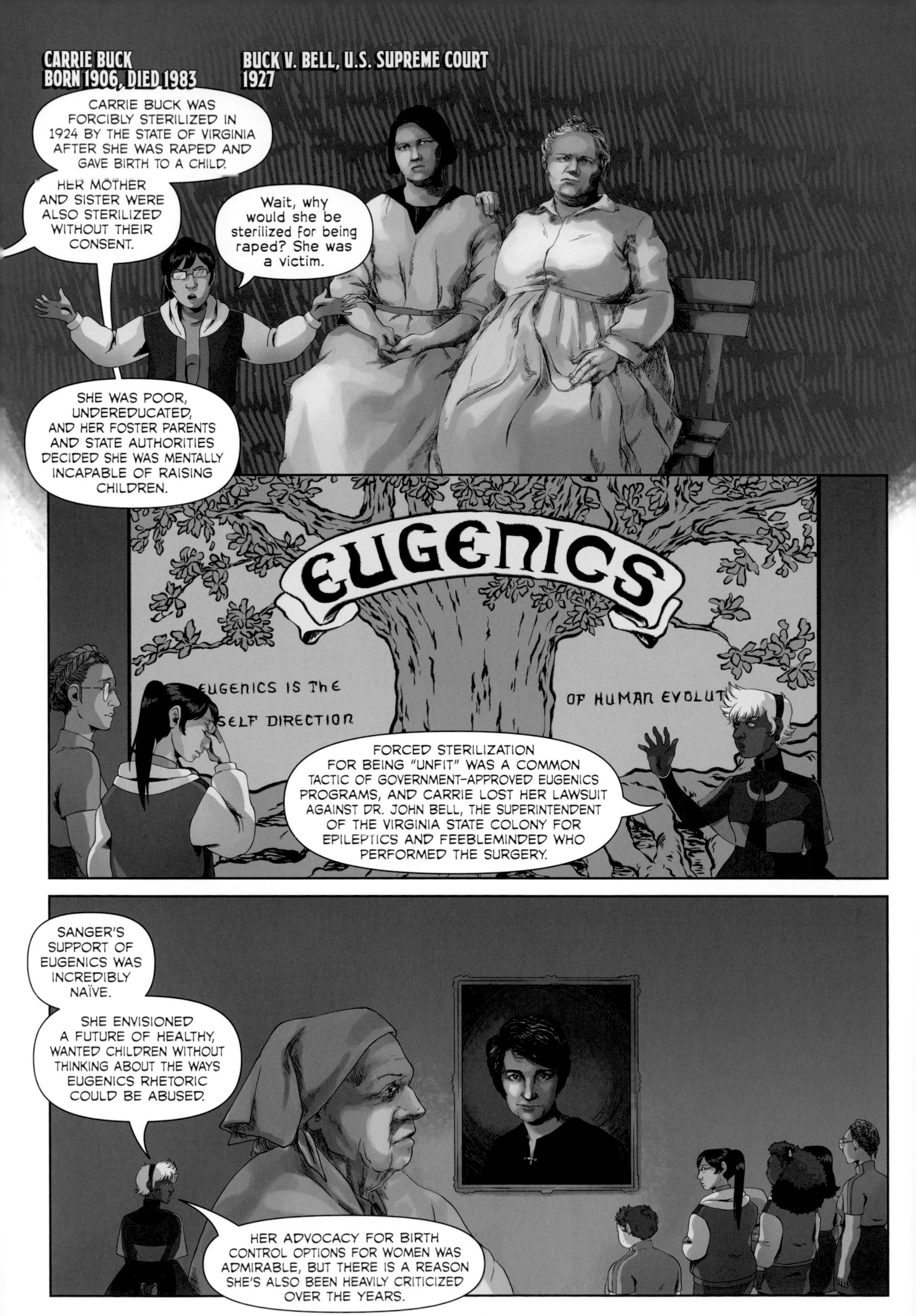
CARRIE BUCK
BORN 1906, DIED 1983
BUCK V. BELL, U.S. SUPREME COURT
1927
CARRIE BUCK WAS FORCIBLY STERILIZED IN 1924 BY THE STATE OF VIRGINIA AFTER SHE WAS RAPED AND GAVE BIRTH TO A CHILD.
HER MOTHER AND SISTER WERE ALSO STERILIZED WITHOUT THEIR CONSENT.
Wait, why would she be sterilized for being raped? She was a victim.
SHE WAS POOR, UNDEREDUCATED, AND HER FOSTER PARENTS AND STATE AUTHORITIES DECIDED SHE WAS MENTALLY INCAPABLE OF RAISING CHILDREN.
EUGENICS
EUGENICS IS THE SELF DIRECTION OF HUMAN EVOLUT
FORCED STERILIZATION FOR BEING "UNFIT" WAS A COMMON TACTIC OF GOVERNMENT-APPROVED EUGENICS PROGRAMS, AND CARRIE LOST HER LAWSUIT AGAINST DR. JOHN BELL, THE SUPERINTENDENT OF THE VIRGINIA STATE COLONY FOR EPILEPTICS AND FEEBLEMINDED WHO PERFORMED THE SURGERY.
SANGER'S SUPPORT OF EUGENICS WAS INCREDIBLY NAÏVE.
SHE ENVISIONED A FUTURE OF HEALTHY, WANTED CHILDREN WITHOUT THINKING ABOUT THE WAYS EUGENICS RHETORIC COULD BE ABUSED.
HER ADVOCACY FOR BIRTH CONTROL OPTIONS FOR WOMEN WAS ADMIRABLE, BUT THERE IS A REASON SHE'S ALSO BEEN HEAVILY CRITICIZED OVER THE YEARS.

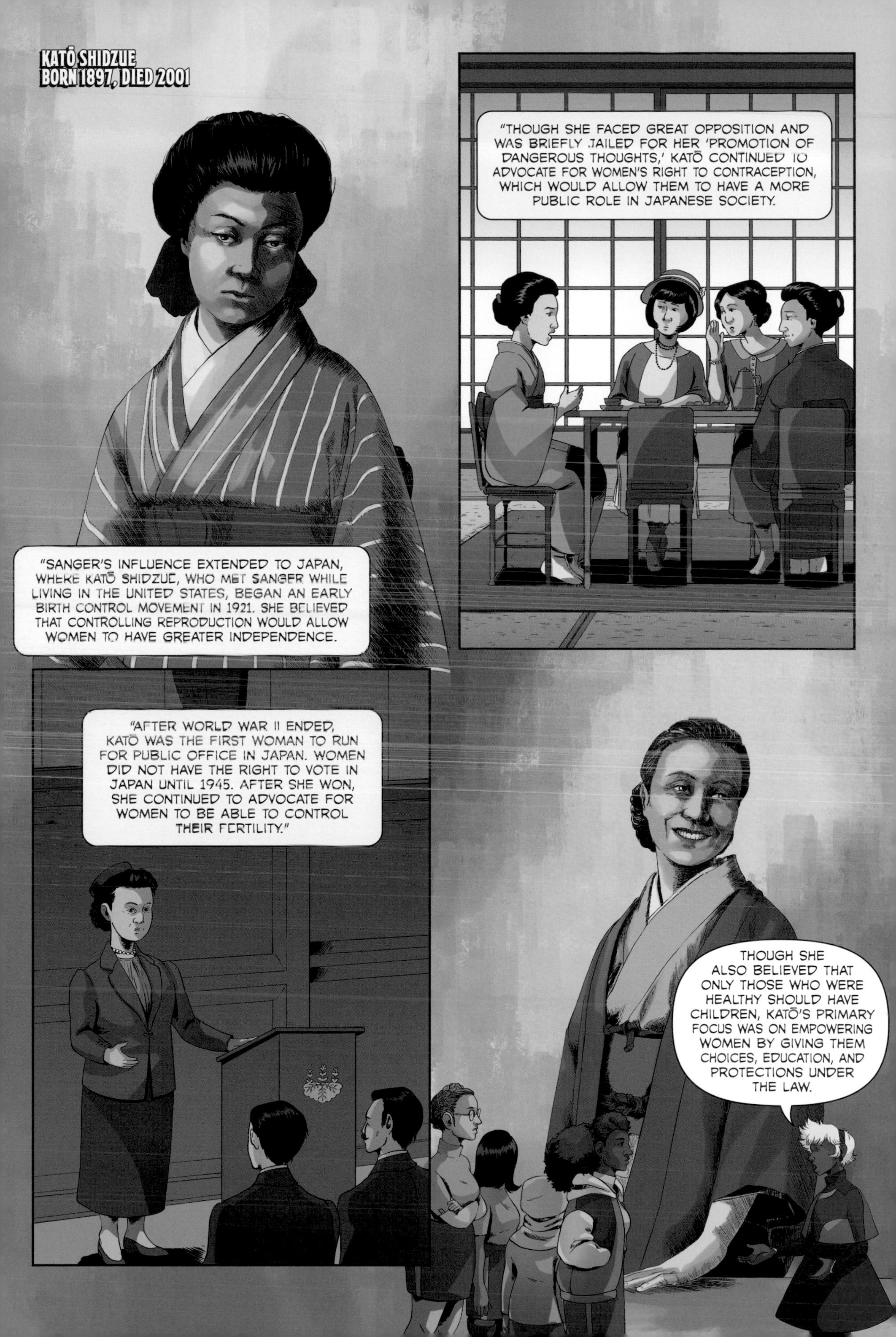
KATŌ SHIDZUE
BORN 1897, DIED 2001
"SANGER'S INFLUENCE EXTENDED TO JAPAN, WHERE KATŌ SHIDZUE, WHO MET SANGER WHILE LIVING IN THE UNITED STATES, BEGAN AN EARLY BIRTH CONTROL MOVEMENT IN 1921. SHE BELIEVED THAT CONTROLLING REPRODUCTION WOULD ALLOW WOMEN TO HAVE GREATER INDEPENDENCE.
"THOUGH SHE FACED GREAT OPPOSITION AND WAS BRIEFLY JAILED FOR HER 'PROMOTION OF DANGEROUS THOUGHTS,' KATŌ CONTINUED TO ADVOCATE FOR WOMEN'S RIGHT TO CONTRACEPTION, WHICH WOULD ALLOW THEM TO HAVE A MORE PUBLIC ROLE IN JAPANESE SOCIETY.
"AFTER WORLD WAR II ENDED, KATŌ WAS THE FIRST WOMAN TO RUN FOR PUBLIC OFFICE IN JAPAN. WOMEN DID NOT HAVE THE RIGHT TO VOTE IN JAPAN UNTIL 1945. AFTER SHE WON, SHE CONTINUED TO ADVOCATE FOR WOMEN TO BE ABLE TO CONTROL THEIR FERTILITY."
THOUGH SHE ALSO BELIEVED THAT ONLY THOSE WHO WERE HEALTHY SHOULD HAVE CHILDREN, KATŌ'S PRIMARY FOCUS WAS ON EMPOWERING WOMEN BY GIVING THEM CHOICES, EDUCATION, AND PROTECTIONS UNDER THE LAW.

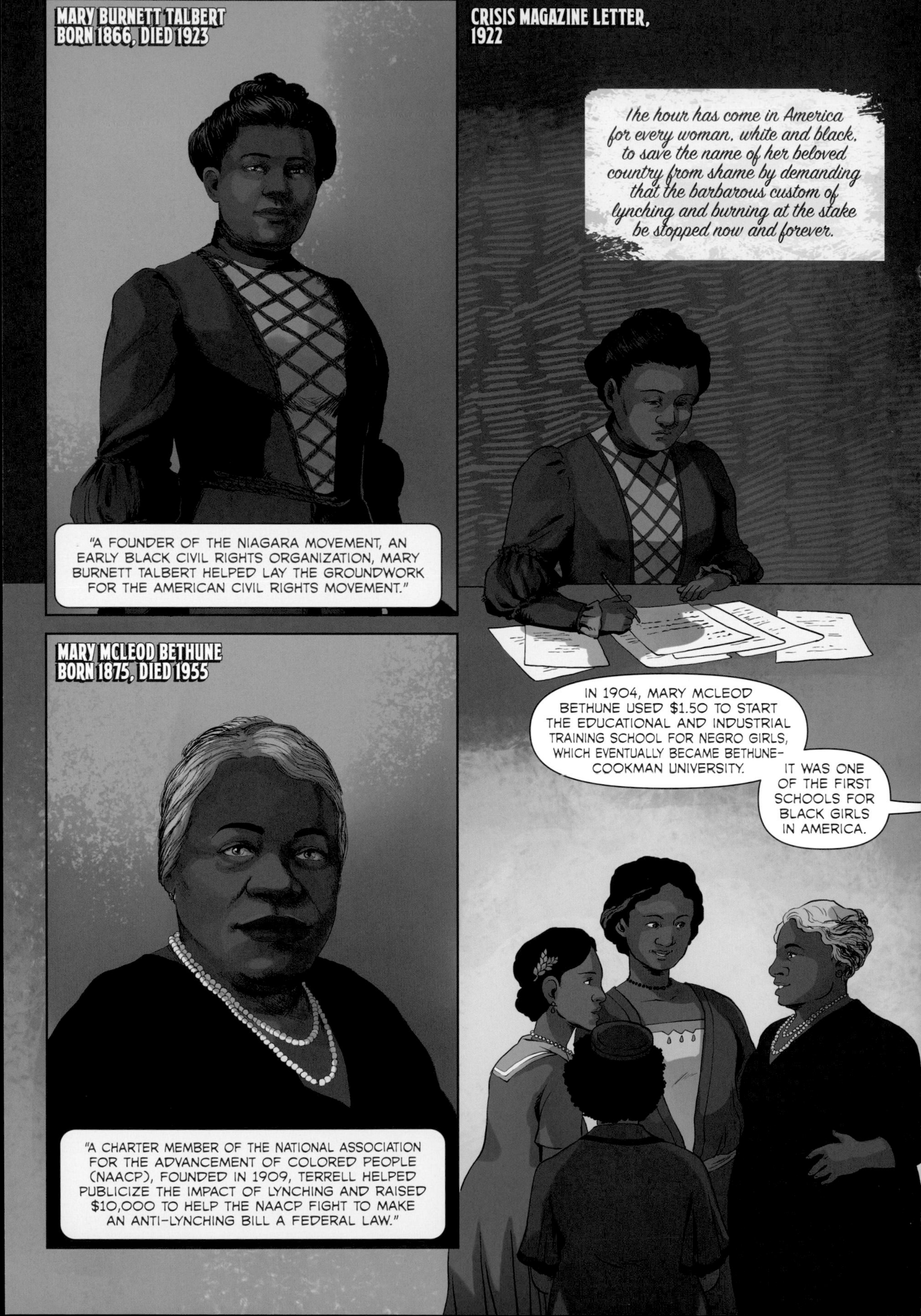
MARY BURNETT TALBERT
BORN 1866, DIED 1923
"A FOUNDER OF THE NIAGARA MOVEMENT, AN EARLY BLACK CIVIL RIGHTS ORGANIZATION, MARY BURNETT TALBERT HELPED LAY THE GROUNDWORK FOR THE AMERICAN CIVIL RIGHTS MOVEMENT."
CRISIS MAGAZINE LETTER, 1922
The hour has come in America for every woman, white and black, to save the name of her beloved country from shame by demanding that the barbarous custom of lynching and burning at the stake be stopped now and forever.
MARY MCLEOD BETHUNE
BORN 1875, DIED 1955
"A CHARTER MEMBER OF THE NATIONAL ASSOCIATION FOR THE ADVANCEMENT OF COLORED PEOPLE (NAACP), FOUNDED IN 1909, TERRELL HELPED PUBLICIZE THE IMPACT OF LYNCHING AND RAISED $10,000 TO HELP THE NAACP FIGHT TO MAKE AN ANTI-LYNCHING BILL A FEDERAL LAW."
IN 1904, MARY MCLEOD BETHUNE USED $1.50 TO START THE EDUCATIONAL AND INDUSTRIAL TRAINING SCHOOL FOR NEGRO GIRLS, WHICH EVENTUALLY BECAME BETHUNE-COOKMAN UNIVERSITY.
IT WAS ONE OF THE FIRST SCHOOLS FOR BLACK GIRLS IN AMERICA.

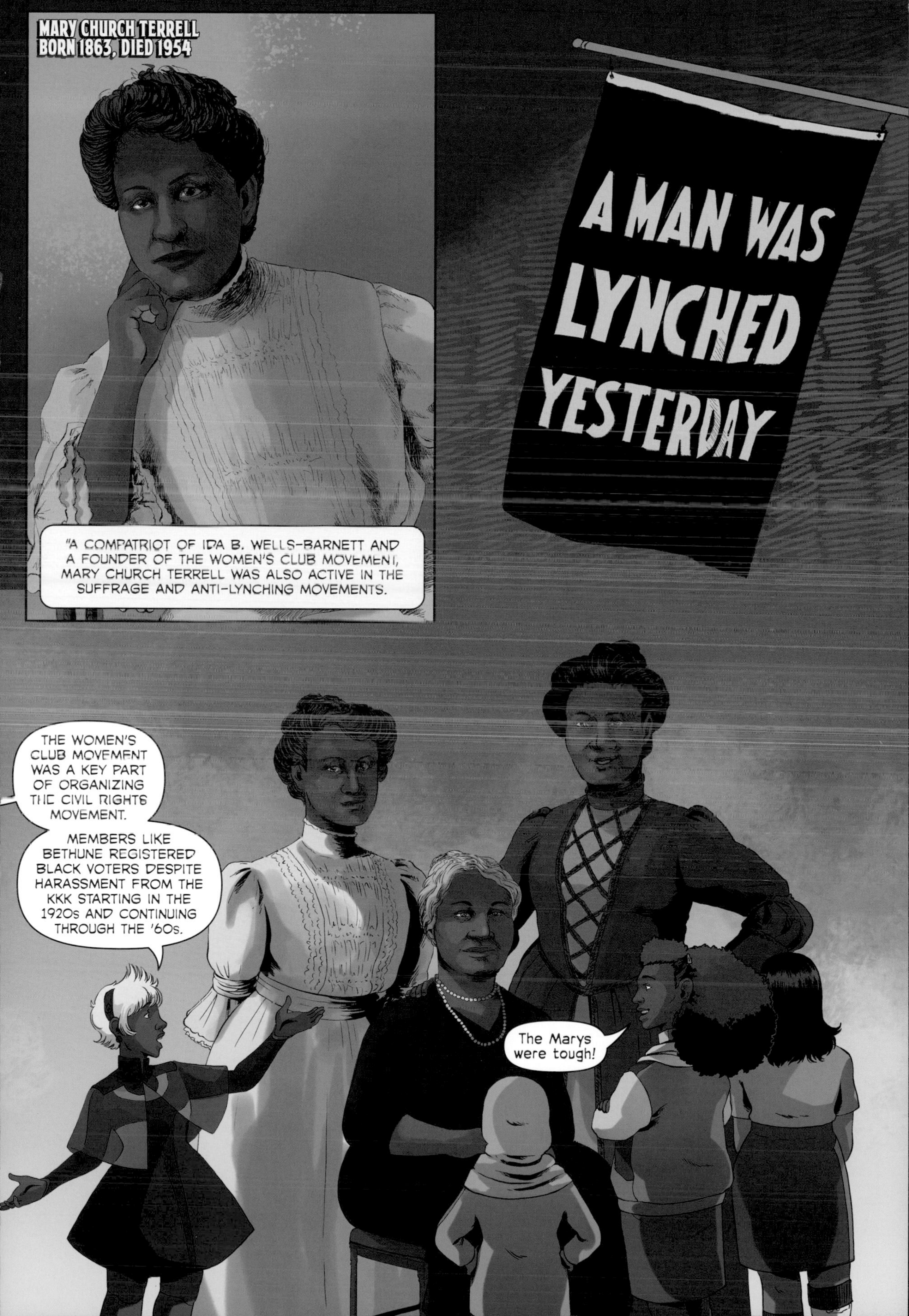
MARY CHURCH TERRELL
BORN 1863, DIED 1954
A MAN WAS LYNCHED YESTERDAY
"A COMPATRIOT OF IDA B. WELLS-BARNETT AND A FOUNDER OF THE WOMEN'S CLUB MOVEMENT, MARY CHURCH TERRELL WAS ALSO ACTIVE IN THE SUFFRAGE AND ANTI-LYNCHING MOVEMENTS.
THE WOMEN'S CLUB MOVEMENT WAS A KEY PART OF ORGANIZING THE CIVIL RIGHTS MOVEMENT.
MEMBERS LIKE BETHUNE REGISTERED BLACK VOTERS DESPITE HARASSMENT FROM THE KKK STARTING IN THE 1920s AND CONTINUING THROUGH THE '60s.
The Marys were tough!

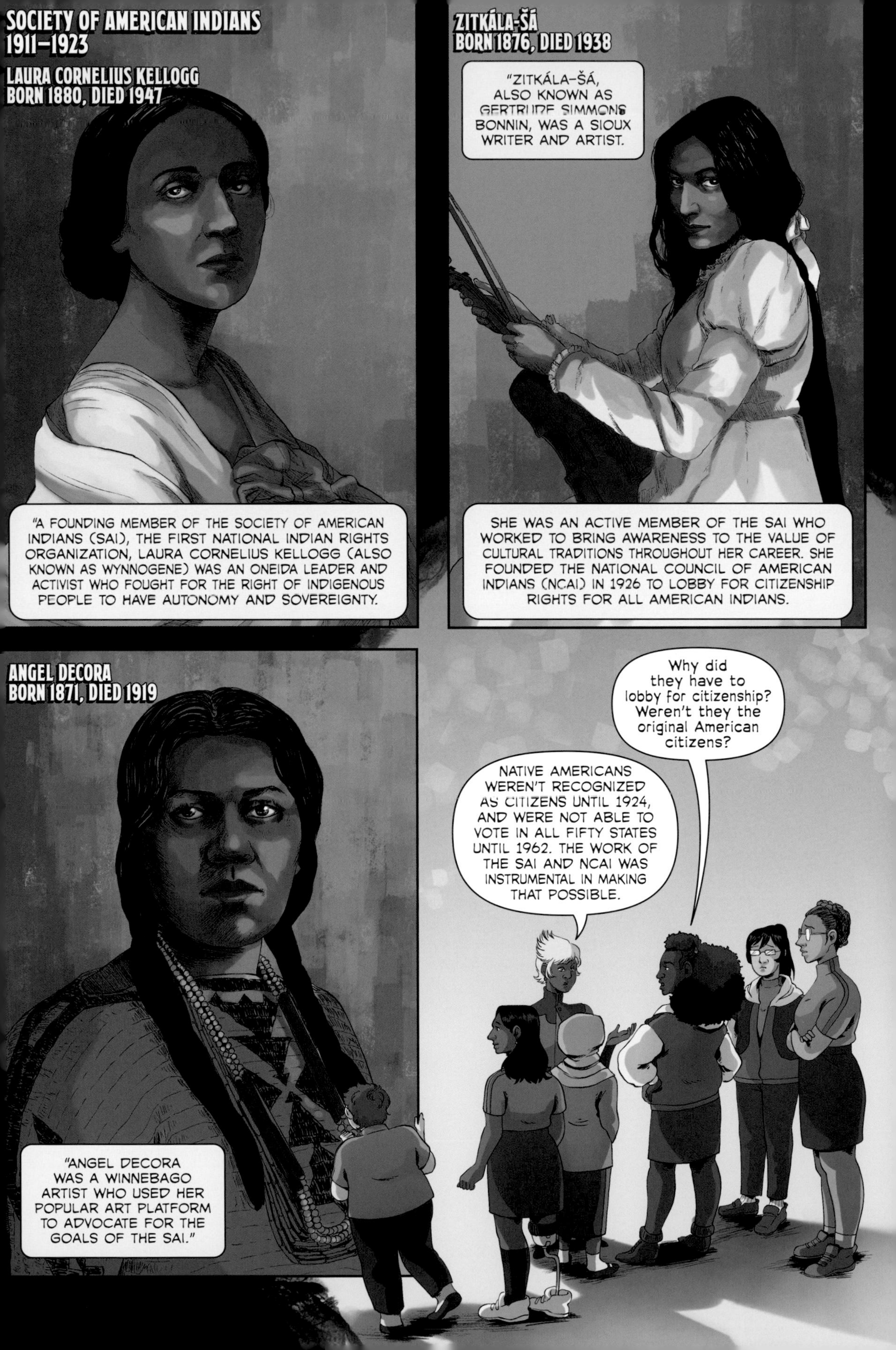
SOCIETY OF AMERICAN INDIANS
1911–1923
LAURA CORNELIUS KELLOGG
BORN 1880, DIED 1947
"A FOUNDING MEMBER OF THE SOCIETY OF AMERICAN INDIANS (SAI), THE FIRST NATIONAL INDIAN RIGHTS ORGANIZATION, LAURA CORNELIUS KELLOGG (ALSO KNOWN AS WYNNOGENE) WAS AN ONEIDA LEADER AND ACTIVIST WHO FOUGHT FOR THE RIGHT OF INDIGENOUS PEOPLE TO HAVE AUTONOMY AND SOVEREIGNTY.
ZITKÁLA-ŠÁ
BORN 1876, DIED 1938
"ZITKÁLA-ŠÁ, ALSO KNOWN AS GERTRUDE SIMMONS BONNIN, WAS A SIOUX WRITER AND ARTIST.
SHE WAS AN ACTIVE MEMBER OF THE SAI WHO WORKED TO BRING AWARENESS TO THE VALUE OF CULTURAL TRADITIONS THROUGHOUT HER CAREER. SHE FOUNDED THE NATIONAL COUNCIL OF AMERICAN INDIANS (NCAI) IN 1926 TO LOBBY FOR CITIZENSHIP RIGHTS FOR ALL AMERICAN INDIANS.
ANGEL DECORA
BORN 1871, DIED 1919
"ANGEL DECORA WAS A WINNEBAGO ARTIST WHO USED HER POPULAR ART PLATFORM TO ADVOCATE FOR THE GOALS OF THE SAI."
Why did they have to lobby for citizenship? Weren't they the original American citizens?
NATIVE AMERICANS WEREN'T RECOGNIZED AS CITIZENS UNTIL 1924, AND WERE NOT ABLE TO VOTE IN ALL FIFTY STATES UNTIL 1962. THE WORK OF THE SAI AND NCAI WAS INSTRUMENTAL IN MAKING THAT POSSIBLE.

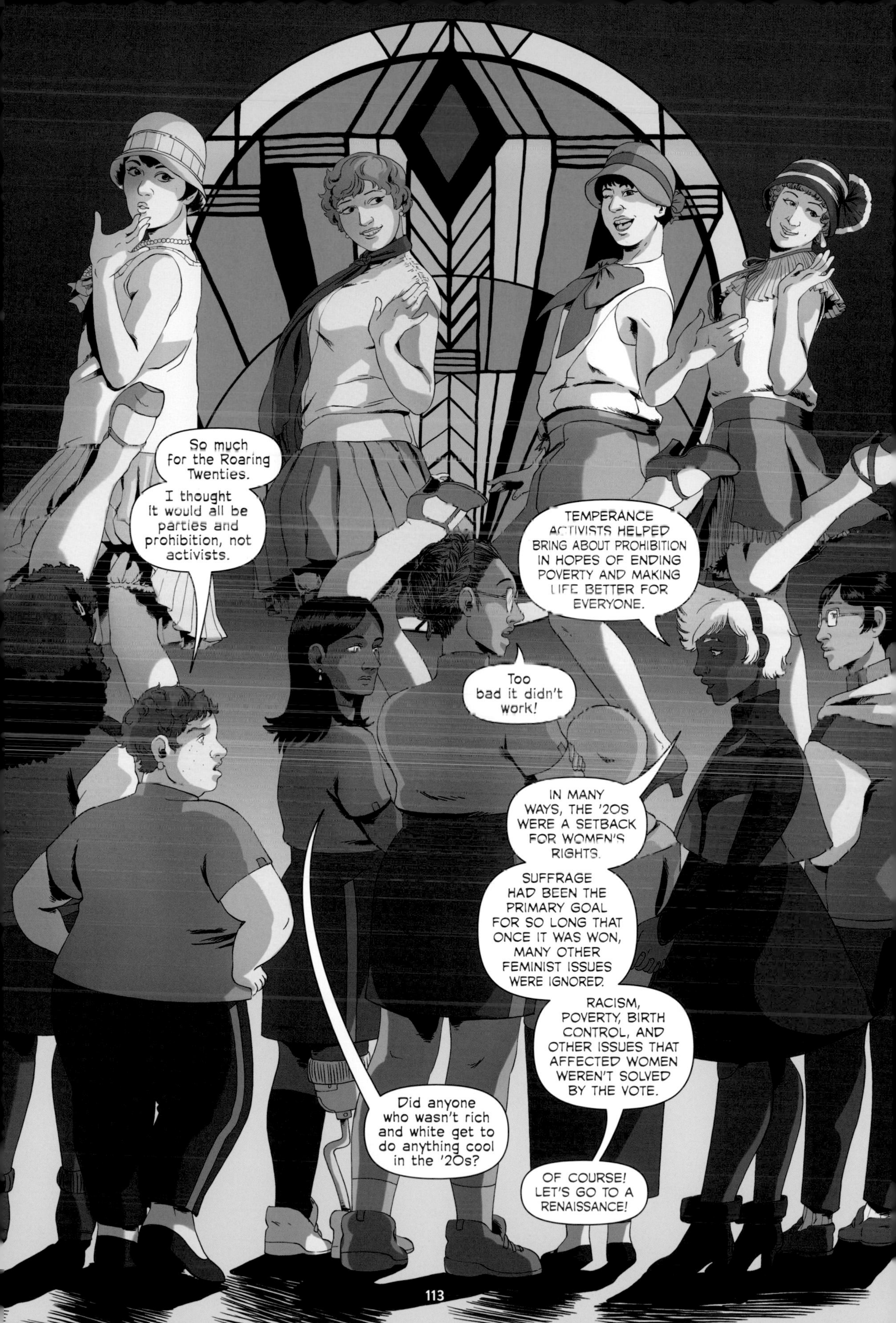

So much for the Roaring Twenties.
I thought it would all be parties and prohibition, not activists.
TEMPERANCE ACTIVISTS HELPED BRING ABOUT PROHIBITION IN HOPES OF ENDING POVERTY AND MAKING LIFE BETTER FOR EVERYONE.
Too bad it didn't work!
IN MANY WAYS, THE '20S WERE A SETBACK FOR WOMEN'S RIGHTS.
SUFFRAGE HAD BEEN THE PRIMARY GOAL FOR SO LONG THAT ONCE IT WAS WON, MANY OTHER FEMINIST ISSUES WERE IGNORED.
RACISM, POVERTY, BIRTH CONTROL, AND OTHER ISSUES THAT AFFECTED WOMEN WEREN'T SOLVED BY THE VOTE.
Did anyone who wasn't rich and white get to do anything cool in the '20s?
OF COURSE! LET'S GO TO A RENAISSANCE!

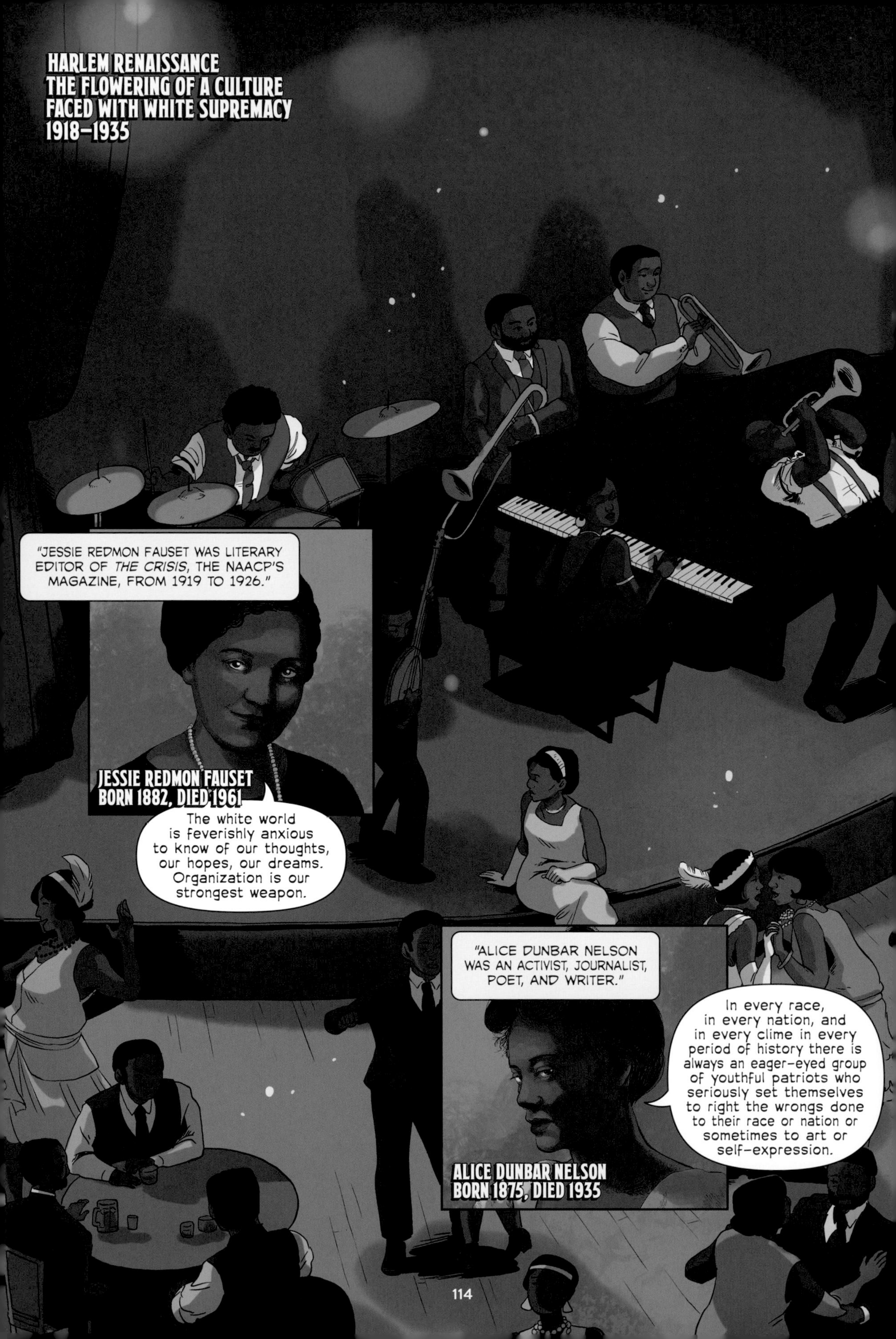
HARLEM RENAISSANCE
THE FLOWERING OF A CULTURE
FACED WITH WHITE SUPREMACY
1918–1935
"JESSIE REDMON FAUSET WAS LITERARY EDITOR OF *THE CRISIS*, THE NAACP'S MAGAZINE, FROM 1919 TO 1926."
JESSIE REDMON FAUSET
BORN 1882, DIED 1961
The white world is feverishly anxious to know of our thoughts, our hopes, our dreams. Organization is our strongest weapon.
"ALICE DUNBAR NELSON WAS AN ACTIVIST, JOURNALIST, POET, AND WRITER."
In every race, in every nation, and in every clime in every period of history there is always an eager-eyed group of youthful patriots who seriously set themselves to right the wrongs done to their race or nation or sometimes to art or self-expression.
ALICE DUNBAR NELSON
BORN 1875, DIED 1935

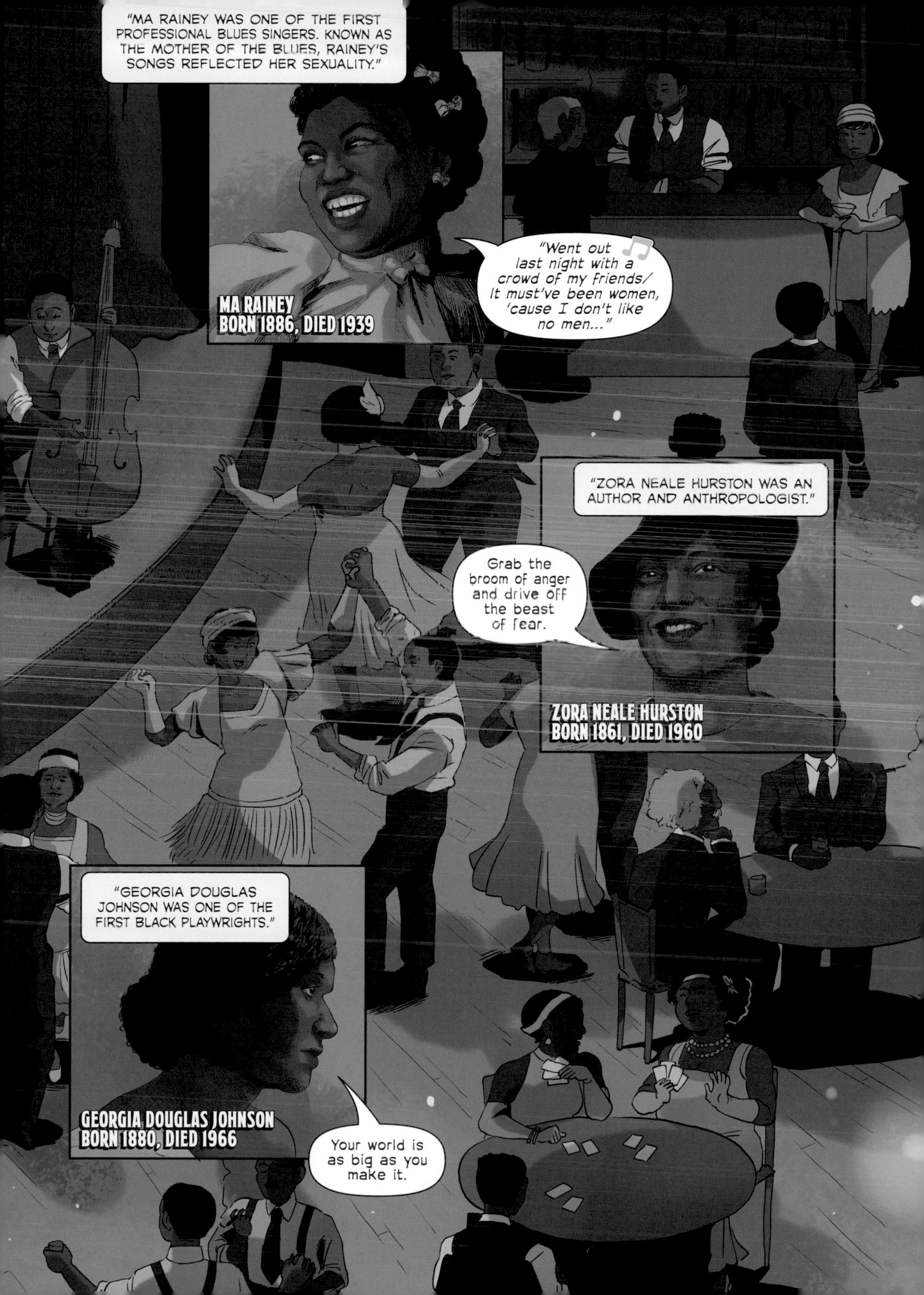
"MA RAINEY WAS ONE OF THE FIRST PROFESSIONAL BLUES SINGERS. KNOWN AS THE MOTHER OF THE BLUES, RAINEY'S SONGS REFLECTED HER SEXUALITY."
MA RAINEY BORN 1886, DIED 1939
"Went out last night with a crowd of my friends/ It must've been women, 'cause I don't like no men..."
"ZORA NEALE HURSTON WAS AN AUTHOR AND ANTHROPOLOGIST."
Grab the broom of anger and drive off the beast of fear.
ZORA NEALE HURSTON BORN 1861, DIED 1960
"GEORGIA DOUGLAS JOHNSON WAS ONE OF THE FIRST BLACK PLAYWRIGHTS."
GEORGIA DOUGLAS JOHNSON BORN 1880, DIED 1966
Your world is as big as you make it.

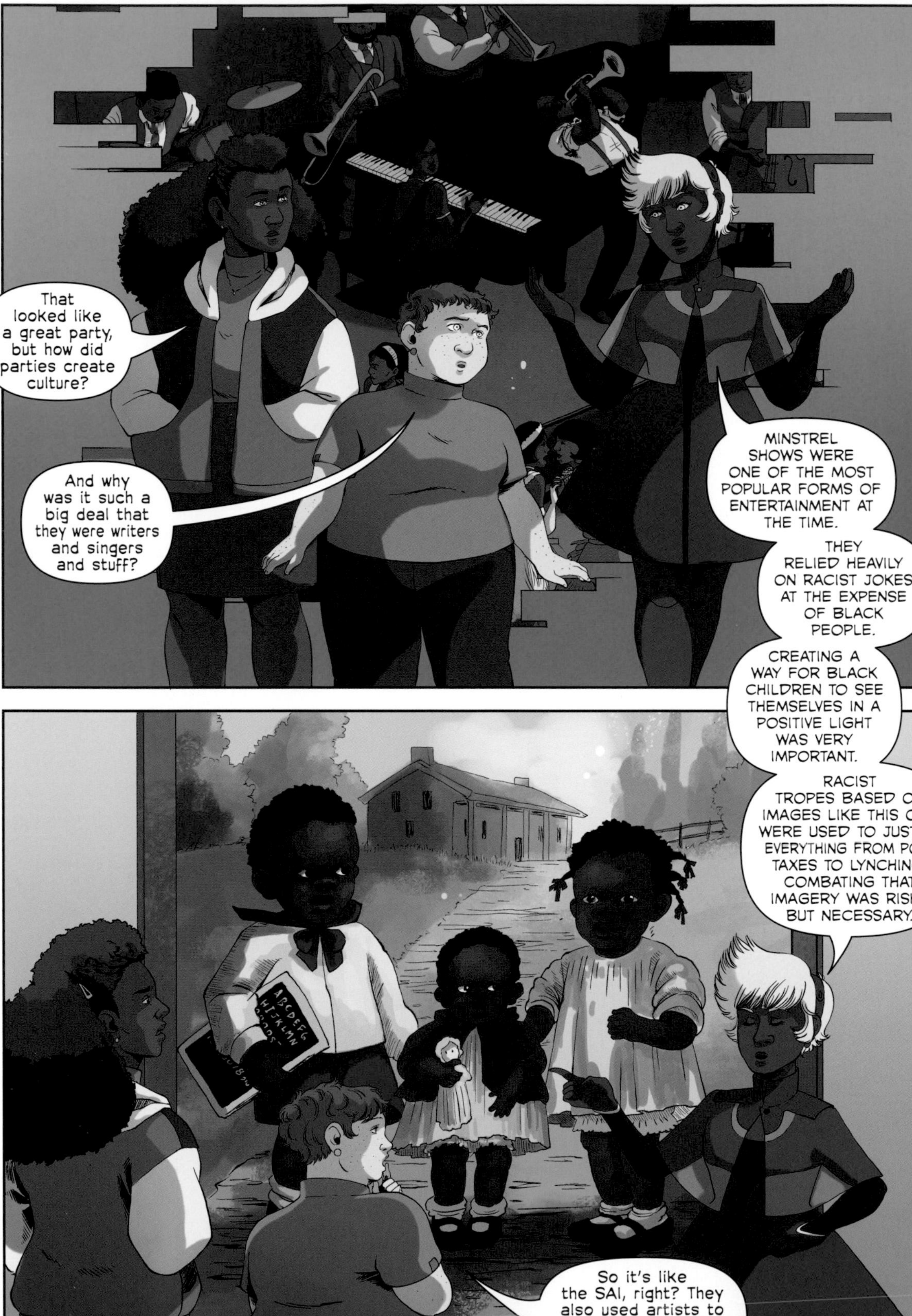
That looked like a great party, but how did parties create culture?
And why was it such a big deal that they were writers and singers and stuff?
MINSTREL SHOWS WERE ONE OF THE MOST POPULAR FORMS OF ENTERTAINMENT AT THE TIME.
THEY RELIED HEAVILY ON RACIST JOKES AT THE EXPENSE OF BLACK PEOPLE.
CREATING A WAY FOR BLACK CHILDREN TO SEE THEMSELVES IN A POSITIVE LIGHT WAS VERY IMPORTANT.
RACIST TROPES BASED ON IMAGES LIKE THIS ONE WERE USED TO JUSTIFY EVERYTHING FROM POLL TAXES TO LYNCHING. COMBATING THAT IMAGERY WAS RISKY, BUT NECESSARY.
So it's like the SAI, right? They also used artists to change the way Native Americans were perceived.

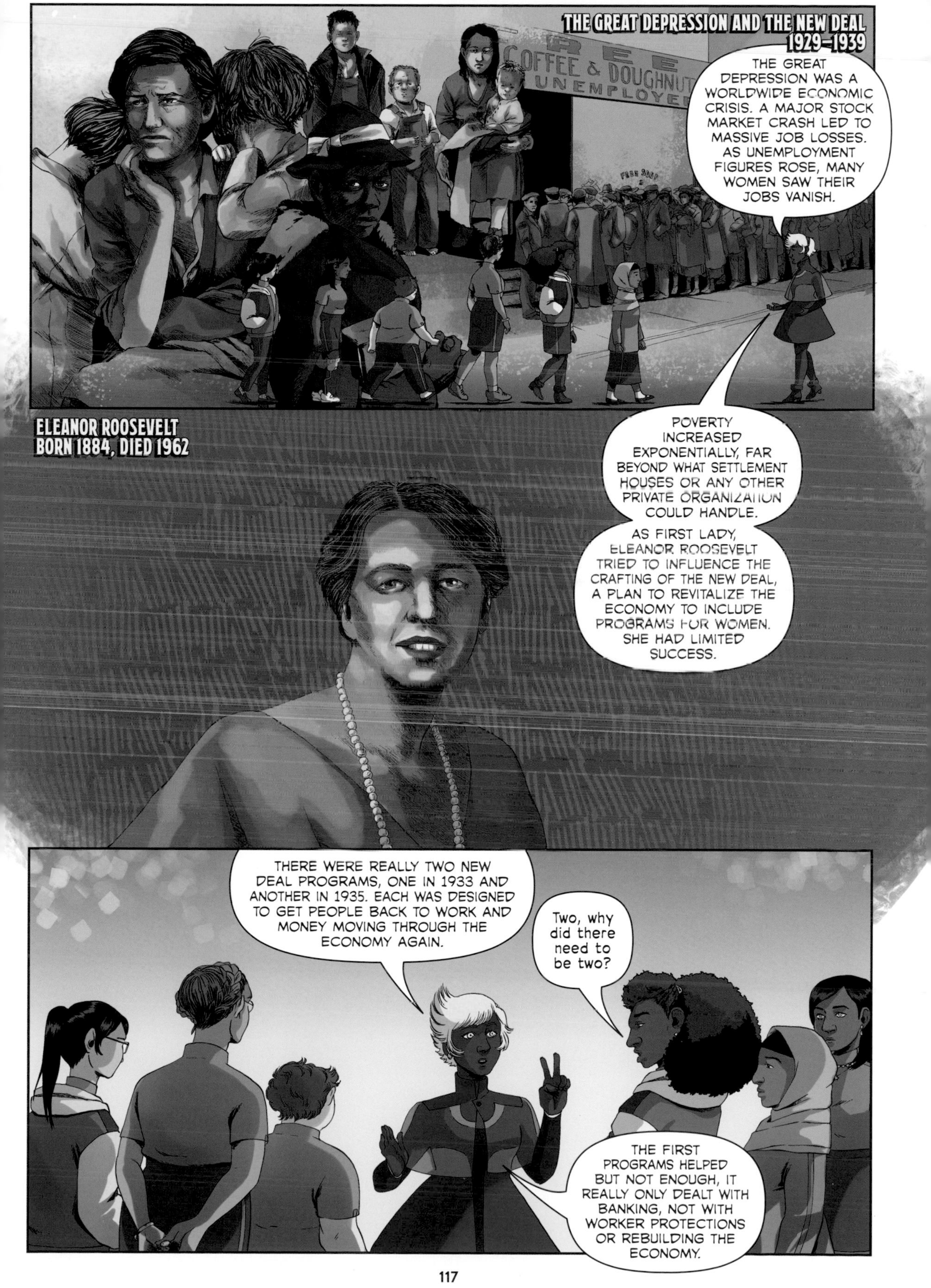
THE GREAT DEPRESSION AND THE NEW DEAL 1929–1939
THE GREAT DEPRESSION WAS A WORLDWIDE ECONOMIC CRISIS. A MAJOR STOCK MARKET CRASH LED TO MASSIVE JOB LOSSES. AS UNEMPLOYMENT FIGURES ROSE, MANY WOMEN SAW THEIR JOBS VANISH.
ELEANOR ROOSEVELT BORN 1884, DIED 1962
POVERTY INCREASED EXPONENTIALLY, FAR BEYOND WHAT SETTLEMENT HOUSES OR ANY OTHER PRIVATE ORGANIZATION COULD HANDLE.
AS FIRST LADY, ELEANOR ROOSEVELT TRIED TO INFLUENCE THE CRAFTING OF THE NEW DEAL, A PLAN TO REVITALIZE THE ECONOMY TO INCLUDE PROGRAMS FOR WOMEN. SHE HAD LIMITED SUCCESS.
THERE WERE REALLY TWO NEW DEAL PROGRAMS, ONE IN 1933 AND ANOTHER IN 1935. EACH WAS DESIGNED TO GET PEOPLE BACK TO WORK AND MONEY MOVING THROUGH THE ECONOMY AGAIN.
Two, why did there need to be two?
THE FIRST PROGRAMS HELPED BUT NOT ENOUGH, IT REALLY ONLY DEALT WITH BANKING, NOT WITH WORKER PROTECTIONS OR REBUILDING THE ECONOMY.

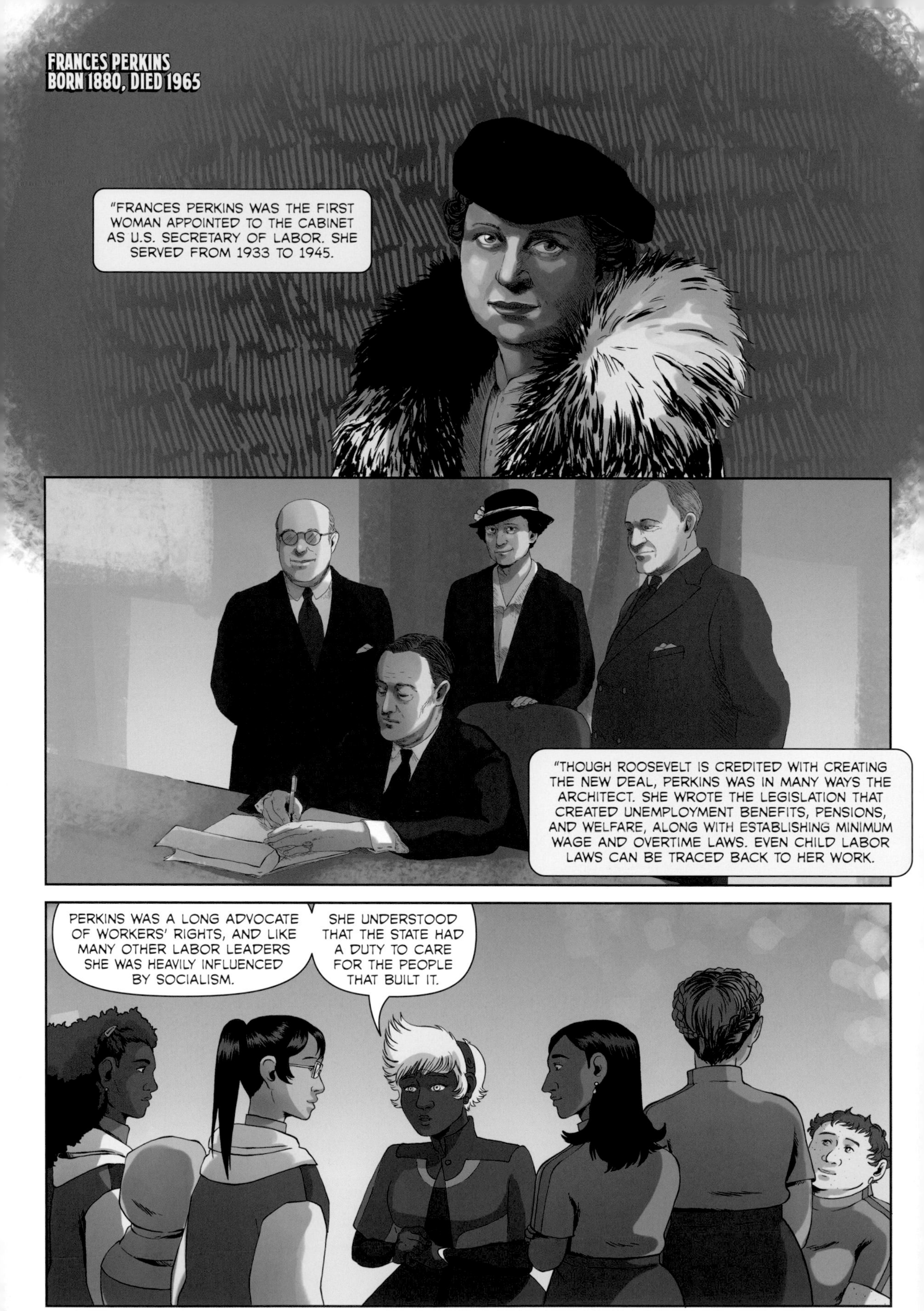
FRANCES PERKINS
BORN 1880, DIED 1965
"FRANCES PERKINS WAS THE FIRST WOMAN APPOINTED TO THE CABINET AS U.S. SECRETARY OF LABOR. SHE SERVED FROM 1933 TO 1945.
"THOUGH ROOSEVELT IS CREDITED WITH CREATING THE NEW DEAL, PERKINS WAS IN MANY WAYS THE ARCHITECT. SHE WROTE THE LEGISLATION THAT CREATED UNEMPLOYMENT BENEFITS, PENSIONS, AND WELFARE, ALONG WITH ESTABLISHING MINIMUM WAGE AND OVERTIME LAWS. EVEN CHILD LABOR LAWS CAN BE TRACED BACK TO HER WORK.
PERKINS WAS A LONG ADVOCATE OF WORKERS' RIGHTS, AND LIKE MANY OTHER LABOR LEADERS SHE WAS HEAVILY INFLUENCED BY SOCIALISM.
SHE UNDERSTOOD THAT THE STATE HAD A DUTY TO CARE FOR THE PEOPLE THAT BUILT IT.

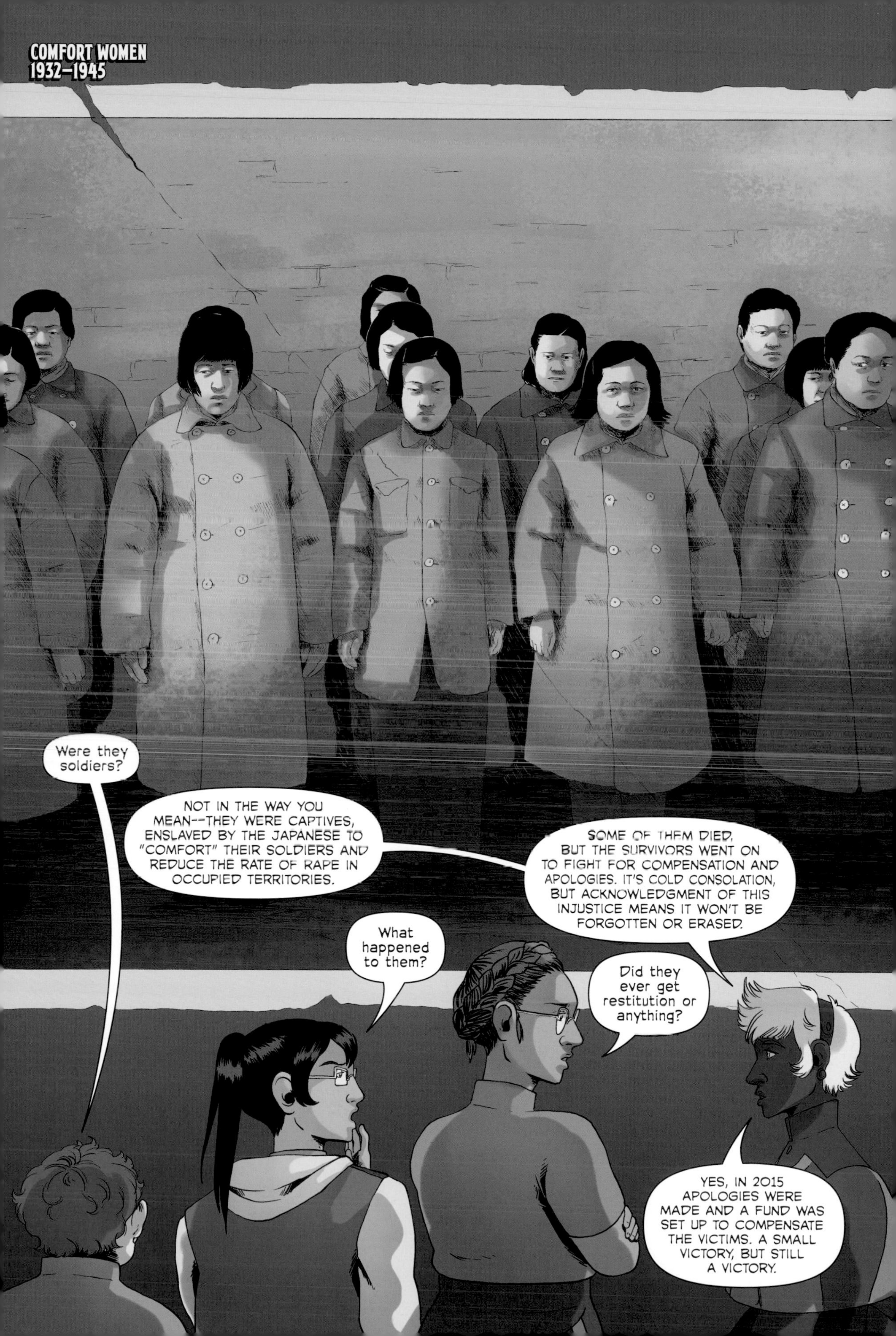
COMFORT WOMEN 1932–1945
Were they soldiers?
NOT IN THE WAY YOU MEAN--THEY WERE CAPTIVES, ENSLAVED BY THE JAPANESE TO "COMFORT" THEIR SOLDIERS AND REDUCE THE RATE OF RAPE IN OCCUPIED TERRITORIES.
What happened to them?
SOME OF THEM DIED, BUT THE SURVIVORS WENT ON TO FIGHT FOR COMPENSATION AND APOLOGIES. IT'S COLD CONSOLATION, BUT ACKNOWLEDGMENT OF THIS INJUSTICE MEANS IT WON'T BE FORGOTTEN OR ERASED.
Did they ever get restitution or anything?
YES, IN 2015 APOLOGIES WERE MADE AND A FUND WAS SET UP TO COMPENSATE THE VICTIMS. A SMALL VICTORY, BUT STILL A VICTORY.

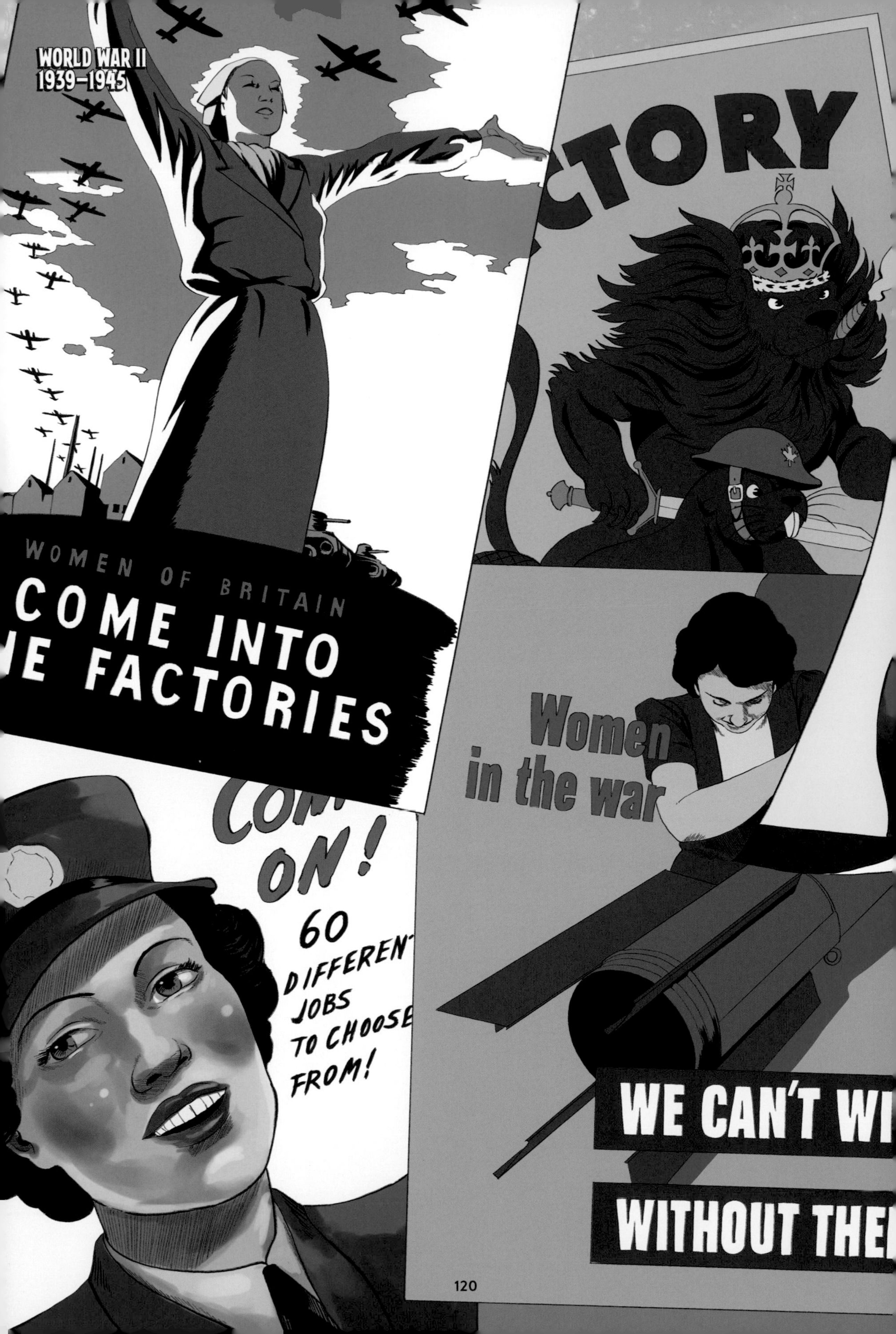
CTORY
WOMEN OF BRITAIN
COME INTO
IE FACTORIES
Women
in the war
COM
ON!
60
DIFFEREN
JOBS
TO CHOOSE
FROM!
WE CAN'T WI
WITHOUT THE

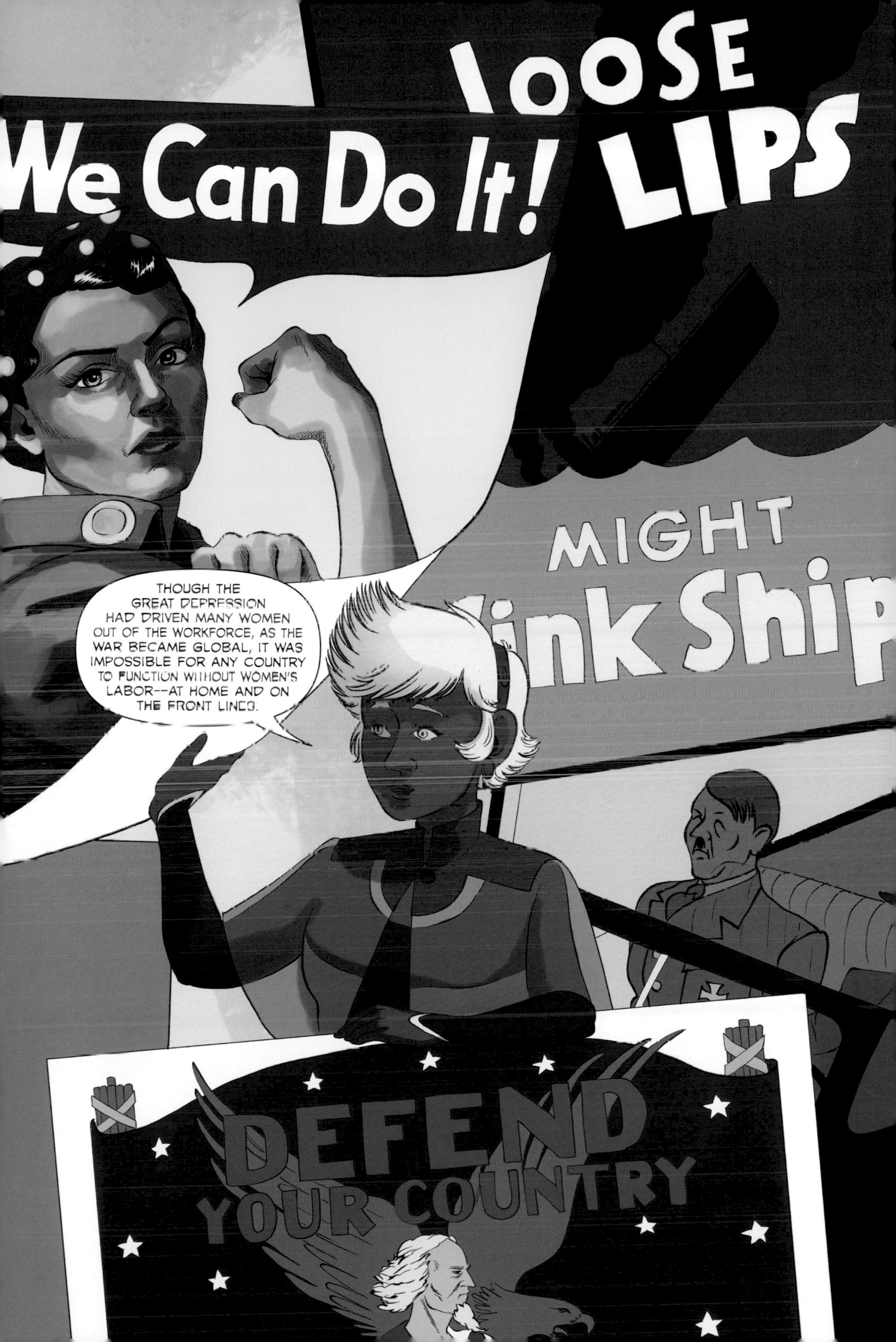
LOOSE LIPS
MIGHT
Sink Ship
We Can Do It!
THOUGH THE GREAT DEPRESSION HAD DRIVEN MANY WOMEN OUT OF THE WORKFORCE, AS THE WAR BECAME GLOBAL, IT WAS IMPOSSIBLE FOR ANY COUNTRY TO FUNCTION WITHOUT WOMEN'S LABOR--AT HOME AND ON THE FRONT LINES.
DEFEND YOUR COUNTRY

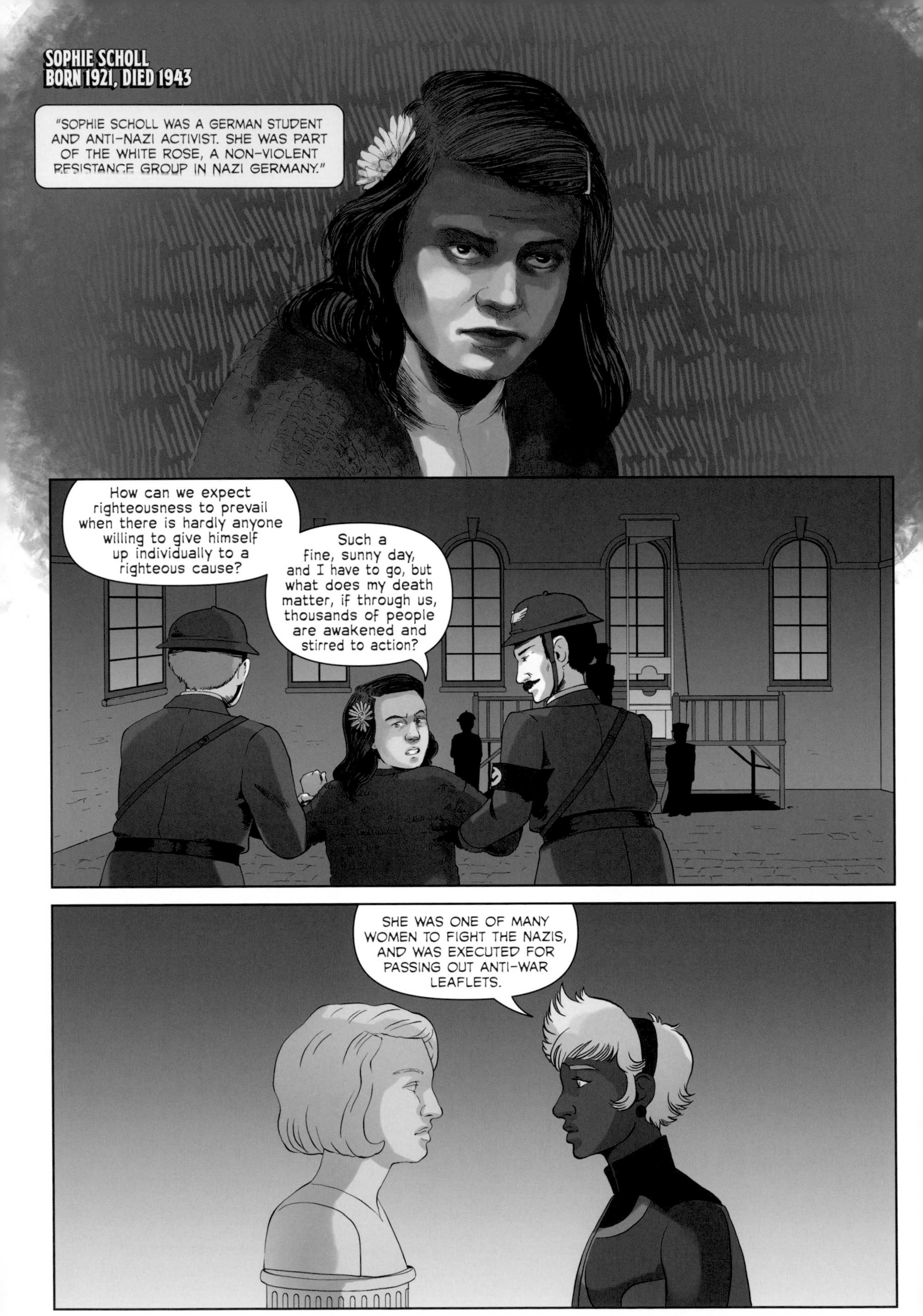
SOPHIE SCHOLL
BORN 1921, DIED 1943
"SOPHIE SCHOLL WAS A GERMAN STUDENT AND ANTI-NAZI ACTIVIST. SHE WAS PART OF THE WHITE ROSE, A NON-VIOLENT RESISTANCE GROUP IN NAZI GERMANY."
How can we expect righteousness to prevail when there is hardly anyone willing to give himself up individually to a righteous cause?
Such a fine, sunny day, and I have to go, but what does my death matter, if through us, thousands of people are awakened and stirred to action?
SHE WAS ONE OF MANY WOMEN TO FIGHT THE NAZIS, AND WAS EXECUTED FOR PASSING OUT ANTI-WAR LEAFLETS.

AGNES MEYER DRISCOLL
BORN 1889, DIED 1971

"DURING THE WAR, MILITARY MESSAGES WERE CODED, SO AS NOT TO BE UNDERSTOOD BY ENEMY FORCES. SPECIALLY TRAINED CODEBREAKERS-- INCLUDING MANY WOMEN--WORKED TO DECIPHER THESE MESSAGES. AGNES MEYER DRISCOLL WAS ONE OF THE FIRST WOMEN IN AMERICA TO WORK ON CRACKING CODED MESSAGES."

ELIZEBETH SMITH FRIEDMAN
BORN 1892, DIED 1980

"WIDELY REGARDED AS AMERICA'S FIRST WOMAN CRYPTANALYST, ELIZEBETH SMITH FRIEDMAN'S CAREER BEGAN WITH DECIPHERING THE MESSAGES OF SMUGGLERS DURING PROHIBITION."

ARLINGTON HALL, VIRGINIA

"THOUGH LITTLE IS KNOWN ABOUT THEM INDIVIDUALLY, THERE WAS EVEN A SEGREGATED CRYPTANALYSIS WING AT ARLINGTON HALL THAT TRACKED WHO WAS DOING BUSINESS WITH AXIS COMPANIES."

BLETCHLEY PARK, ENGLAND

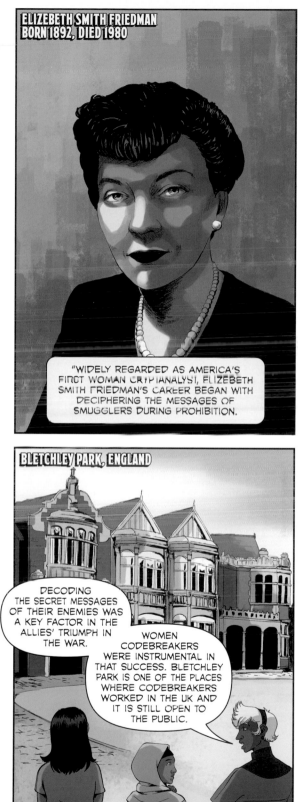

DECODING THE SECRET MESSAGES OF THEIR ENEMIES WAS A KEY FACTOR IN THE ALLIES' TRIUMPH IN THE WAR.

WOMEN CODEBREAKERS WERE INSTRUMENTAL IN THAT SUCCESS. BLETCHLEY PARK IS ONE OF THE PLACES WHERE CODEBREAKERS WORKED IN THE UK AND IT IS STILL OPEN TO THE PUBLIC.

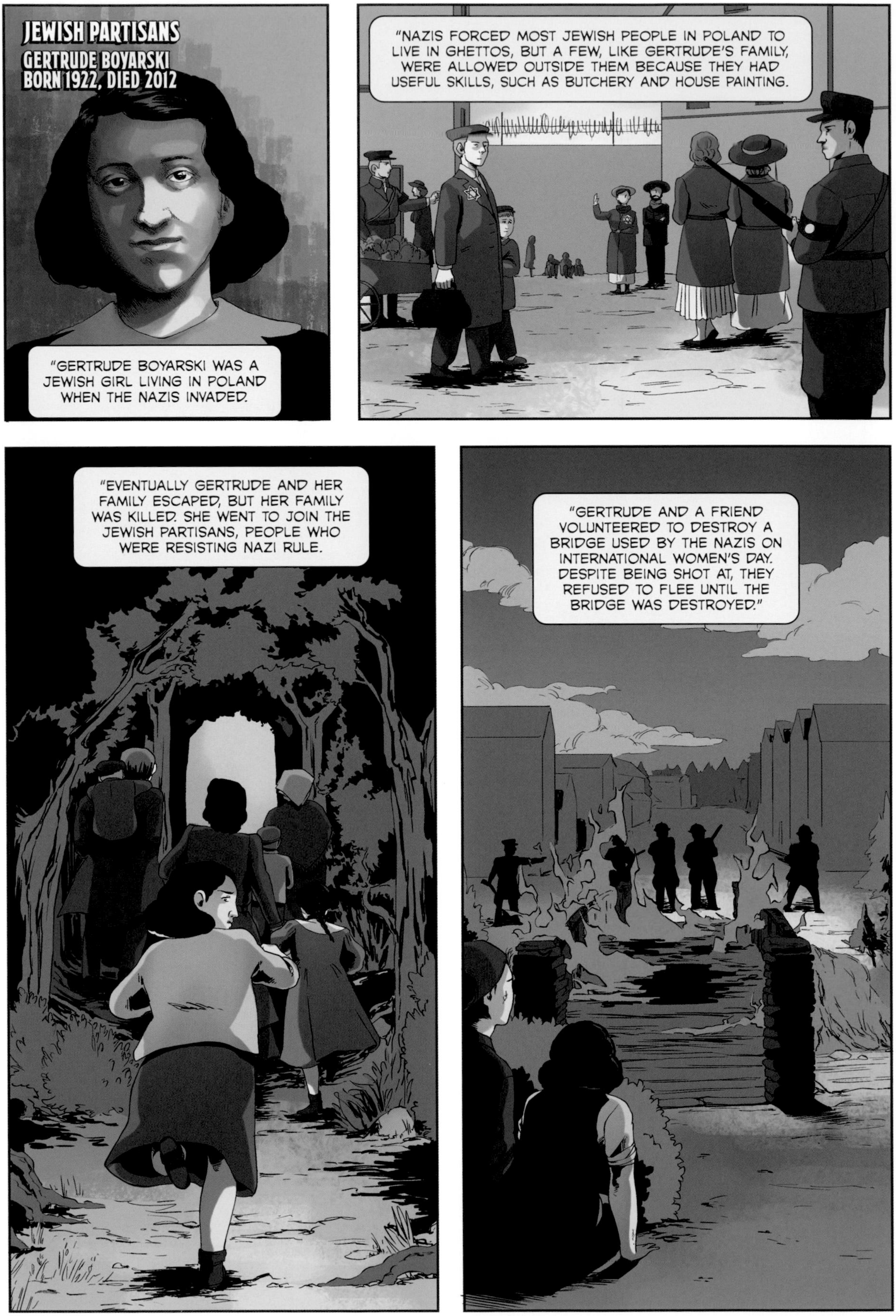
JEWISH PARTISANS
GERTRUDE BOYARSKI
BORN 1922, DIED 2012
"GERTRUDE BOYARSKI WAS A JEWISH GIRL LIVING IN POLAND WHEN THE NAZIS INVADED.
"NAZIS FORCED MOST JEWISH PEOPLE IN POLAND TO LIVE IN GHETTOS, BUT A FEW, LIKE GERTRUDE'S FAMILY, WERE ALLOWED OUTSIDE THEM BECAUSE THEY HAD USEFUL SKILLS, SUCH AS BUTCHERY AND HOUSE PAINTING.
"EVENTUALLY GERTRUDE AND HER FAMILY ESCAPED, BUT HER FAMILY WAS KILLED. SHE WENT TO JOIN THE JEWISH PARTISANS, PEOPLE WHO WERE RESISTING NAZI RULE.
"GERTRUDE AND A FRIEND VOLUNTEERED TO DESTROY A BRIDGE USED BY THE NAZIS ON INTERNATIONAL WOMEN'S DAY. DESPITE BEING SHOT AT, THEY REFUSED TO FLEE UNTIL THE BRIDGE WAS DESTROYED."

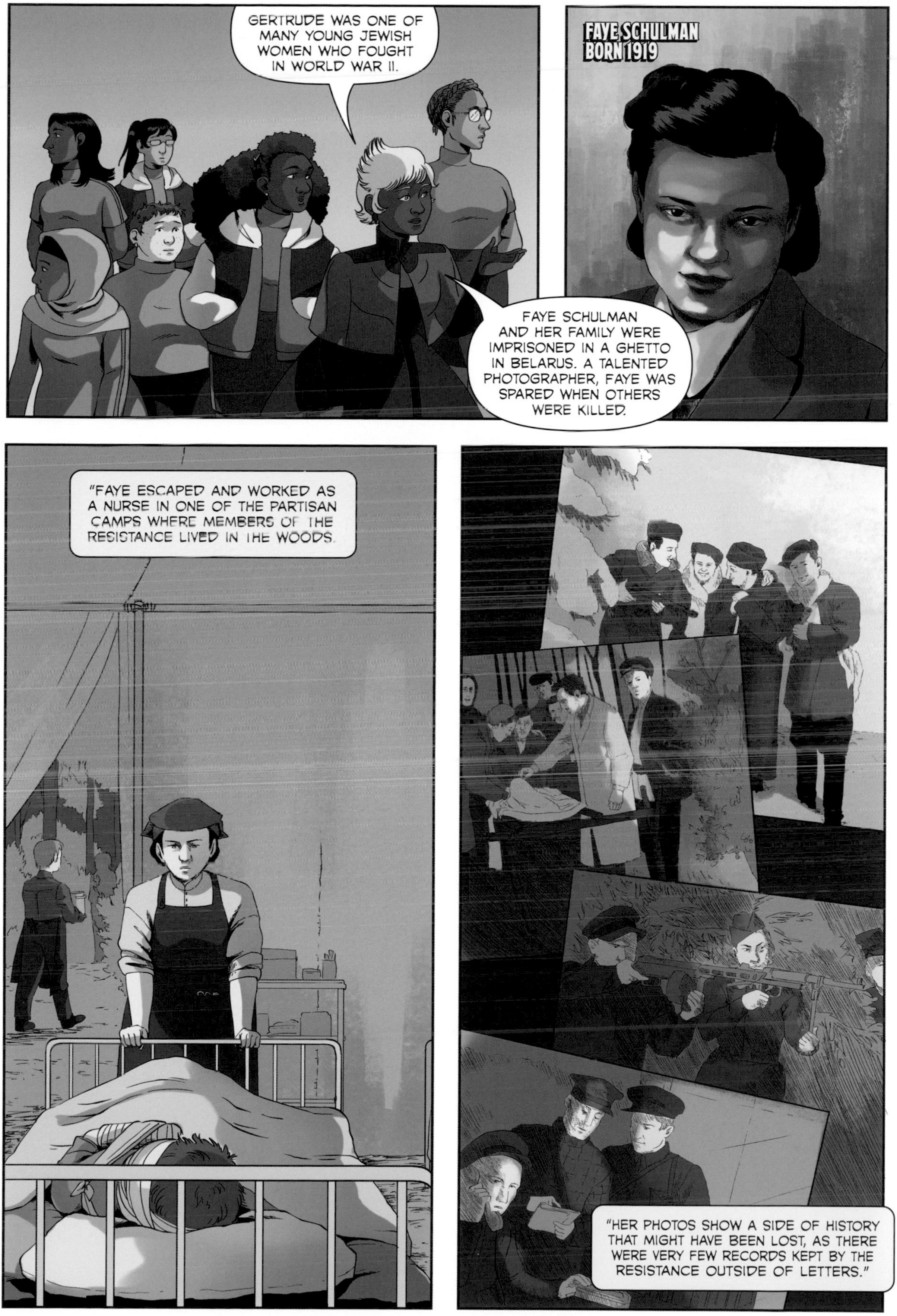
GERTRUDE WAS ONE OF MANY YOUNG JEWISH WOMEN WHO FOUGHT IN WORLD WAR II.
FAYE SCHULMAN BORN 1919
FAYE SCHULMAN AND HER FAMILY WERE IMPRISONED IN A GHETTO IN BELARUS. A TALENTED PHOTOGRAPHER, FAYE WAS SPARED WHEN OTHERS WERE KILLED.
"FAYE ESCAPED AND WORKED AS A NURSE IN ONE OF THE PARTISAN CAMPS WHERE MEMBERS OF THE RESISTANCE LIVED IN THE WOODS.
"HER PHOTOS SHOW A SIDE OF HISTORY THAT MIGHT HAVE BEEN LOST, AS THERE WERE VERY FEW RECORDS KEPT BY THE RESISTANCE OUTSIDE OF LETTERS."

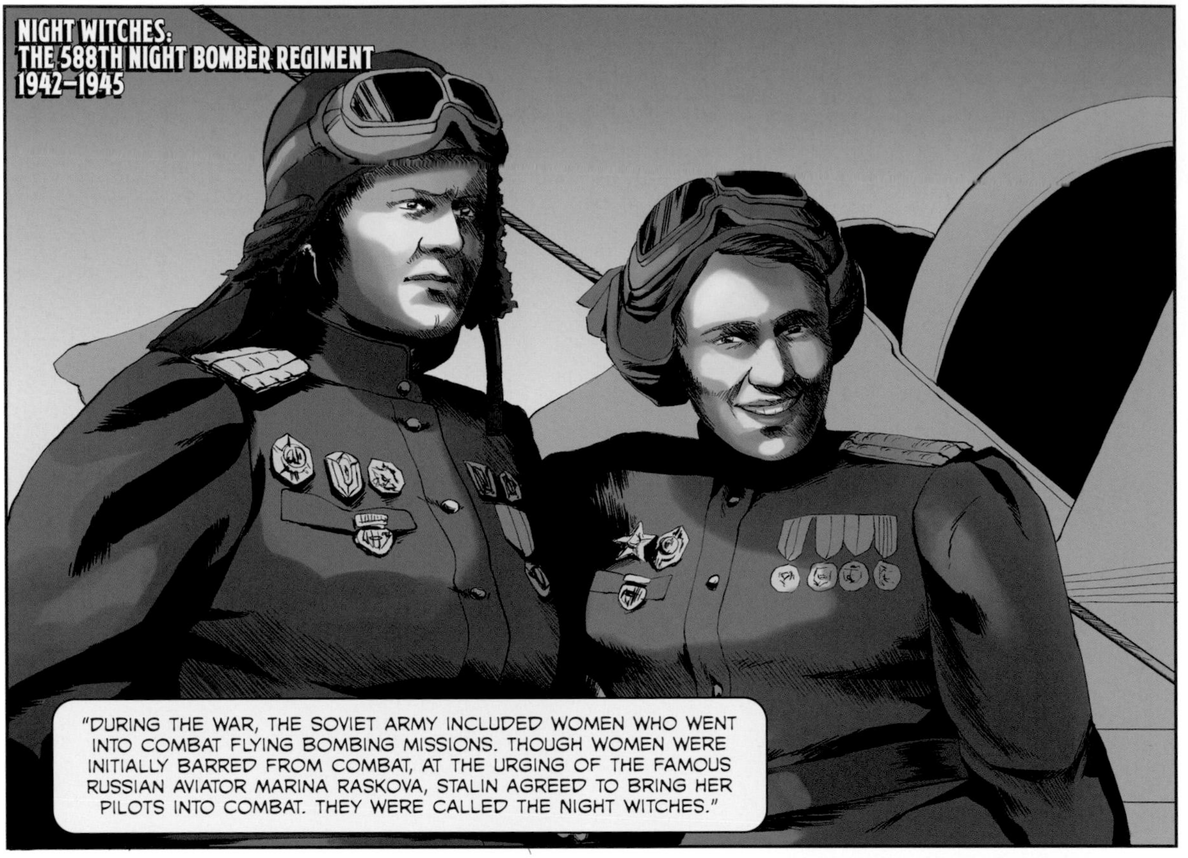
NIGHT WITCHES:
THE 588TH NIGHT BOMBER REGIMENT
1942–1945
"DURING THE WAR, THE SOVIET ARMY INCLUDED WOMEN WHO WENT INTO COMBAT FLYING BOMBING MISSIONS. THOUGH WOMEN WERE INITIALLY BARRED FROM COMBAT, AT THE URGING OF THE FAMOUS RUSSIAN AVIATOR MARINA RASKOVA, STALIN AGREED TO BRING HER PILOTS INTO COMBAT. THEY WERE CALLED THE NIGHT WITCHES."

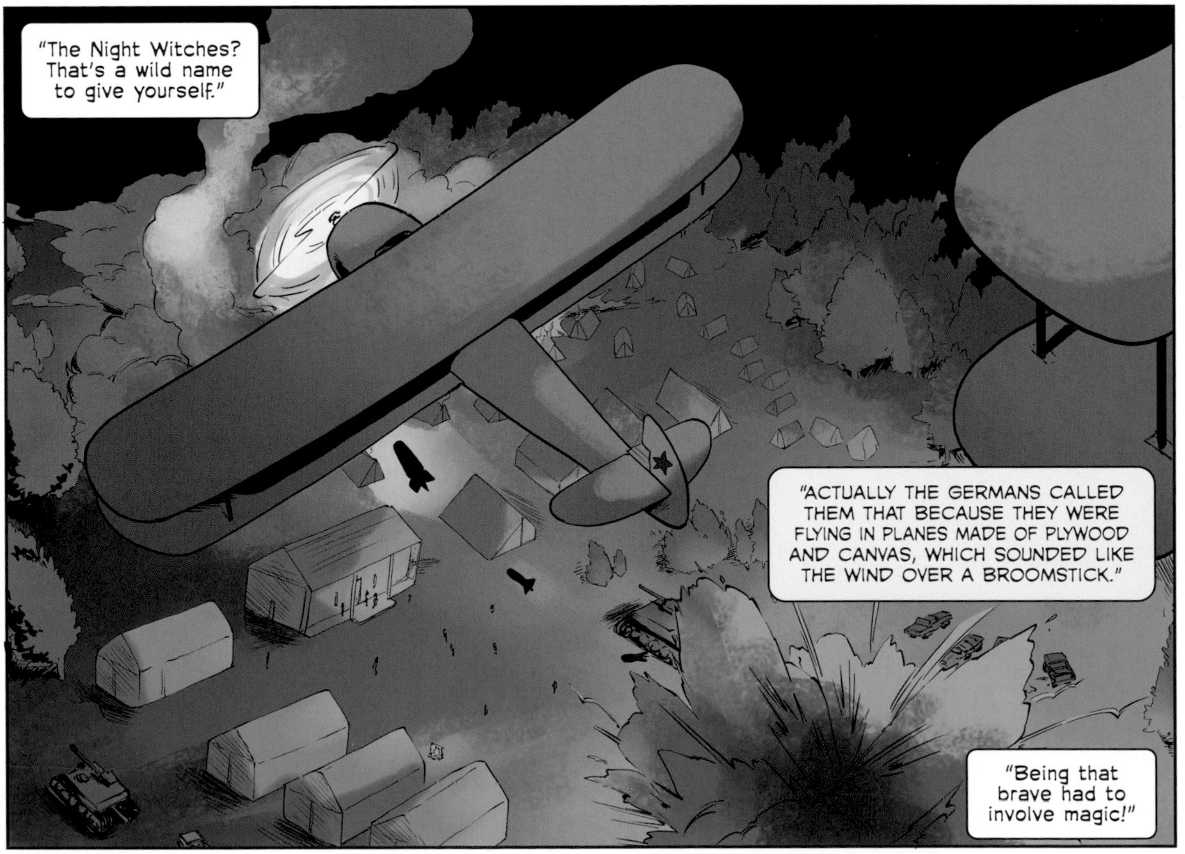
"The Night Witches? That's a wild name to give yourself."
"ACTUALLY THE GERMANS CALLED THEM THAT BECAUSE THEY WERE FLYING IN PLANES MADE OF PLYWOOD AND CANVAS, WHICH SOUNDED LIKE THE WIND OVER A BROOMSTICK."
"Being that brave had to involve magic!"

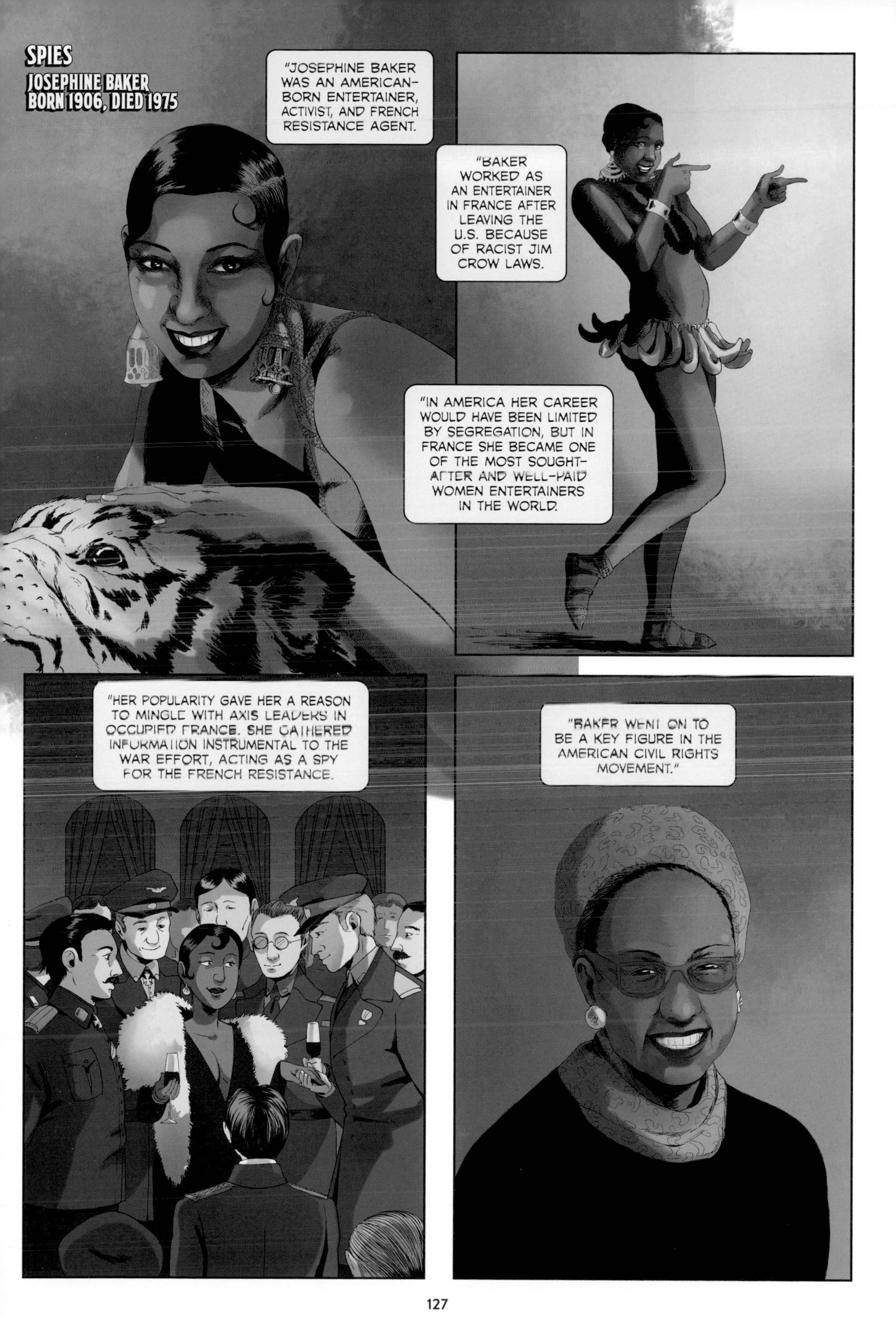
SPIES
JOSEPHINE BAKER
BORN 1906, DIED 1975
"JOSEPHINE BAKER WAS AN AMERICAN-BORN ENTERTAINER, ACTIVIST, AND FRENCH RESISTANCE AGENT.
"BAKER WORKED AS AN ENTERTAINER IN FRANCE AFTER LEAVING THE U.S. BECAUSE OF RACIST JIM CROW LAWS.
"IN AMERICA HER CAREER WOULD HAVE BEEN LIMITED BY SEGREGATION, BUT IN FRANCE SHE BECAME ONE OF THE MOST SOUGHT-AFTER AND WELL-PAID WOMEN ENTERTAINERS IN THE WORLD.
"HER POPULARITY GAVE HER A REASON TO MINGLE WITH AXIS LEADERS IN OCCUPIED FRANCE. SHE GATHERED INFORMATION INSTRUMENTAL TO THE WAR EFFORT, ACTING AS A SPY FOR THE FRENCH RESISTANCE.
"BAKER WENT ON TO BE A KEY FIGURE IN THE AMERICAN CIVIL RIGHTS MOVEMENT."

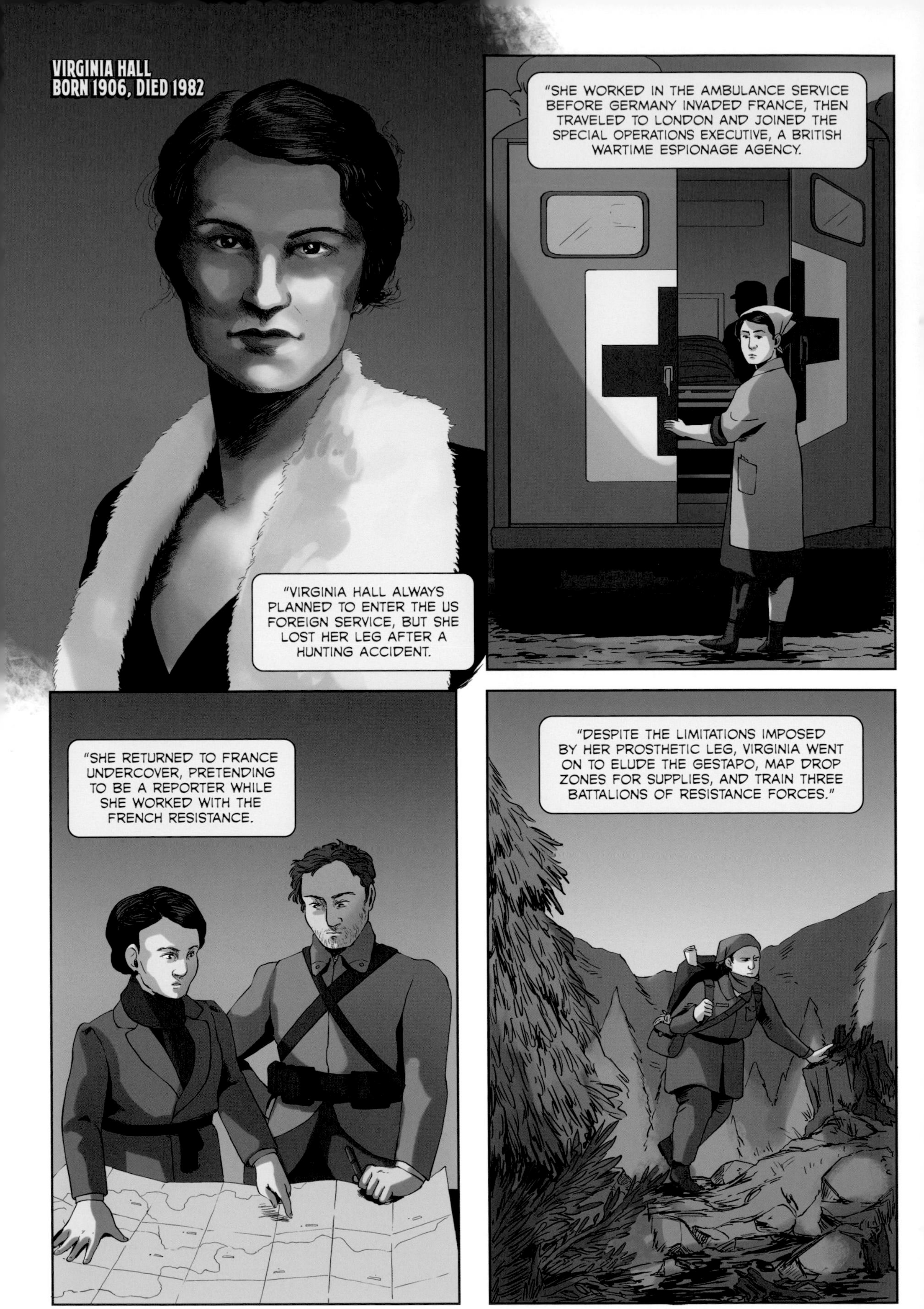
VIRGINIA HALL
BORN 1906, DIED 1982
"VIRGINIA HALL ALWAYS PLANNED TO ENTER THE US FOREIGN SERVICE, BUT SHE LOST HER LEG AFTER A HUNTING ACCIDENT.
"SHE WORKED IN THE AMBULANCE SERVICE BEFORE GERMANY INVADED FRANCE, THEN TRAVELED TO LONDON AND JOINED THE SPECIAL OPERATIONS EXECUTIVE, A BRITISH WARTIME ESPIONAGE AGENCY.
"SHE RETURNED TO FRANCE UNDERCOVER, PRETENDING TO BE A REPORTER WHILE SHE WORKED WITH THE FRENCH RESISTANCE.
"DESPITE THE LIMITATIONS IMPOSED BY HER PROSTHETIC LEG, VIRGINIA WENT ON TO ELUDE THE GESTAPO, MAP DROP ZONES FOR SUPPLIES, AND TRAIN THREE BATTALIONS OF RESISTANCE FORCES."

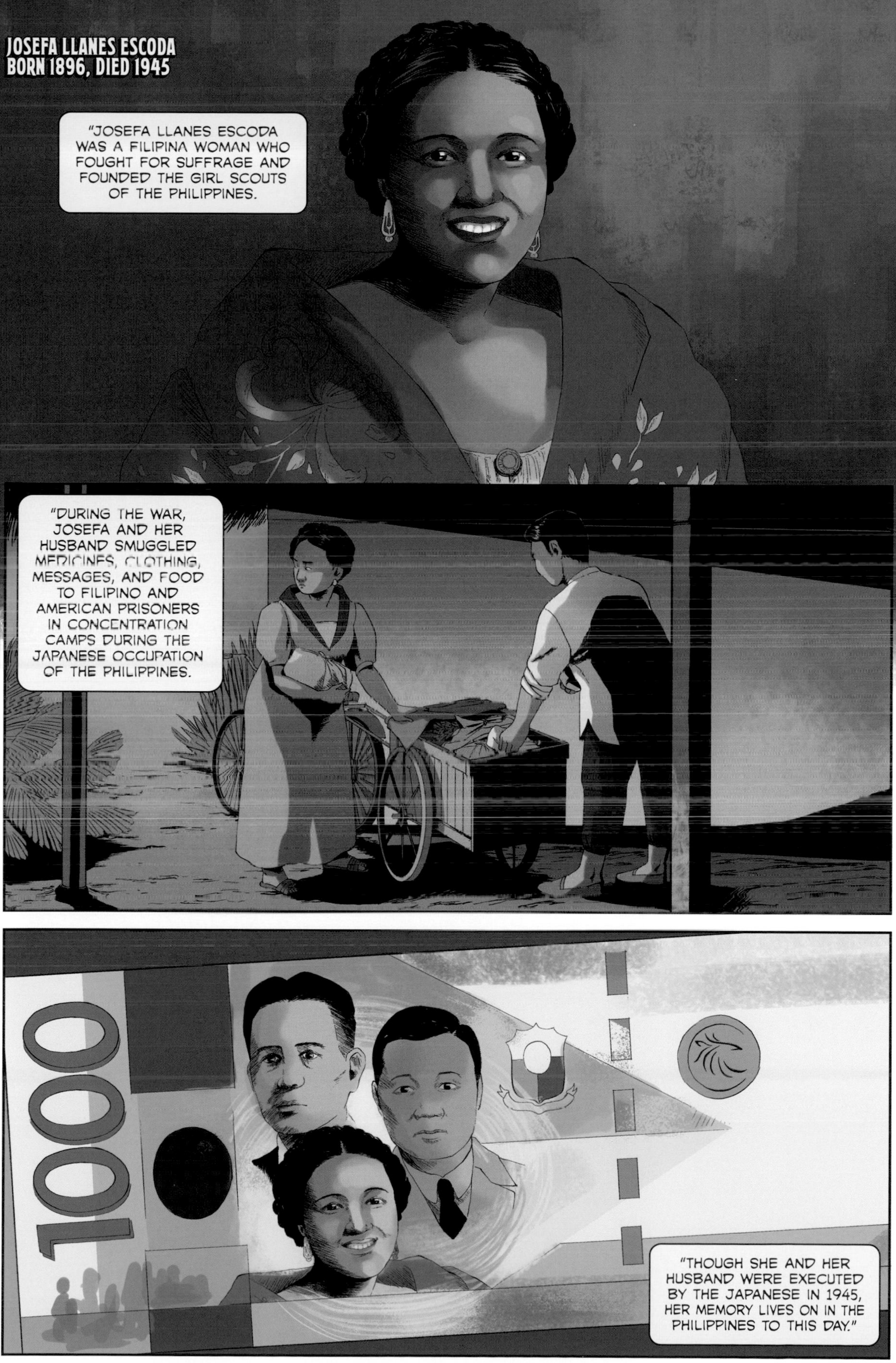
JOSEFA LLANES ESCODA
BORN 1896, DIED 1945
"JOSEFA LLANES ESCODA WAS A FILIPINA WOMAN WHO FOUGHT FOR SUFFRAGE AND FOUNDED THE GIRL SCOUTS OF THE PHILIPPINES.
"DURING THE WAR, JOSEFA AND HER HUSBAND SMUGGLED MEDICINES, CLOTHING, MESSAGES, AND FOOD TO FILIPINO AND AMERICAN PRISONERS IN CONCENTRATION CAMPS DURING THE JAPANESE OCCUPATION OF THE PHILIPPINES.
1000
"THOUGH SHE AND HER HUSBAND WERE EXECUTED BY THE JAPANESE IN 1945, HER MEMORY LIVES ON IN THE PHILIPPINES TO THIS DAY."

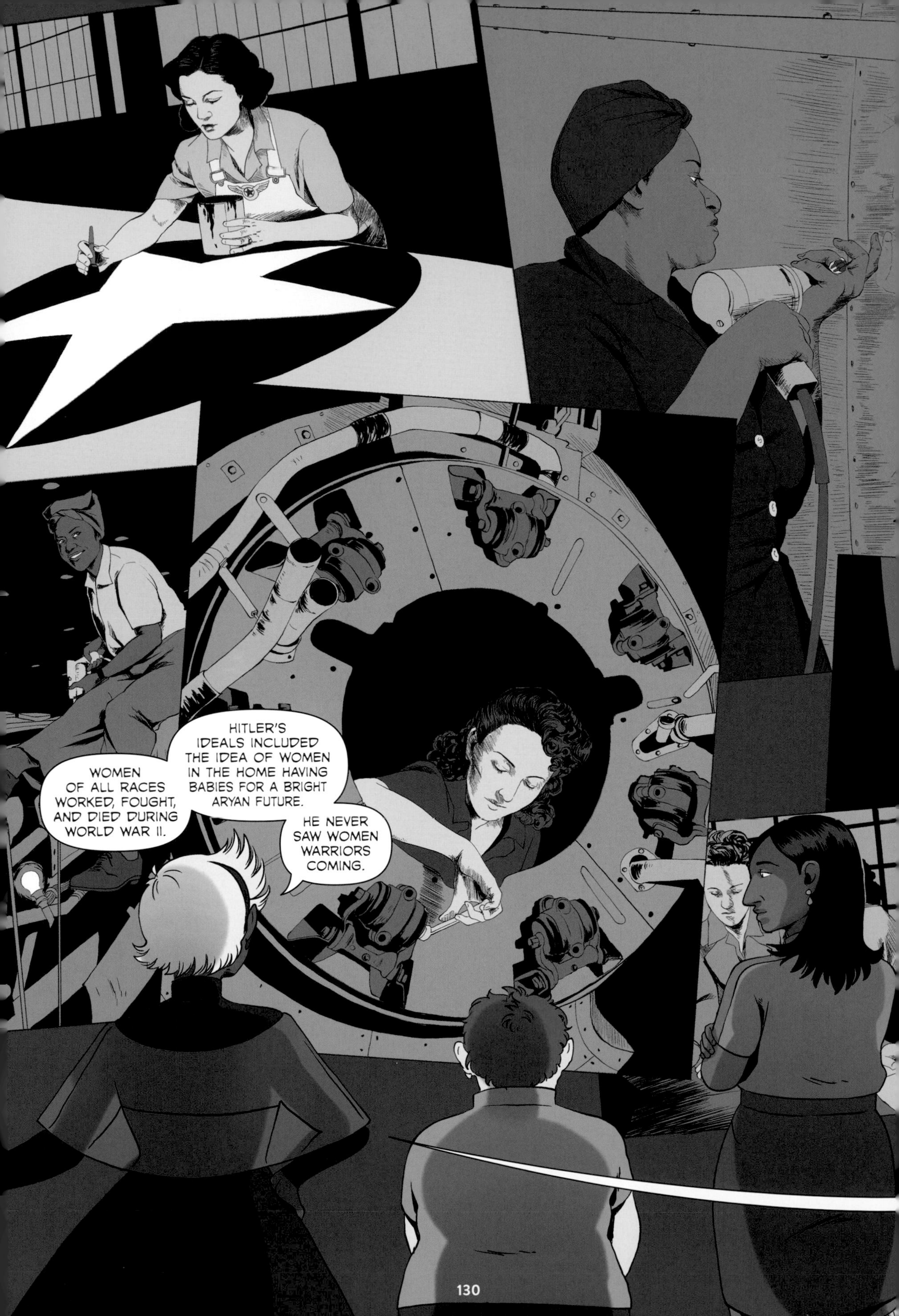
WOMEN OF ALL RACES WORKED, FOUGHT, AND DIED DURING WORLD WAR II.
HITLER'S IDEALS INCLUDED THE IDEA OF WOMEN IN THE HOME HAVING BABIES FOR A BRIGHT ARYAN FUTURE.
HE NEVER SAW WOMEN WARRIORS COMING.

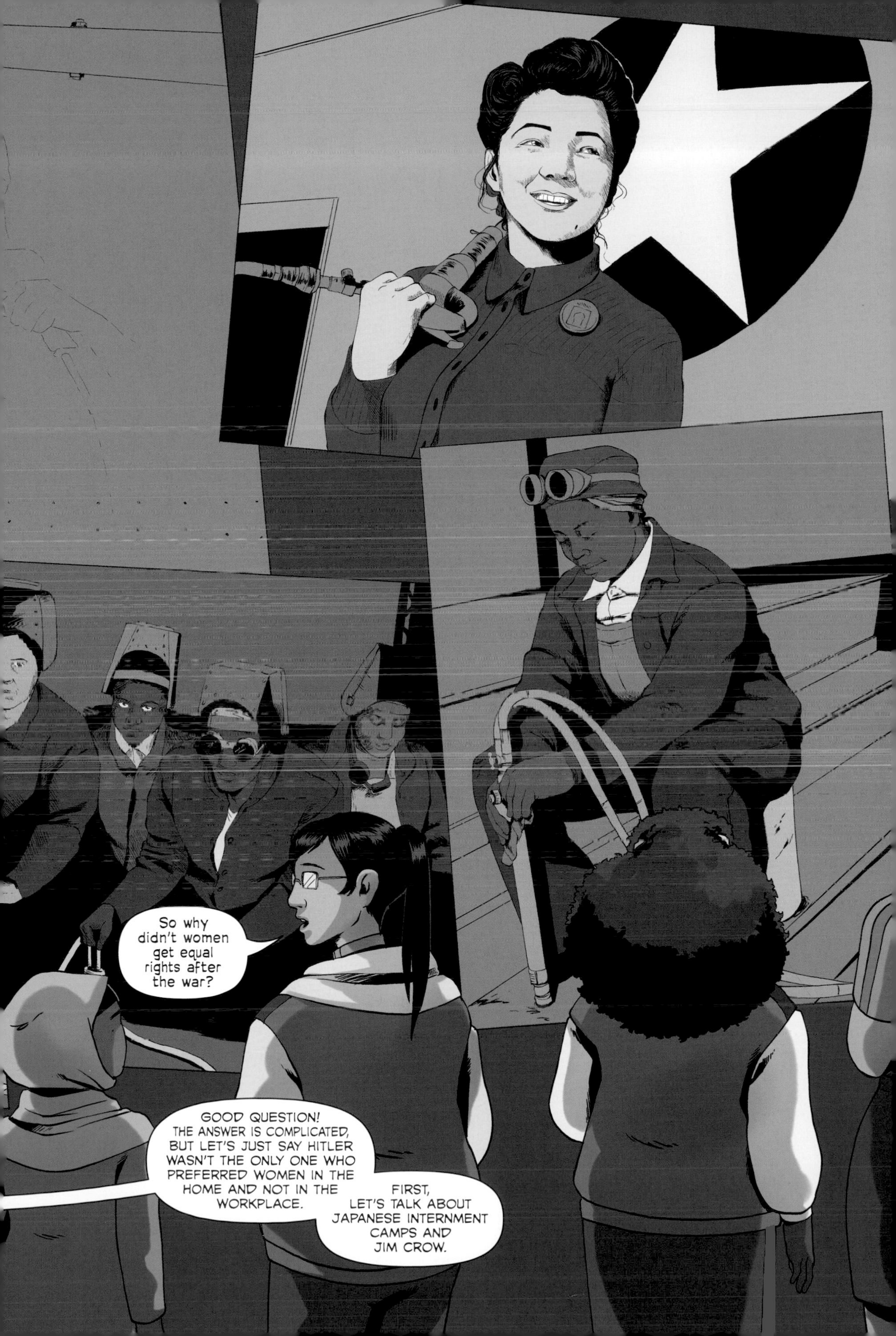
So why didn't women get equal rights after the war?
GOOD QUESTION! THE ANSWER IS COMPLICATED, BUT LET'S JUST SAY HITLER WASN'T THE ONLY ONE WHO PREFERRED WOMEN IN THE HOME AND NOT IN THE WORKPLACE.
FIRST, LET'S TALK ABOUT JAPANESE INTERNMENT CAMPS AND JIM CROW.

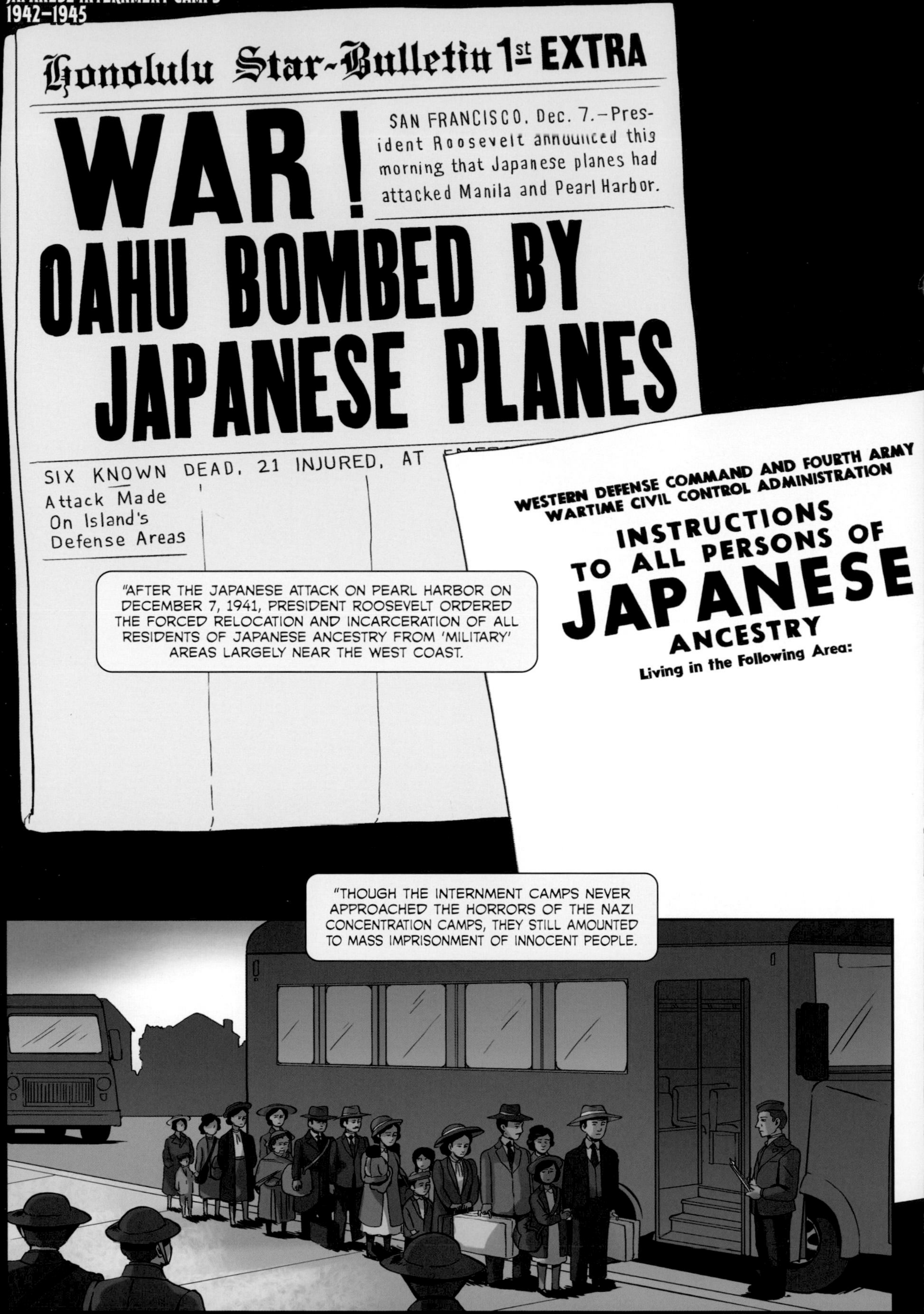
Honolulu Star-Bulletin 1st EXTRA
WAR!
SAN FRANCISCO, Dec. 7.—President Roosevelt announced this morning that Japanese planes had attacked Manila and Pearl Harbor.
OAHU BOMBED BY JAPANESE PLANES
SIX KNOWN DEAD, 21 INJURED, AT
Attack Made On Island's Defense Areas
"AFTER THE JAPANESE ATTACK ON PEARL HARBOR ON DECEMBER 7, 1941, PRESIDENT ROOSEVELT ORDERED THE FORCED RELOCATION AND INCARCERATION OF ALL RESIDENTS OF JAPANESE ANCESTRY FROM 'MILITARY' AREAS LARGELY NEAR THE WEST COAST.
WESTERN DEFENSE COMMAND AND FOURTH ARMY
WARTIME CIVIL CONTROL ADMINISTRATION
INSTRUCTIONS TO ALL PERSONS OF JAPANESE ANCESTRY
Living in the Following Area:
"THOUGH THE INTERNMENT CAMPS NEVER APPROACHED THE HORRORS OF THE NAZI CONCENTRATION CAMPS, THEY STILL AMOUNTED TO MASS IMPRISONMENT OF INNOCENT PEOPLE.

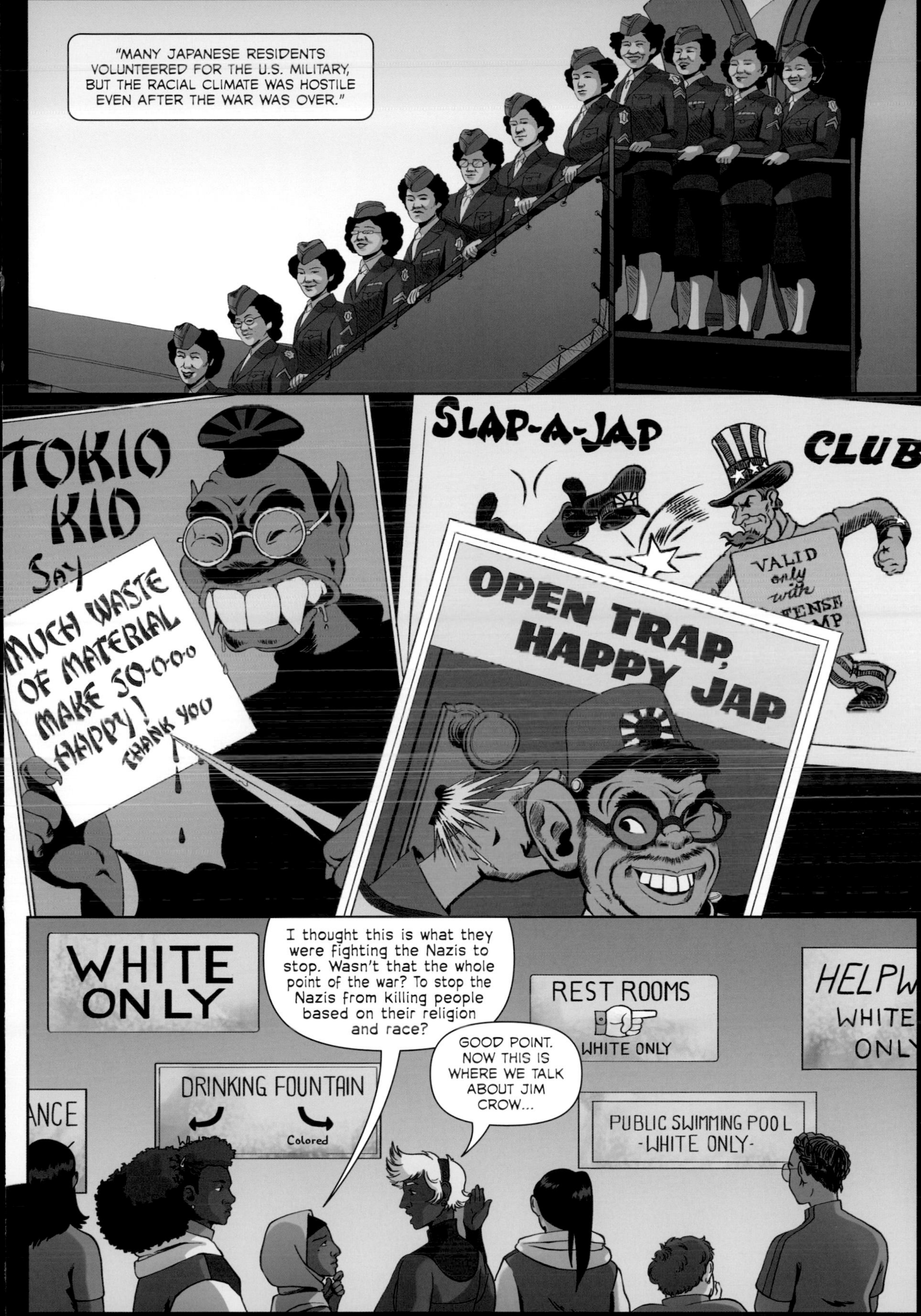
"MANY JAPANESE RESIDENTS VOLUNTEERED FOR THE U.S. MILITARY, BUT THE RACIAL CLIMATE WAS HOSTILE EVEN AFTER THE WAR WAS OVER."
TOKIO KID SAY
MUCH WASTE OF MATERIAL MAKE SO-O-O-O HAPPY! THANK YOU
SLAP-A-JAP CLUB
VALID only with
OPEN TRAP, HAPPY JAP
WHITE ONLY
I thought this is what they were fighting the Nazis to stop. Wasn't that the whole point of the war? To stop the Nazis from killing people based on their religion and race?
REST ROOMS
WHITE ONLY
GOOD POINT. NOW THIS IS WHERE WE TALK ABOUT JIM CROW...
DRINKING FOUNTAIN
Colored
PUBLIC SWIMMING POOL -WHITE ONLY-

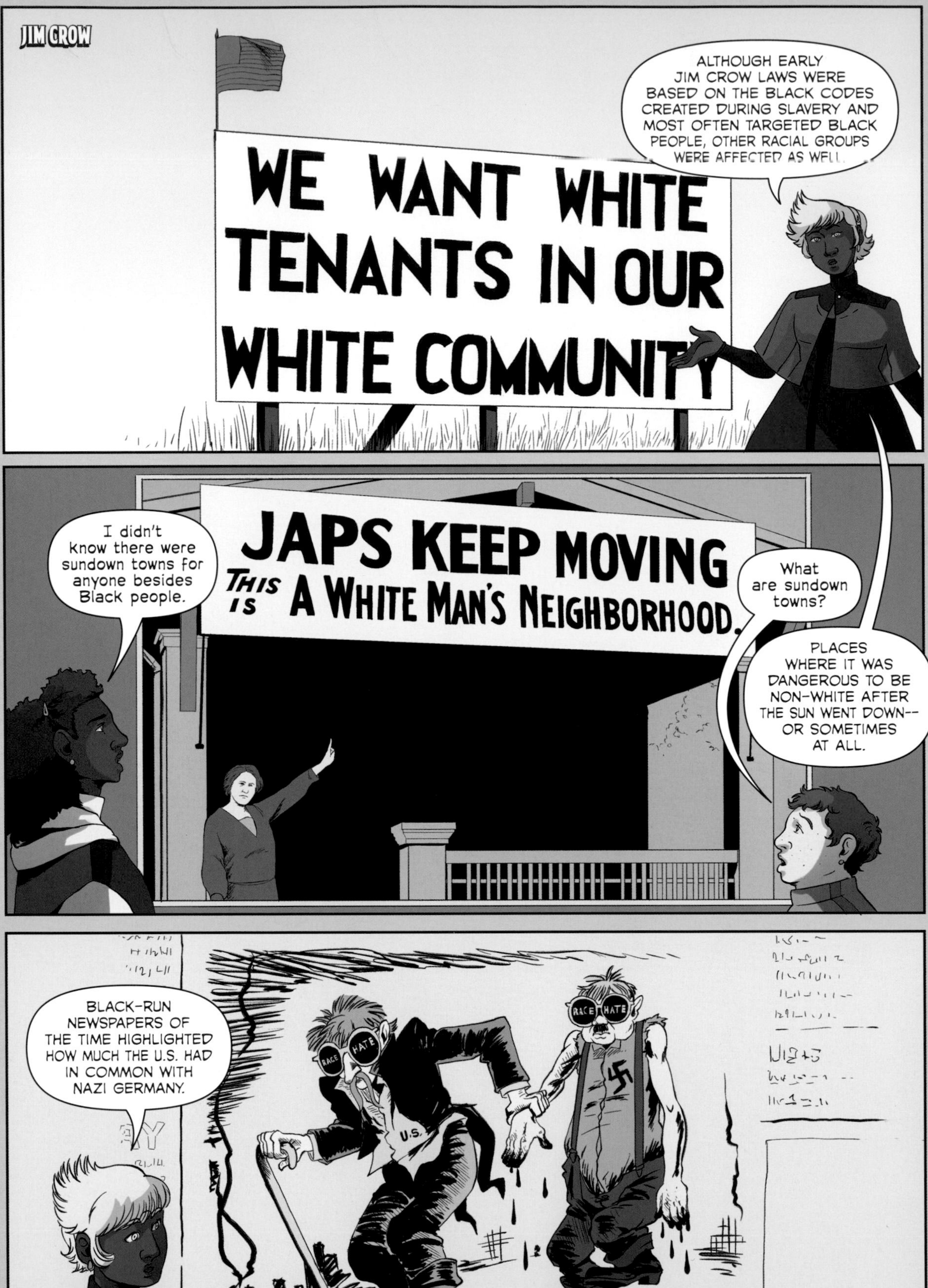
ALTHOUGH EARLY JIM CROW LAWS WERE BASED ON THE BLACK CODES CREATED DURING SLAVERY AND MOST OFTEN TARGETED BLACK PEOPLE, OTHER RACIAL GROUPS WERE AFFECTED AS WELL.
WE WANT WHITE TENANTS IN OUR WHITE COMMUNITY
JAPS KEEP MOVING
THIS IS A WHITE MAN'S NEIGHBORHOOD.
I didn't know there were sundown towns for anyone besides Black people.
What are sundown towns?
PLACES WHERE IT WAS DANGEROUS TO BE NON-WHITE AFTER THE SUN WENT DOWN--OR SOMETIMES AT ALL.
BLACK-RUN NEWSPAPERS OF THE TIME HIGHLIGHTED HOW MUCH THE U.S. HAD IN COMMON WITH NAZI GERMANY.
RACE HATE
RACE HATE
U.S.
GERMANY
Blind Leading The Blind

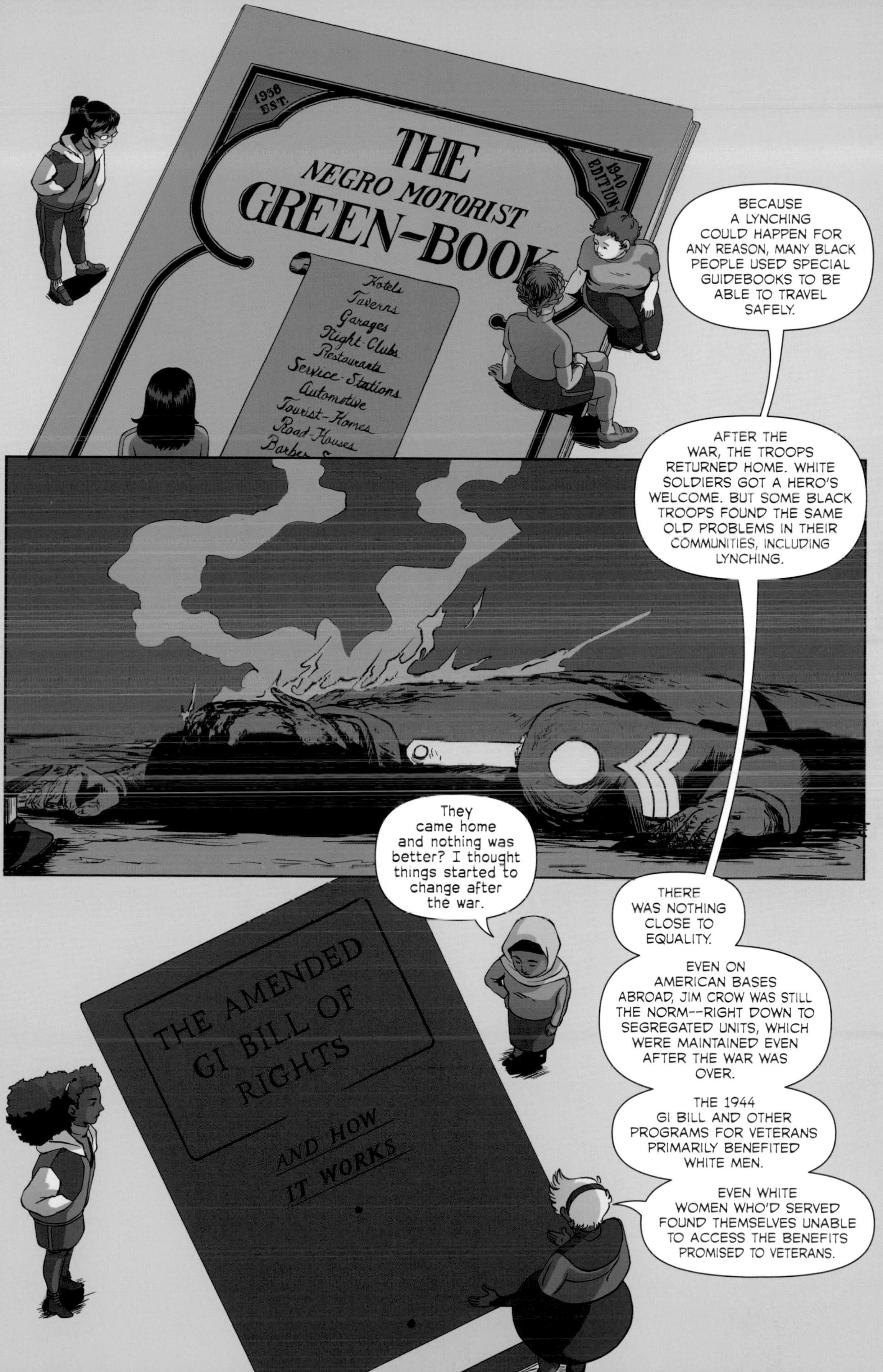

1936 EST.
THE NEGRO MOTORIST GREEN-BOOK
1940 EDITION
Hotels
Taverns
Garages
Night-Clubs
Restaurants
Service-Stations
Automotive
Tourist-Homes
Road-Houses
BECAUSE A LYNCHING COULD HAPPEN FOR ANY REASON, MANY BLACK PEOPLE USED SPECIAL GUIDEBOOKS TO BE ABLE TO TRAVEL SAFELY.
AFTER THE WAR, THE TROOPS RETURNED HOME. WHITE SOLDIERS GOT A HERO'S WELCOME. BUT SOME BLACK TROOPS FOUND THE SAME OLD PROBLEMS IN THEIR COMMUNITIES, INCLUDING LYNCHING.
They came home and nothing was better? I thought things started to change after the war.
THERE WAS NOTHING CLOSE TO EQUALITY.
EVEN ON AMERICAN BASES ABROAD, JIM CROW WAS STILL THE NORM--RIGHT DOWN TO SEGREGATED UNITS, WHICH WERE MAINTAINED EVEN AFTER THE WAR WAS OVER.
THE 1944 GI BILL AND OTHER PROGRAMS FOR VETERANS PRIMARILY BENEFITED WHITE MEN.
EVEN WHITE WOMEN WHO'D SERVED FOUND THEMSELVES UNABLE TO ACCESS THE BENEFITS PROMISED TO VETERANS.
THE AMENDED GI BILL OF RIGHTS
AND HOW IT WORKS

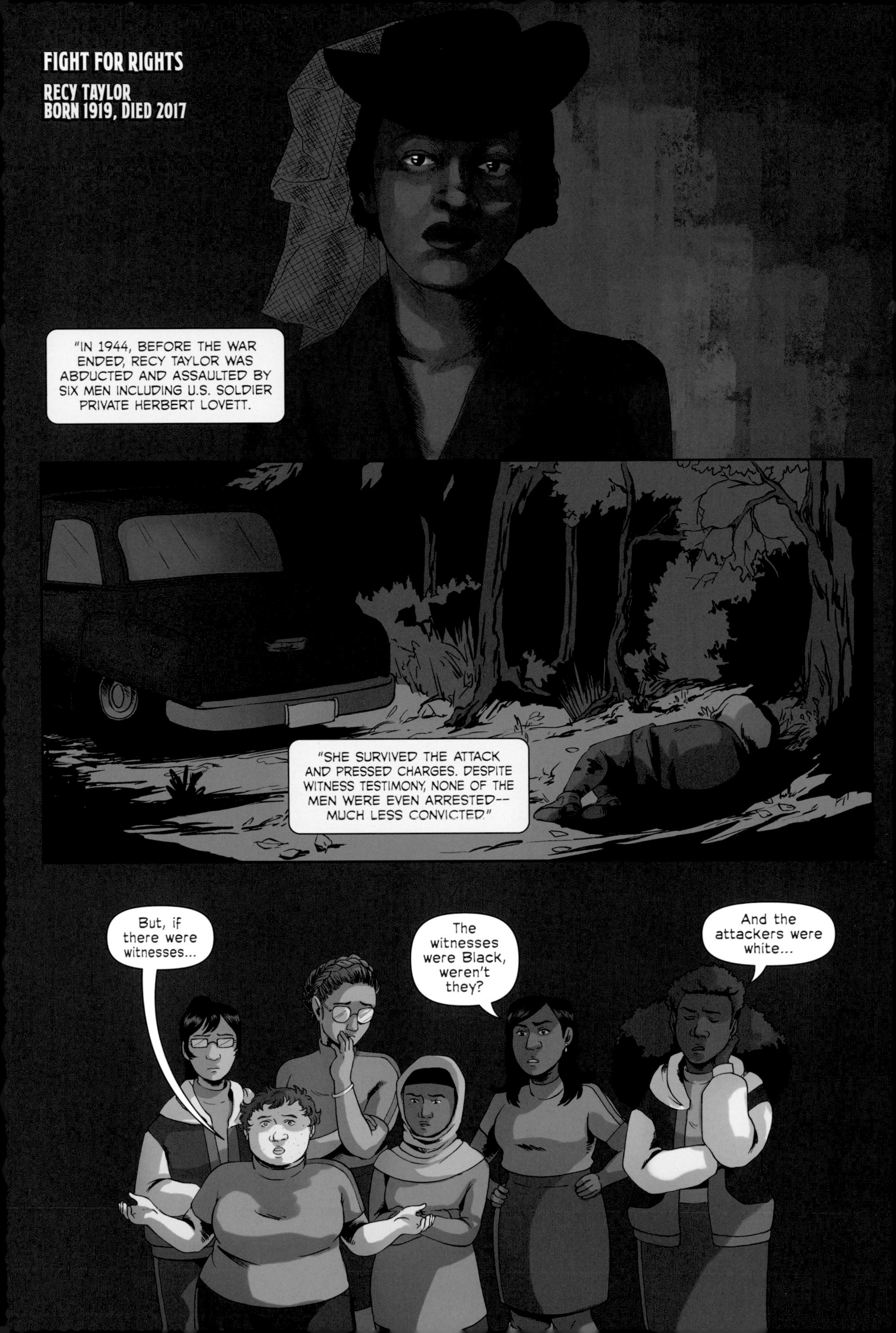
FIGHT FOR RIGHTS
RECY TAYLOR
BORN 1919, DIED 2017
"IN 1944, BEFORE THE WAR ENDED, RECY TAYLOR WAS ABDUCTED AND ASSAULTED BY SIX MEN INCLUDING U.S. SOLDIER PRIVATE HERBERT LOVETT.
"SHE SURVIVED THE ATTACK AND PRESSED CHARGES. DESPITE WITNESS TESTIMONY, NONE OF THE MEN WERE EVEN ARRESTED-- MUCH LESS CONVICTED."
But, if there were witnesses...
The witnesses were Black, weren't they?
And the attackers were white...

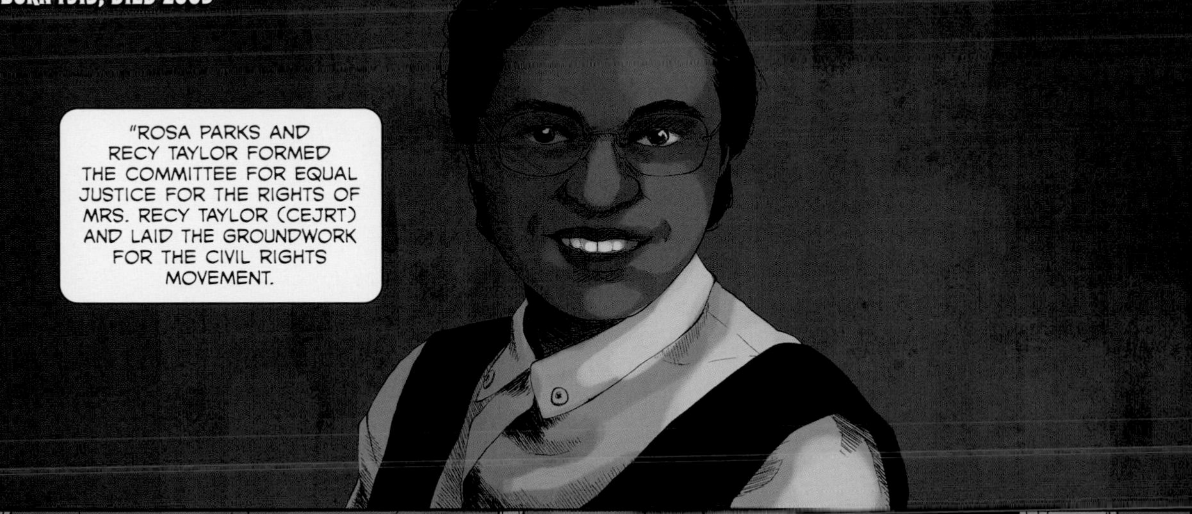
"ROSA PARKS AND RECY TAYLOR FORMED THE COMMITTEE FOR EQUAL JUSTICE FOR THE RIGHTS OF MRS. RECY TAYLOR (CEJRT) AND LAID THE GROUNDWORK FOR THE CIVIL RIGHTS MOVEMENT.

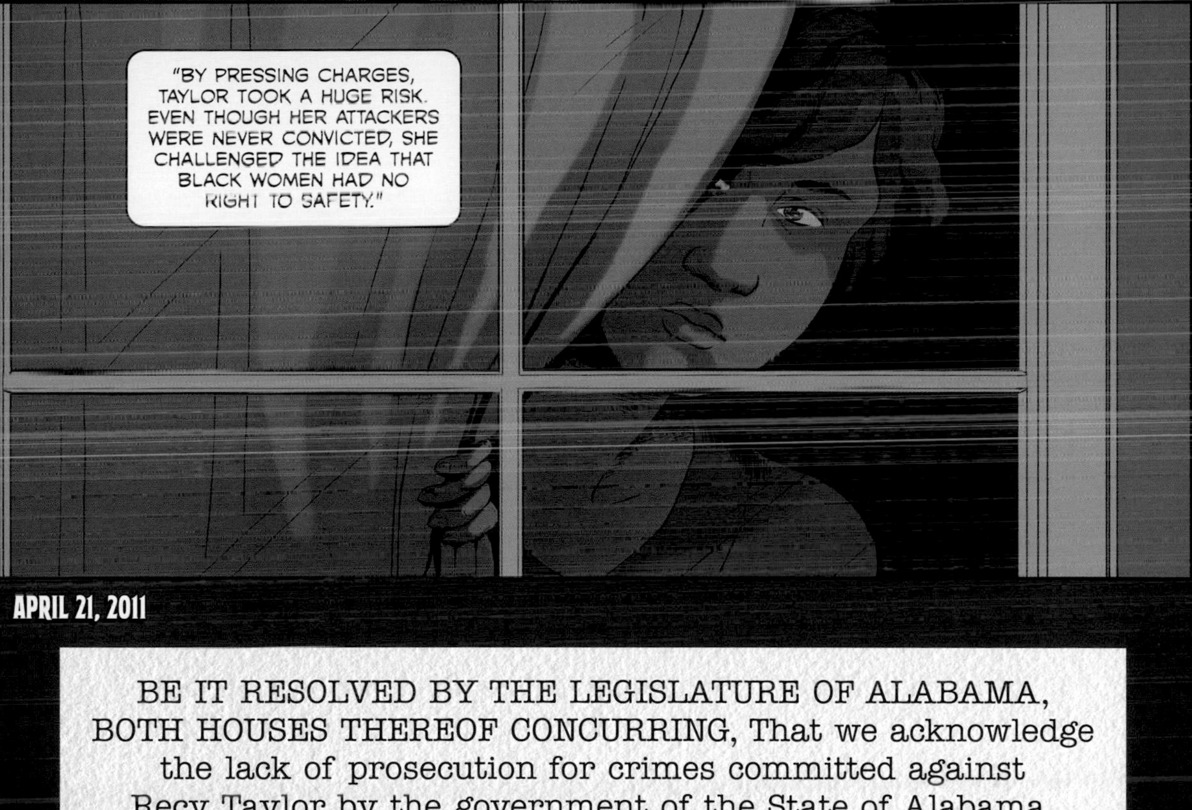
"BY PRESSING CHARGES, TAYLOR TOOK A HUGE RISK. EVEN THOUGH HER ATTACKERS WERE NEVER CONVICTED, SHE CHALLENGED THE IDEA THAT BLACK WOMEN HAD NO RIGHT TO SAFETY."

APRIL 21, 2011

BE IT RESOLVED BY THE LEGISLATURE OF ALABAMA, BOTH HOUSES THEREOF CONCURRING, That we acknowledge the lack of prosecution for crimes committed against Recy Taylor by the government of the State of Alabama, that we declare such failure to act was, and is, morally abhorrent and repugnant, and that we do hereby express profound regret for the role played by the government of the State of Alabama in failing to prosecute the crimes.

BE IT FURTHER RESOLVED, That we express our deepest sympathies and solemn regrets to Recy Taylor and her family and friends.

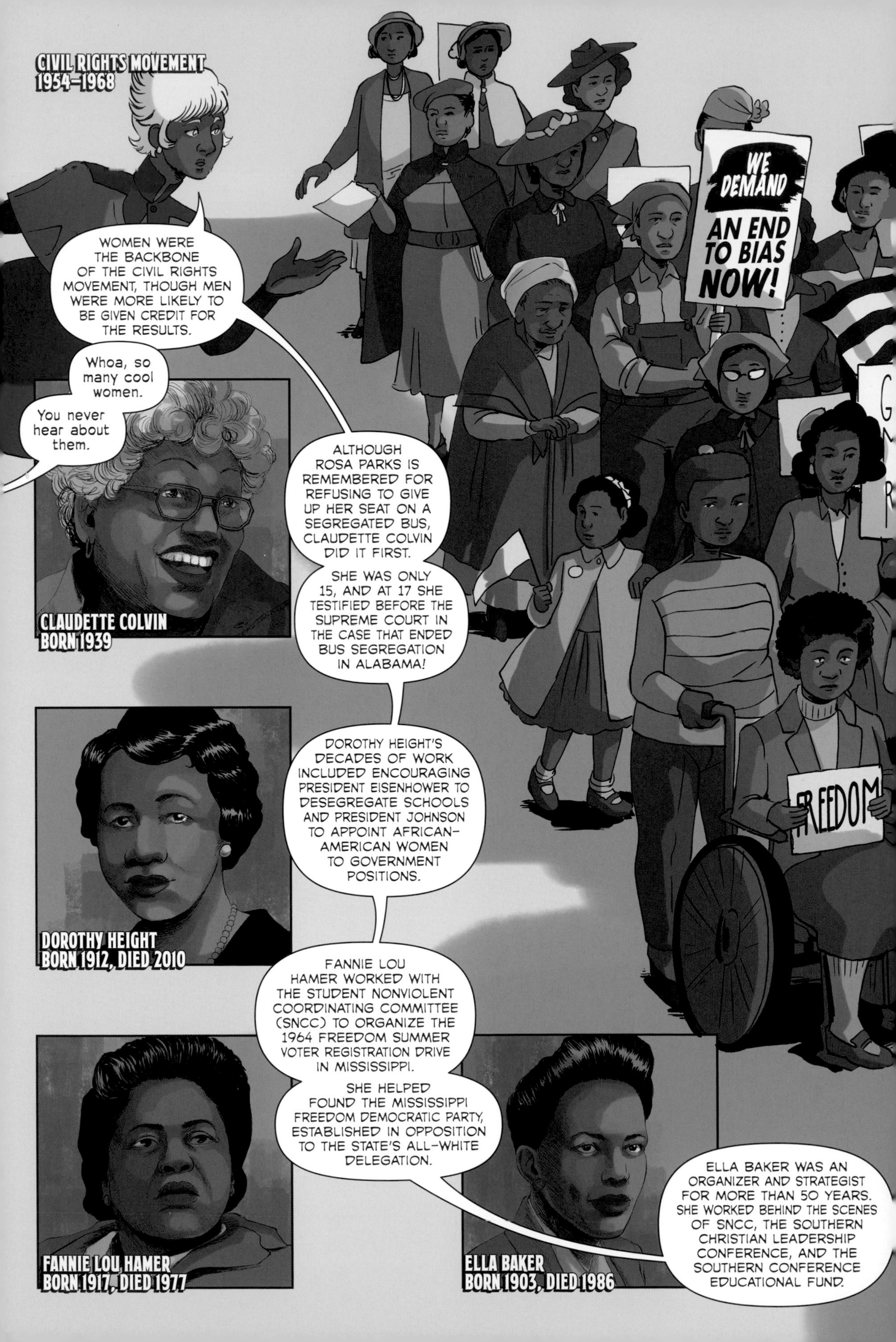
CIVIL RIGHTS MOVEMENT
1954–1968
WOMEN WERE THE BACKBONE OF THE CIVIL RIGHTS MOVEMENT, THOUGH MEN WERE MORE LIKELY TO BE GIVEN CREDIT FOR THE RESULTS.
Whoa, so many cool women.
You never hear about them.
WE DEMAND
AN END TO BIAS NOW!
CLAUDETTE COLVIN
BORN 1939
ALTHOUGH ROSA PARKS IS REMEMBERED FOR REFUSING TO GIVE UP HER SEAT ON A SEGREGATED BUS, CLAUDETTE COLVIN DID IT FIRST.
SHE WAS ONLY 15, AND AT 17 SHE TESTIFIED BEFORE THE SUPREME COURT IN THE CASE THAT ENDED BUS SEGREGATION IN ALABAMA!
DOROTHY HEIGHT
BORN 1912, DIED 2010
DOROTHY HEIGHT'S DECADES OF WORK INCLUDED ENCOURAGING PRESIDENT EISENHOWER TO DESEGREGATE SCHOOLS AND PRESIDENT JOHNSON TO APPOINT AFRICAN-AMERICAN WOMEN TO GOVERNMENT POSITIONS.
FREEDOM
FANNIE LOU HAMER WORKED WITH THE STUDENT NONVIOLENT COORDINATING COMMITTEE (SNCC) TO ORGANIZE THE 1964 FREEDOM SUMMER VOTER REGISTRATION DRIVE IN MISSISSIPPI.
SHE HELPED FOUND THE MISSISSIPPI FREEDOM DEMOCRATIC PARTY, ESTABLISHED IN OPPOSITION TO THE STATE'S ALL-WHITE DELEGATION.
FANNIE LOU HAMER
BORN 1917, DIED 1977
ELLA BAKER
BORN 1903, DIED 1986
ELLA BAKER WAS AN ORGANIZER AND STRATEGIST FOR MORE THAN 50 YEARS. SHE WORKED BEHIND THE SCENES OF SNCC, THE SOUTHERN CHRISTIAN LEADERSHIP CONFERENCE, AND THE SOUTHERN CONFERENCE EDUCATIONAL FUND.

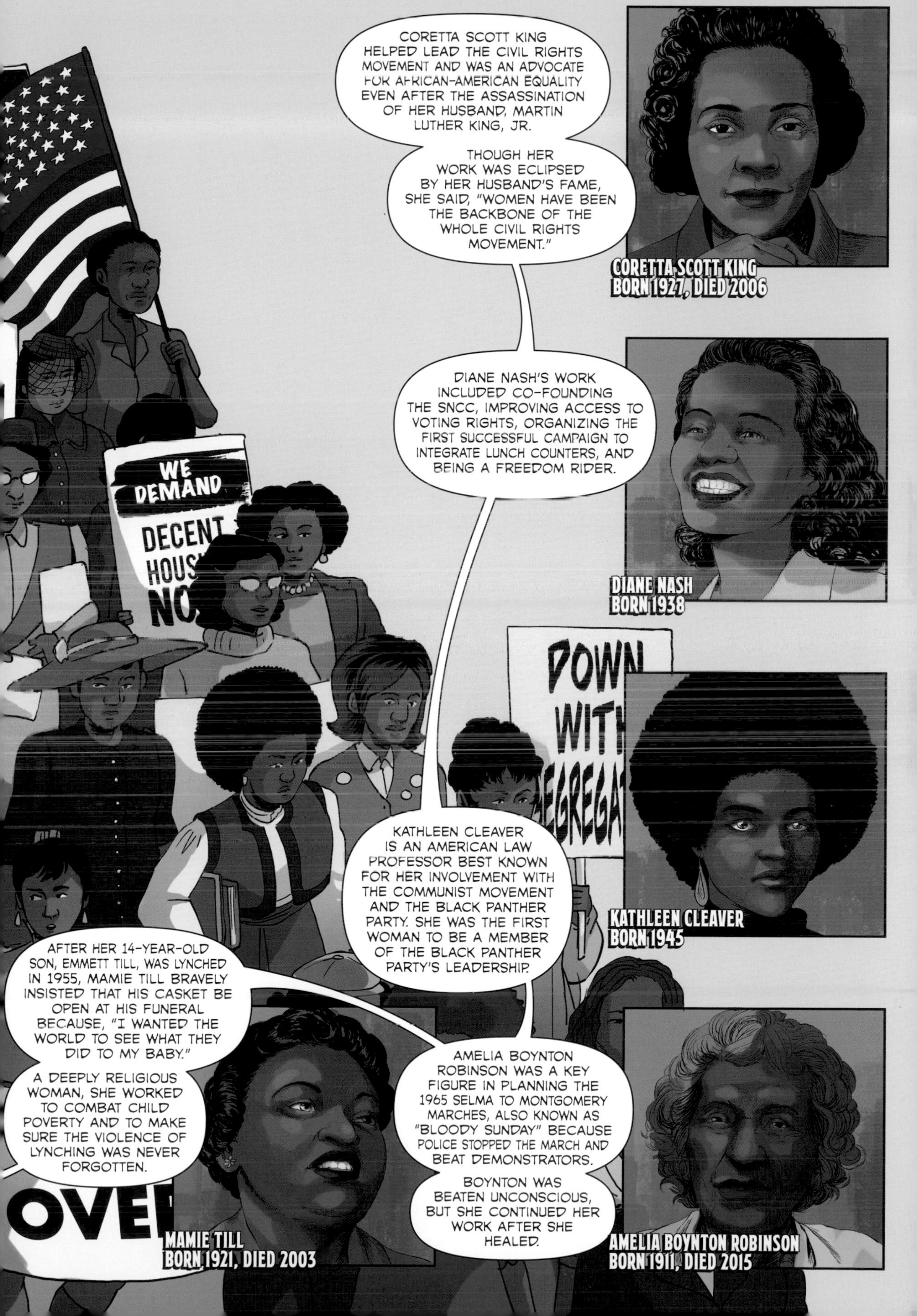
CORETTA SCOTT KING HELPED LEAD THE CIVIL RIGHTS MOVEMENT AND WAS AN ADVOCATE FOR AFRICAN-AMERICAN EQUALITY EVEN AFTER THE ASSASSINATION OF HER HUSBAND, MARTIN LUTHER KING, JR.
THOUGH HER WORK WAS ECLIPSED BY HER HUSBAND'S FAME, SHE SAID, "WOMEN HAVE BEEN THE BACKBONE OF THE WHOLE CIVIL RIGHTS MOVEMENT."
CORETTA SCOTT KING
BORN 1927, DIED 2006
WE DEMAND
DECENT HOUS
NO
DIANE NASH'S WORK INCLUDED CO-FOUNDING THE SNCC, IMPROVING ACCESS TO VOTING RIGHTS, ORGANIZING THE FIRST SUCCESSFUL CAMPAIGN TO INTEGRATE LUNCH COUNTERS, AND BEING A FREEDOM RIDER.
DIANE NASH
BORN 1938
DOWN WITH
KATHLEEN CLEAVER IS AN AMERICAN LAW PROFESSOR BEST KNOWN FOR HER INVOLVEMENT WITH THE COMMUNIST MOVEMENT AND THE BLACK PANTHER PARTY. SHE WAS THE FIRST WOMAN TO BE A MEMBER OF THE BLACK PANTHER PARTY'S LEADERSHIP.
KATHLEEN CLEAVER
BORN 1945
AFTER HER 14-YEAR-OLD SON, EMMETT TILL, WAS LYNCHED IN 1955, MAMIE TILL BRAVELY INSISTED THAT HIS CASKET BE OPEN AT HIS FUNERAL BECAUSE, "I WANTED THE WORLD TO SEE WHAT THEY DID TO MY BABY."
A DEEPLY RELIGIOUS WOMAN, SHE WORKED TO COMBAT CHILD POVERTY AND TO MAKE SURE THE VIOLENCE OF LYNCHING WAS NEVER FORGOTTEN.
OVE
MAMIE TILL
BORN 1921, DIED 2003
AMELIA BOYNTON ROBINSON WAS A KEY FIGURE IN PLANNING THE 1965 SELMA TO MONTGOMERY MARCHES, ALSO KNOWN AS "BLOODY SUNDAY" BECAUSE POLICE STOPPED THE MARCH AND BEAT DEMONSTRATORS.
BOYNTON WAS BEATEN UNCONSCIOUS, BUT SHE CONTINUED HER WORK AFTER SHE HEALED.
AMELIA BOYNTON ROBINSON
BORN 1911, DIED 2015

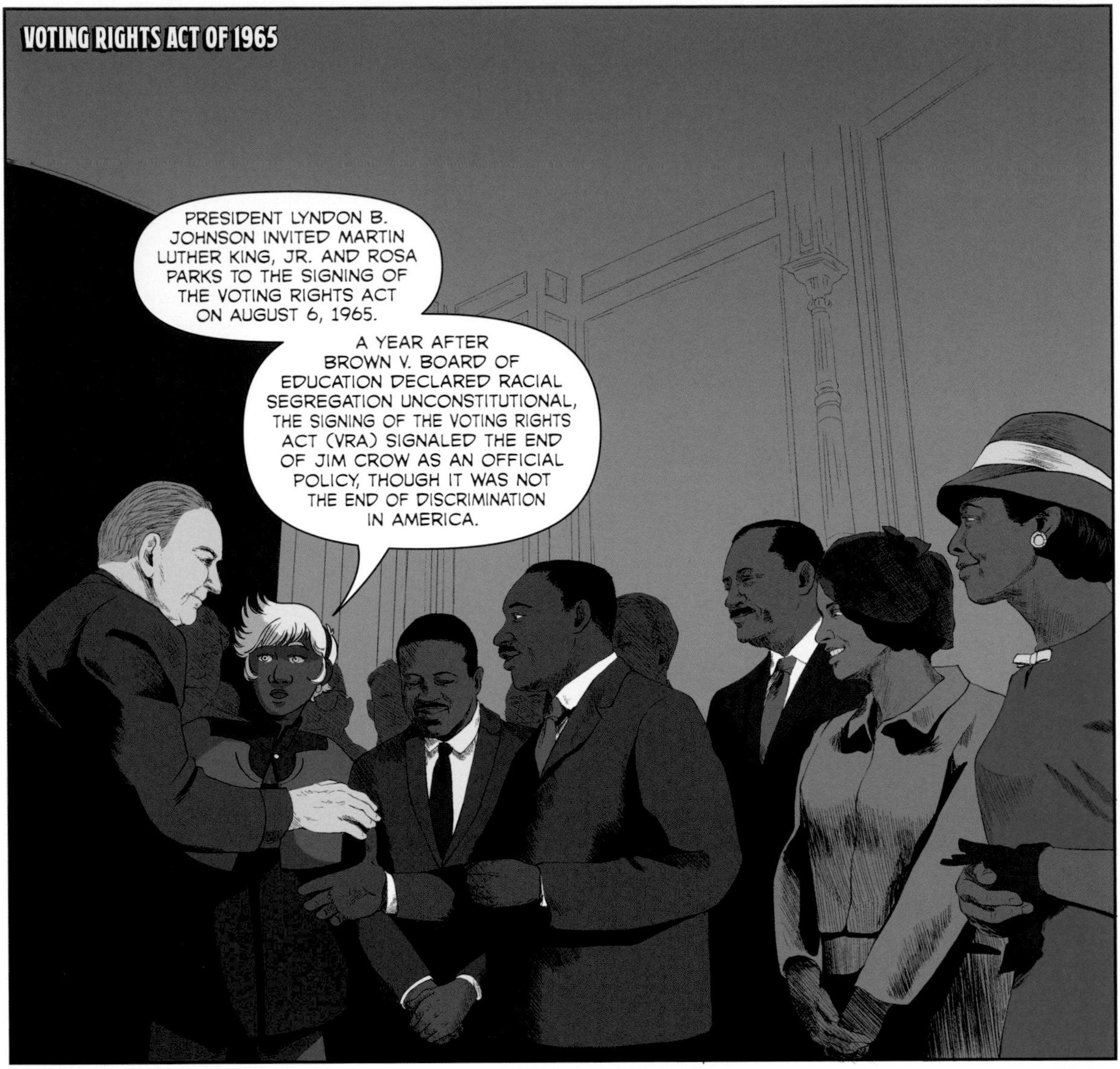
VOTING RIGHTS ACT OF 1965
PRESIDENT LYNDON B. JOHNSON INVITED MARTIN LUTHER KING, JR. AND ROSA PARKS TO THE SIGNING OF THE VOTING RIGHTS ACT ON AUGUST 6, 1965.
A YEAR AFTER BROWN V. BOARD OF EDUCATION DECLARED RACIAL SEGREGATION UNCONSTITUTIONAL, THE SIGNING OF THE VOTING RIGHTS ACT (VRA) SIGNALED THE END OF JIM CROW AS AN OFFICIAL POLICY, THOUGH IT WAS NOT THE END OF DISCRIMINATION IN AMERICA.

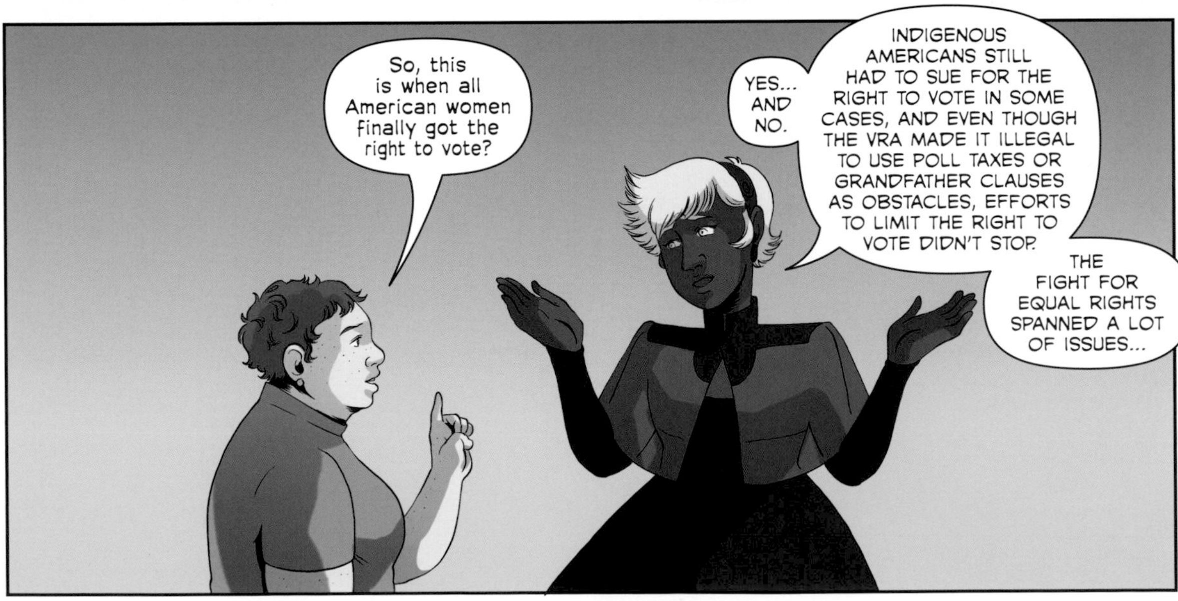
So, this is when all American women finally got the right to vote?
YES... AND NO.
INDIGENOUS AMERICANS STILL HAD TO SUE FOR THE RIGHT TO VOTE IN SOME CASES, AND EVEN THOUGH THE VRA MADE IT ILLEGAL TO USE POLL TAXES OR GRANDFATHER CLAUSES AS OBSTACLES, EFFORTS TO LIMIT THE RIGHT TO VOTE DIDN'T STOP.
THE FIGHT FOR EQUAL RIGHTS SPANNED A LOT OF ISSUES...

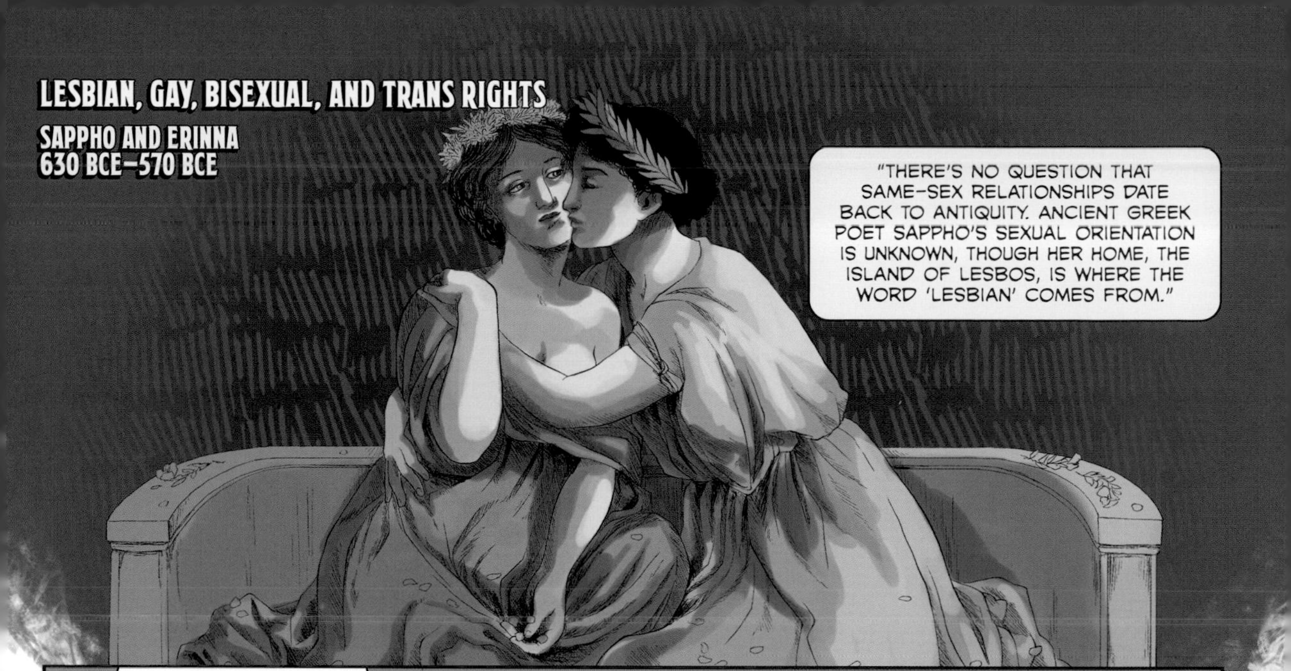
LESBIAN, GAY, BISEXUAL, AND TRANS RIGHTS
SAPPHO AND ERINNA
630 BCE–570 BCE
"THERE'S NO QUESTION THAT SAME-SEX RELATIONSHIPS DATE BACK TO ANTIQUITY. ANCIENT GREEK POET SAPPHO'S SEXUAL ORIENTATION IS UNKNOWN, THOUGH HER HOME, THE ISLAND OF LESBOS, IS WHERE THE WORD 'LESBIAN' COMES FROM."

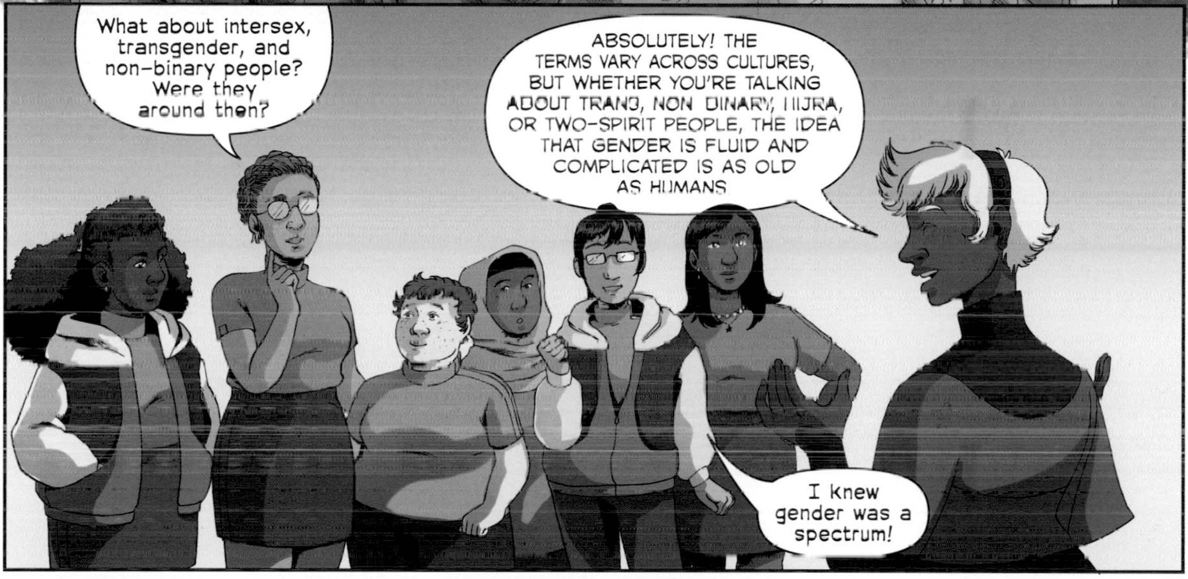
What about intersex, transgender, and non-binary people? Were they around then?
ABSOLUTELY! THE TERMS VARY ACROSS CULTURES, BUT WHETHER YOU'RE TALKING ABOUT TRANS, NON-BINARY, HIJRA, OR TWO-SPIRIT PEOPLE, THE IDEA THAT GENDER IS FLUID AND COMPLICATED IS AS OLD AS HUMANS.
I knew gender was a spectrum!

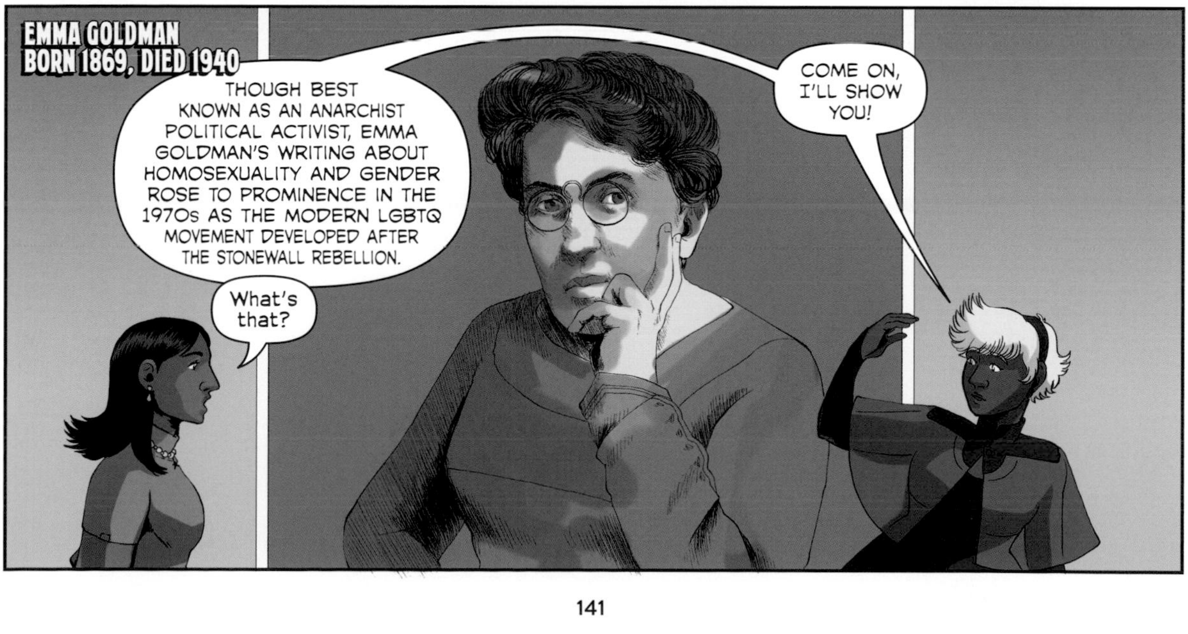
EMMA GOLDMAN
BORN 1869, DIED 1940
THOUGH BEST KNOWN AS AN ANARCHIST POLITICAL ACTIVIST, EMMA GOLDMAN'S WRITING ABOUT HOMOSEXUALITY AND GENDER ROSE TO PROMINENCE IN THE 1970s AS THE MODERN LGBTQ MOVEMENT DEVELOPED AFTER THE STONEWALL REBELLION.
COME ON, I'LL SHOW YOU!
What's that?

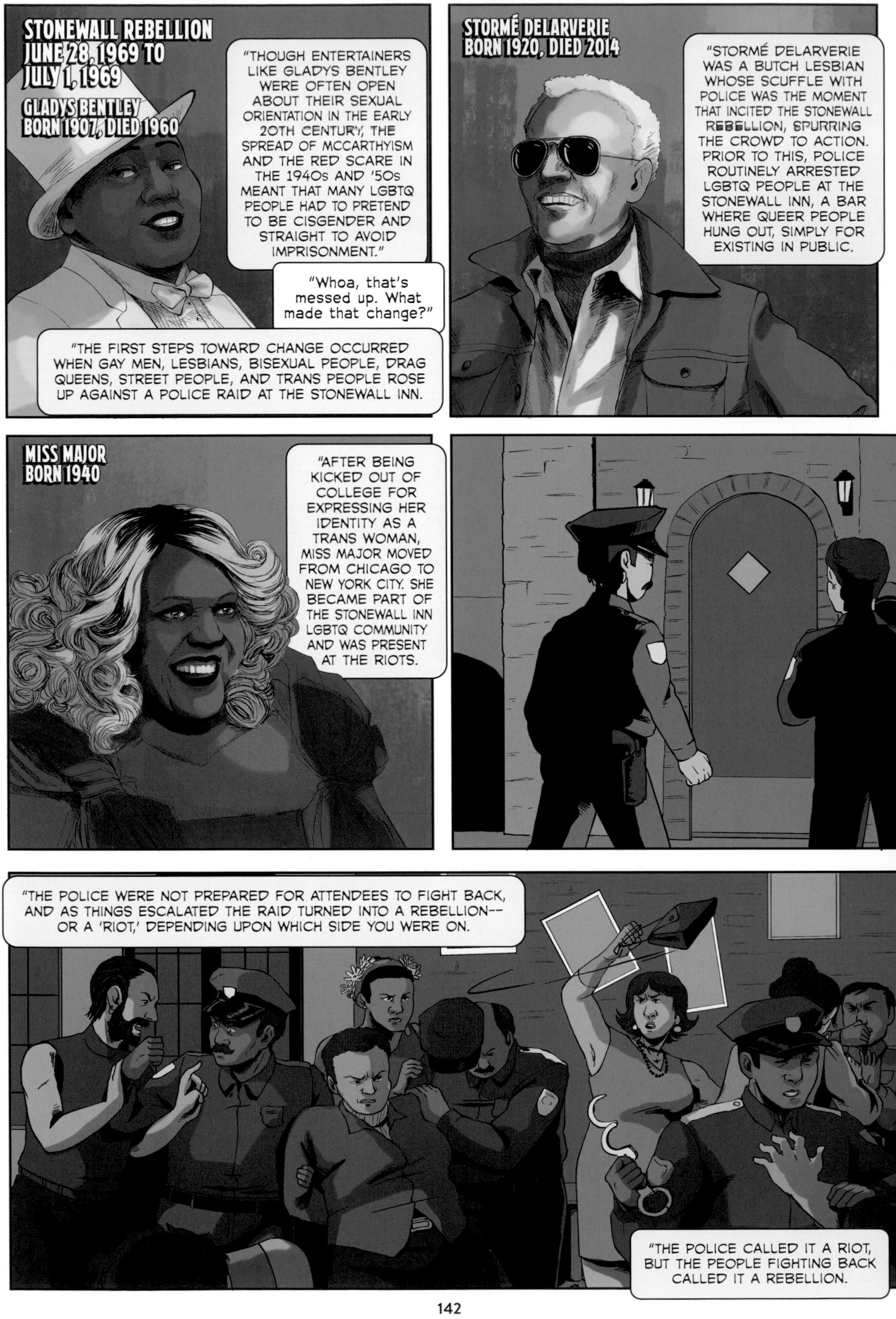
STONEWALL REBELLION JUNE 28, 1969 TO JULY 1, 1969
GLADYS BENTLEY BORN 1907, DIED 1960
"THOUGH ENTERTAINERS LIKE GLADYS BENTLEY WERE OFTEN OPEN ABOUT THEIR SEXUAL ORIENTATION IN THE EARLY 20TH CENTURY, THE SPREAD OF MCCARTHYISM AND THE RED SCARE IN THE 1940s AND '50s MEANT THAT MANY LGBTQ PEOPLE HAD TO PRETEND TO BE CISGENDER AND STRAIGHT TO AVOID IMPRISONMENT."
"Whoa, that's messed up. What made that change?"
"THE FIRST STEPS TOWARD CHANGE OCCURRED WHEN GAY MEN, LESBIANS, BISEXUAL PEOPLE, DRAG QUEENS, STREET PEOPLE, AND TRANS PEOPLE ROSE UP AGAINST A POLICE RAID AT THE STONEWALL INN.
STORMÉ DELARVERIE BORN 1920, DIED 2014
"STORMÉ DELARVERIE WAS A BUTCH LESBIAN WHOSE SCUFFLE WITH POLICE WAS THE MOMENT THAT INCITED THE STONEWALL REBELLION, SPURRING THE CROWD TO ACTION. PRIOR TO THIS, POLICE ROUTINELY ARRESTED LGBTQ PEOPLE AT THE STONEWALL INN, A BAR WHERE QUEER PEOPLE HUNG OUT, SIMPLY FOR EXISTING IN PUBLIC.
MISS MAJOR BORN 1940
"AFTER BEING KICKED OUT OF COLLEGE FOR EXPRESSING HER IDENTITY AS A TRANS WOMAN, MISS MAJOR MOVED FROM CHICAGO TO NEW YORK CITY. SHE BECAME PART OF THE STONEWALL INN LGBTQ COMMUNITY AND WAS PRESENT AT THE RIOTS.
"THE POLICE WERE NOT PREPARED FOR ATTENDEES TO FIGHT BACK, AND AS THINGS ESCALATED THE RAID TURNED INTO A REBELLION-- OR A 'RIOT,' DEPENDING UPON WHICH SIDE YOU WERE ON.
"THE POLICE CALLED IT A RIOT, BUT THE PEOPLE FIGHTING BACK CALLED IT A REBELLION.

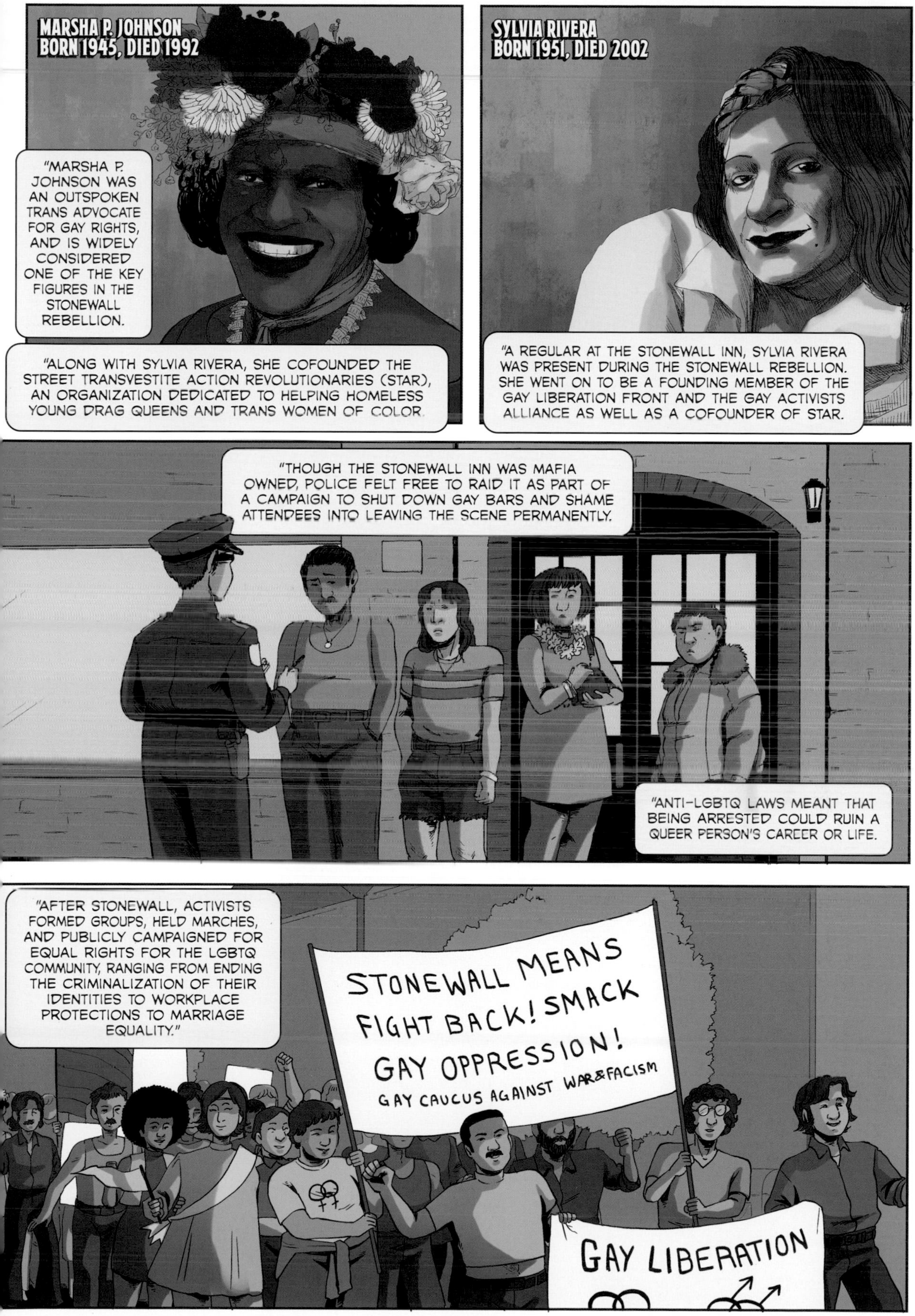
MARSHA P. JOHNSON
BORN 1945, DIED 1992
"MARSHA P. JOHNSON WAS AN OUTSPOKEN TRANS ADVOCATE FOR GAY RIGHTS, AND IS WIDELY CONSIDERED ONE OF THE KEY FIGURES IN THE STONEWALL REBELLION.
"ALONG WITH SYLVIA RIVERA, SHE COFOUNDED THE STREET TRANSVESTITE ACTION REVOLUTIONARIES (STAR), AN ORGANIZATION DEDICATED TO HELPING HOMELESS YOUNG DRAG QUEENS AND TRANS WOMEN OF COLOR.
SYLVIA RIVERA
BORN 1951, DIED 2002
"A REGULAR AT THE STONEWALL INN, SYLVIA RIVERA WAS PRESENT DURING THE STONEWALL REBELLION. SHE WENT ON TO BE A FOUNDING MEMBER OF THE GAY LIBERATION FRONT AND THE GAY ACTIVISTS ALLIANCE AS WELL AS A COFOUNDER OF STAR.
"THOUGH THE STONEWALL INN WAS MAFIA OWNED, POLICE FELT FREE TO RAID IT AS PART OF A CAMPAIGN TO SHUT DOWN GAY BARS AND SHAME ATTENDEES INTO LEAVING THE SCENE PERMANENTLY.
"ANTI-LGBTQ LAWS MEANT THAT BEING ARRESTED COULD RUIN A QUEER PERSON'S CAREER OR LIFE.
"AFTER STONEWALL, ACTIVISTS FORMED GROUPS, HELD MARCHES, AND PUBLICLY CAMPAIGNED FOR EQUAL RIGHTS FOR THE LGBTQ COMMUNITY, RANGING FROM ENDING THE CRIMINALIZATION OF THEIR IDENTITIES TO WORKPLACE PROTECTIONS TO MARRIAGE EQUALITY."
STONEWALL MEANS FIGHT BACK! SMACK GAY OPPRESSION!
GAY CAUCUS AGAINST WAR&FACISM
GAY LIBERATION

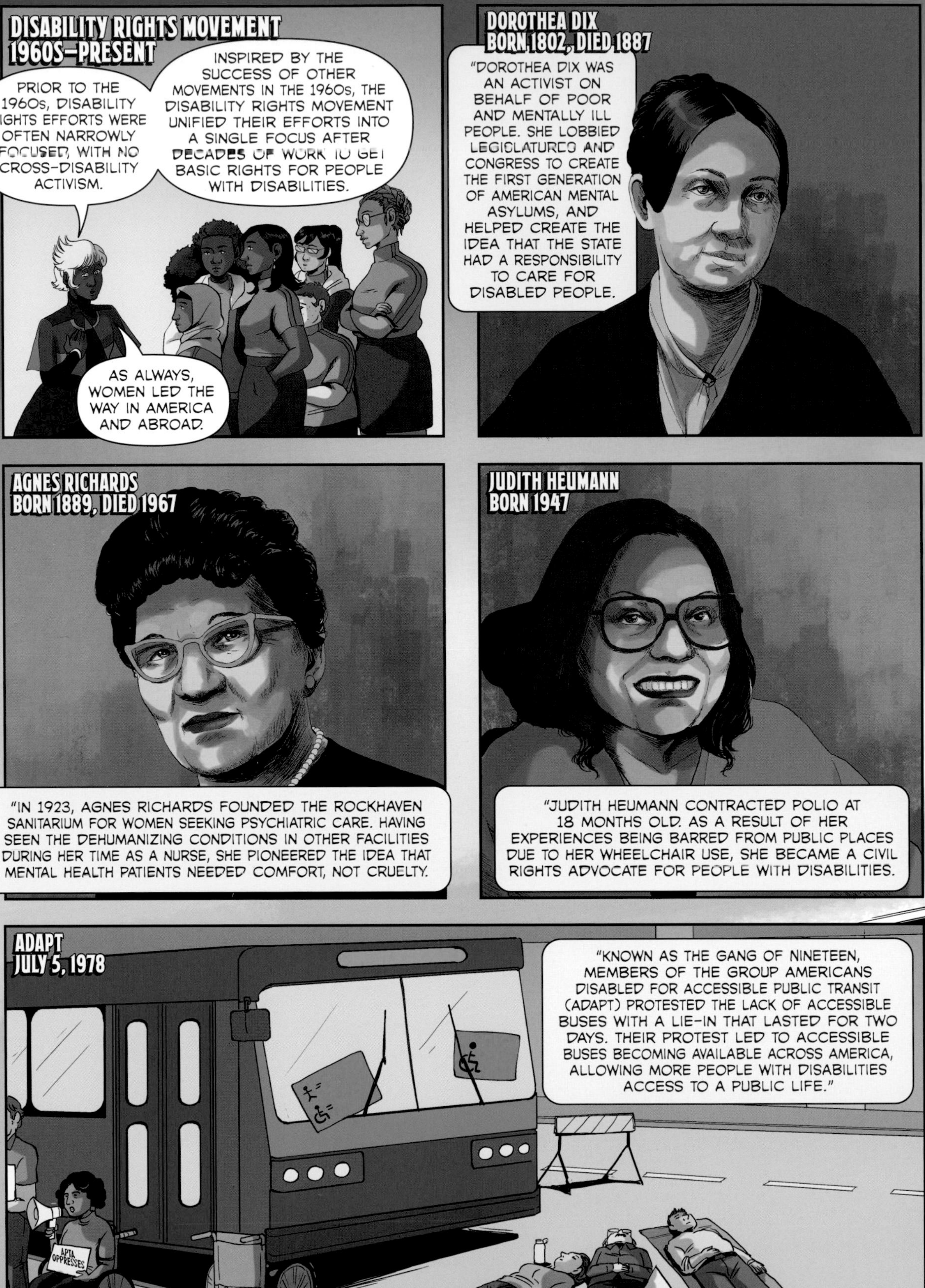
DISABILITY RIGHTS MOVEMENT
1960S–PRESENT
PRIOR TO THE 1960s, DISABILITY RIGHTS EFFORTS WERE OFTEN NARROWLY FOCUSED, WITH NO CROSS-DISABILITY ACTIVISM.
INSPIRED BY THE SUCCESS OF OTHER MOVEMENTS IN THE 1960s, THE DISABILITY RIGHTS MOVEMENT UNIFIED THEIR EFFORTS INTO A SINGLE FOCUS AFTER DECADES OF WORK TO GET BASIC RIGHTS FOR PEOPLE WITH DISABILITIES.
AS ALWAYS, WOMEN LED THE WAY IN AMERICA AND ABROAD.
DOROTHEA DIX
BORN 1802, DIED 1887
"DOROTHEA DIX WAS AN ACTIVIST ON BEHALF OF POOR AND MENTALLY ILL PEOPLE. SHE LOBBIED LEGISLATURES AND CONGRESS TO CREATE THE FIRST GENERATION OF AMERICAN MENTAL ASYLUMS, AND HELPED CREATE THE IDEA THAT THE STATE HAD A RESPONSIBILITY TO CARE FOR DISABLED PEOPLE.
AGNES RICHARDS
BORN 1889, DIED 1967
"IN 1923, AGNES RICHARDS FOUNDED THE ROCKHAVEN SANITARIUM FOR WOMEN SEEKING PSYCHIATRIC CARE. HAVING SEEN THE DEHUMANIZING CONDITIONS IN OTHER FACILITIES DURING HER TIME AS A NURSE, SHE PIONEERED THE IDEA THAT MENTAL HEALTH PATIENTS NEEDED COMFORT, NOT CRUELTY.
JUDITH HEUMANN
BORN 1947
"JUDITH HEUMANN CONTRACTED POLIO AT 18 MONTHS OLD. AS A RESULT OF HER EXPERIENCES BEING BARRED FROM PUBLIC PLACES DUE TO HER WHEELCHAIR USE, SHE BECAME A CIVIL RIGHTS ADVOCATE FOR PEOPLE WITH DISABILITIES.
ADAPT
JULY 5, 1978
"KNOWN AS THE GANG OF NINETEEN, MEMBERS OF THE GROUP AMERICANS DISABLED FOR ACCESSIBLE PUBLIC TRANSIT (ADAPT) PROTESTED THE LACK OF ACCESSIBLE BUSES WITH A LIE-IN THAT LASTED FOR TWO DAYS. THEIR PROTEST LED TO ACCESSIBLE BUSES BECOMING AVAILABLE ACROSS AMERICA, ALLOWING MORE PEOPLE WITH DISABILITIES ACCESS TO A PUBLIC LIFE."
APTA OPPRESSES

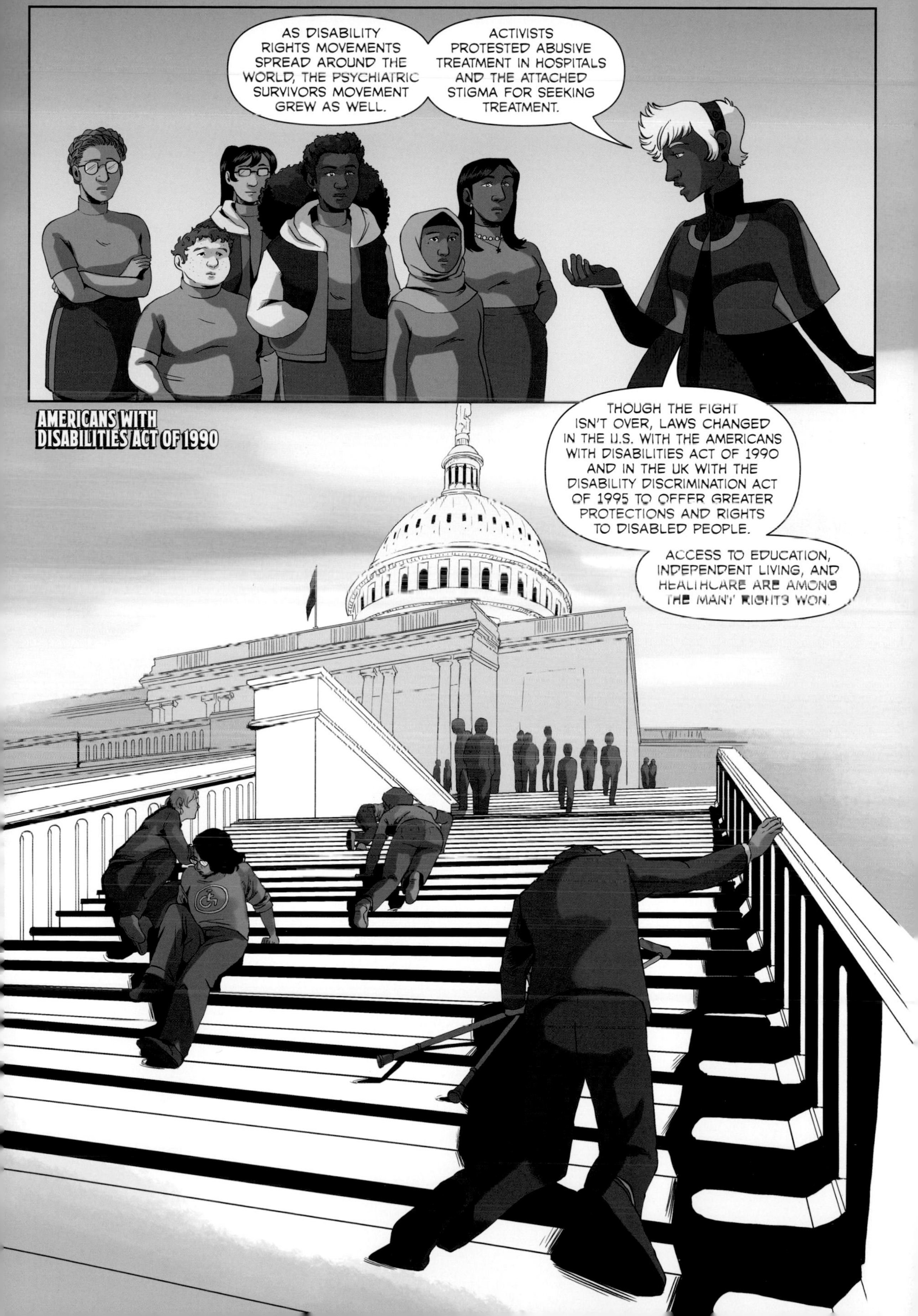
AS DISABILITY RIGHTS MOVEMENTS SPREAD AROUND THE WORLD, THE PSYCHIATRIC SURVIVORS MOVEMENT GREW AS WELL.
ACTIVISTS PROTESTED ABUSIVE TREATMENT IN HOSPITALS AND THE ATTACHED STIGMA FOR SEEKING TREATMENT.
AMERICANS WITH DISABILITIES ACT OF 1990
THOUGH THE FIGHT ISN'T OVER, LAWS CHANGED IN THE U.S. WITH THE AMERICANS WITH DISABILITIES ACT OF 1990 AND IN THE UK WITH THE DISABILITY DISCRIMINATION ACT OF 1995 TO OFFER GREATER PROTECTIONS AND RIGHTS TO DISABLED PEOPLE.
ACCESS TO EDUCATION, INDEPENDENT LIVING, AND HEALTHCARE ARE AMONG THE MANY RIGHTS WON.

CHAPTER 6
WOMEN'S RIGHTS, 1960s TO 1980s: FROM THE SEXUAL REVOLUTION TO THE AIDS CRISIS

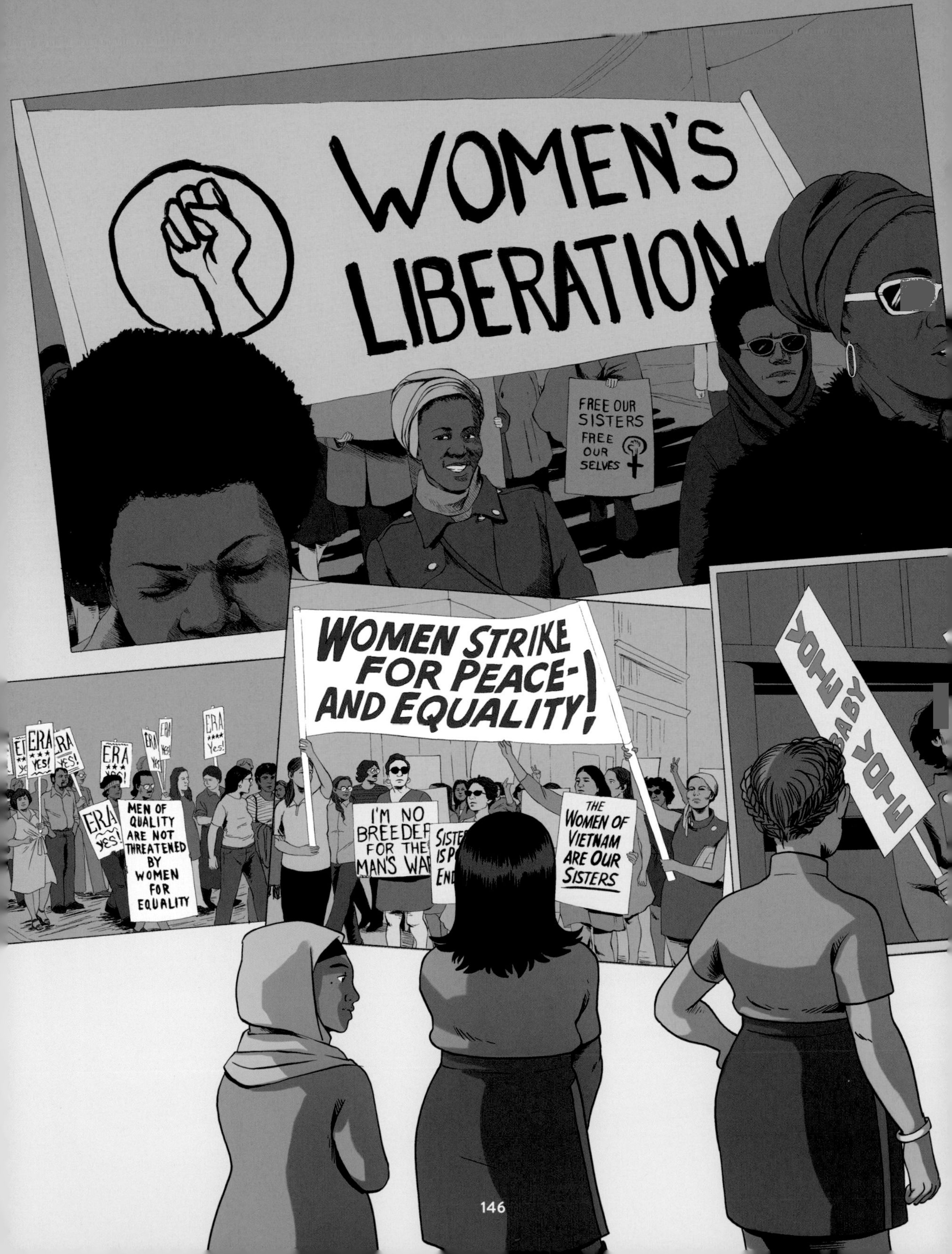
WOMEN'S LIBERATION
FREE OUR SISTERS FREE OUR SELVES
WOMEN STRIKE FOR PEACE- AND EQUALITY!
ERA YES!
ERA ★★★ Yes!
MEN OF QUALITY ARE NOT THREATENED BY WOMEN FOR EQUALITY
I'M NO BREEDE FOR THE MAN'S WA
THE WOMEN OF VIETNAM ARE OUR SISTERS

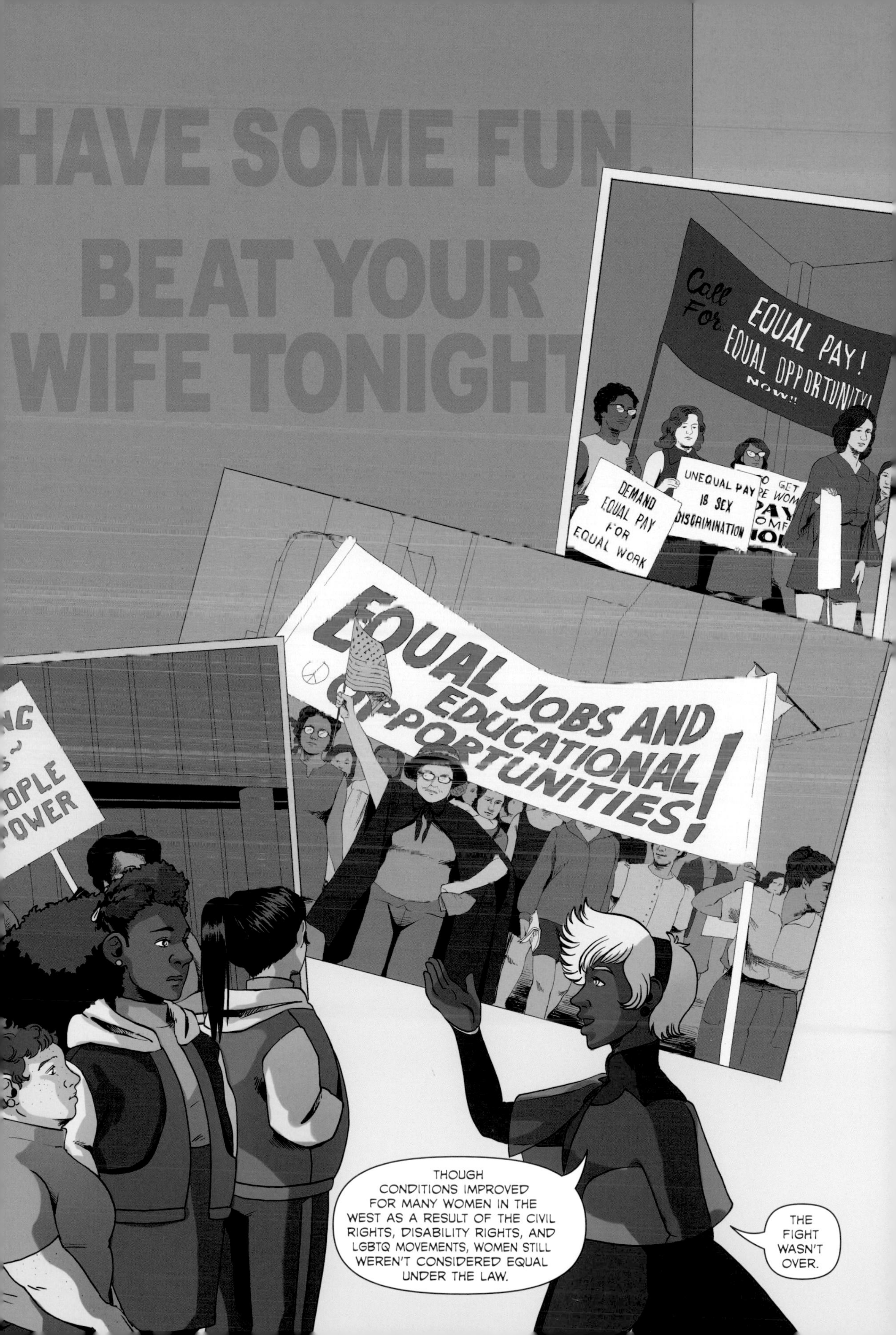

HAVE SOME FUN. BEAT YOUR WIFE TONIGHT
Call For... EQUAL PAY! EQUAL OPPORTUNITY! NOW!!
DEMAND EQUAL PAY FOR EQUAL WORK
UNEQUAL PAY IS SEX DISCRIMINATION
EQUAL JOBS AND EDUCATIONAL OPPORTUNITIES!
THOUGH CONDITIONS IMPROVED FOR MANY WOMEN IN THE WEST AS A RESULT OF THE CIVIL RIGHTS, DISABILITY RIGHTS, AND LGBTQ MOVEMENTS, WOMEN STILL WEREN'T CONSIDERED EQUAL UNDER THE LAW.
THE FIGHT WASN'T OVER.

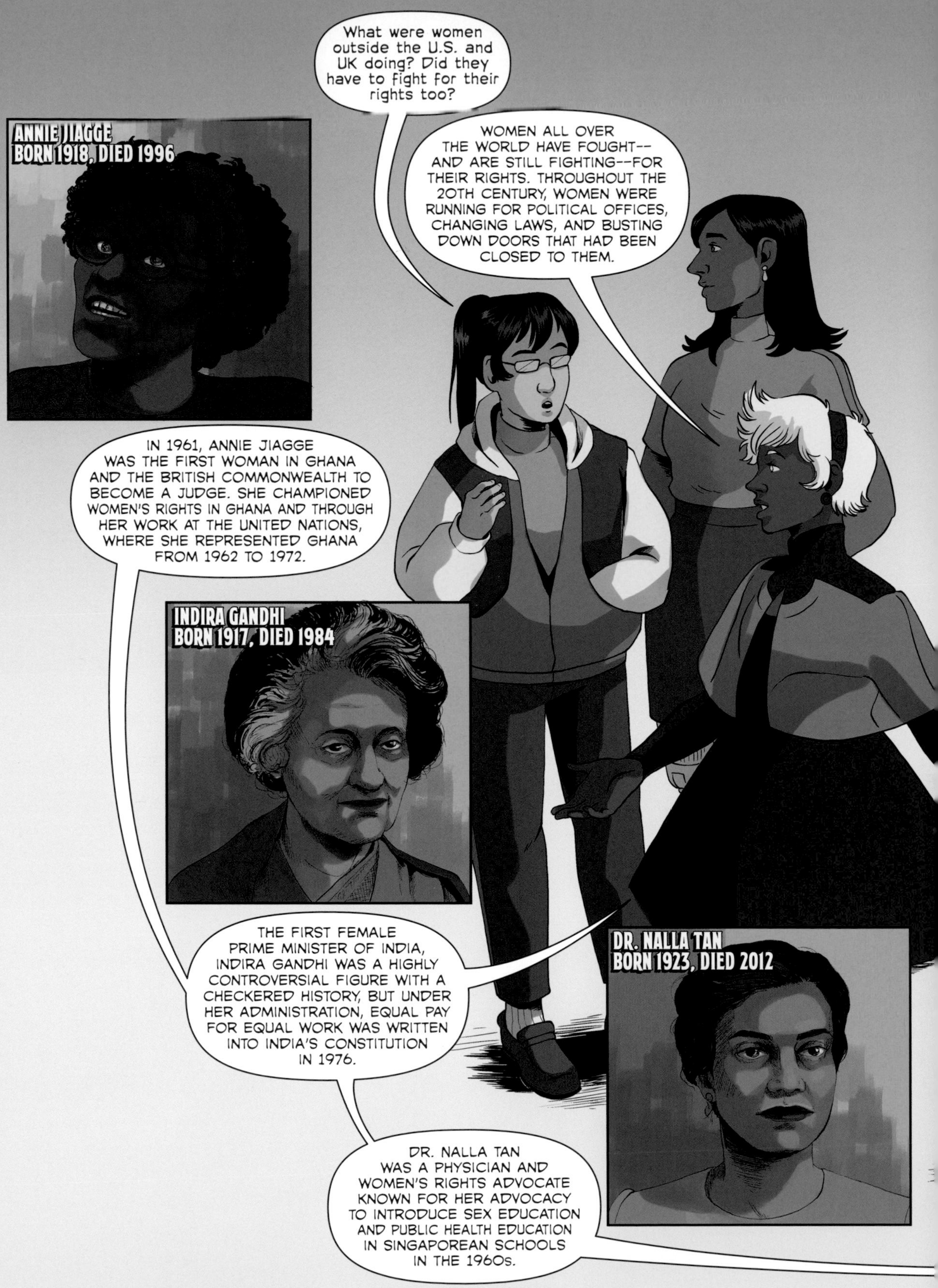
What were women outside the U.S. and UK doing? Did they have to fight for their rights too?
WOMEN ALL OVER THE WORLD HAVE FOUGHT--AND ARE STILL FIGHTING--FOR THEIR RIGHTS. THROUGHOUT THE 20TH CENTURY, WOMEN WERE RUNNING FOR POLITICAL OFFICES, CHANGING LAWS, AND BUSTING DOWN DOORS THAT HAD BEEN CLOSED TO THEM.
ANNIE JIAGGE BORN 1918, DIED 1996
IN 1961, ANNIE JIAGGE WAS THE FIRST WOMAN IN GHANA AND THE BRITISH COMMONWEALTH TO BECOME A JUDGE. SHE CHAMPIONED WOMEN'S RIGHTS IN GHANA AND THROUGH HER WORK AT THE UNITED NATIONS, WHERE SHE REPRESENTED GHANA FROM 1962 TO 1972.
INDIRA GANDHI BORN 1917, DIED 1984
THE FIRST FEMALE PRIME MINISTER OF INDIA, INDIRA GANDHI WAS A HIGHLY CONTROVERSIAL FIGURE WITH A CHECKERED HISTORY, BUT UNDER HER ADMINISTRATION, EQUAL PAY FOR EQUAL WORK WAS WRITTEN INTO INDIA'S CONSTITUTION IN 1976.
DR. NALLA TAN BORN 1923, DIED 2012
DR. NALLA TAN WAS A PHYSICIAN AND WOMEN'S RIGHTS ADVOCATE KNOWN FOR HER ADVOCACY TO INTRODUCE SEX EDUCATION AND PUBLIC HEALTH EDUCATION IN SINGAPOREAN SCHOOLS IN THE 1960s.

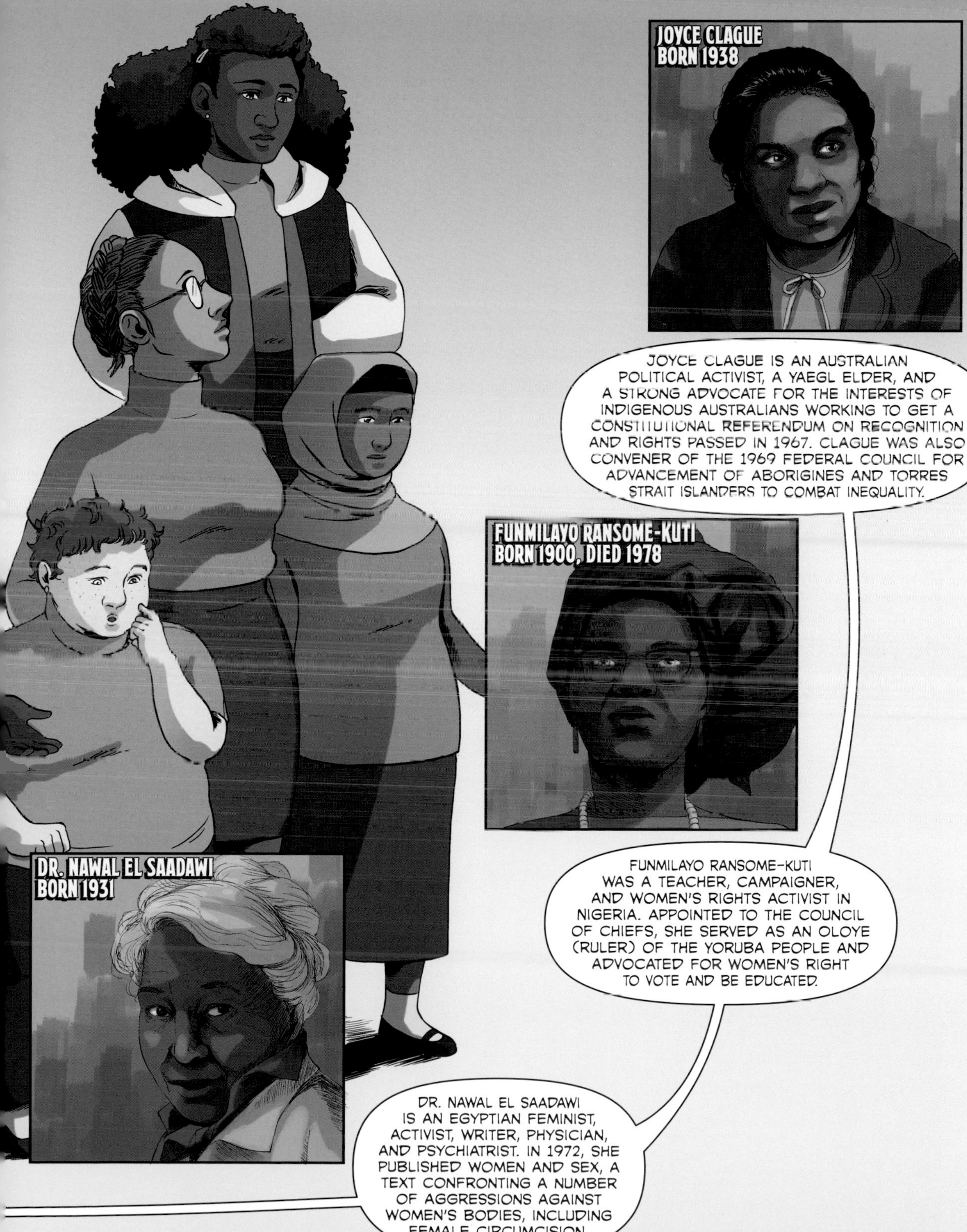
JOYCE CLAGUE
BORN 1938
JOYCE CLAGUE IS AN AUSTRALIAN POLITICAL ACTIVIST, A YAEGL ELDER, AND A STRONG ADVOCATE FOR THE INTERESTS OF INDIGENOUS AUSTRALIANS WORKING TO GET A CONSTITUTIONAL REFERENDUM ON RECOGNITION AND RIGHTS PASSED IN 1967. CLAGUE WAS ALSO CONVENER OF THE 1969 FEDERAL COUNCIL FOR ADVANCEMENT OF ABORIGINES AND TORRES STRAIT ISLANDERS TO COMBAT INEQUALITY.
FUNMILAYO RANSOME-KUTI
BORN 1900, DIED 1978
FUNMILAYO RANSOME-KUTI WAS A TEACHER, CAMPAIGNER, AND WOMEN'S RIGHTS ACTIVIST IN NIGERIA. APPOINTED TO THE COUNCIL OF CHIEFS, SHE SERVED AS AN OLOYE (RULER) OF THE YORUBA PEOPLE AND ADVOCATED FOR WOMEN'S RIGHT TO VOTE AND BE EDUCATED.
DR. NAWAL EL SAADAWI
BORN 1931
DR. NAWAL EL SAADAWI IS AN EGYPTIAN FEMINIST, ACTIVIST, WRITER, PHYSICIAN, AND PSYCHIATRIST. IN 1972, SHE PUBLISHED WOMEN AND SEX, A TEXT CONFRONTING A NUMBER OF AGGRESSIONS AGAINST WOMEN'S BODIES, INCLUDING FEMALE CIRCUMCISION.

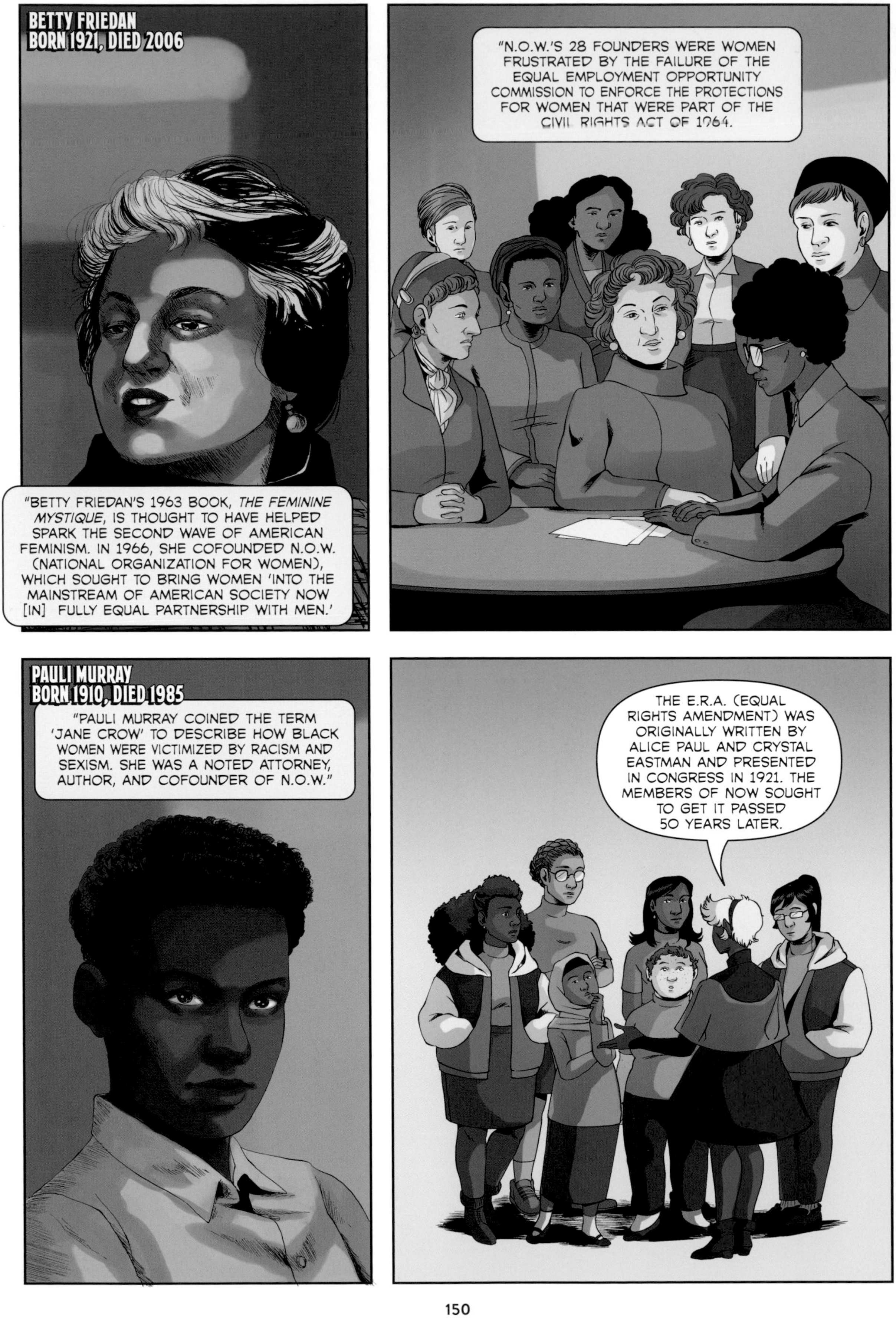
BETTY FRIEDAN
BORN 1921, DIED 2006
"BETTY FRIEDAN'S 1963 BOOK, *THE FEMININE MYSTIQUE*, IS THOUGHT TO HAVE HELPED SPARK THE SECOND WAVE OF AMERICAN FEMINISM. IN 1966, SHE COFOUNDED N.O.W. (NATIONAL ORGANIZATION FOR WOMEN), WHICH SOUGHT TO BRING WOMEN 'INTO THE MAINSTREAM OF AMERICAN SOCIETY NOW [IN] FULLY EQUAL PARTNERSHIP WITH MEN.'
"N.O.W.'S 28 FOUNDERS WERE WOMEN FRUSTRATED BY THE FAILURE OF THE EQUAL EMPLOYMENT OPPORTUNITY COMMISSION TO ENFORCE THE PROTECTIONS FOR WOMEN THAT WERE PART OF THE CIVIL RIGHTS ACT OF 1964.
PAULI MURRAY
BORN 1910, DIED 1985
"PAULI MURRAY COINED THE TERM 'JANE CROW' TO DESCRIBE HOW BLACK WOMEN WERE VICTIMIZED BY RACISM AND SEXISM. SHE WAS A NOTED ATTORNEY, AUTHOR, AND COFOUNDER OF N.O.W."
THE E.R.A. (EQUAL RIGHTS AMENDMENT) WAS ORIGINALLY WRITTEN BY ALICE PAUL AND CRYSTAL EASTMAN AND PRESENTED IN CONGRESS IN 1921. THE MEMBERS OF NOW SOUGHT TO GET IT PASSED 50 YEARS LATER.

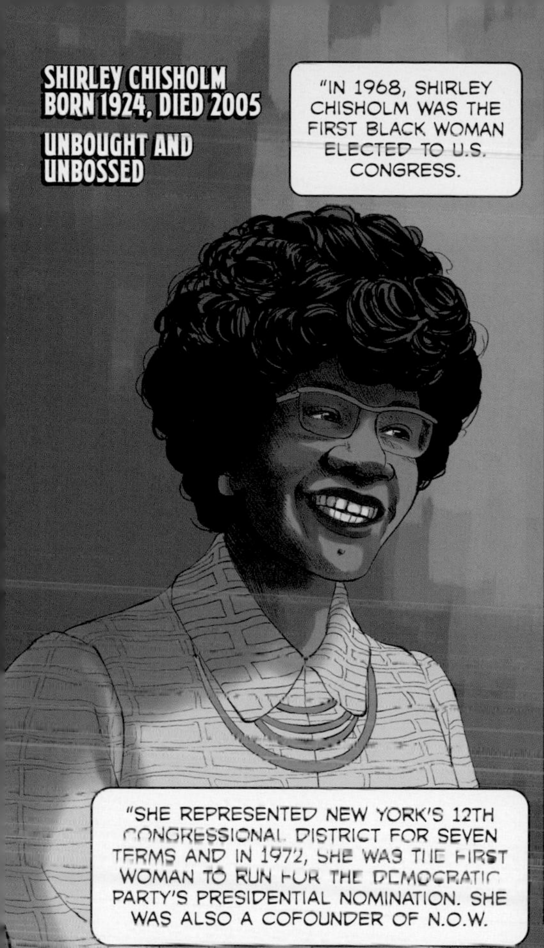
SHIRLEY CHISHOLM
BORN 1924, DIED 2005
UNBOUGHT AND UNBOSSED
"IN 1968, SHIRLEY CHISHOLM WAS THE FIRST BLACK WOMAN ELECTED TO U.S. CONGRESS.
"SHE REPRESENTED NEW YORK'S 12TH CONGRESSIONAL DISTRICT FOR SEVEN TERMS AND IN 1972, SHE WAS THE FIRST WOMAN TO RUN FOR THE DEMOCRATIC PARTY'S PRESIDENTIAL NOMINATION. SHE WAS ALSO A COFOUNDER OF N.O.W.

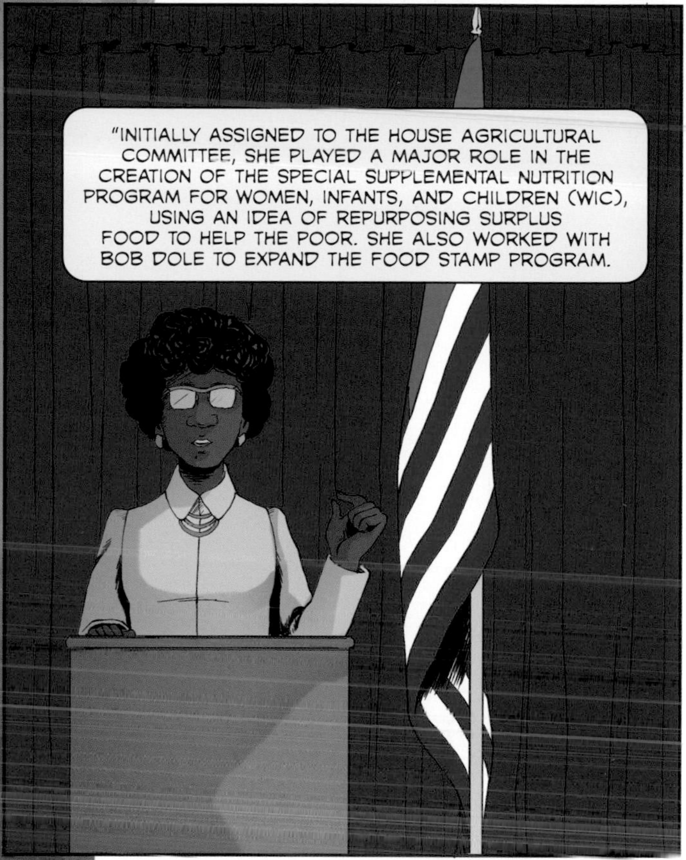
"INITIALLY ASSIGNED TO THE HOUSE AGRICULTURAL COMMITTEE, SHE PLAYED A MAJOR ROLE IN THE CREATION OF THE SPECIAL SUPPLEMENTAL NUTRITION PROGRAM FOR WOMEN, INFANTS, AND CHILDREN (WIC), USING AN IDEA OF REPURPOSING SURPLUS FOOD TO HELP THE POOR. SHE ALSO WORKED WITH BOB DOLE TO EXPAND THE FOOD STAMP PROGRAM.

"Discrimination against women, solely on the basis of their sex, is so widespread that it seems to many persons normal, natural, and right. Legal expression of prejudice on the grounds of religious or political belief has become a minor problem in our society. Prejudice on the basis of race is, at least, under systematic attack. There is reason for optimism that it will start to die with the present older generation. It is time we act to assure full equality of opportunity to those citizens who, although in a majority, suffer the restrictions that are commonly imposed on minorities, to women."

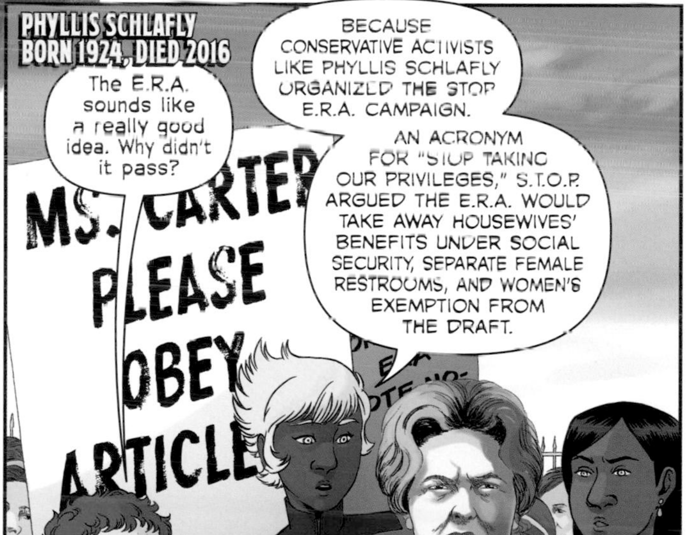
PHYLLIS SCHLAFLY
BORN 1924, DIED 2016
The E.R.A. sounds like a really good idea. Why didn't it pass?
BECAUSE CONSERVATIVE ACTIVISTS LIKE PHYLLIS SCHLAFLY ORGANIZED THE STOP E.R.A. CAMPAIGN.
AN ACRONYM FOR "STOP TAKING OUR PRIVILEGES," S.T.O.P. ARGUED THE E.R.A. WOULD TAKE AWAY HOUSEWIVES' BENEFITS UNDER SOCIAL SECURITY, SEPARATE FEMALE RESTROOMS, AND WOMEN'S EXEMPTION FROM THE DRAFT.
MS. CARTER PLEASE OBEY ARTICLE
NONE OF THAT WAS TRUE, BUT SHE KNEW IT WOULD SWAY PEOPLE TO VOTE AGAINST THE E.R.A.
STOP ERA
That's atrocious. Thanks for nothin', Phyllis.

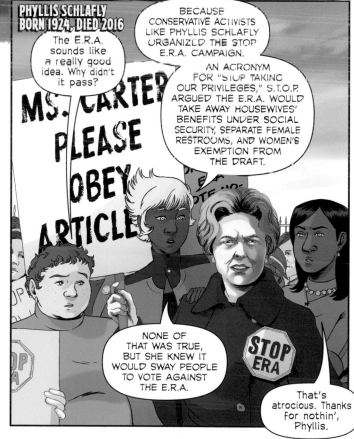

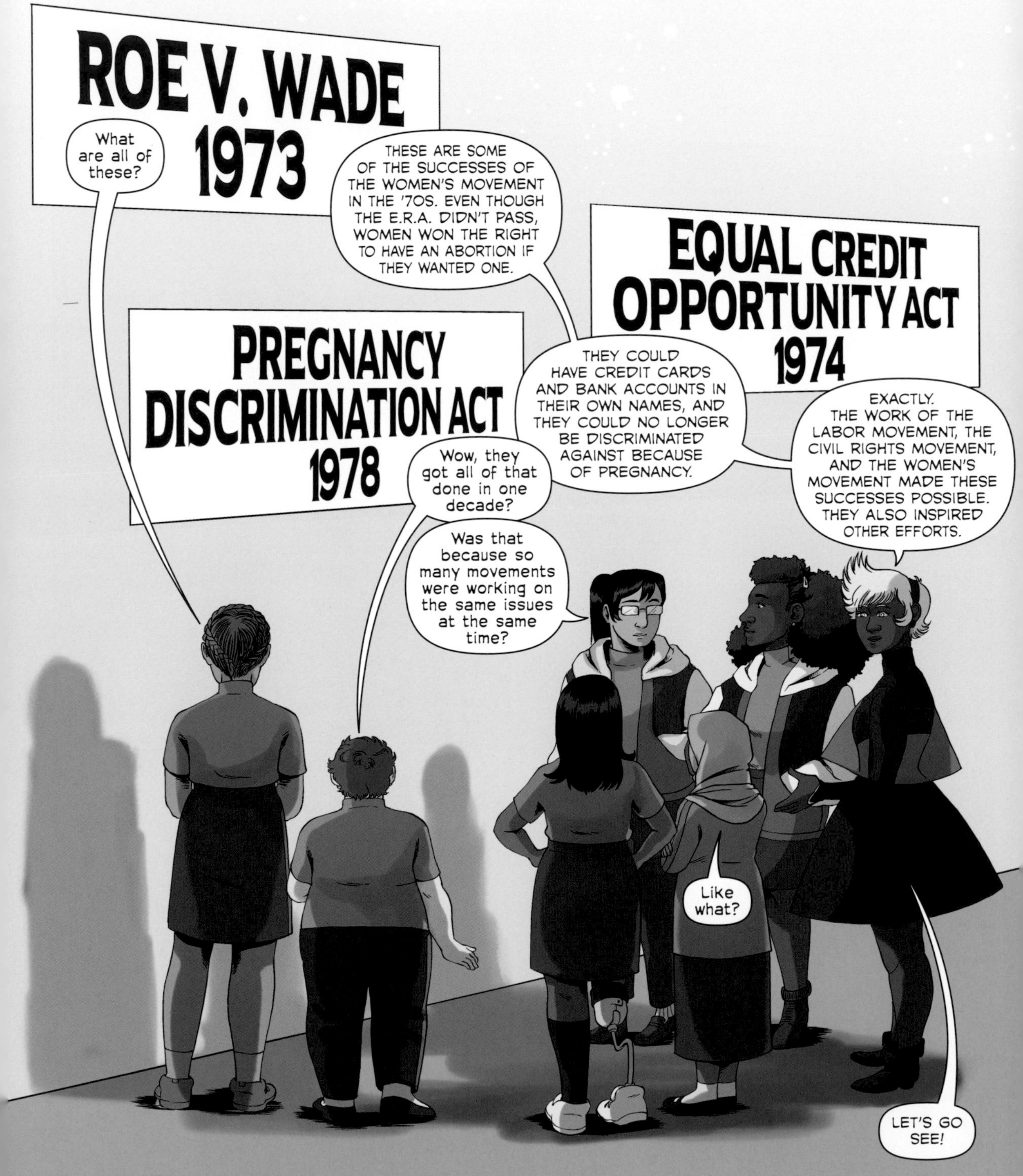
ROE V. WADE 1973
What are all of these?
THESE ARE SOME OF THE SUCCESSES OF THE WOMEN'S MOVEMENT IN THE '70S. EVEN THOUGH THE E.R.A. DIDN'T PASS, WOMEN WON THE RIGHT TO HAVE AN ABORTION IF THEY WANTED ONE.
EQUAL CREDIT OPPORTUNITY ACT 1974
PREGNANCY DISCRIMINATION ACT 1978
THEY COULD HAVE CREDIT CARDS AND BANK ACCOUNTS IN THEIR OWN NAMES, AND THEY COULD NO LONGER BE DISCRIMINATED AGAINST BECAUSE OF PREGNANCY.
Wow, they got all of that done in one decade?
Was that because so many movements were working on the same issues at the same time?
EXACTLY. THE WORK OF THE LABOR MOVEMENT, THE CIVIL RIGHTS MOVEMENT, AND THE WOMEN'S MOVEMENT MADE THESE SUCCESSES POSSIBLE. THEY ALSO INSPIRED OTHER EFFORTS.
Like what?
LET'S GO SEE!

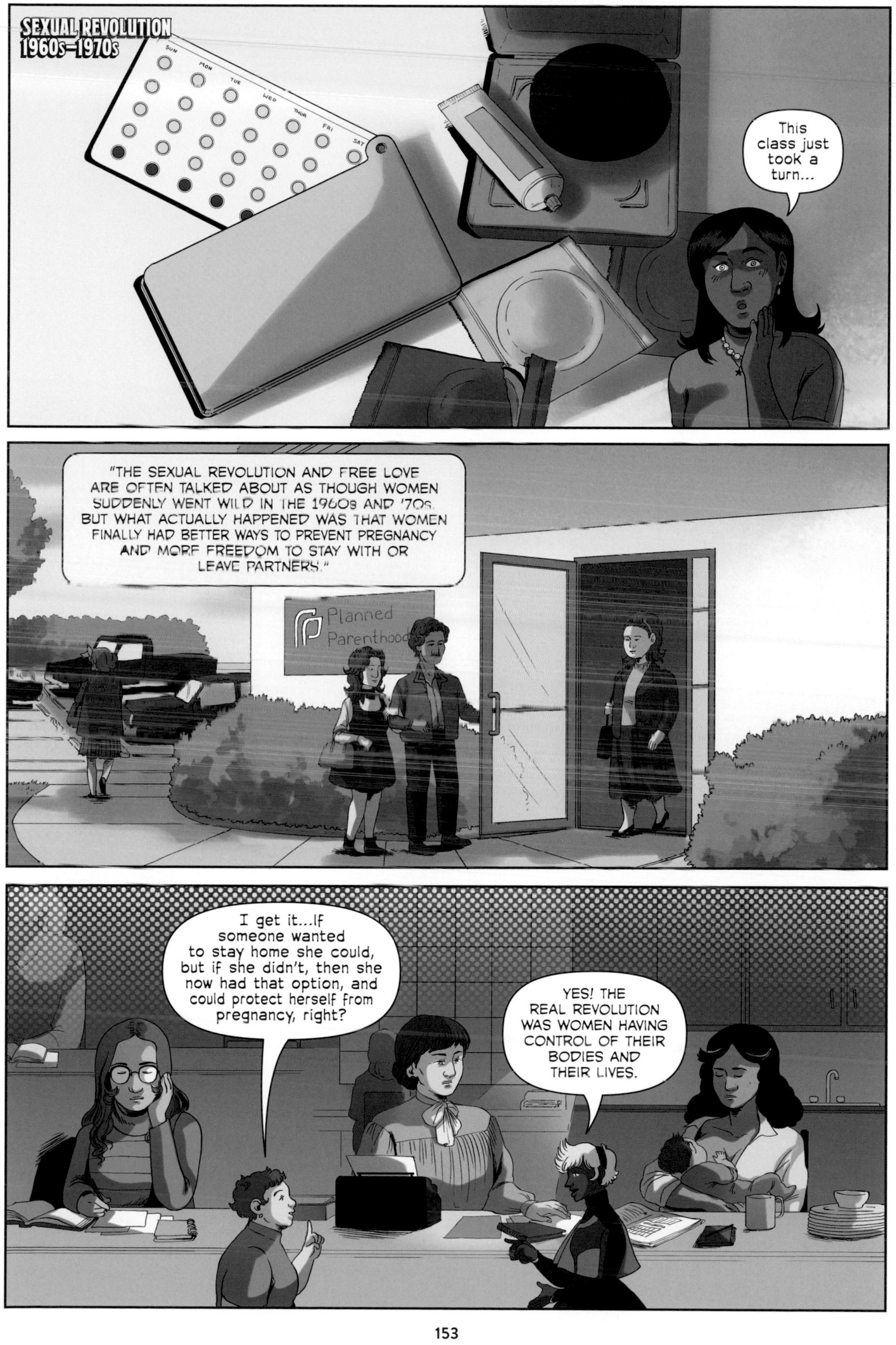
SEXUAL REVOLUTION 1960s–1970s
SUN
MON
TUE
WED
THUR
FRI
SAT
This class just took a turn...
"THE SEXUAL REVOLUTION AND FREE LOVE ARE OFTEN TALKED ABOUT AS THOUGH WOMEN SUDDENLY WENT WILD IN THE 1960s AND '70s. BUT WHAT ACTUALLY HAPPENED WAS THAT WOMEN FINALLY HAD BETTER WAYS TO PREVENT PREGNANCY AND MORE FREEDOM TO STAY WITH OR LEAVE PARTNERS."
Planned Parenthood
I get it...If someone wanted to stay home she could, but if she didn't, then she now had that option, and could protect herself from pregnancy, right?
YES! THE REAL REVOLUTION WAS WOMEN HAVING CONTROL OF THEIR BODIES AND THEIR LIVES.

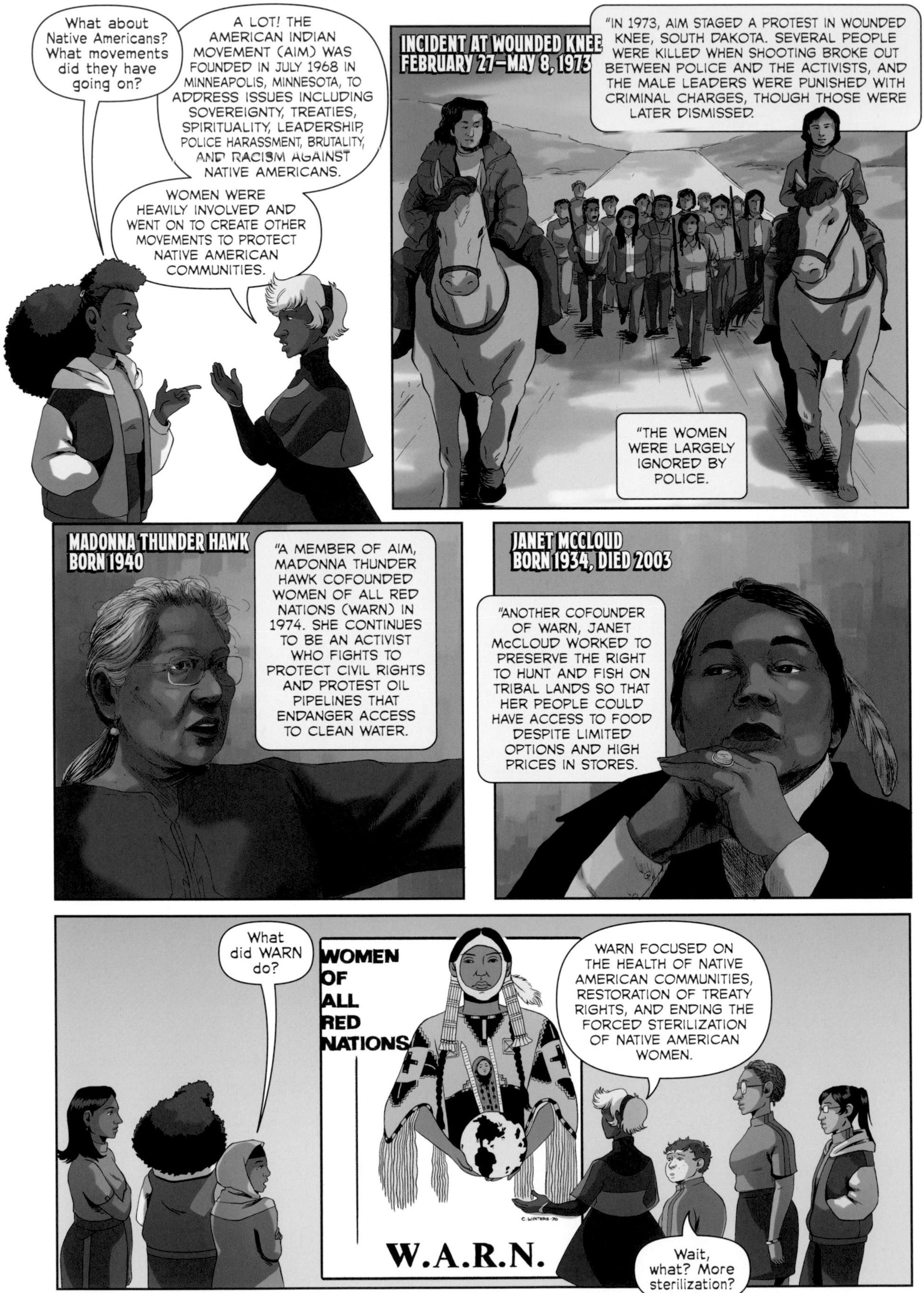

What about Native Americans? What movements did they have going on?
A LOT! THE AMERICAN INDIAN MOVEMENT (AIM) WAS FOUNDED IN JULY 1968 IN MINNEAPOLIS, MINNESOTA, TO ADDRESS ISSUES INCLUDING SOVEREIGNTY, TREATIES, SPIRITUALITY, LEADERSHIP, POLICE HARASSMENT, BRUTALITY, AND RACISM AGAINST NATIVE AMERICANS.
WOMEN WERE HEAVILY INVOLVED AND WENT ON TO CREATE OTHER MOVEMENTS TO PROTECT NATIVE AMERICAN COMMUNITIES.
INCIDENT AT WOUNDED KNEE
FEBRUARY 27–MAY 8, 1973
"IN 1973, AIM STAGED A PROTEST IN WOUNDED KNEE, SOUTH DAKOTA. SEVERAL PEOPLE WERE KILLED WHEN SHOOTING BROKE OUT BETWEEN POLICE AND THE ACTIVISTS, AND THE MALE LEADERS WERE PUNISHED WITH CRIMINAL CHARGES, THOUGH THOSE WERE LATER DISMISSED.
"THE WOMEN WERE LARGELY IGNORED BY POLICE.
MADONNA THUNDER HAWK
BORN 1940
"A MEMBER OF AIM, MADONNA THUNDER HAWK COFOUNDED WOMEN OF ALL RED NATIONS (WARN) IN 1974. SHE CONTINUES TO BE AN ACTIVIST WHO FIGHTS TO PROTECT CIVIL RIGHTS AND PROTEST OIL PIPELINES THAT ENDANGER ACCESS TO CLEAN WATER.
JANET McCLOUD
BORN 1934, DIED 2003
"ANOTHER COFOUNDER OF WARN, JANET McCLOUD WORKED TO PRESERVE THE RIGHT TO HUNT AND FISH ON TRIBAL LANDS SO THAT HER PEOPLE COULD HAVE ACCESS TO FOOD DESPITE LIMITED OPTIONS AND HIGH PRICES IN STORES.
What did WARN do?
WOMEN OF ALL RED NATIONS
C. WINTERS '70
W.A.R.N.
WARN FOCUSED ON THE HEALTH OF NATIVE AMERICAN COMMUNITIES, RESTORATION OF TREATY RIGHTS, AND ENDING THE FORCED STERILIZATION OF NATIVE AMERICAN WOMEN.
Wait, what? More sterilization?

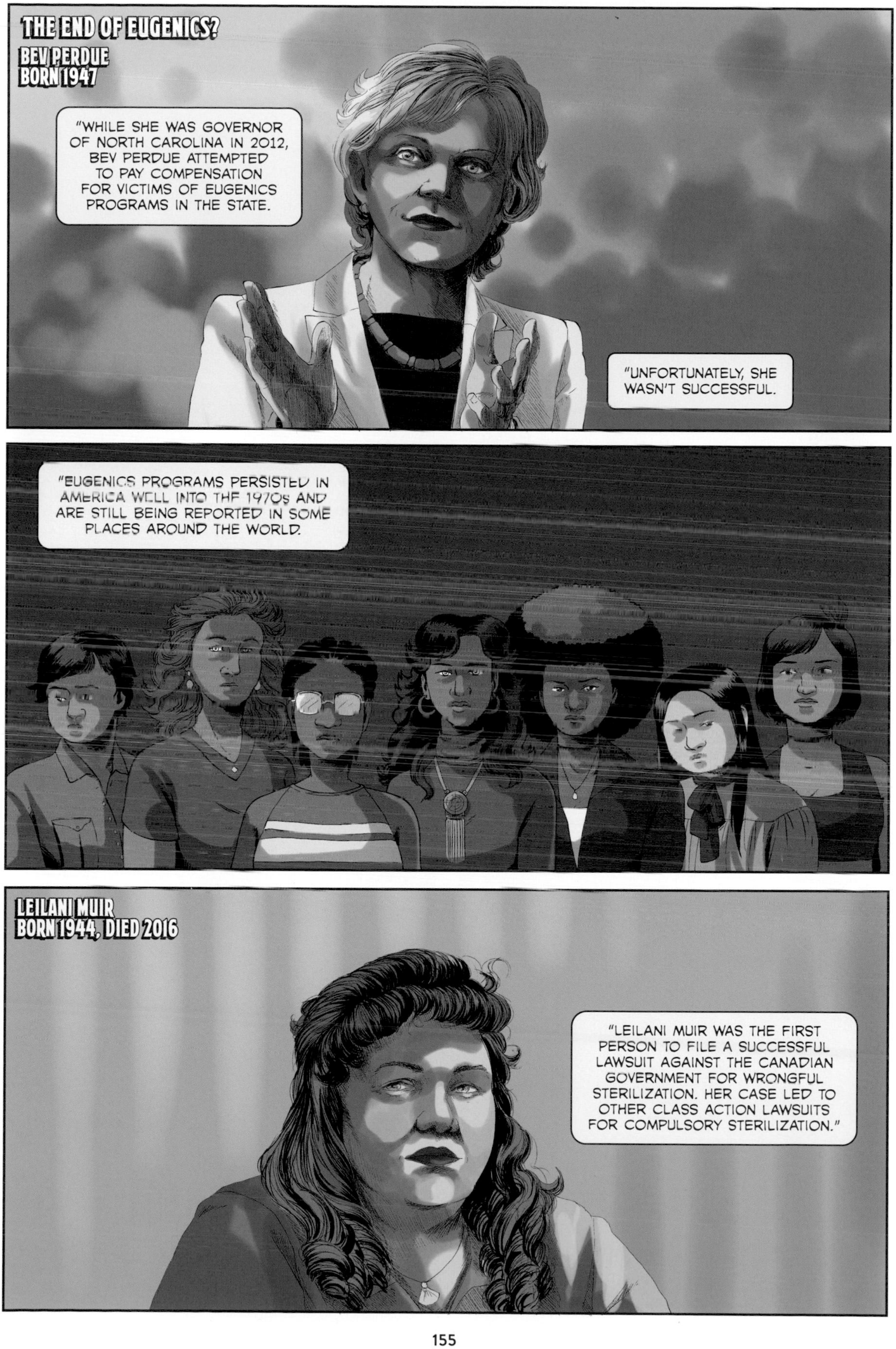
THE END OF EUGENICS?
BEV PERDUE
BORN 1947
"WHILE SHE WAS GOVERNOR OF NORTH CAROLINA IN 2012, BEV PERDUE ATTEMPTED TO PAY COMPENSATION FOR VICTIMS OF EUGENICS PROGRAMS IN THE STATE.
"UNFORTUNATELY, SHE WASN'T SUCCESSFUL.
"EUGENICS PROGRAMS PERSISTED IN AMERICA WELL INTO THE 1970s AND ARE STILL BEING REPORTED IN SOME PLACES AROUND THE WORLD.
LEILANI MUIR
BORN 1944, DIED 2016
"LEILANI MUIR WAS THE FIRST PERSON TO FILE A SUCCESSFUL LAWSUIT AGAINST THE CANADIAN GOVERNMENT FOR WRONGFUL STERILIZATION. HER CASE LED TO OTHER CLASS ACTION LAWSUITS FOR COMPULSORY STERILIZATION."

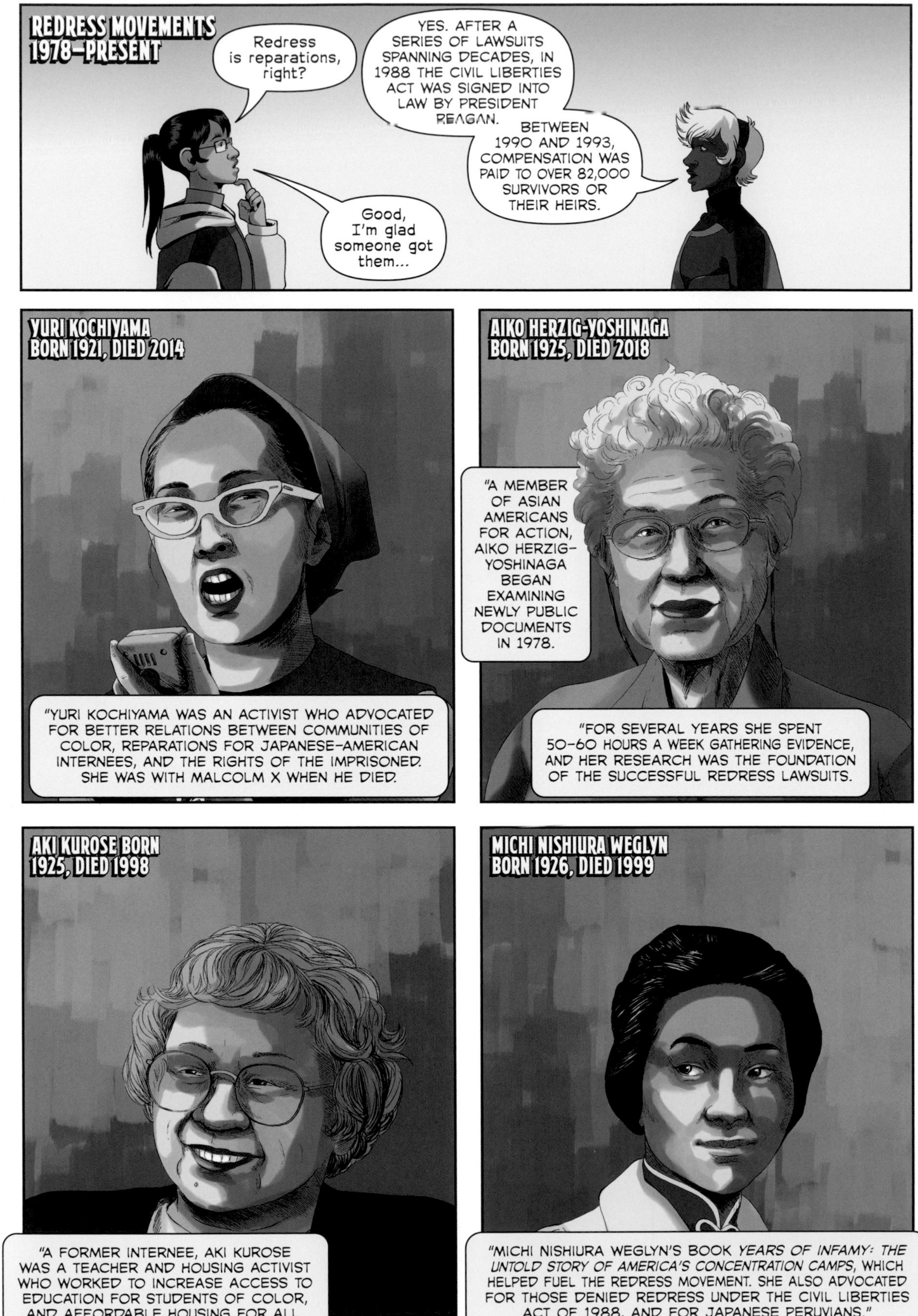
REDRESS MOVEMENTS 1978–PRESENT
Redress is reparations, right?
YES. AFTER A SERIES OF LAWSUITS SPANNING DECADES, IN 1988 THE CIVIL LIBERTIES ACT WAS SIGNED INTO LAW BY PRESIDENT REAGAN.
BETWEEN 1990 AND 1993, COMPENSATION WAS PAID TO OVER 82,000 SURVIVORS OR THEIR HEIRS.
Good, I'm glad someone got them...
YURI KOCHIYAMA BORN 1921, DIED 2014
"YURI KOCHIYAMA WAS AN ACTIVIST WHO ADVOCATED FOR BETTER RELATIONS BETWEEN COMMUNITIES OF COLOR, REPARATIONS FOR JAPANESE-AMERICAN INTERNEES, AND THE RIGHTS OF THE IMPRISONED. SHE WAS WITH MALCOLM X WHEN HE DIED.
AIKO HERZIG-YOSHINAGA BORN 1925, DIED 2018
"A MEMBER OF ASIAN AMERICANS FOR ACTION, AIKO HERZIG-YOSHINAGA BEGAN EXAMINING NEWLY PUBLIC DOCUMENTS IN 1978.
"FOR SEVERAL YEARS SHE SPENT 50–60 HOURS A WEEK GATHERING EVIDENCE, AND HER RESEARCH WAS THE FOUNDATION OF THE SUCCESSFUL REDRESS LAWSUITS.
AKI KUROSE BORN 1925, DIED 1998
"A FORMER INTERNEE, AKI KUROSE WAS A TEACHER AND HOUSING ACTIVIST WHO WORKED TO INCREASE ACCESS TO EDUCATION FOR STUDENTS OF COLOR, AND AFFORDABLE HOUSING FOR ALL.
MICHI NISHIURA WEGLYN BORN 1926, DIED 1999
"MICHI NISHIURA WEGLYN'S BOOK *YEARS OF INFAMY: THE UNTOLD STORY OF AMERICA'S CONCENTRATION CAMPS*, WHICH HELPED FUEL THE REDRESS MOVEMENT. SHE ALSO ADVOCATED FOR THOSE DENIED REDRESS UNDER THE CIVIL LIBERTIES ACT OF 1988, AND FOR JAPANESE PERUVIANS."

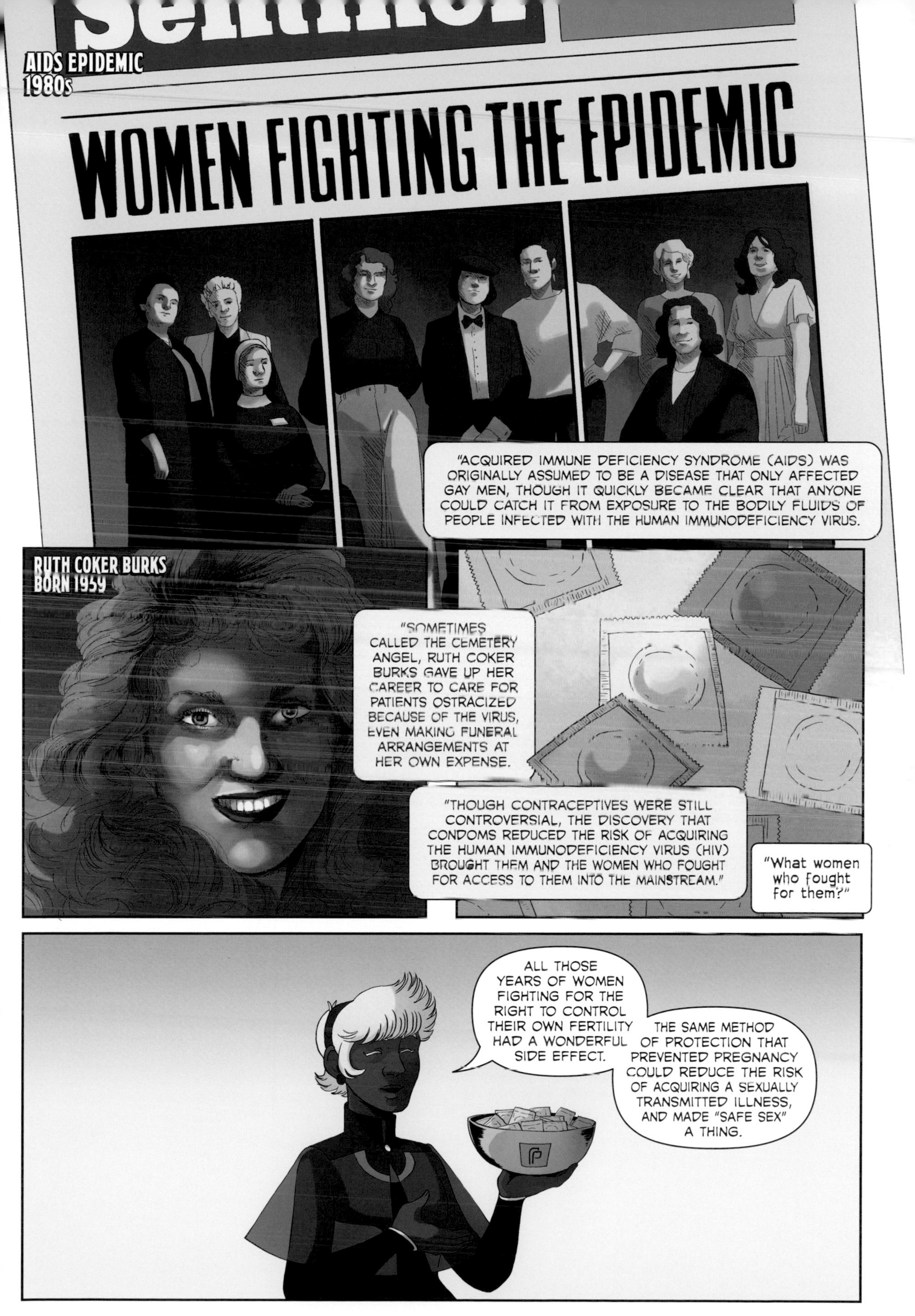
AIDS EPIDEMIC 1980s
WOMEN FIGHTING THE EPIDEMIC
"ACQUIRED IMMUNE DEFICIENCY SYNDROME (AIDS) WAS ORIGINALLY ASSUMED TO BE A DISEASE THAT ONLY AFFECTED GAY MEN, THOUGH IT QUICKLY BECAME CLEAR THAT ANYONE COULD CATCH IT FROM EXPOSURE TO THE BODILY FLUIDS OF PEOPLE INFECTED WITH THE HUMAN IMMUNODEFICIENCY VIRUS.
RUTH COKER BURKS BORN 1959
"SOMETIMES CALLED THE CEMETERY ANGEL, RUTH COKER BURKS GAVE UP HER CAREER TO CARE FOR PATIENTS OSTRACIZED BECAUSE OF THE VIRUS, EVEN MAKING FUNERAL ARRANGEMENTS AT HER OWN EXPENSE.
"THOUGH CONTRACEPTIVES WERE STILL CONTROVERSIAL, THE DISCOVERY THAT CONDOMS REDUCED THE RISK OF ACQUIRING THE HUMAN IMMUNODEFICIENCY VIRUS (HIV) BROUGHT THEM AND THE WOMEN WHO FOUGHT FOR ACCESS TO THEM INTO THE MAINSTREAM."
"What women who fought for them?"
ALL THOSE YEARS OF WOMEN FIGHTING FOR THE RIGHT TO CONTROL THEIR OWN FERTILITY HAD A WONDERFUL SIDE EFFECT.
THE SAME METHOD OF PROTECTION THAT PREVENTED PREGNANCY COULD REDUCE THE RISK OF ACQUIRING A SEXUALLY TRANSMITTED ILLNESS, AND MADE "SAFE SEX" A THING.

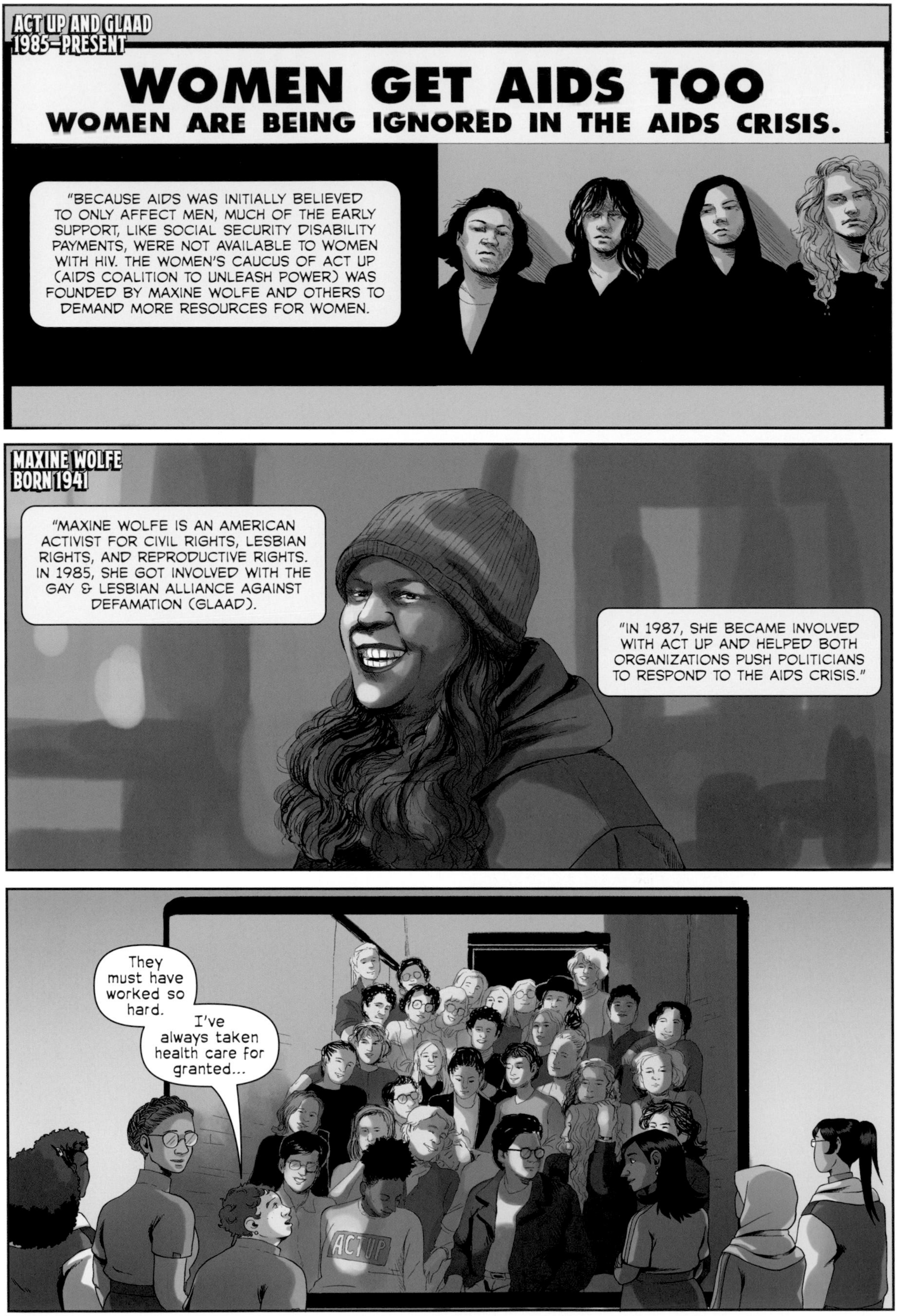
ACT UP AND GLAAD
1985–PRESENT
WOMEN GET AIDS TOO
WOMEN ARE BEING IGNORED IN THE AIDS CRISIS.
"BECAUSE AIDS WAS INITIALLY BELIEVED TO ONLY AFFECT MEN, MUCH OF THE EARLY SUPPORT, LIKE SOCIAL SECURITY DISABILITY PAYMENTS, WERE NOT AVAILABLE TO WOMEN WITH HIV. THE WOMEN'S CAUCUS OF ACT UP (AIDS COALITION TO UNLEASH POWER) WAS FOUNDED BY MAXINE WOLFE AND OTHERS TO DEMAND MORE RESOURCES FOR WOMEN.
MAXINE WOLFE
BORN 1941
"MAXINE WOLFE IS AN AMERICAN ACTIVIST FOR CIVIL RIGHTS, LESBIAN RIGHTS, AND REPRODUCTIVE RIGHTS. IN 1985, SHE GOT INVOLVED WITH THE GAY & LESBIAN ALLIANCE AGAINST DEFAMATION (GLAAD).
"IN 1987, SHE BECAME INVOLVED WITH ACT UP AND HELPED BOTH ORGANIZATIONS PUSH POLITICIANS TO RESPOND TO THE AIDS CRISIS."
They must have worked so hard.
I've always taken health care for granted...
ACT UP

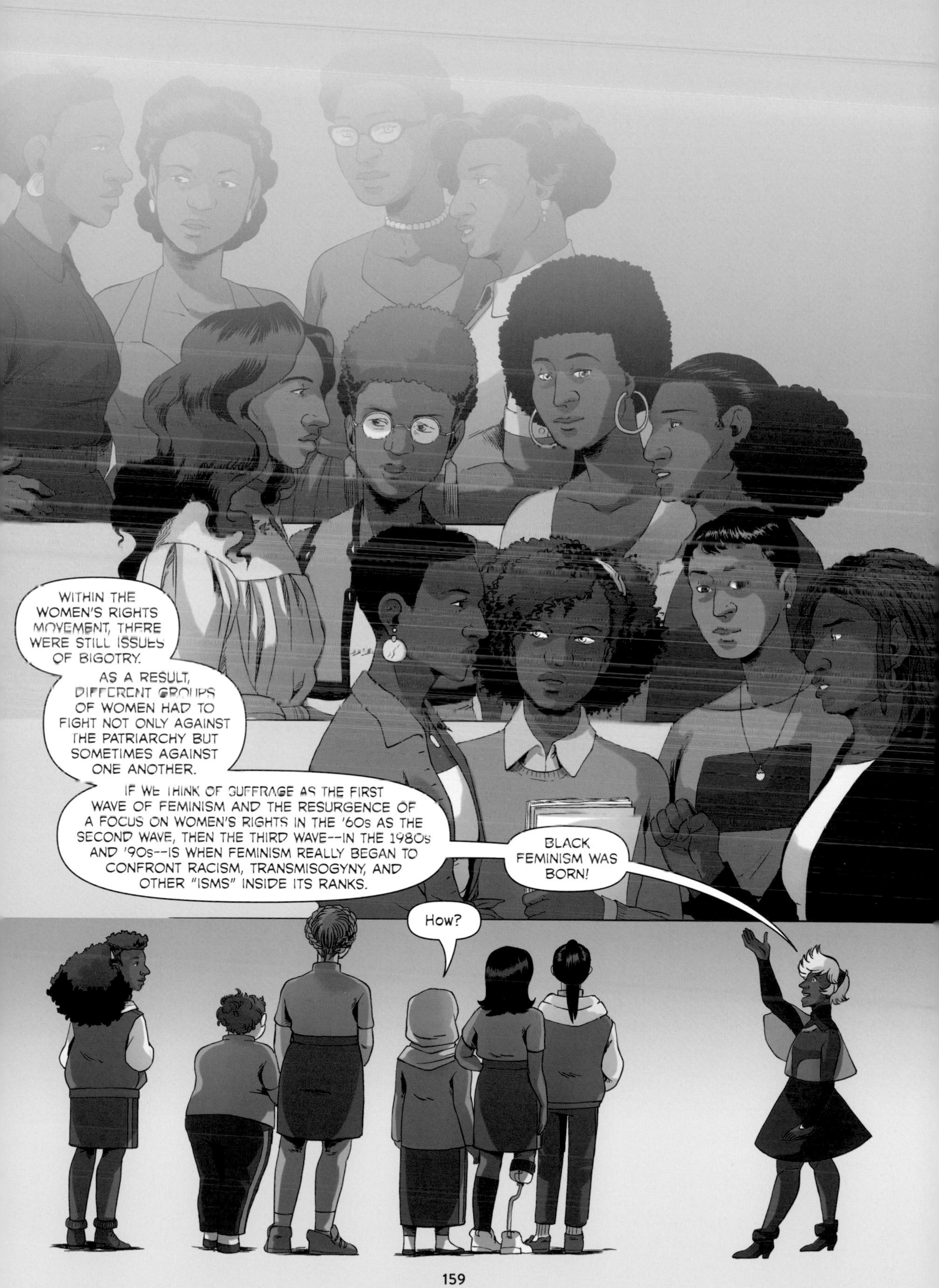
WITHIN THE WOMEN'S RIGHTS MOVEMENT, THERE WERE STILL ISSUES OF BIGOTRY.
AS A RESULT, DIFFERENT GROUPS OF WOMEN HAD TO FIGHT NOT ONLY AGAINST THE PATRIARCHY BUT SOMETIMES AGAINST ONE ANOTHER.
IF WE THINK OF SUFFRAGE AS THE FIRST WAVE OF FEMINISM AND THE RESURGENCE OF A FOCUS ON WOMEN'S RIGHTS IN THE '60s AS THE SECOND WAVE, THEN THE THIRD WAVE--IN THE 1980s AND '90s--IS WHEN FEMINISM REALLY BEGAN TO CONFRONT RACISM, TRANSMISOGYNY, AND OTHER "ISMS" INSIDE ITS RANKS.
BLACK FEMINISM WAS BORN!
How?

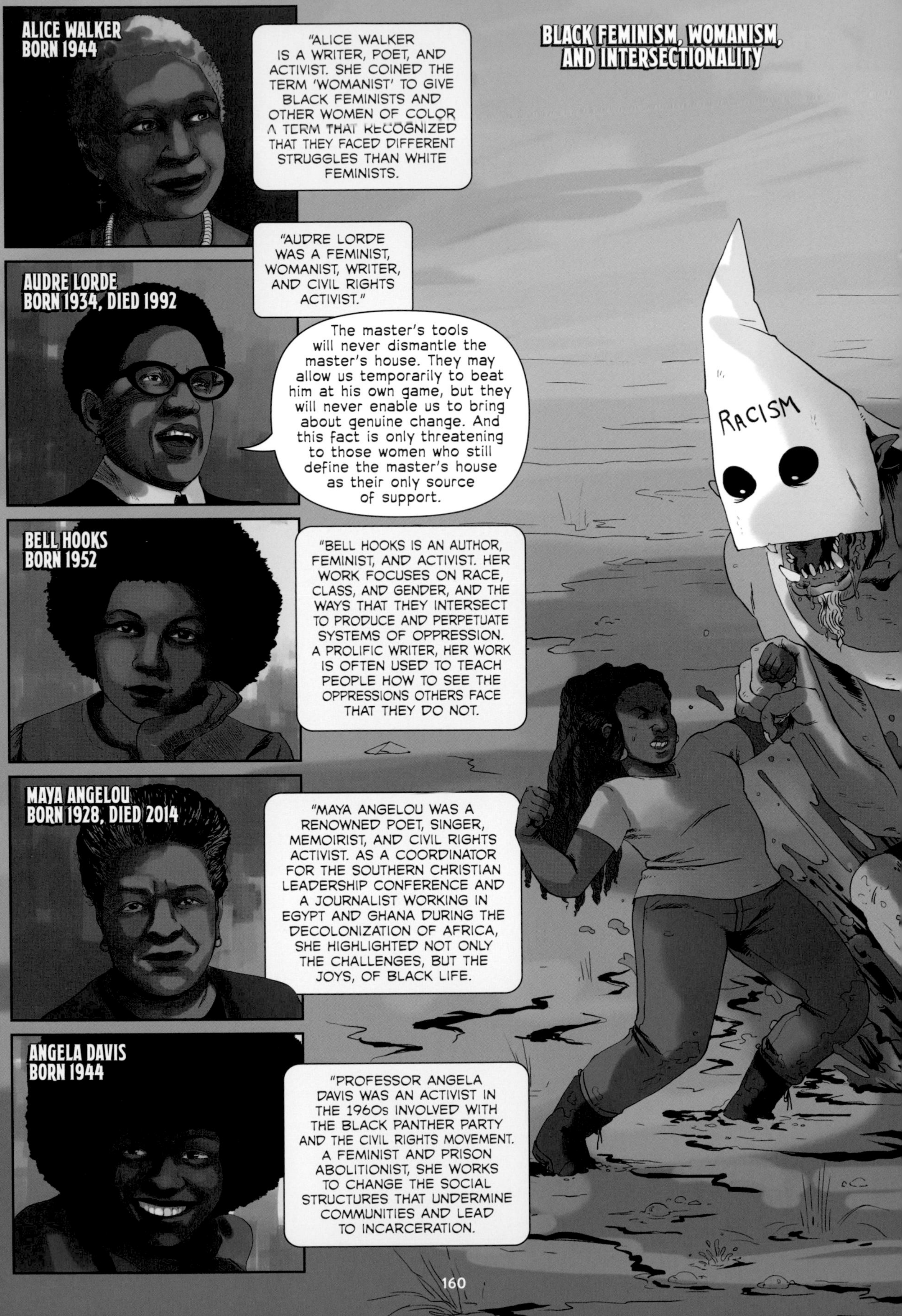

BLACK FEMINISM, WOMANISM, AND INTERSECTIONALITY
ALICE WALKER BORN 1944
"ALICE WALKER IS A WRITER, POET, AND ACTIVIST. SHE COINED THE TERM 'WOMANIST' TO GIVE BLACK FEMINISTS AND OTHER WOMEN OF COLOR A TERM THAT RECOGNIZED THAT THEY FACED DIFFERENT STRUGGLES THAN WHITE FEMINISTS.
AUDRE LORDE BORN 1934, DIED 1992
"AUDRE LORDE WAS A FEMINIST, WOMANIST, WRITER, AND CIVIL RIGHTS ACTIVIST."
The master's tools will never dismantle the master's house. They may allow us temporarily to beat him at his own game, but they will never enable us to bring about genuine change. And this fact is only threatening to those women who still define the master's house as their only source of support.
RACISM
BELL HOOKS BORN 1952
"BELL HOOKS IS AN AUTHOR, FEMINIST, AND ACTIVIST. HER WORK FOCUSES ON RACE, CLASS, AND GENDER, AND THE WAYS THAT THEY INTERSECT TO PRODUCE AND PERPETUATE SYSTEMS OF OPPRESSION. A PROLIFIC WRITER, HER WORK IS OFTEN USED TO TEACH PEOPLE HOW TO SEE THE OPPRESSIONS OTHERS FACE THAT THEY DO NOT.
MAYA ANGELOU BORN 1928, DIED 2014
"MAYA ANGELOU WAS A RENOWNED POET, SINGER, MEMOIRIST, AND CIVIL RIGHTS ACTIVIST. AS A COORDINATOR FOR THE SOUTHERN CHRISTIAN LEADERSHIP CONFERENCE AND A JOURNALIST WORKING IN EGYPT AND GHANA DURING THE DECOLONIZATION OF AFRICA, SHE HIGHLIGHTED NOT ONLY THE CHALLENGES, BUT THE JOYS, OF BLACK LIFE.
ANGELA DAVIS BORN 1944
"PROFESSOR ANGELA DAVIS WAS AN ACTIVIST IN THE 1960s INVOLVED WITH THE BLACK PANTHER PARTY AND THE CIVIL RIGHTS MOVEMENT. A FEMINIST AND PRISON ABOLITIONIST, SHE WORKS TO CHANGE THE SOCIAL STRUCTURES THAT UNDERMINE COMMUNITIES AND LEAD TO INCARCERATION.

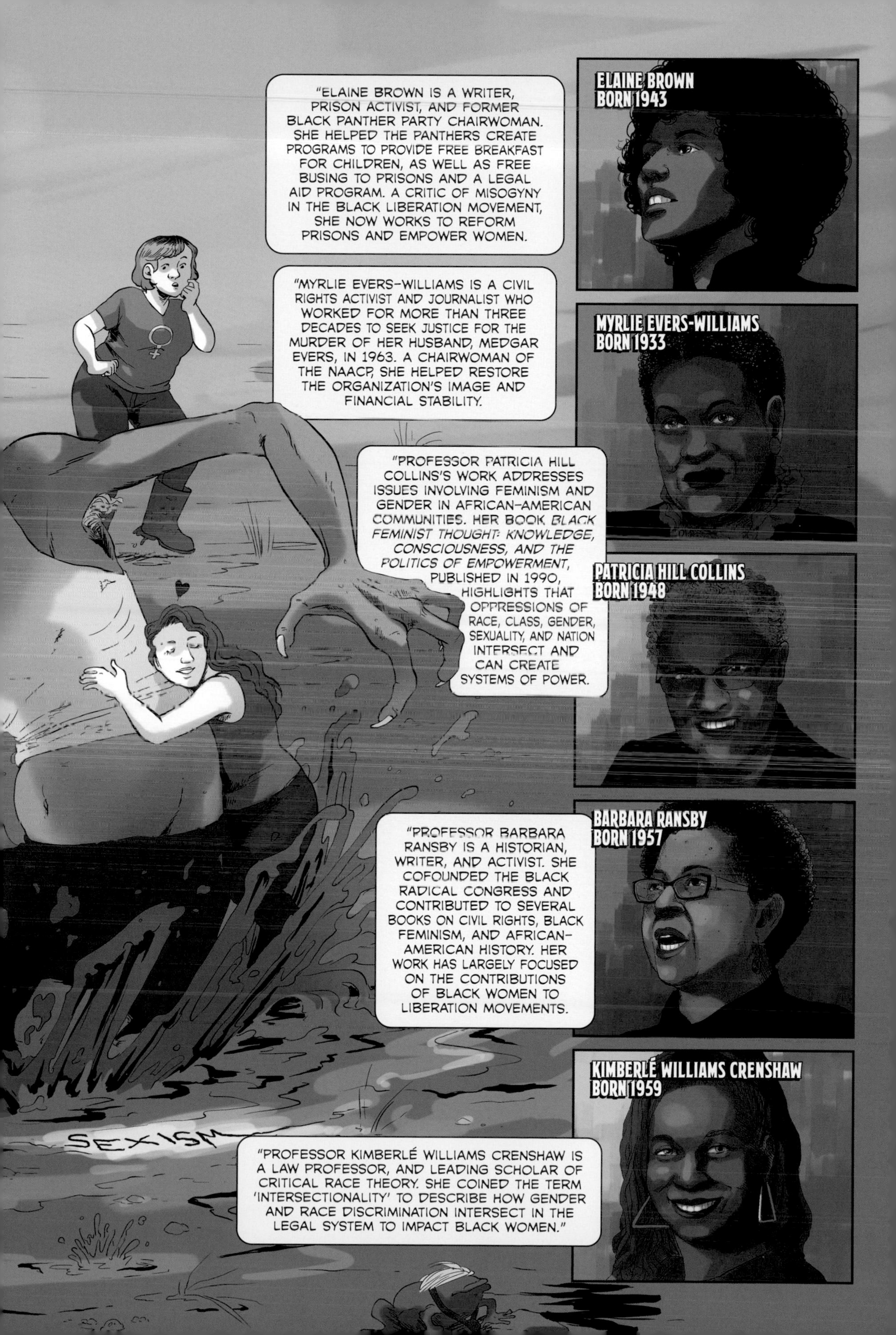
ELAINE BROWN
BORN 1943
"ELAINE BROWN IS A WRITER, PRISON ACTIVIST, AND FORMER BLACK PANTHER PARTY CHAIRWOMAN. SHE HELPED THE PANTHERS CREATE PROGRAMS TO PROVIDE FREE BREAKFAST FOR CHILDREN, AS WELL AS FREE BUSING TO PRISONS AND A LEGAL AID PROGRAM. A CRITIC OF MISOGYNY IN THE BLACK LIBERATION MOVEMENT, SHE NOW WORKS TO REFORM PRISONS AND EMPOWER WOMEN.
MYRLIE EVERS-WILLIAMS
BORN 1933
"MYRLIE EVERS-WILLIAMS IS A CIVIL RIGHTS ACTIVIST AND JOURNALIST WHO WORKED FOR MORE THAN THREE DECADES TO SEEK JUSTICE FOR THE MURDER OF HER HUSBAND, MEDGAR EVERS, IN 1963. A CHAIRWOMAN OF THE NAACP, SHE HELPED RESTORE THE ORGANIZATION'S IMAGE AND FINANCIAL STABILITY.
PATRICIA HILL COLLINS
BORN 1948
"PROFESSOR PATRICIA HILL COLLINS'S WORK ADDRESSES ISSUES INVOLVING FEMINISM AND GENDER IN AFRICAN-AMERICAN COMMUNITIES. HER BOOK *BLACK FEMINIST THOUGHT: KNOWLEDGE, CONSCIOUSNESS, AND THE POLITICS OF EMPOWERMENT*, PUBLISHED IN 1990, HIGHLIGHTS THAT OPPRESSIONS OF RACE, CLASS, GENDER, SEXUALITY, AND NATION INTERSECT AND CAN CREATE SYSTEMS OF POWER.
BARBARA RANSBY
BORN 1957
"PROFESSOR BARBARA RANSBY IS A HISTORIAN, WRITER, AND ACTIVIST. SHE COFOUNDED THE BLACK RADICAL CONGRESS AND CONTRIBUTED TO SEVERAL BOOKS ON CIVIL RIGHTS, BLACK FEMINISM, AND AFRICAN-AMERICAN HISTORY. HER WORK HAS LARGELY FOCUSED ON THE CONTRIBUTIONS OF BLACK WOMEN TO LIBERATION MOVEMENTS.
KIMBERLÉ WILLIAMS CRENSHAW
BORN 1959
SEXISM
"PROFESSOR KIMBERLÉ WILLIAMS CRENSHAW IS A LAW PROFESSOR, AND LEADING SCHOLAR OF CRITICAL RACE THEORY. SHE COINED THE TERM 'INTERSECTIONALITY' TO DESCRIBE HOW GENDER AND RACE DISCRIMINATION INTERSECT IN THE LEGAL SYSTEM TO IMPACT BLACK WOMEN."

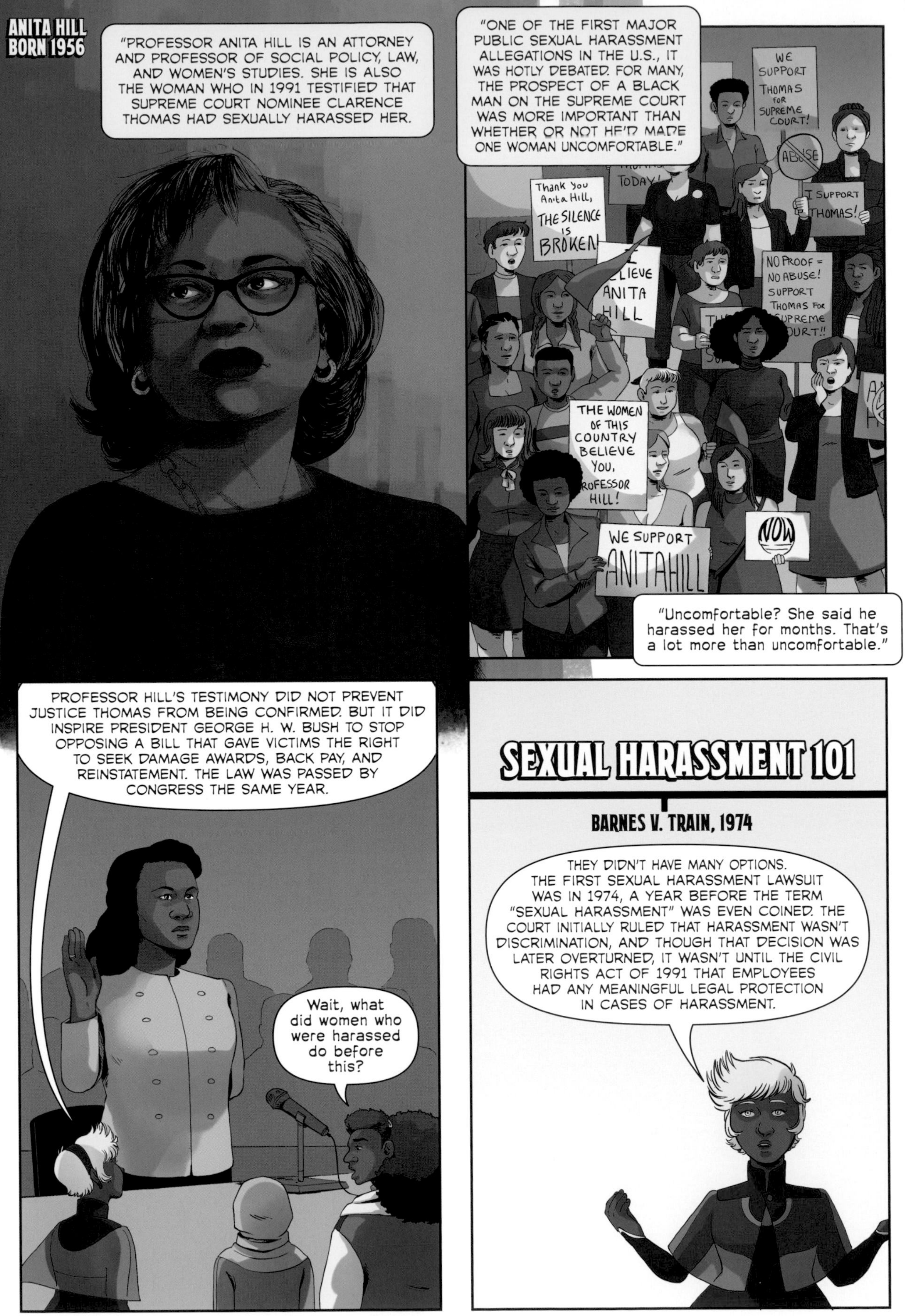

ANITA HILL BORN 1956
"PROFESSOR ANITA HILL IS AN ATTORNEY AND PROFESSOR OF SOCIAL POLICY, LAW, AND WOMEN'S STUDIES. SHE IS ALSO THE WOMAN WHO IN 1991 TESTIFIED THAT SUPREME COURT NOMINEE CLARENCE THOMAS HAD SEXUALLY HARASSED HER.
"ONE OF THE FIRST MAJOR PUBLIC SEXUAL HARASSMENT ALLEGATIONS IN THE U.S., IT WAS HOTLY DEBATED. FOR MANY, THE PROSPECT OF A BLACK MAN ON THE SUPREME COURT WAS MORE IMPORTANT THAN WHETHER OR NOT HE'D MADE ONE WOMAN UNCOMFORTABLE."
WE SUPPORT THOMAS FOR SUPREME COURT!
ABUSE
TODAY!
Thank You Anita Hill, THE SILENCE IS BROKEN
I SUPPORT THOMAS!
NO PROOF = NO ABUSE! SUPPORT THOMAS FOR SUPREME COURT!!
BELIEVE ANITA HILL
THE WOMEN OF THIS COUNTRY BELIEVE YOU, PROFESSOR HILL!
WE SUPPORT ANITAHILL
NOW
"Uncomfortable? She said he harassed her for months. That's a lot more than uncomfortable."
PROFESSOR HILL'S TESTIMONY DID NOT PREVENT JUSTICE THOMAS FROM BEING CONFIRMED. BUT IT DID INSPIRE PRESIDENT GEORGE H. W. BUSH TO STOP OPPOSING A BILL THAT GAVE VICTIMS THE RIGHT TO SEEK DAMAGE AWARDS, BACK PAY, AND REINSTATEMENT. THE LAW WAS PASSED BY CONGRESS THE SAME YEAR.
Wait, what did women who were harassed do before this?
SEXUAL HARASSMENT 101
BARNES V. TRAIN, 1974
THEY DIDN'T HAVE MANY OPTIONS. THE FIRST SEXUAL HARASSMENT LAWSUIT WAS IN 1974, A YEAR BEFORE THE TERM "SEXUAL HARASSMENT" WAS EVEN COINED. THE COURT INITIALLY RULED THAT HARASSMENT WASN'T DISCRIMINATION, AND THOUGH THAT DECISION WAS LATER OVERTURNED, IT WASN'T UNTIL THE CIVIL RIGHTS ACT OF 1991 THAT EMPLOYEES HAD ANY MEANINGFUL LEGAL PROTECTION IN CASES OF HARASSMENT.

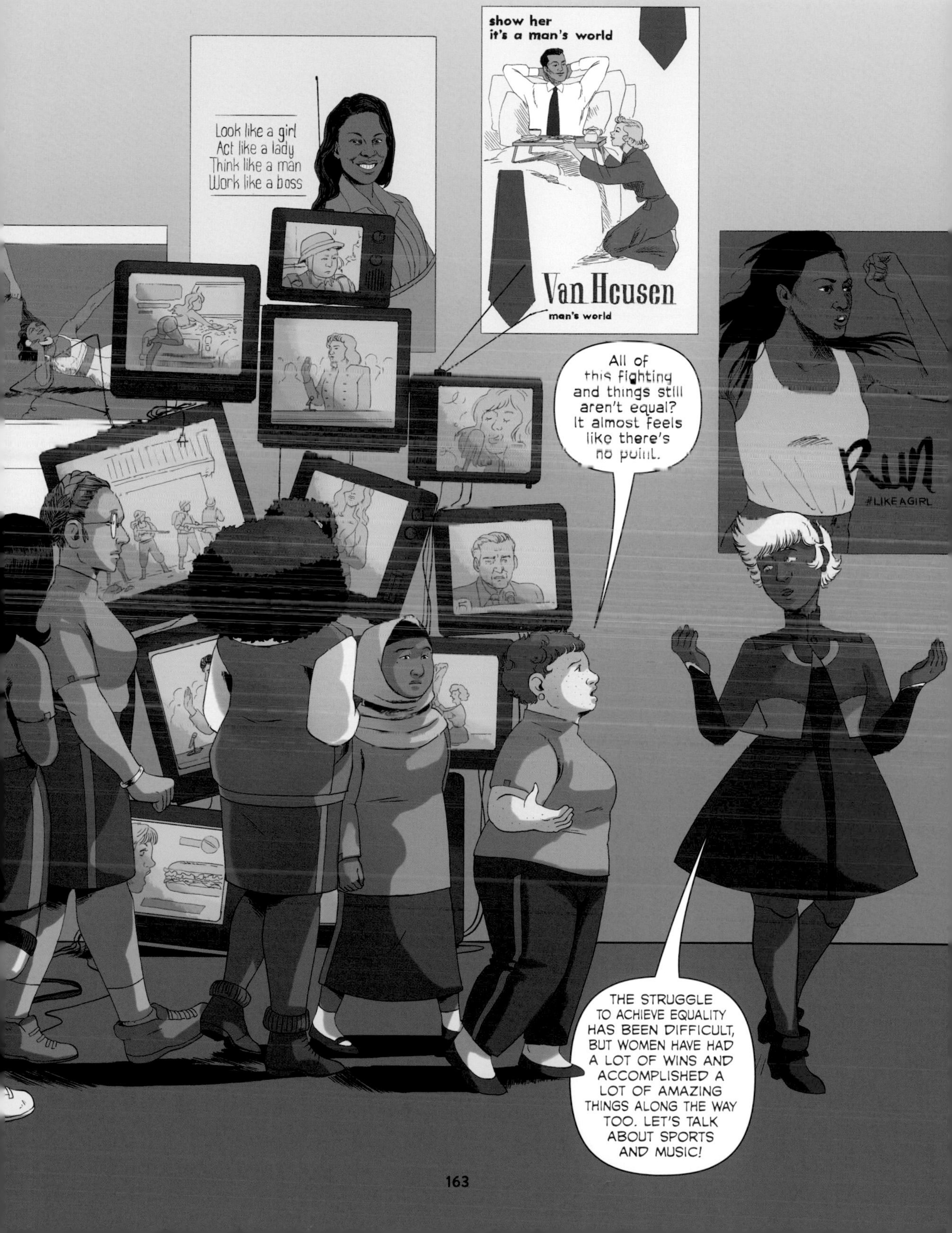
Look like a girl
Act like a lady
Think like a man
Work like a boss
show her
it's a man's world
Van Heusen
man's world
RUN
#LIKEAGIRL
All of this fighting and things still aren't equal? It almost feels like there's no point.
THE STRUGGLE TO ACHIEVE EQUALITY HAS BEEN DIFFICULT, BUT WOMEN HAVE HAD A LOT OF WINS AND ACCOMPLISHED A LOT OF AMAZING THINGS ALONG THE WAY TOO. LET'S TALK ABOUT SPORTS AND MUSIC!

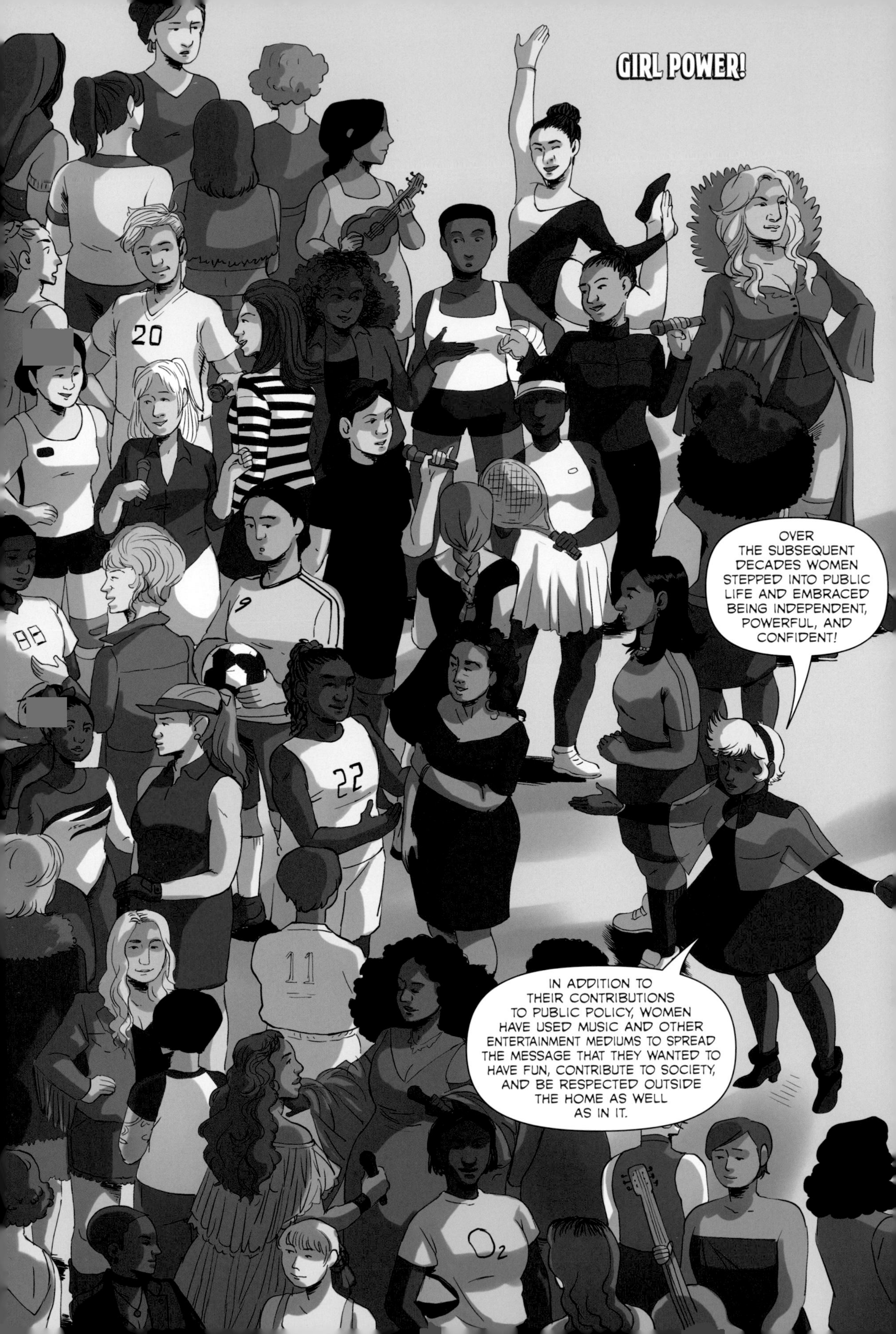
GIRL POWER!
OVER THE SUBSEQUENT DECADES WOMEN STEPPED INTO PUBLIC LIFE AND EMBRACED BEING INDEPENDENT, POWERFUL, AND CONFIDENT!
IN ADDITION TO THEIR CONTRIBUTIONS TO PUBLIC POLICY, WOMEN HAVE USED MUSIC AND OTHER ENTERTAINMENT MEDIUMS TO SPREAD THE MESSAGE THAT THEY WANTED TO HAVE FUN, CONTRIBUTE TO SOCIETY, AND BE RESPECTED OUTSIDE THE HOME AS WELL AS IN IT.

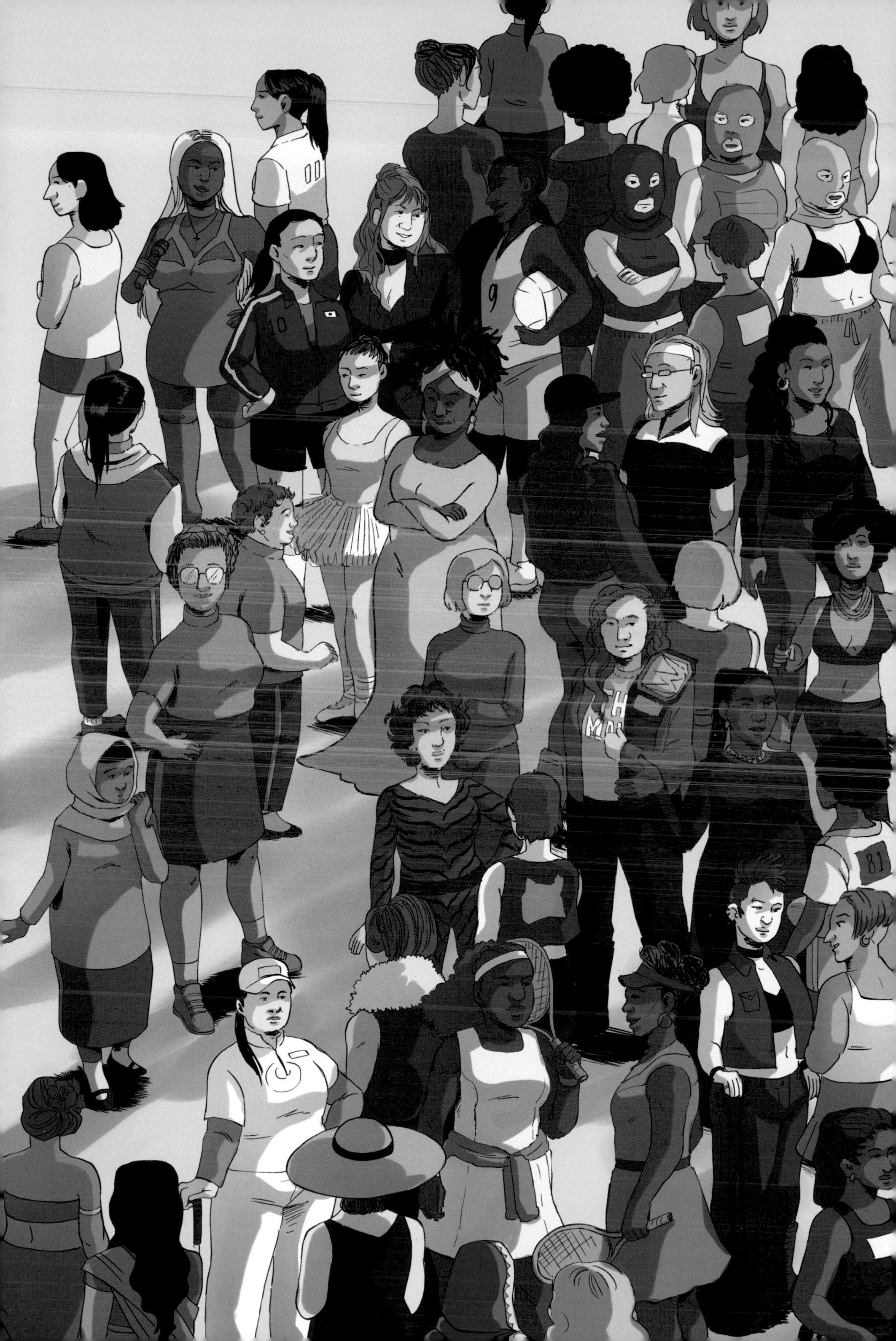
00
10
9
81

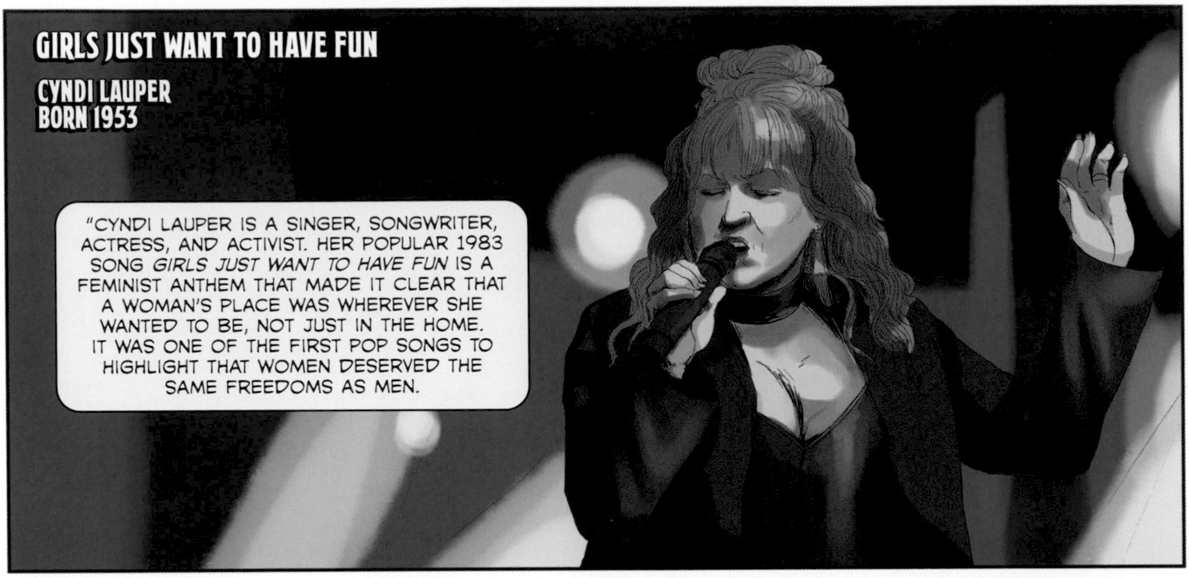
GIRLS JUST WANT TO HAVE FUN
CYNDI LAUPER
BORN 1953
"CYNDI LAUPER IS A SINGER, SONGWRITER, ACTRESS, AND ACTIVIST. HER POPULAR 1983 SONG *GIRLS JUST WANT TO HAVE FUN* IS A FEMINIST ANTHEM THAT MADE IT CLEAR THAT A WOMAN'S PLACE WAS WHEREVER SHE WANTED TO BE, NOT JUST IN THE HOME. IT WAS ONE OF THE FIRST POP SONGS TO HIGHLIGHT THAT WOMEN DESERVED THE SAME FREEDOMS AS MEN.

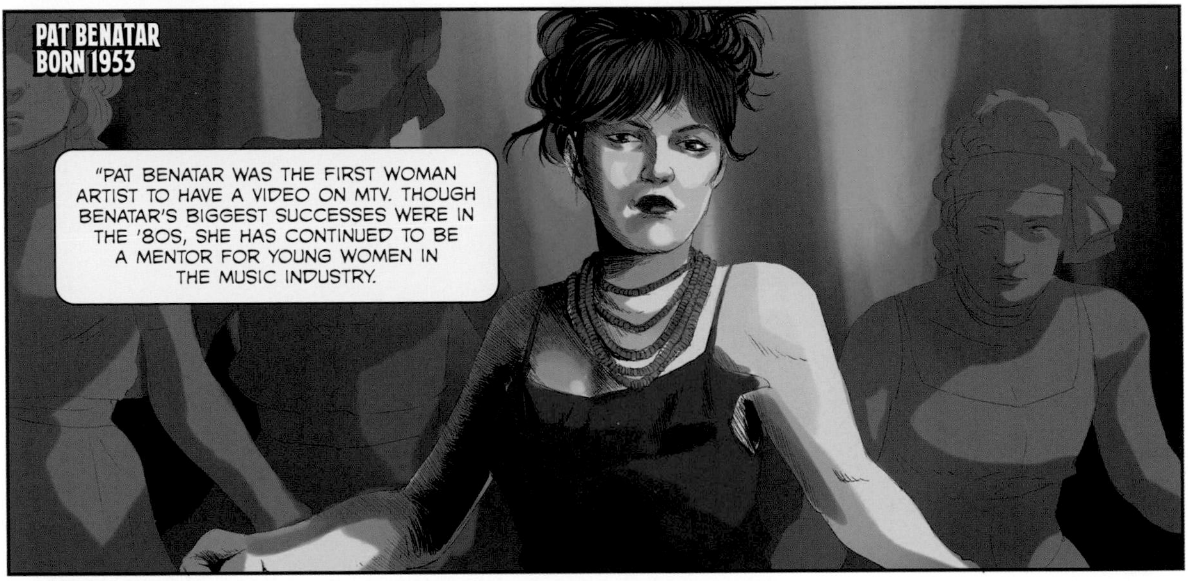
PAT BENATAR
BORN 1953
"PAT BENATAR WAS THE FIRST WOMAN ARTIST TO HAVE A VIDEO ON MTV. THOUGH BENATAR'S BIGGEST SUCCESSES WERE IN THE '80S, SHE HAS CONTINUED TO BE A MENTOR FOR YOUNG WOMEN IN THE MUSIC INDUSTRY.

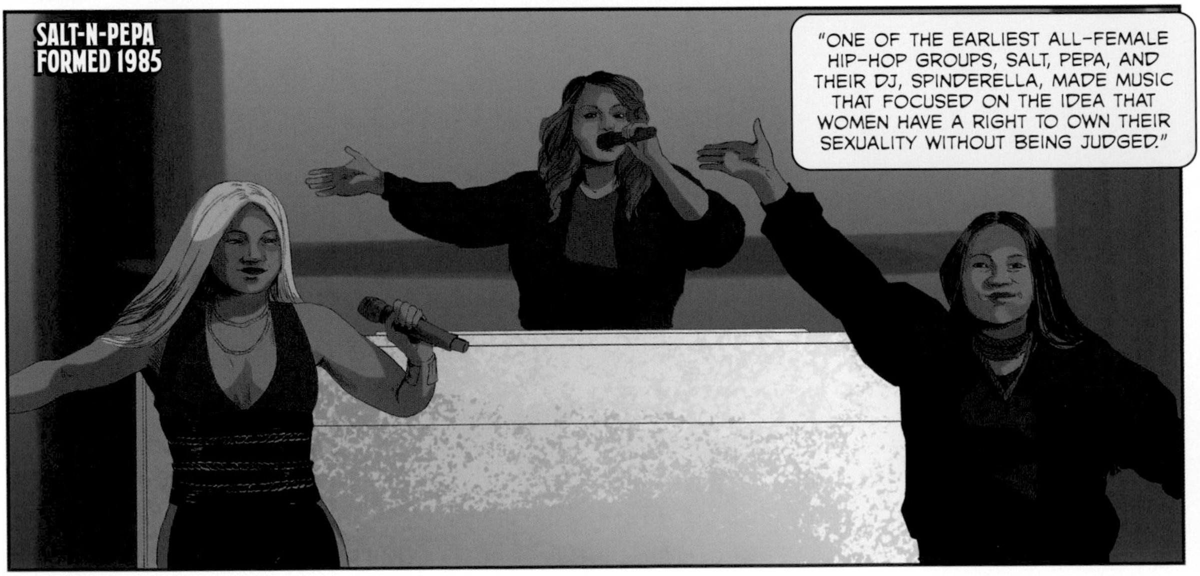
SALT-N-PEPA
FORMED 1985
"ONE OF THE EARLIEST ALL-FEMALE HIP-HOP GROUPS, SALT, PEPA, AND THEIR DJ, SPINDERELLA, MADE MUSIC THAT FOCUSED ON THE IDEA THAT WOMEN HAVE A RIGHT TO OWN THEIR SEXUALITY WITHOUT BEING JUDGED."

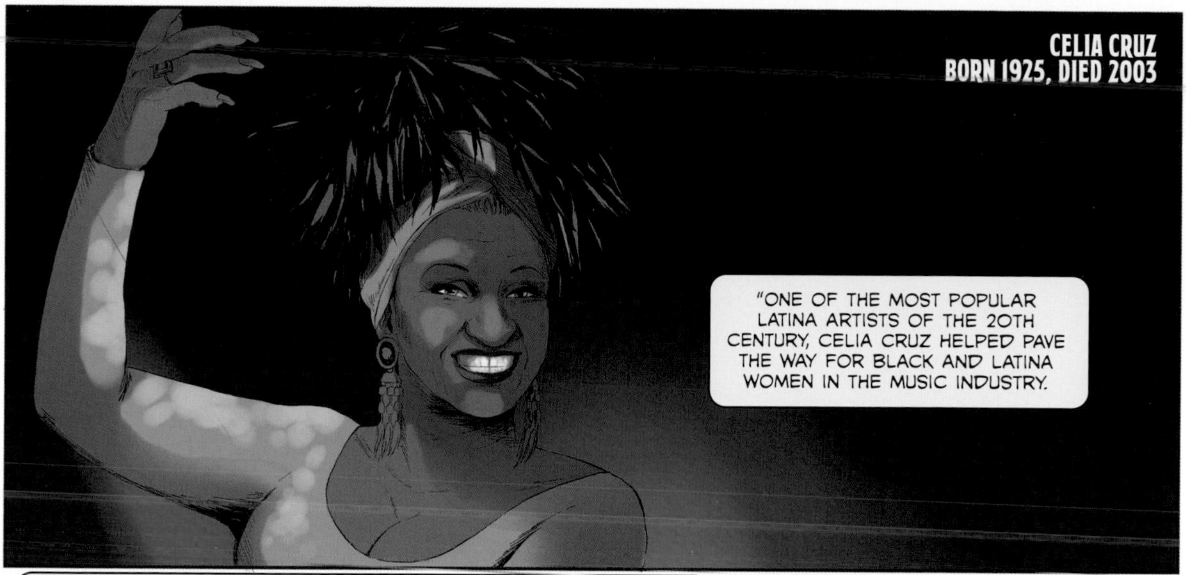
CELIA CRUZ
BORN 1925, DIED 2003
"ONE OF THE MOST POPULAR LATINA ARTISTS OF THE 20TH CENTURY, CELIA CRUZ HELPED PAVE THE WAY FOR BLACK AND LATINA WOMEN IN THE MUSIC INDUSTRY.

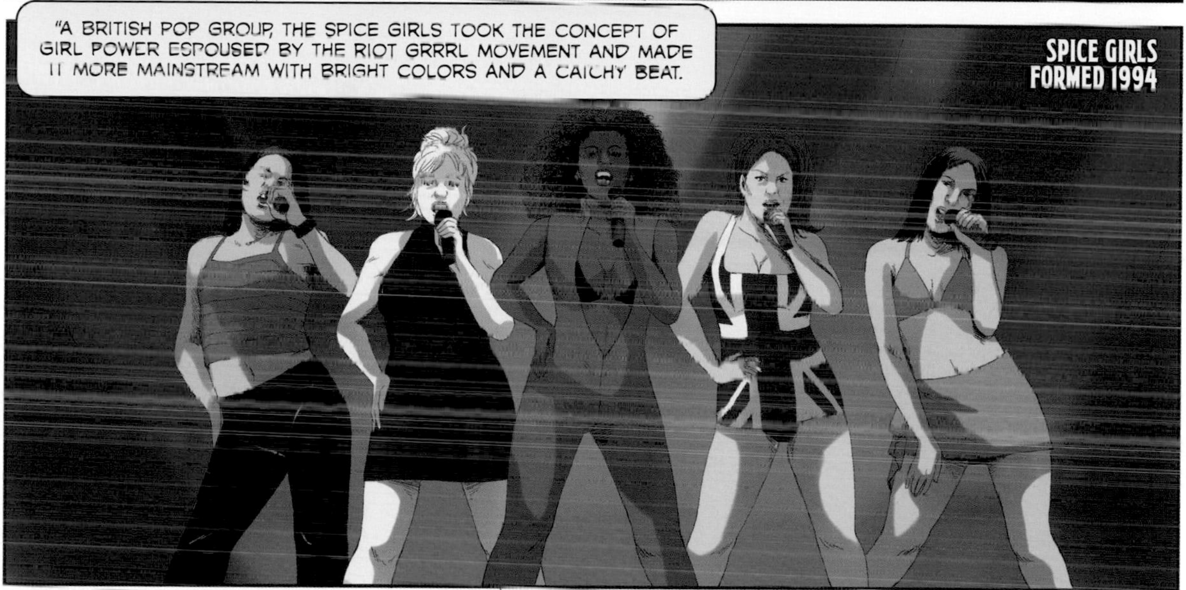
"A BRITISH POP GROUP, THE SPICE GIRLS TOOK THE CONCEPT OF GIRL POWER ESPOUSED BY THE RIOT GRRRL MOVEMENT AND MADE IT MORE MAINSTREAM WITH BRIGHT COLORS AND A CATCHY BEAT.
SPICE GIRLS
FORMED 1994

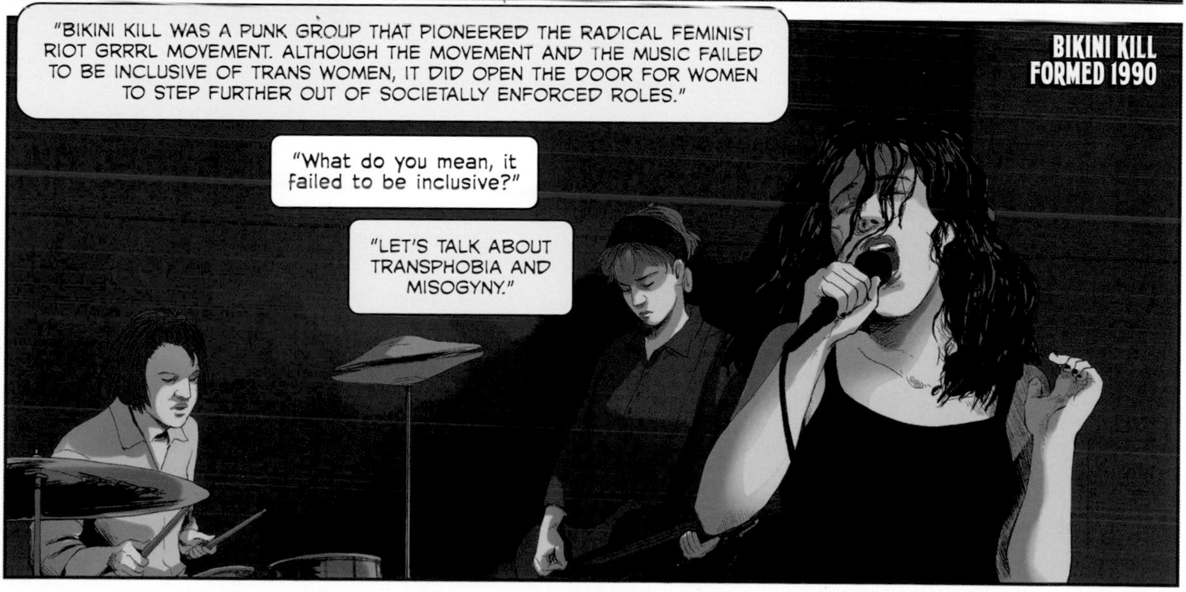
"BIKINI KILL WAS A PUNK GROUP THAT PIONEERED THE RADICAL FEMINIST RIOT GRRRL MOVEMENT. ALTHOUGH THE MOVEMENT AND THE MUSIC FAILED TO BE INCLUSIVE OF TRANS WOMEN, IT DID OPEN THE DOOR FOR WOMEN TO STEP FURTHER OUT OF SOCIETALLY ENFORCED ROLES."
BIKINI KILL
FORMED 1990
"What do you mean, it failed to be inclusive?"
"LET'S TALK ABOUT TRANSPHOBIA AND MISOGYNY."

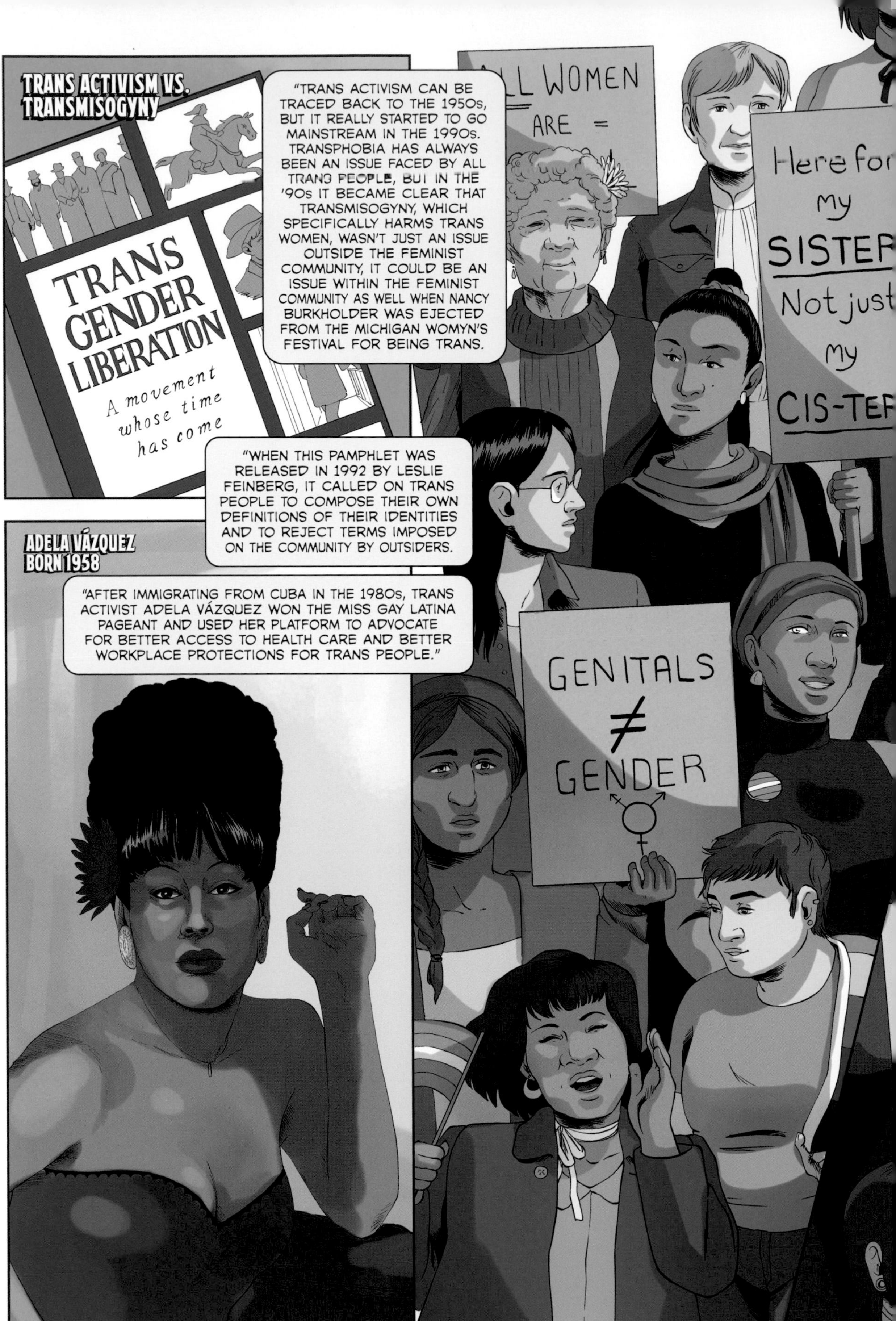

TRANS ACTIVISM VS. TRANSMISOGYNY
"TRANS ACTIVISM CAN BE TRACED BACK TO THE 1950s, BUT IT REALLY STARTED TO GO MAINSTREAM IN THE 1990s. TRANSPHOBIA HAS ALWAYS BEEN AN ISSUE FACED BY ALL TRANS PEOPLE, BUT IN THE '90s IT BECAME CLEAR THAT TRANSMISOGYNY, WHICH SPECIFICALLY HARMS TRANS WOMEN, WASN'T JUST AN ISSUE OUTSIDE THE FEMINIST COMMUNITY, IT COULD BE AN ISSUE WITHIN THE FEMINIST COMMUNITY AS WELL WHEN NANCY BURKHOLDER WAS EJECTED FROM THE MICHIGAN WOMYN'S FESTIVAL FOR BEING TRANS.
TRANS GENDER LIBERATION
A movement whose time has come
"WHEN THIS PAMPHLET WAS RELEASED IN 1992 BY LESLIE FEINBERG, IT CALLED ON TRANS PEOPLE TO COMPOSE THEIR OWN DEFINITIONS OF THEIR IDENTITIES AND TO REJECT TERMS IMPOSED ON THE COMMUNITY BY OUTSIDERS.
ADELA VÁZQUEZ BORN 1958
"AFTER IMMIGRATING FROM CUBA IN THE 1980s, TRANS ACTIVIST ADELA VÁZQUEZ WON THE MISS GAY LATINA PAGEANT AND USED HER PLATFORM TO ADVOCATE FOR BETTER ACCESS TO HEALTH CARE AND BETTER WORKPLACE PROTECTIONS FOR TRANS PEOPLE."
LL WOMEN
ARE =
Here for
my
SISTER
Not just
my
CIS-TE
GENITALS
≠
GENDER

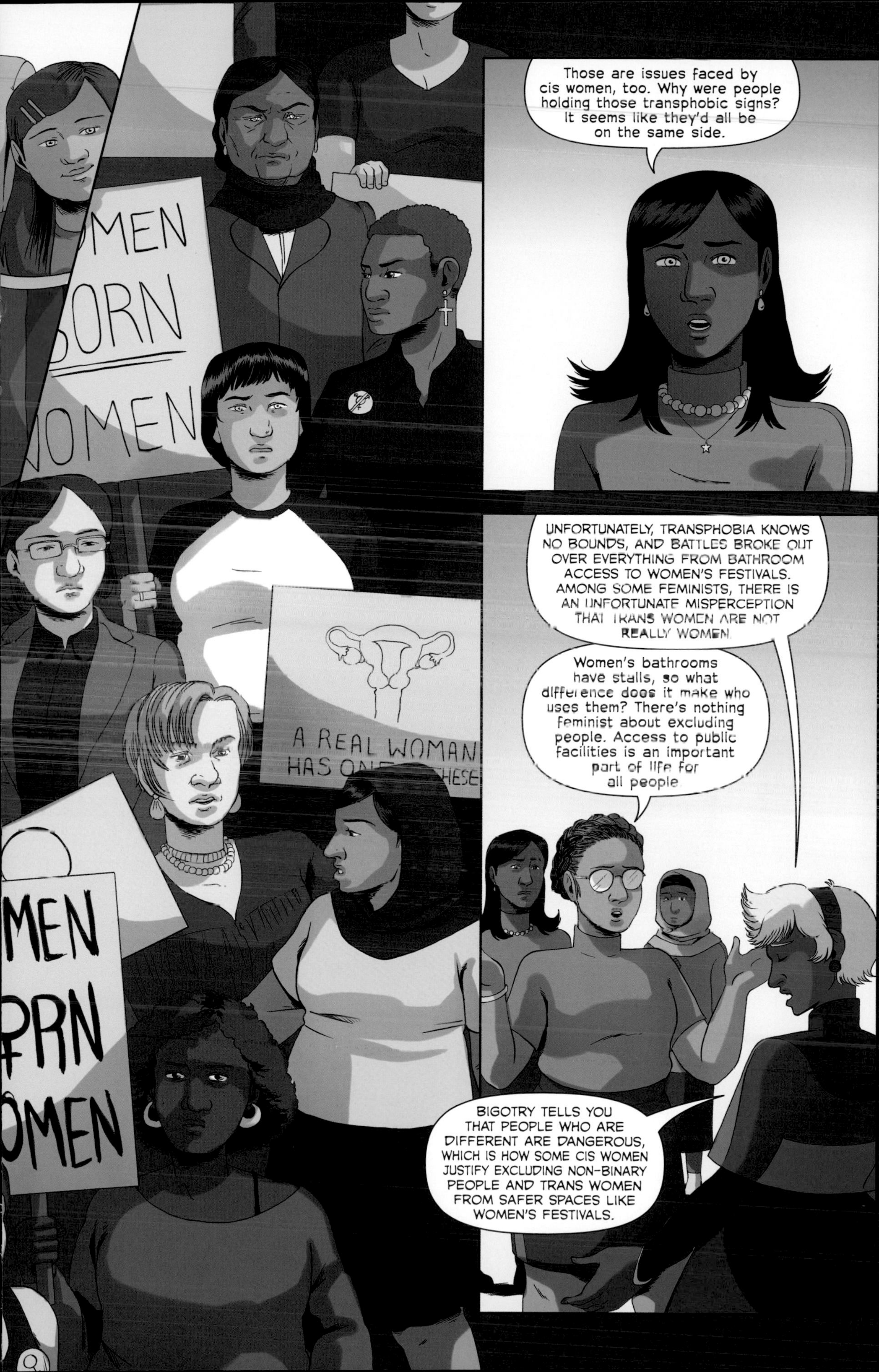
BORN
A REAL WOMAN
Those are issues faced by cis women, too. Why were people holding those transphobic signs? It seems like they'd all be on the same side.
UNFORTUNATELY, TRANSPHOBIA KNOWS NO BOUNDS, AND BATTLES BROKE OUT OVER EVERYTHING FROM BATHROOM ACCESS TO WOMEN'S FESTIVALS. AMONG SOME FEMINISTS, THERE IS AN UNFORTUNATE MISPERCEPTION THAT TRANS WOMEN ARE NOT REALLY WOMEN.
Women's bathrooms have stalls, so what difference does it make who uses them? There's nothing feminist about excluding people. Access to public facilities is an important part of life for all people.
BIGOTRY TELLS YOU THAT PEOPLE WHO ARE DIFFERENT ARE DANGEROUS, WHICH IS HOW SOME CIS WOMEN JUSTIFY EXCLUDING NON-BINARY PEOPLE AND TRANS WOMEN FROM SAFER SPACES LIKE WOMEN'S FESTIVALS.

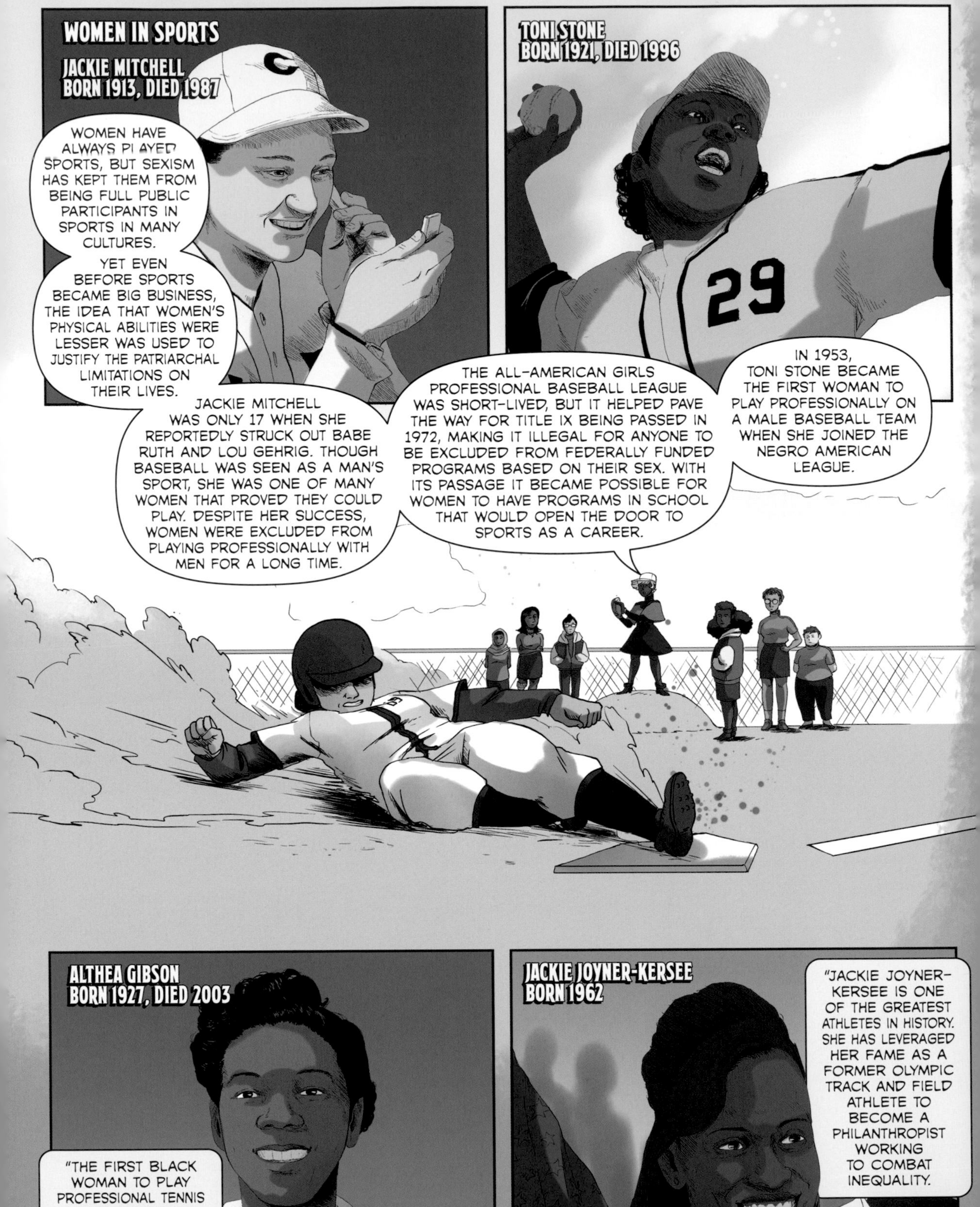
WOMEN IN SPORTS
JACKIE MITCHELL BORN 1913, DIED 1987
WOMEN HAVE ALWAYS PLAYED SPORTS, BUT SEXISM HAS KEPT THEM FROM BEING FULL PUBLIC PARTICIPANTS IN SPORTS IN MANY CULTURES.
YET EVEN BEFORE SPORTS BECAME BIG BUSINESS, THE IDEA THAT WOMEN'S PHYSICAL ABILITIES WERE LESSER WAS USED TO JUSTIFY THE PATRIARCHAL LIMITATIONS ON THEIR LIVES.
TONI STONE BORN 1921, DIED 1996
29
JACKIE MITCHELL WAS ONLY 17 WHEN SHE REPORTEDLY STRUCK OUT BABE RUTH AND LOU GEHRIG. THOUGH BASEBALL WAS SEEN AS A MAN'S SPORT, SHE WAS ONE OF MANY WOMEN THAT PROVED THEY COULD PLAY. DESPITE HER SUCCESS, WOMEN WERE EXCLUDED FROM PLAYING PROFESSIONALLY WITH MEN FOR A LONG TIME.
THE ALL-AMERICAN GIRLS PROFESSIONAL BASEBALL LEAGUE WAS SHORT-LIVED, BUT IT HELPED PAVE THE WAY FOR TITLE IX BEING PASSED IN 1972, MAKING IT ILLEGAL FOR ANYONE TO BE EXCLUDED FROM FEDERALLY FUNDED PROGRAMS BASED ON THEIR SEX. WITH ITS PASSAGE IT BECAME POSSIBLE FOR WOMEN TO HAVE PROGRAMS IN SCHOOL THAT WOULD OPEN THE DOOR TO SPORTS AS A CAREER.
IN 1953, TONI STONE BECAME THE FIRST WOMAN TO PLAY PROFESSIONALLY ON A MALE BASEBALL TEAM WHEN SHE JOINED THE NEGRO AMERICAN LEAGUE.
ALTHEA GIBSON BORN 1927, DIED 2003
"THE FIRST BLACK WOMAN TO PLAY PROFESSIONAL TENNIS INTERNATIONALLY, ALTHEA GIBSON WENT ON TO BE A PROFESSIONAL GOLFER AND A KEY FIGURE IN BRINGING ACCESS TO SPORTS TO UNDERSERVED COMMUNITIES.
JACKIE JOYNER-KERSEE BORN 1962
"JACKIE JOYNER-KERSEE IS ONE OF THE GREATEST ATHLETES IN HISTORY. SHE HAS LEVERAGED HER FAME AS A FORMER OLYMPIC TRACK AND FIELD ATHLETE TO BECOME A PHILANTHROPIST WORKING TO COMBAT INEQUALITY.

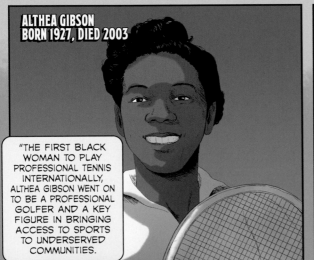

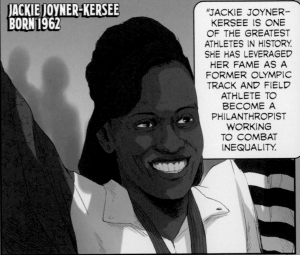

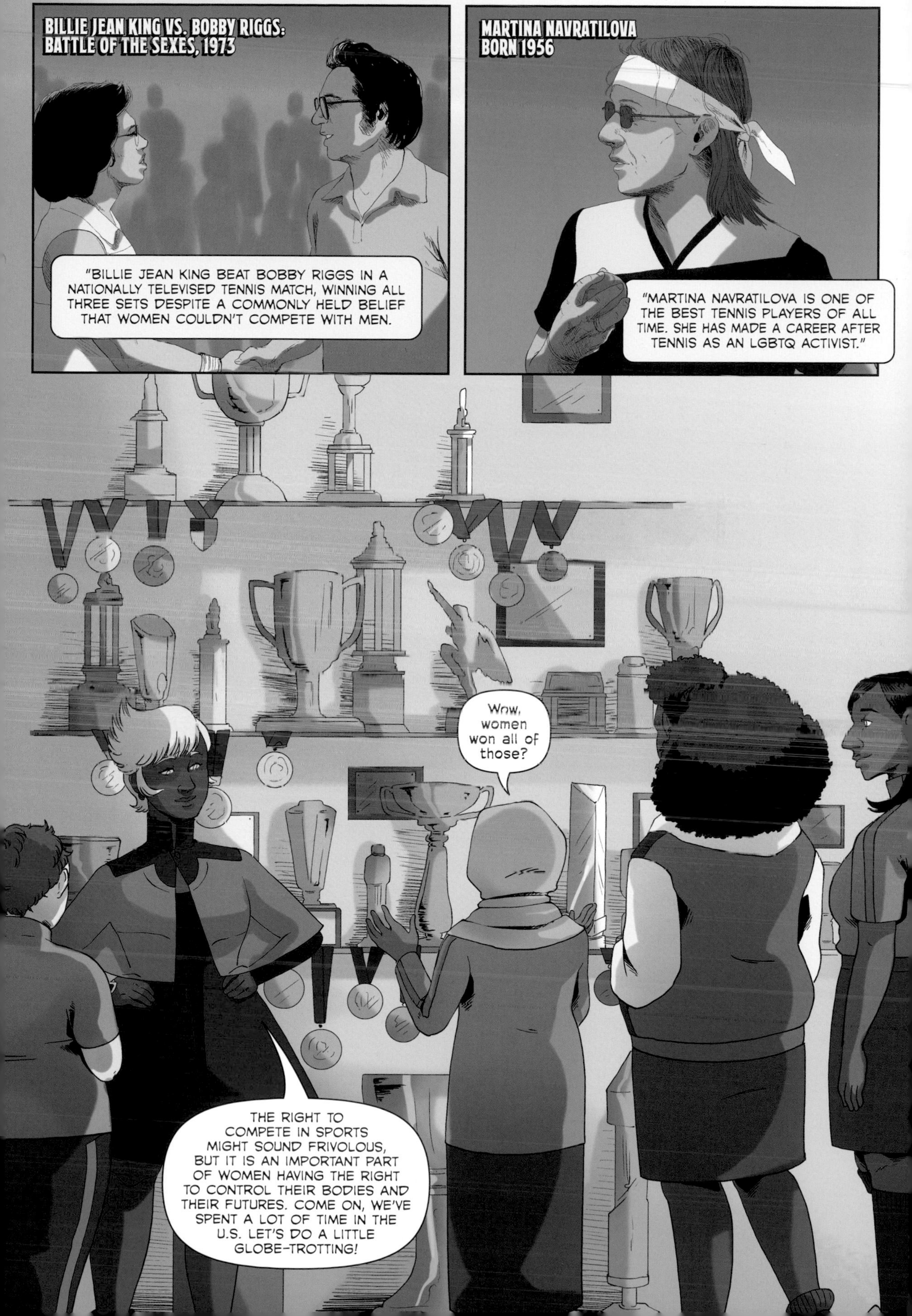

BILLIE JEAN KING VS. BOBBY RIGGS: BATTLE OF THE SEXES, 1973
"BILLIE JEAN KING BEAT BOBBY RIGGS IN A NATIONALLY TELEVISED TENNIS MATCH, WINNING ALL THREE SETS DESPITE A COMMONLY HELD BELIEF THAT WOMEN COULDN'T COMPETE WITH MEN.
MARTINA NAVRATILOVA BORN 1956
"MARTINA NAVRATILOVA IS ONE OF THE BEST TENNIS PLAYERS OF ALL TIME. SHE HAS MADE A CAREER AFTER TENNIS AS AN LGBTQ ACTIVIST."
Wow, women won all of those?
THE RIGHT TO COMPETE IN SPORTS MIGHT SOUND FRIVOLOUS, BUT IT IS AN IMPORTANT PART OF WOMEN HAVING THE RIGHT TO CONTROL THEIR BODIES AND THEIR FUTURES. COME ON, WE'VE SPENT A LOT OF TIME IN THE U.S. LET'S DO A LITTLE GLOBE-TROTTING!

WOMEN'S LEADERSHIP AROUND THE WORLD

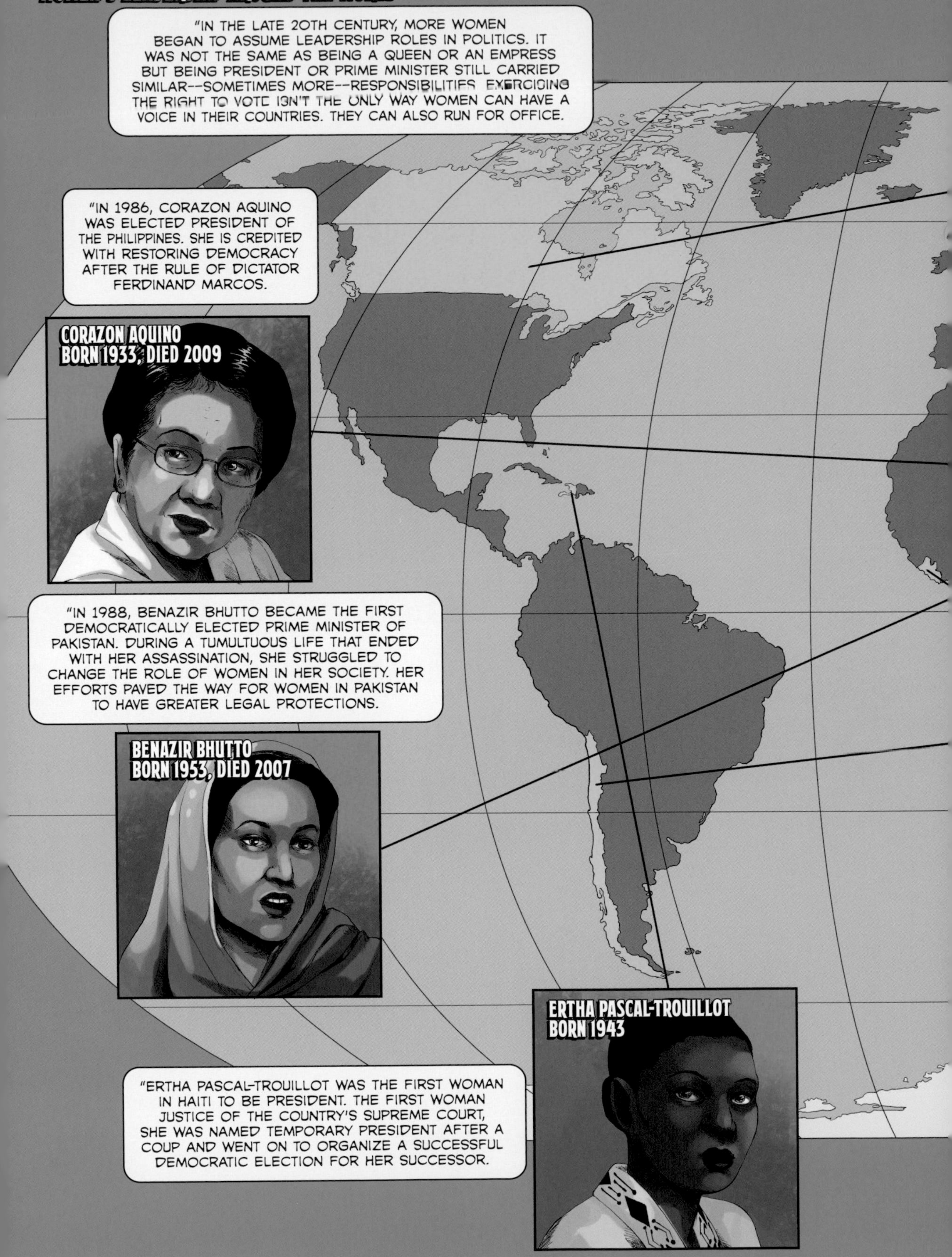
"IN THE LATE 20TH CENTURY, MORE WOMEN BEGAN TO ASSUME LEADERSHIP ROLES IN POLITICS. IT WAS NOT THE SAME AS BEING A QUEEN OR AN EMPRESS BUT BEING PRESIDENT OR PRIME MINISTER STILL CARRIED SIMILAR--SOMETIMES MORE--RESPONSIBILITIES. EXERCISING THE RIGHT TO VOTE ISN'T THE ONLY WAY WOMEN CAN HAVE A VOICE IN THEIR COUNTRIES. THEY CAN ALSO RUN FOR OFFICE.
"IN 1986, CORAZON AQUINO WAS ELECTED PRESIDENT OF THE PHILIPPINES. SHE IS CREDITED WITH RESTORING DEMOCRACY AFTER THE RULE OF DICTATOR FERDINAND MARCOS.
CORAZON AQUINO BORN 1933, DIED 2009
"IN 1988, BENAZIR BHUTTO BECAME THE FIRST DEMOCRATICALLY ELECTED PRIME MINISTER OF PAKISTAN. DURING A TUMULTUOUS LIFE THAT ENDED WITH HER ASSASSINATION, SHE STRUGGLED TO CHANGE THE ROLE OF WOMEN IN HER SOCIETY. HER EFFORTS PAVED THE WAY FOR WOMEN IN PAKISTAN TO HAVE GREATER LEGAL PROTECTIONS.
BENAZIR BHUTTO BORN 1953, DIED 2007
ERTHA PASCAL-TROUILLOT BORN 1943
"ERTHA PASCAL-TROUILLOT WAS THE FIRST WOMAN IN HAITI TO BE PRESIDENT. THE FIRST WOMAN JUSTICE OF THE COUNTRY'S SUPREME COURT, SHE WAS NAMED TEMPORARY PRESIDENT AFTER A COUP AND WENT ON TO ORGANIZE A SUCCESSFUL DEMOCRATIC ELECTION FOR HER SUCCESSOR.

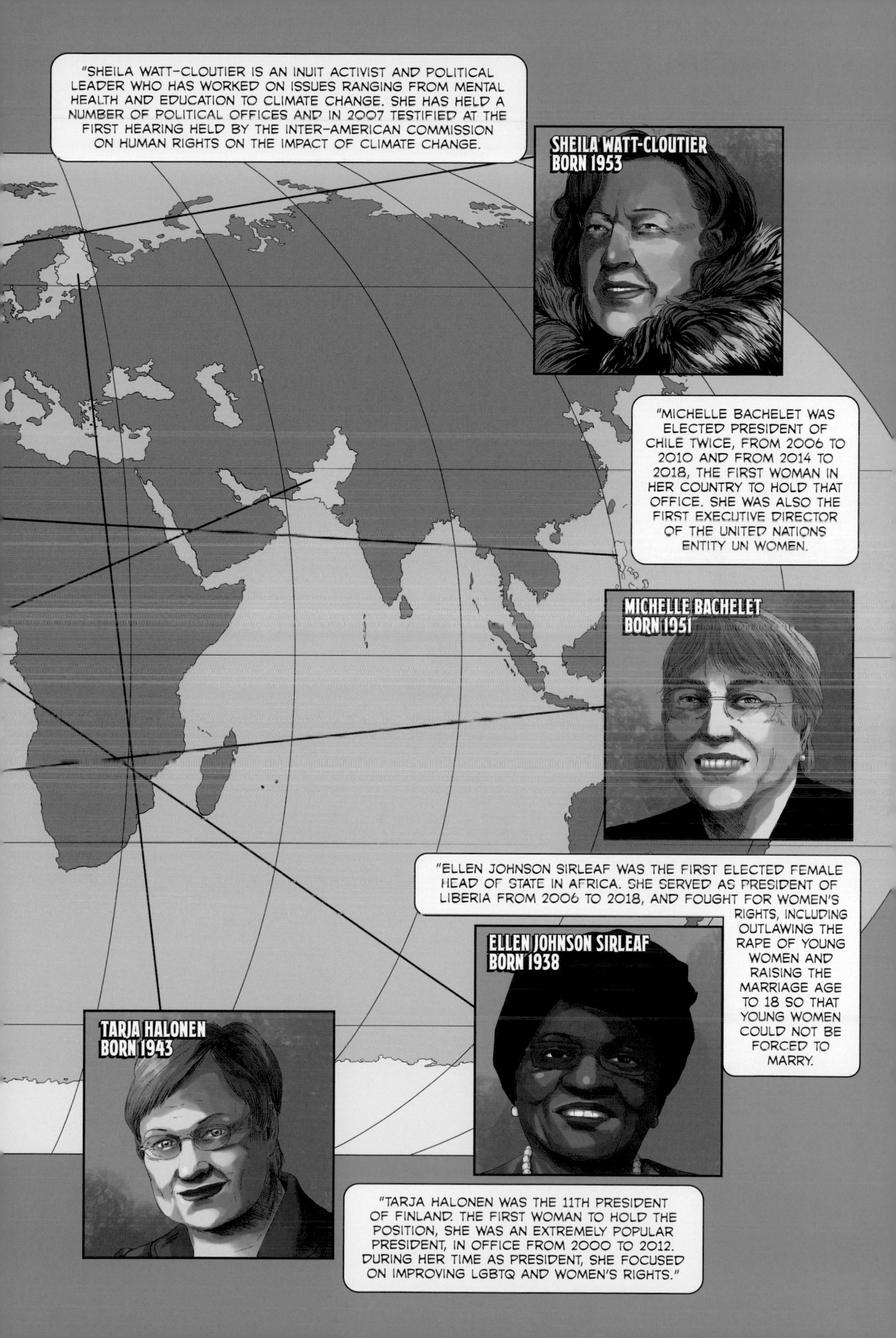
"SHEILA WATT-CLOUTIER IS AN INUIT ACTIVIST AND POLITICAL LEADER WHO HAS WORKED ON ISSUES RANGING FROM MENTAL HEALTH AND EDUCATION TO CLIMATE CHANGE. SHE HAS HELD A NUMBER OF POLITICAL OFFICES AND IN 2007 TESTIFIED AT THE FIRST HEARING HELD BY THE INTER-AMERICAN COMMISSION ON HUMAN RIGHTS ON THE IMPACT OF CLIMATE CHANGE.
SHEILA WATT-CLOUTIER BORN 1953
"MICHELLE BACHELET WAS ELECTED PRESIDENT OF CHILE TWICE, FROM 2006 TO 2010 AND FROM 2014 TO 2018, THE FIRST WOMAN IN HER COUNTRY TO HOLD THAT OFFICE. SHE WAS ALSO THE FIRST EXECUTIVE DIRECTOR OF THE UNITED NATIONS ENTITY UN WOMEN.
MICHELLE BACHELET BORN 1951
"ELLEN JOHNSON SIRLEAF WAS THE FIRST ELECTED FEMALE HEAD OF STATE IN AFRICA. SHE SERVED AS PRESIDENT OF LIBERIA FROM 2006 TO 2018, AND FOUGHT FOR WOMEN'S RIGHTS, INCLUDING OUTLAWING THE RAPE OF YOUNG WOMEN AND RAISING THE MARRIAGE AGE TO 18 SO THAT YOUNG WOMEN COULD NOT BE FORCED TO MARRY.
ELLEN JOHNSON SIRLEAF BORN 1938
TARJA HALONEN BORN 1943
"TARJA HALONEN WAS THE 11TH PRESIDENT OF FINLAND. THE FIRST WOMAN TO HOLD THE POSITION, SHE WAS AN EXTREMELY POPULAR PRESIDENT, IN OFFICE FROM 2000 TO 2012. DURING HER TIME AS PRESIDENT, SHE FOCUSED ON IMPROVING LGBTQ AND WOMEN'S RIGHTS."

CHAPTER 7
FEMINISMS: CORPORATE, INCLUSIVE, AND MORE!

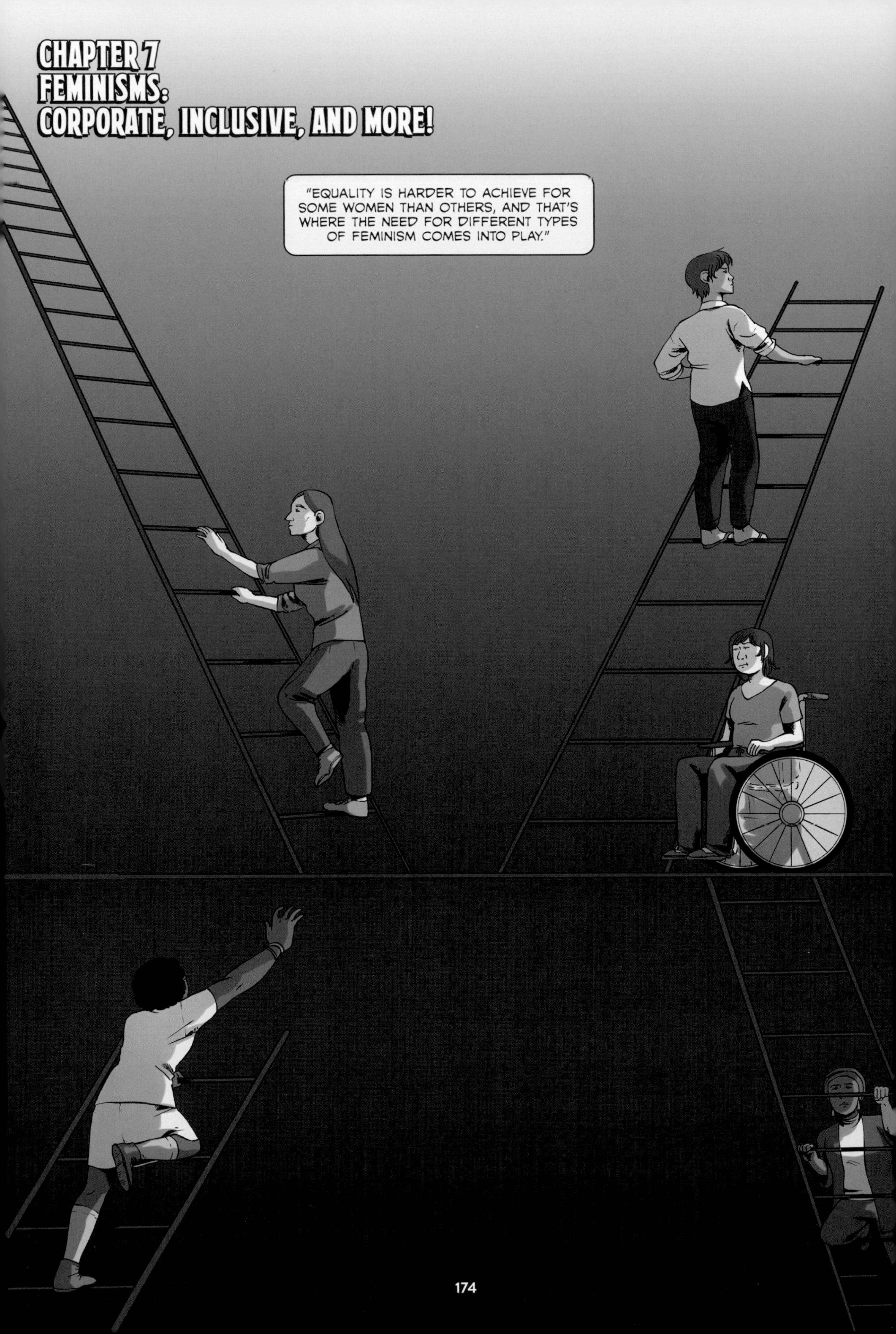
"EQUALITY IS HARDER TO ACHIEVE FOR SOME WOMEN THAN OTHERS, AND THAT'S WHERE THE NEED FOR DIFFERENT TYPES OF FEMINISM COMES INTO PLAY."

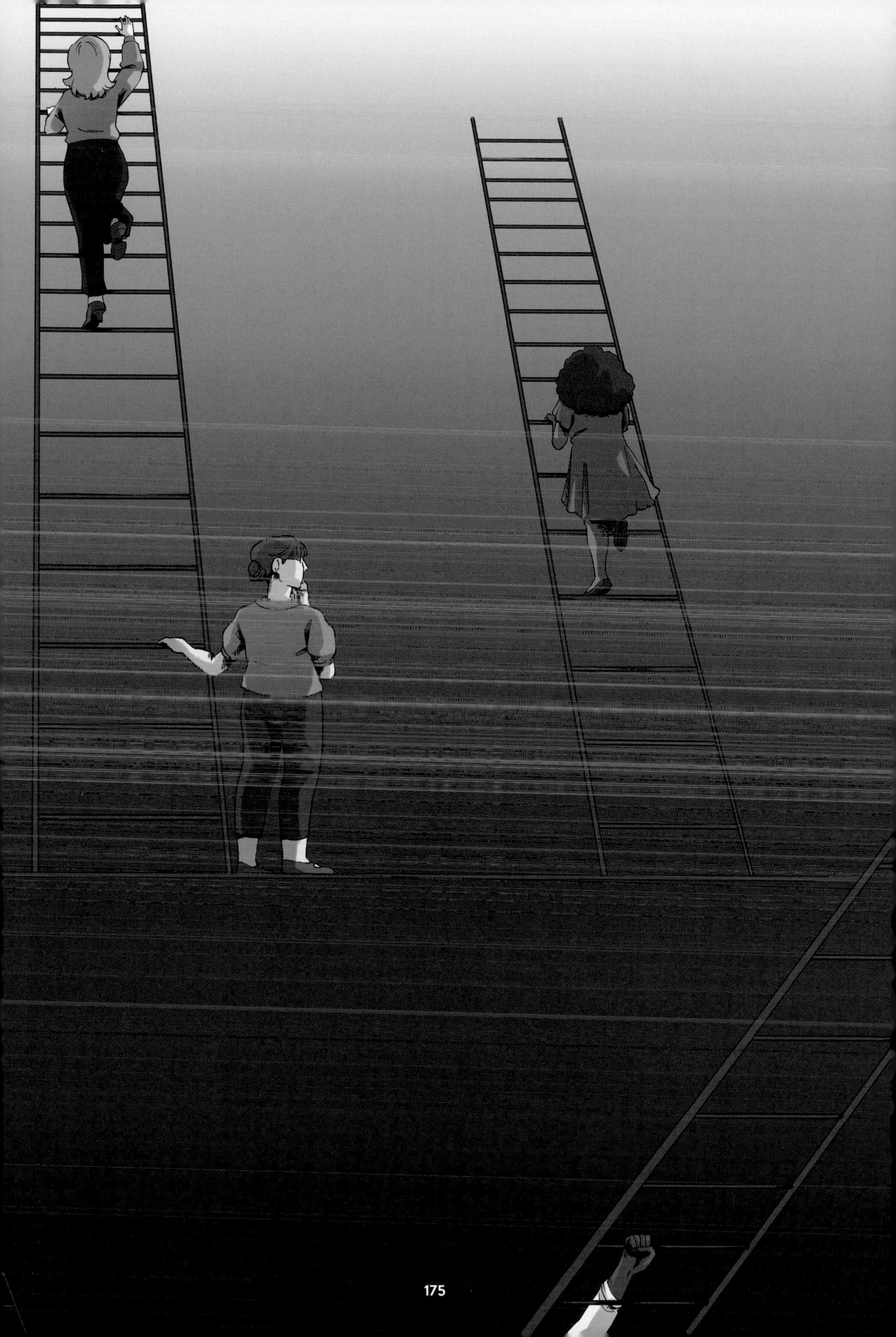

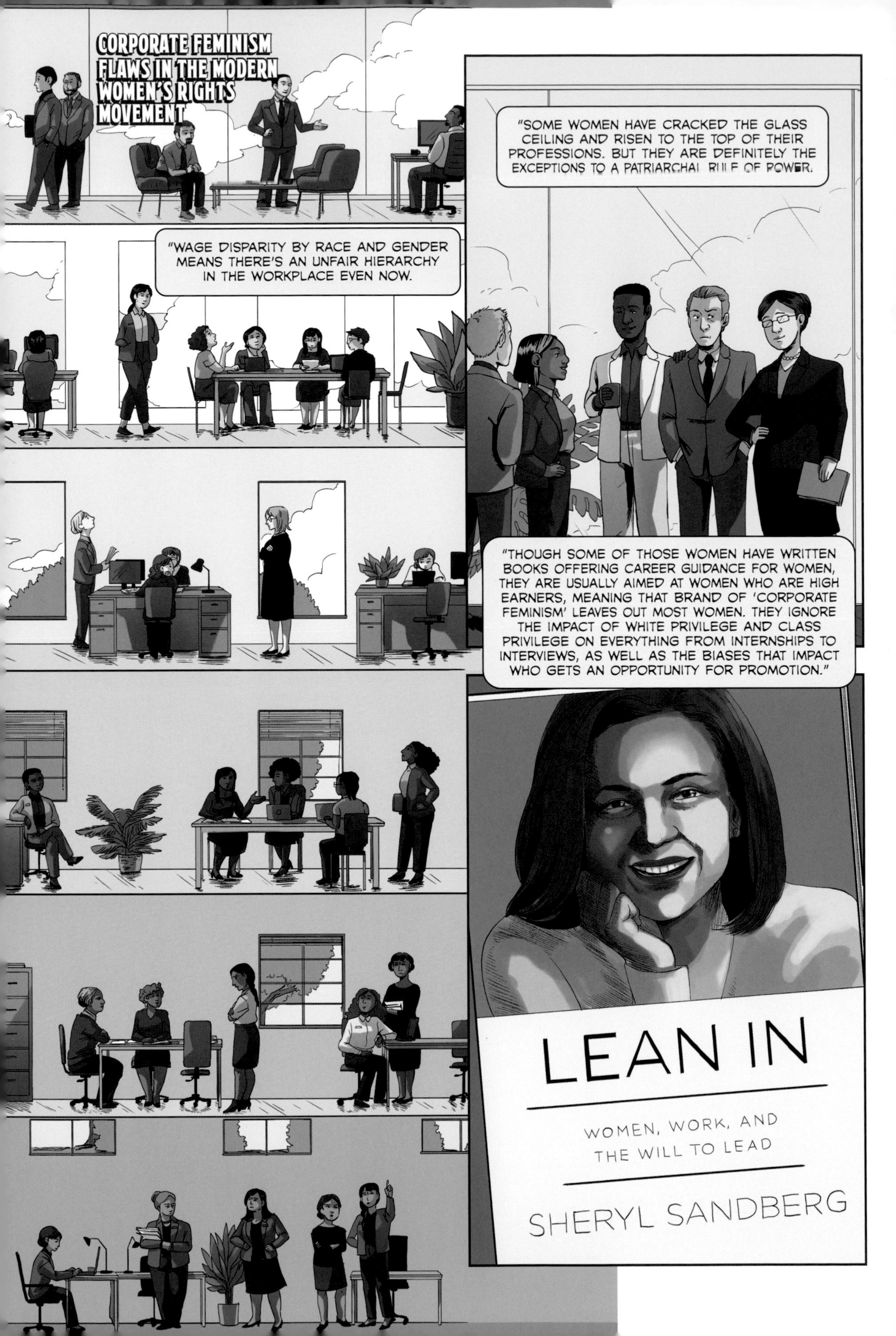
CORPORATE FEMINISM
FLAWS IN THE MODERN WOMEN'S RIGHTS MOVEMENT
"WAGE DISPARITY BY RACE AND GENDER MEANS THERE'S AN UNFAIR HIERARCHY IN THE WORKPLACE EVEN NOW.
"SOME WOMEN HAVE CRACKED THE GLASS CEILING AND RISEN TO THE TOP OF THEIR PROFESSIONS. BUT THEY ARE DEFINITELY THE EXCEPTIONS TO A PATRIARCHAL RULE OF POWER.
"THOUGH SOME OF THOSE WOMEN HAVE WRITTEN BOOKS OFFERING CAREER GUIDANCE FOR WOMEN, THEY ARE USUALLY AIMED AT WOMEN WHO ARE HIGH EARNERS, MEANING THAT BRAND OF 'CORPORATE FEMINISM' LEAVES OUT MOST WOMEN. THEY IGNORE THE IMPACT OF WHITE PRIVILEGE AND CLASS PRIVILEGE ON EVERYTHING FROM INTERNSHIPS TO INTERVIEWS, AS WELL AS THE BIASES THAT IMPACT WHO GETS AN OPPORTUNITY FOR PROMOTION."
LEAN IN
WOMEN, WORK, AND THE WILL TO LEAD
SHERYL SANDBERG

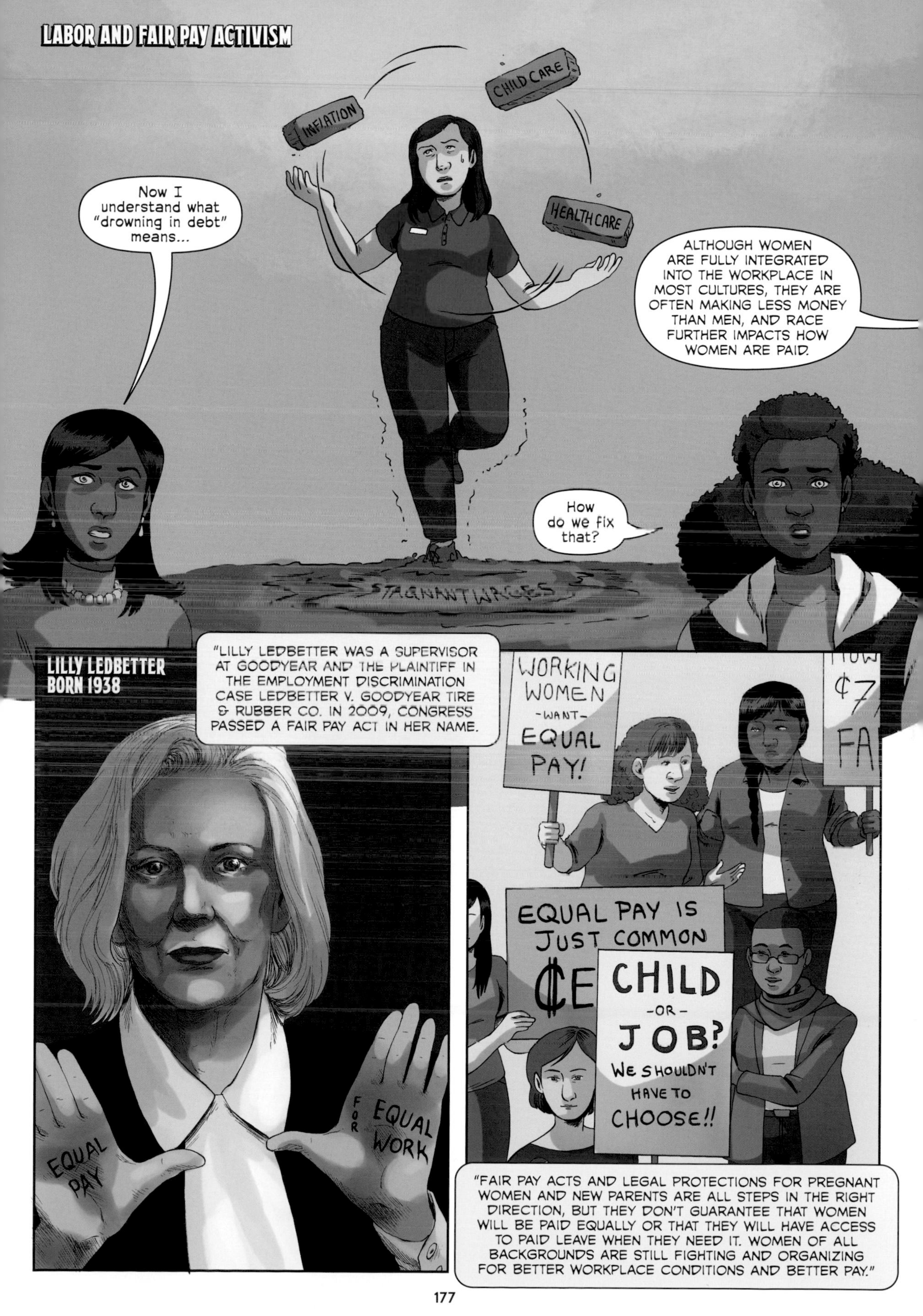
LABOR AND FAIR PAY ACTIVISM
INFLATION
CHILD CARE
HEALTH CARE
Now I understand what "drowning in debt" means...
ALTHOUGH WOMEN ARE FULLY INTEGRATED INTO THE WORKPLACE IN MOST CULTURES, THEY ARE OFTEN MAKING LESS MONEY THAN MEN, AND RACE FURTHER IMPACTS HOW WOMEN ARE PAID.
How do we fix that?
STAGNANT WAGES
LILLY LEDBETTER
BORN 1938
"LILLY LEDBETTER WAS A SUPERVISOR AT GOODYEAR AND THE PLAINTIFF IN THE EMPLOYMENT DISCRIMINATION CASE LEDBETTER V. GOODYEAR TIRE & RUBBER CO. IN 2009, CONGRESS PASSED A FAIR PAY ACT IN HER NAME.
EQUAL PAY
FOR EQUAL WORK
WORKING WOMEN -WANT- EQUAL PAY!
EQUAL PAY IS JUST COMMON ¢E
CHILD -OR- JOB? WE SHOULDN'T HAVE TO CHOOSE!!
"FAIR PAY ACTS AND LEGAL PROTECTIONS FOR PREGNANT WOMEN AND NEW PARENTS ARE ALL STEPS IN THE RIGHT DIRECTION, BUT THEY DON'T GUARANTEE THAT WOMEN WILL BE PAID EQUALLY OR THAT THEY WILL HAVE ACCESS TO PAID LEAVE WHEN THEY NEED IT. WOMEN OF ALL BACKGROUNDS ARE STILL FIGHTING AND ORGANIZING FOR BETTER WORKPLACE CONDITIONS AND BETTER PAY."

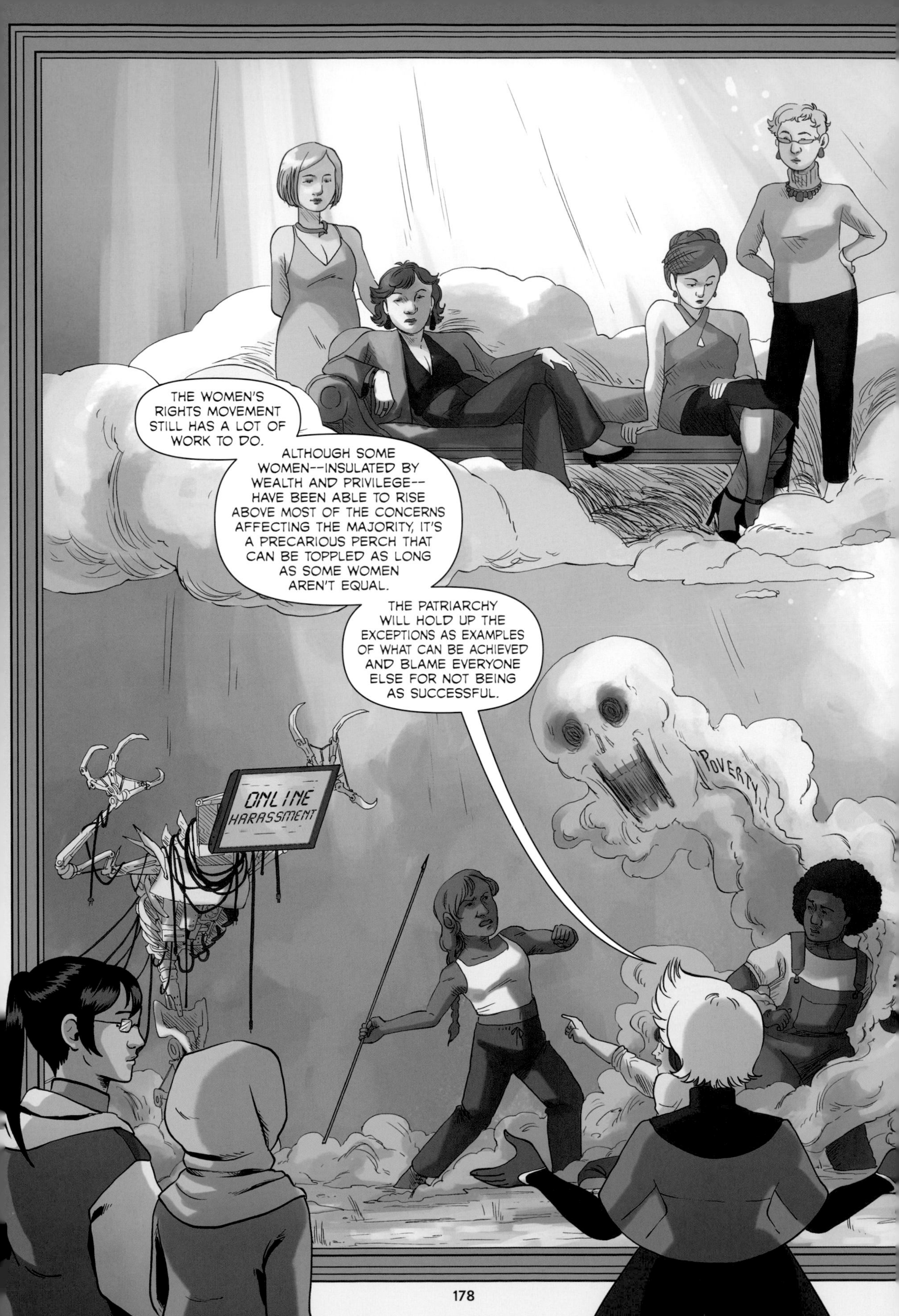
THE WOMEN'S RIGHTS MOVEMENT STILL HAS A LOT OF WORK TO DO.
ALTHOUGH SOME WOMEN--INSULATED BY WEALTH AND PRIVILEGE--HAVE BEEN ABLE TO RISE ABOVE MOST OF THE CONCERNS AFFECTING THE MAJORITY, IT'S A PRECARIOUS PERCH THAT CAN BE TOPPLED AS LONG AS SOME WOMEN AREN'T EQUAL.
THE PATRIARCHY WILL HOLD UP THE EXCEPTIONS AS EXAMPLES OF WHAT CAN BE ACHIEVED AND BLAME EVERYONE ELSE FOR NOT BEING AS SUCCESSFUL.
POVERTY
ONLINE HARASSMENT

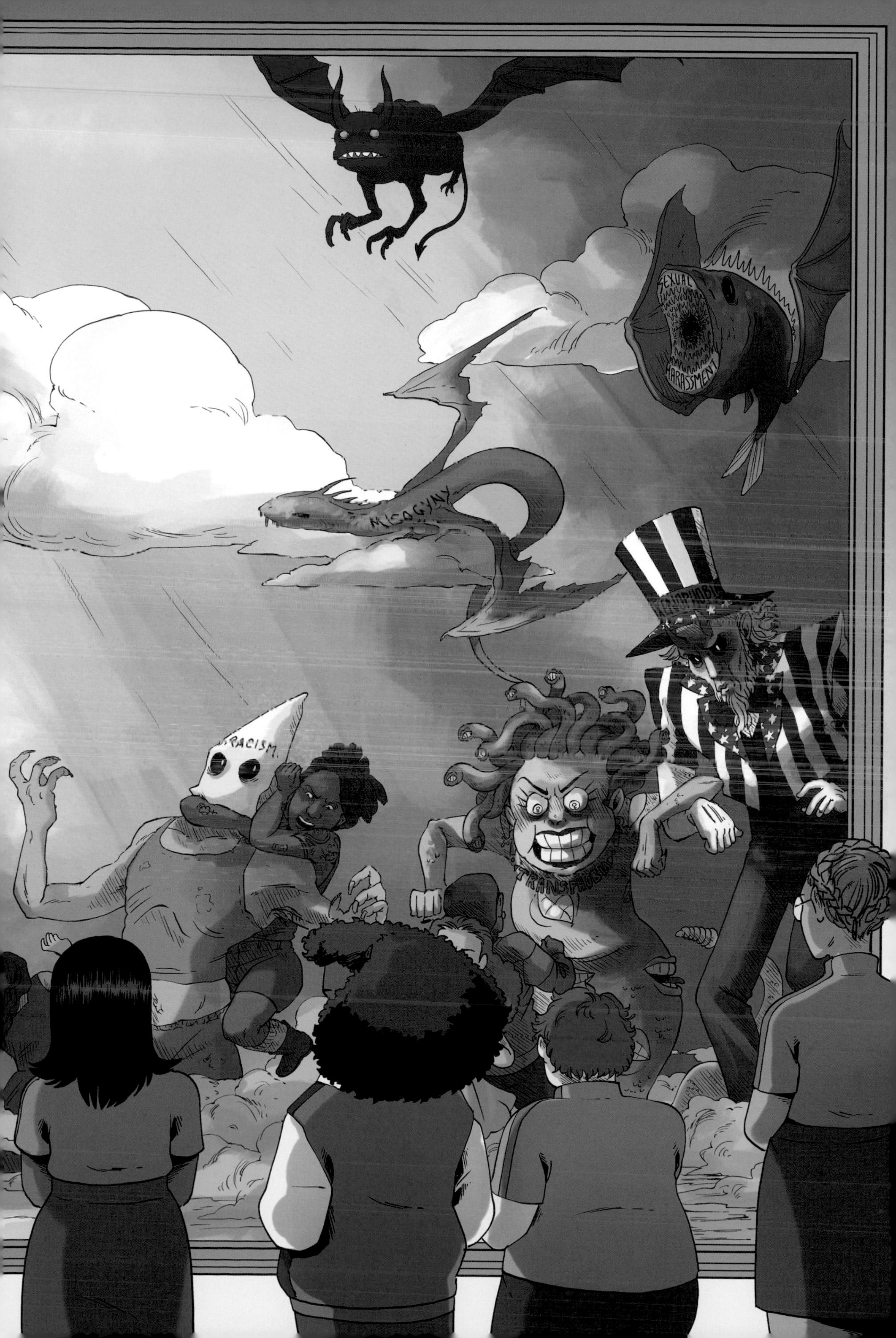
SEXUAL HARASSMENT
MISOGYNY
RACISM.
TRANSPHOBIA

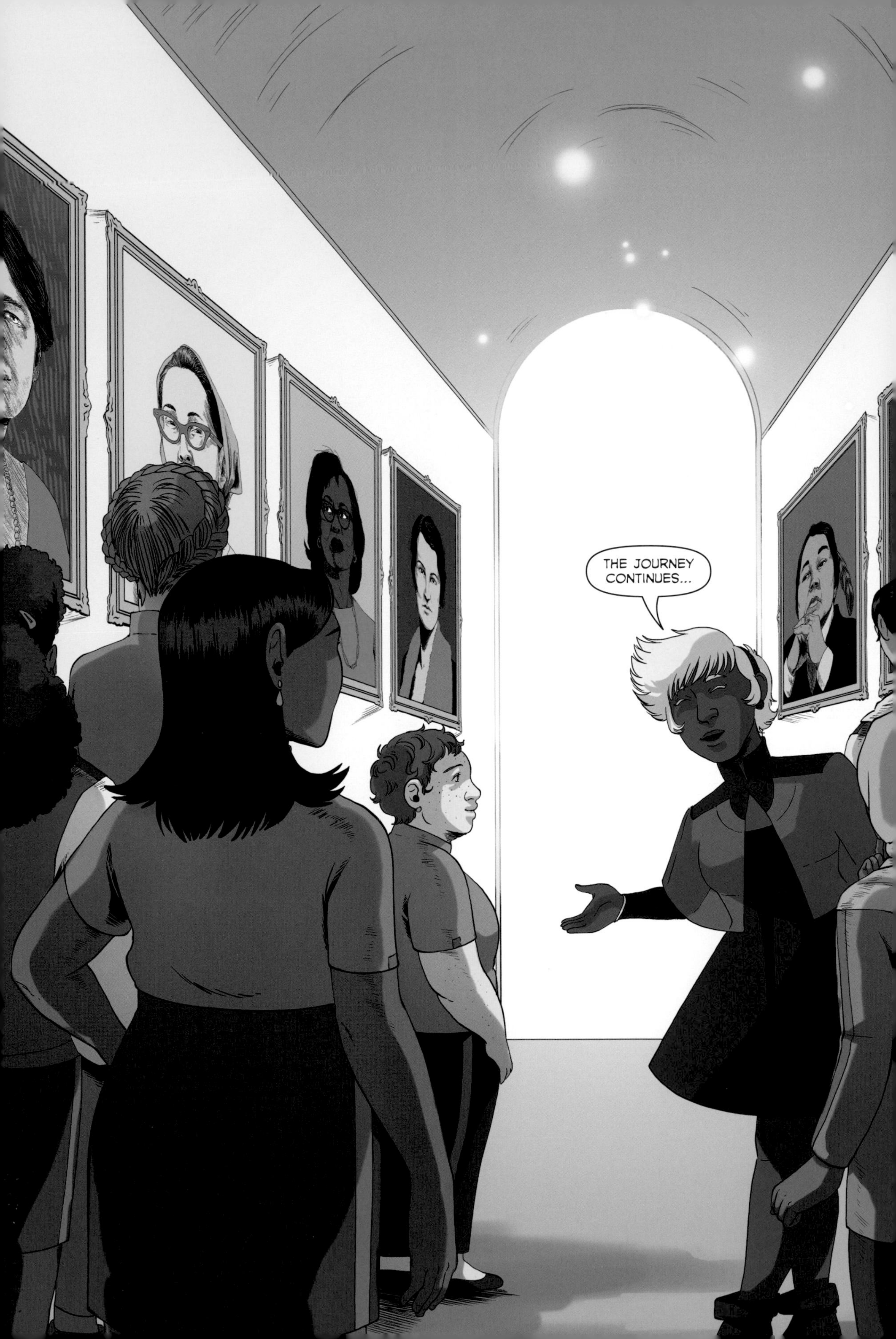
THE JOURNEY CONTINUES...

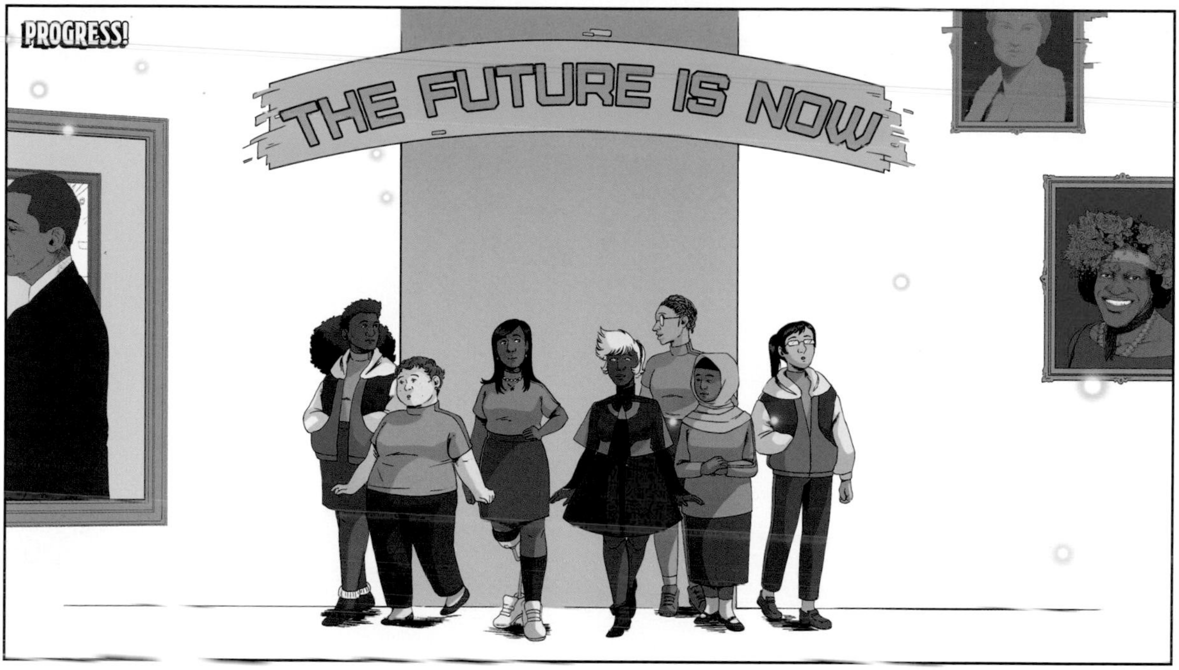
PROGRESS!
THE FUTURE IS NOW

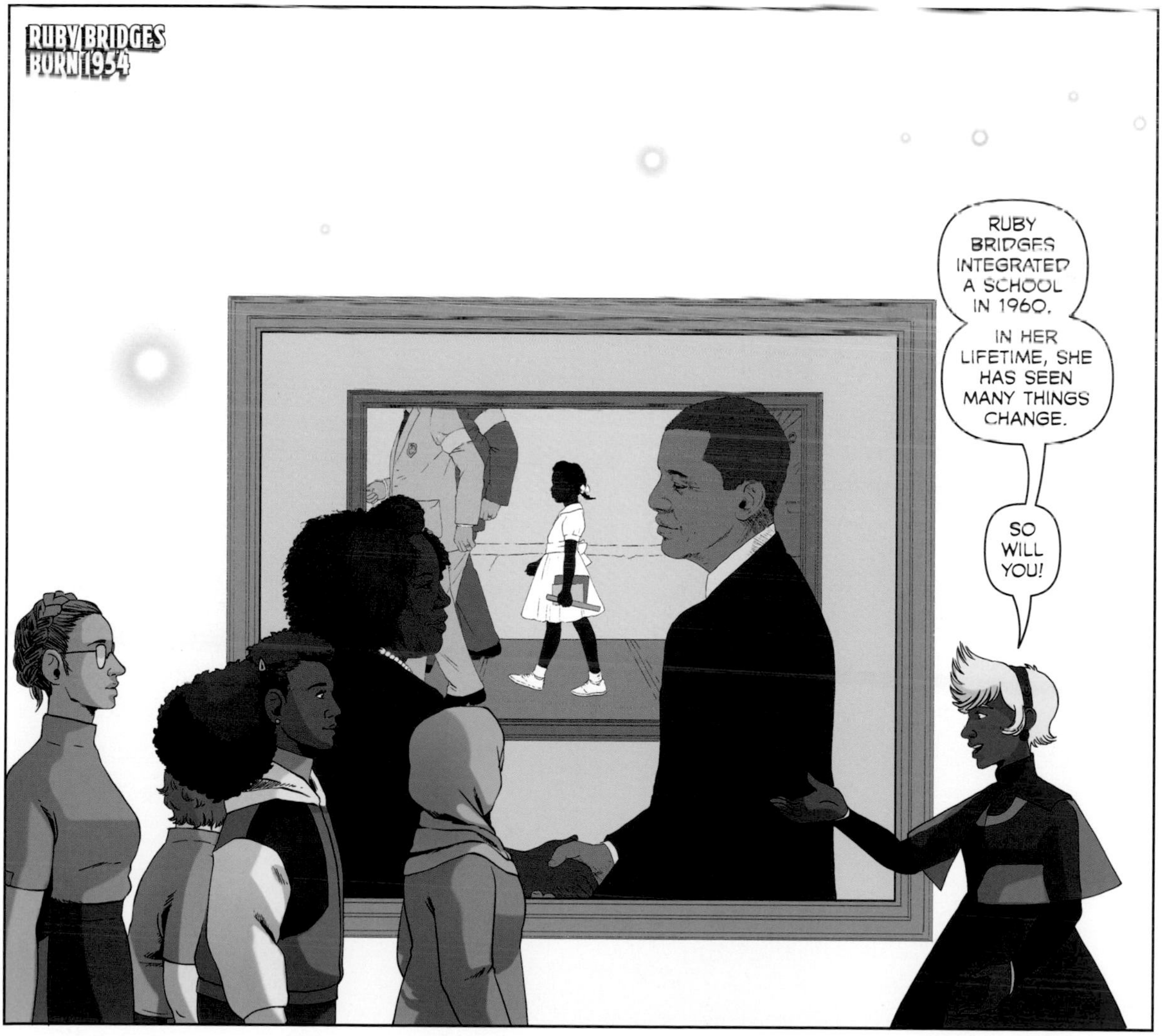
RUBY BRIDGES
BORN 1954
RUBY BRIDGES INTEGRATED A SCHOOL IN 1960.
IN HER LIFETIME, SHE HAS SEEN MANY THINGS CHANGE.
SO WILL YOU!

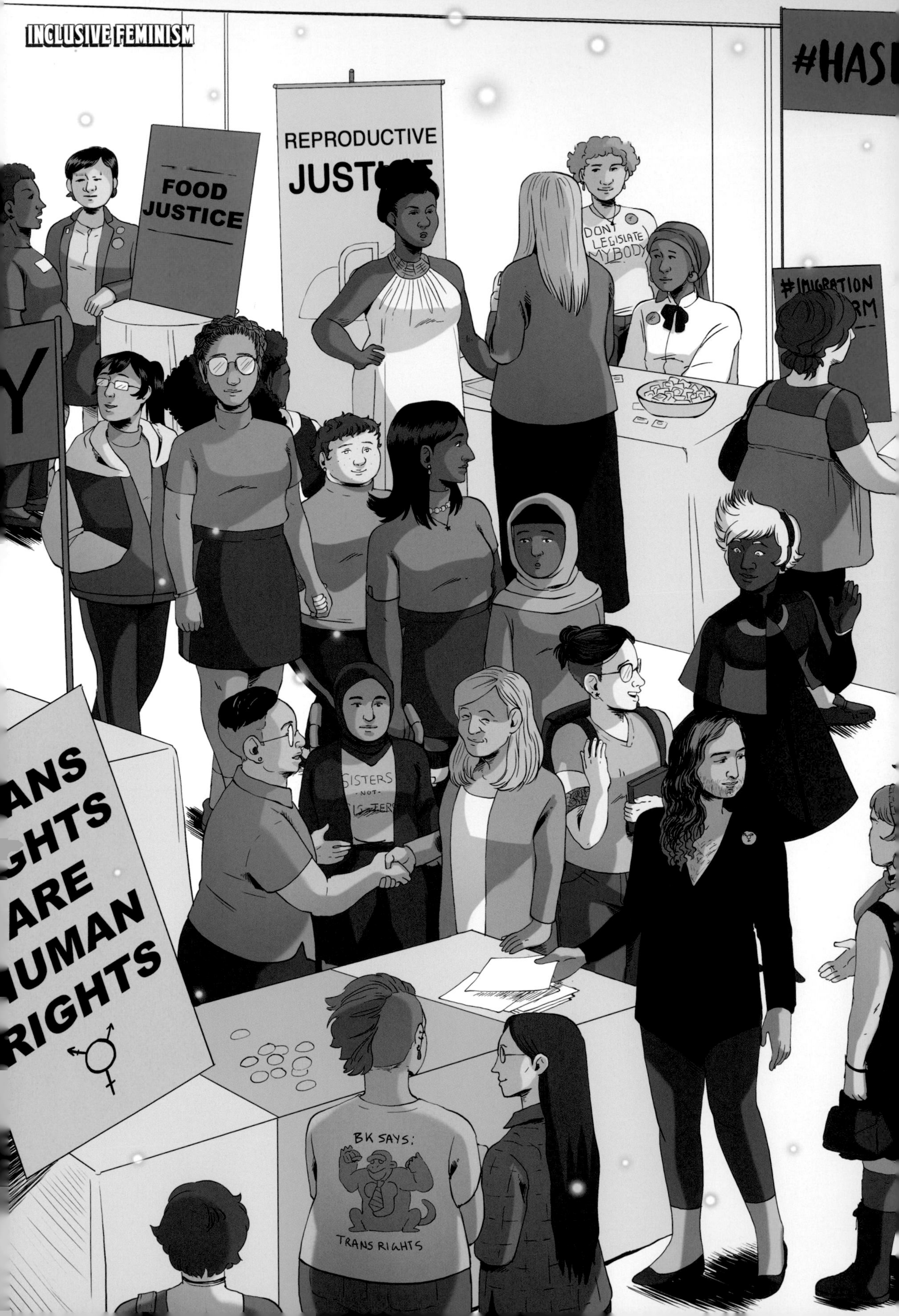
FOOD
JUSTICE
REPRODUCTIVE
DONT
LEGISLATE
MYBODY
#IMIGRATION
BK SAYS:
TRANS RIGHTS

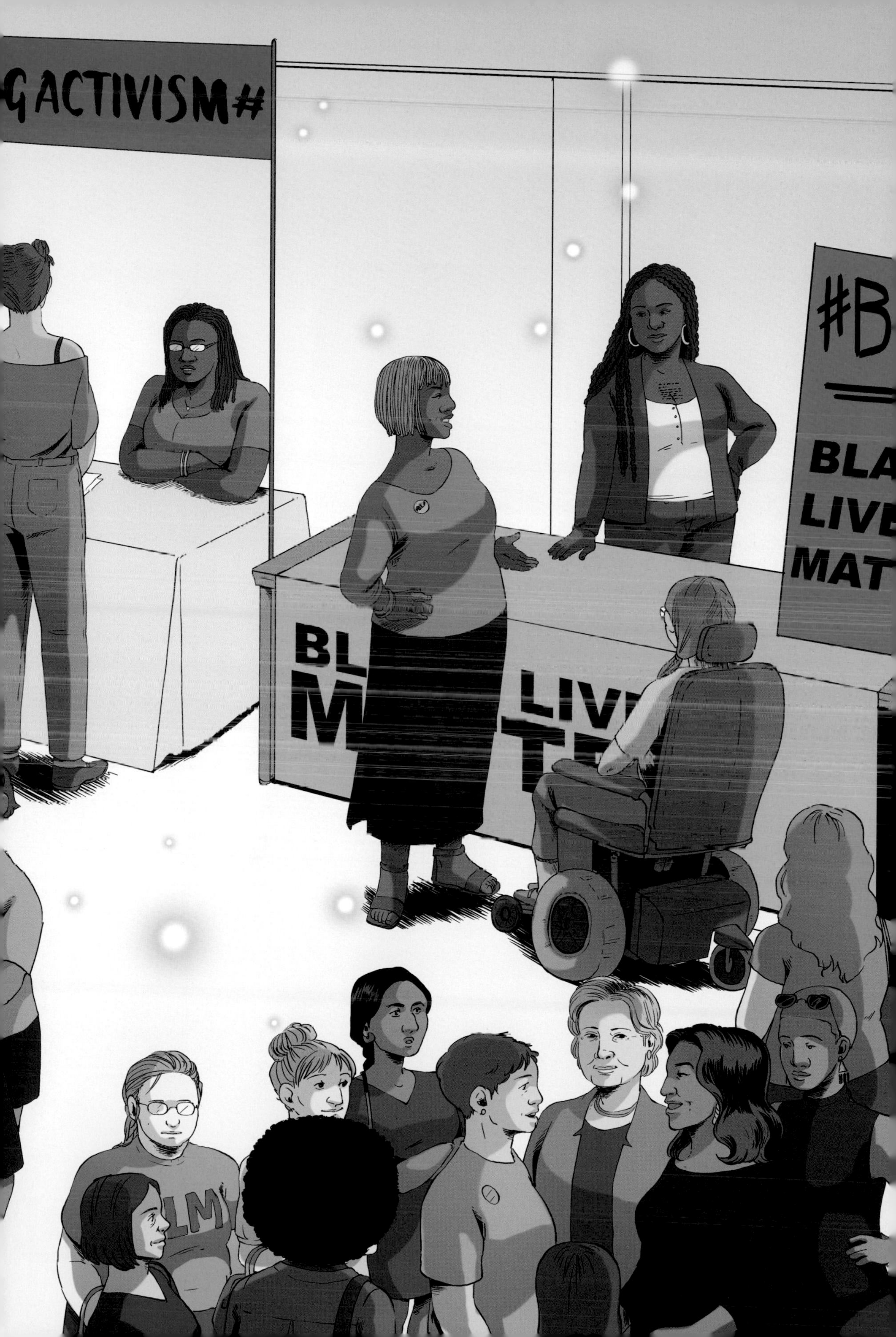
GACTIVISM#
#B
BLA
LIVE
MAT
BL
M
LIVE
LM

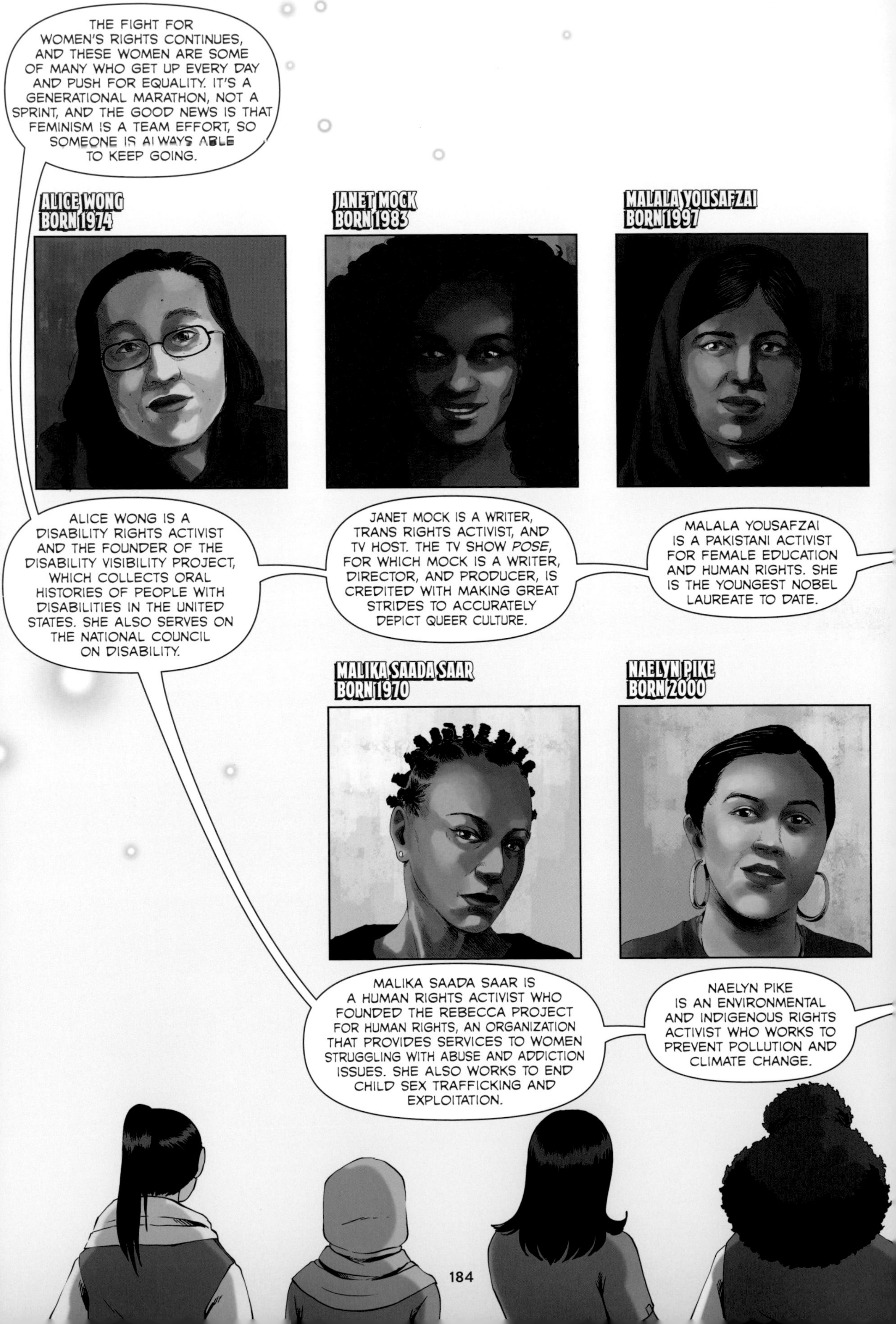
THE FIGHT FOR WOMEN'S RIGHTS CONTINUES, AND THESE WOMEN ARE SOME OF MANY WHO GET UP EVERY DAY AND PUSH FOR EQUALITY. IT'S A GENERATIONAL MARATHON, NOT A SPRINT, AND THE GOOD NEWS IS THAT FEMINISM IS A TEAM EFFORT, SO SOMEONE IS ALWAYS ABLE TO KEEP GOING.
ALICE WONG BORN 1974
JANET MOCK BORN 1983
MALALA YOUSAFZAI BORN 1997
ALICE WONG IS A DISABILITY RIGHTS ACTIVIST AND THE FOUNDER OF THE DISABILITY VISIBILITY PROJECT, WHICH COLLECTS ORAL HISTORIES OF PEOPLE WITH DISABILITIES IN THE UNITED STATES. SHE ALSO SERVES ON THE NATIONAL COUNCIL ON DISABILITY.
JANET MOCK IS A WRITER, TRANS RIGHTS ACTIVIST, AND TV HOST. THE TV SHOW *POSE*, FOR WHICH MOCK IS A WRITER, DIRECTOR, AND PRODUCER, IS CREDITED WITH MAKING GREAT STRIDES TO ACCURATELY DEPICT QUEER CULTURE.
MALALA YOUSAFZAI IS A PAKISTANI ACTIVIST FOR FEMALE EDUCATION AND HUMAN RIGHTS. SHE IS THE YOUNGEST NOBEL LAUREATE TO DATE.
MALIKA SAADA SAAR BORN 1970
NAELYN PIKE BORN 2000
MALIKA SAADA SAAR IS A HUMAN RIGHTS ACTIVIST WHO FOUNDED THE REBECCA PROJECT FOR HUMAN RIGHTS, AN ORGANIZATION THAT PROVIDES SERVICES TO WOMEN STRUGGLING WITH ABUSE AND ADDICTION ISSUES. SHE ALSO WORKS TO END CHILD SEX TRAFFICKING AND EXPLOITATION.
NAELYN PIKE IS AN ENVIRONMENTAL AND INDIGENOUS RIGHTS ACTIVIST WHO WORKS TO PREVENT POLLUTION AND CLIMATE CHANGE.

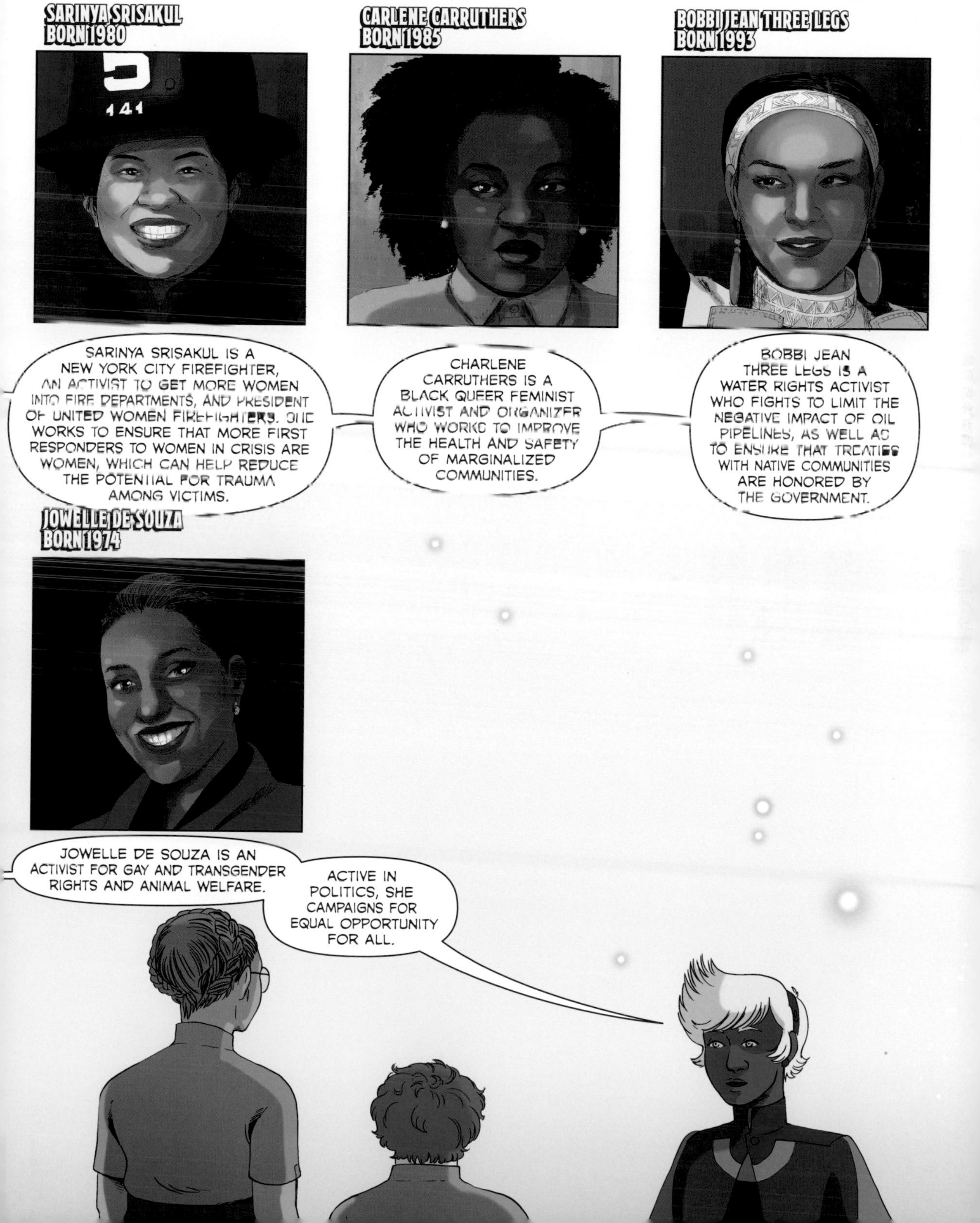

SARINYA SRISAKUL
BORN 1980
141
CARLENE CARRUTHERS
BORN 1985
BOBBI JEAN THREE LEGS
BORN 1993
SARINYA SRISAKUL IS A NEW YORK CITY FIREFIGHTER, AN ACTIVIST TO GET MORE WOMEN INTO FIRE DEPARTMENTS, AND PRESIDENT OF UNITED WOMEN FIREFIGHTERS. SHE WORKS TO ENSURE THAT MORE FIRST RESPONDERS TO WOMEN IN CRISIS ARE WOMEN, WHICH CAN HELP REDUCE THE POTENTIAL FOR TRAUMA AMONG VICTIMS.
CHARLENE CARRUTHERS IS A BLACK QUEER FEMINIST ACTIVIST AND ORGANIZER WHO WORKS TO IMPROVE THE HEALTH AND SAFETY OF MARGINALIZED COMMUNITIES.
BOBBI JEAN THREE LEGS IS A WATER RIGHTS ACTIVIST WHO FIGHTS TO LIMIT THE NEGATIVE IMPACT OF OIL PIPELINES, AS WELL AS TO ENSURE THAT TREATIES WITH NATIVE COMMUNITIES ARE HONORED BY THE GOVERNMENT.
JOWELLE DE SOUZA
BORN 1974
JOWELLE DE SOUZA IS AN ACTIVIST FOR GAY AND TRANSGENDER RIGHTS AND ANIMAL WELFARE.
ACTIVE IN POLITICS, SHE CAMPAIGNS FOR EQUAL OPPORTUNITY FOR ALL.

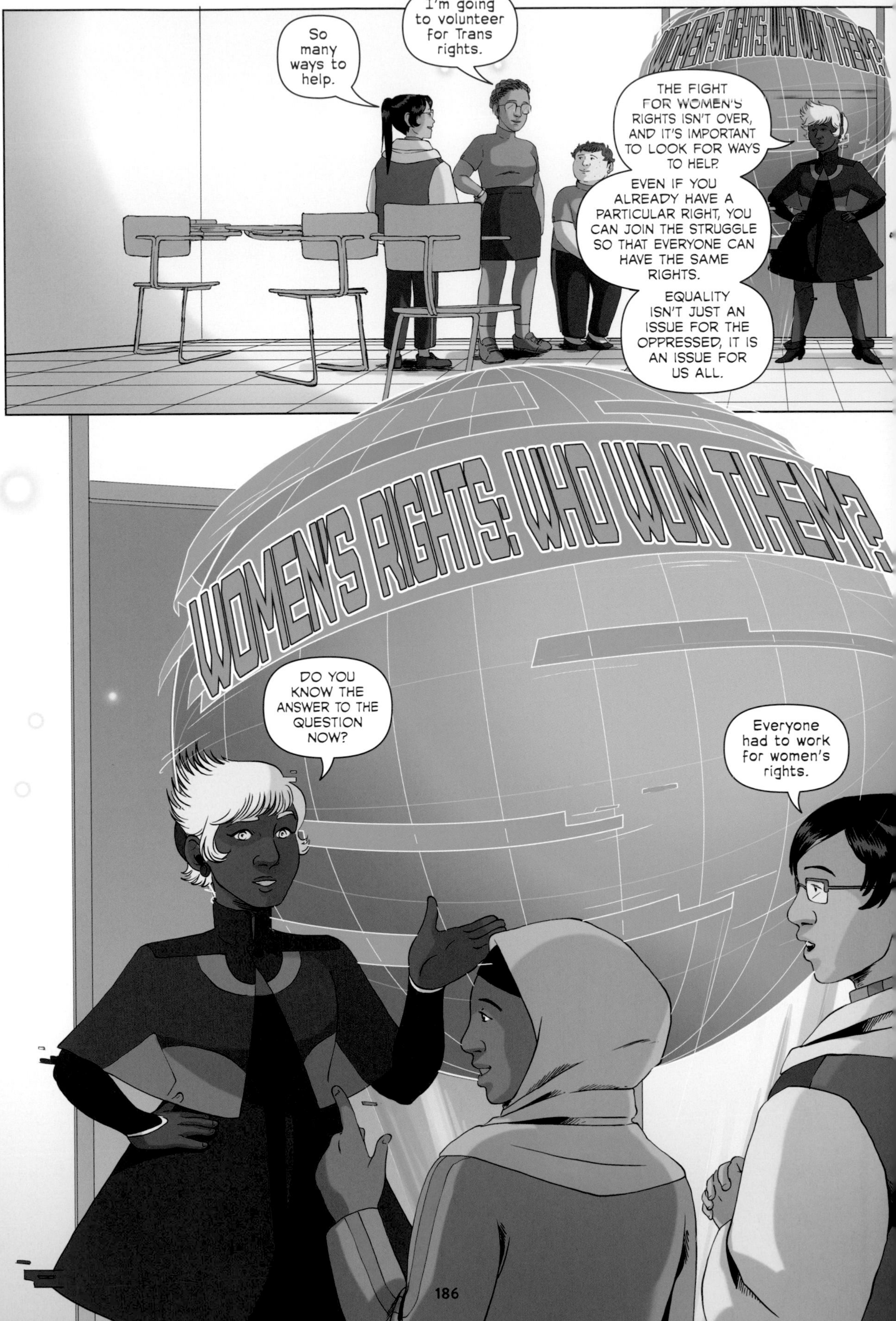
So many ways to help.
I'm going to volunteer for Trans rights.
WOMEN'S RIGHTS: WHO WON THEM?
THE FIGHT FOR WOMEN'S RIGHTS ISN'T OVER, AND IT'S IMPORTANT TO LOOK FOR WAYS TO HELP.
EVEN IF YOU ALREADY HAVE A PARTICULAR RIGHT, YOU CAN JOIN THE STRUGGLE SO THAT EVERYONE CAN HAVE THE SAME RIGHTS.
EQUALITY ISN'T JUST AN ISSUE FOR THE OPPRESSED, IT IS AN ISSUE FOR US ALL.
WOMEN'S RIGHTS: WHO WON THEM?
DO YOU KNOW THE ANSWER TO THE QUESTION NOW?
Everyone had to work for women's rights.

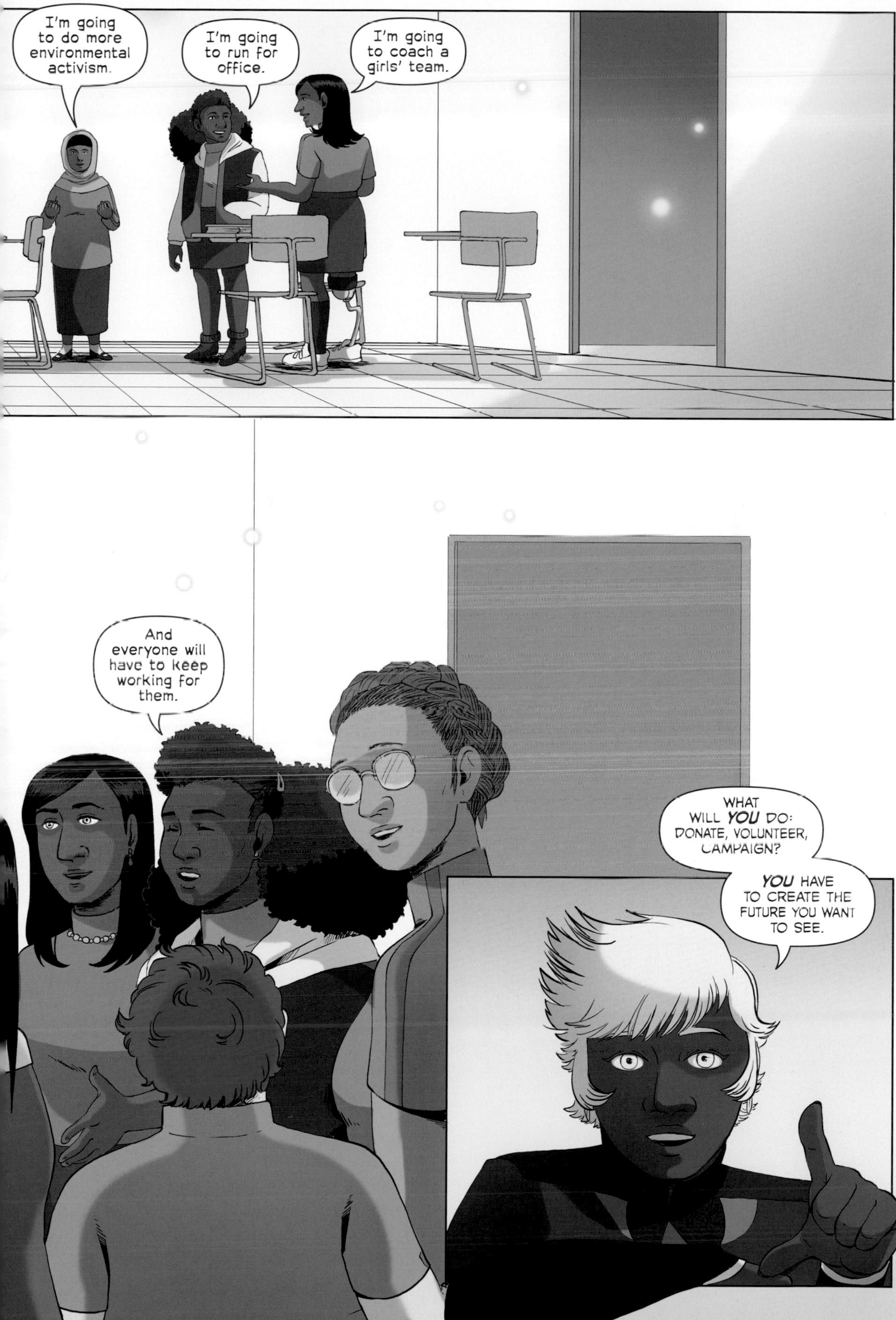
I'm going to do more environmental activism.
I'm going to run for office.
I'm going to coach a girls' team.
And everyone will have to keep working for them.
WHAT WILL *YOU* DO: DONATE, VOLUNTEER, CAMPAIGN?
YOU HAVE TO CREATE THE FUTURE YOU WANT TO SEE.

ABOUT THE AUTHOR

Mikki Kendall lives and works in Chicago where she wields words and raises a family. She has a couple of degrees, a couple of kids, and one patient husbeast. A graduate of the University of Illinois at Urbana Champaign and DePaul University, Mikki has been blogging since 2003 under the pen name Karnythia. She has written about topics ranging from Chicago violence to police brutality, from parenting to racial representation in media, and from reproductive health to food insecurity. She has also covered abortion, education, and politics.

In August of 2013, Mikki started the hashtag #solidarityisforwhitewomen, which sparked a global conversation about racism, solidarity, representation, and access to resources in feminist circles. Her other viral hashtags (including #fasttailedgirls, #notjusthello, #abuserdynamics, #millenialmammy, #notyourmandingo, and others) were designed to make room for hard conversations about feminist issues. She has written for NBC Think, *Washington Post*, *The Guardian*, *Ebony*, *Essence*, *Publishers Weekly*, Global Comment, Salon, xoJane, The Toast, and other online and print outlets. She has also been published in several fiction and nonfiction anthologies. Her professional comics work includes *Swords of Sorrow* with Dynamite Comics, and Action Lab's *Princeless Series*.

ABOUT THE ARTIST

She's here, she's queer, and she's ready to make comics! A. D'Amico is an Ohio-born illustrator who loves all things tea, historical fashion, and fantasy. She graduated from the Columbus College of Art & Design with a BFA in Illustration in 2016, and has been freelancing in comics, watercolor art, and digital illustrations in her (sadly cat-less) home in Michigan ever since.

ACKNOWLEDGMENTS

FROM MIKKI

Thank you to my ancestors, my community, my family, and my friends. To the Husbeast, Rugrat, and Karndilla . . . thank you. I love you. This is for Mariah who wasn't legally allowed to read but made sure her daughters could do what she had not; for Penny Rose who did what it took; for Dorothy, Denise, Karyce, Penny, and Maria. Thanks to Lisa, Pint, Jamie, Chesya, Jackie, Julia, Gatorface, CJ, Justine, Nora, Tempest, Cat, Heather, Sydette, De Ana, Carole, Erin, Beth, and so many others who helped me when I needed it . . . even when that involved a good swift kick in the pants. Thank you to the librarians and the teachers who helped. Chicago, you built me; I hope I did you proud.

FROM A. D'AMICO

This book happened because of my sister, my grandmothers, my aunts, my mom (and my dad, too) who taught me to ask questions, follow what's inside of me, and tell the stories that matter.

Thanks to everyone who shaped my education from the early years: Ms. Fairchild, who helped me learn that I like to learn; St. P.; and Ms. Smith, who worked with me during my most difficult years. During my formal education in the arts, Laurenn McCubbin (the McCubbomb), Adam Osgood, Rob Loss, Mike Laughead, and so many others showed me how to apply this crazy artistic obsession I've always had in skillful and poignant ways. Thank you.

Thanks also to the friends that have stood by me and given me laughs and perspective for over a decade: Rachel, Emily, Maddie, Caroline, and Molly (to name just a few), and the Felners, my second set of parents.

Finally, many thanks to Mikki, Kaitlin, Chloe, Erica, and Shari for the expertise they brought to this project. It wouldn't have even begun to happen without them.

INDEX

D

E

F

G

H

Hill, Anita, 162
Hitler, Adolf, 130, 131
HIV (Human Immunodeficiency
      Virus), 157–58
hooks, bell, 160
Hull House, 98–99, 100
Hurston, Zora Neale, 115

I

India, 43, 59, 148
intersectionality, 161
intersex people, 141
Irene, Empress, 44–45
Isabella I of Castile, Queen, 50
Isabella of France, Queen, 48
Islamic culture, 24, 37, 80
IWW (Industrial Workers of the World),
      92, 93, 96, 97

J

Jamaica, 58
Japan, 30, 109, 119
Japanese internment camps, 132–33, 156
Jiagge, Annie, 148
Jim Crow laws, 127, 134–35, 140
Jindeok, Queen, 41
Jingū, Empress, 30, 36
Johnson, Georgia Douglas, 115
Johnson, Lyndon B., 138, 140
Johnson, Marsha P., 143
Jones, Mary Harris, 97
Joyner-Kersee, Jackie, 170

K

Keller, Helen, 103
Kelley, Florence, 99
Kellogg, Laura Cornelius, 112
King, Billie Jean, 171
King, Coretta Scott, 139
King, Martin Luther, Jr., 139, 140
Kochiyama, Yuri, 156
Korea, 30, 40–41
Kurose, Aki, 156

L

labor movement, 91–97, 118, 152
Lathrop, Julia Clifford, 98
Lauper, Cyndi, 166

Ledbetter, Lilly, 177
Lemlich, Clara, 89
lesbians, 141
LGBTQ movement, 141–43
Liberia, 173
Lincoln, Abraham, 76
Lorde, Audre, 160
Louis VII, King, 46
Lovett, Herbert, 136
Ludlow Massacre, 93
lynching, 81, 82, 110–11, 116, 135, 139

M

mahr, 80
Major, Miss, 142
Malcolm X, 156
Manu, 43
Manusmriti, 43
Marcos, Ferdinand, 172
Margaret I, Queen, 49
Maroons, 58
Mary, Queen of Scots, 51, 52
Mary I, Queen, 51
Mayans, 16, 37
McCloud, Janet, 154
Mencius, 42
minstrel shows, 116
Mitchell, Jackie, 170
Mock, Janet, 184
Morocco, 22–24
Mortimer, Roger, 48
Mott, Lucretia, 63
Muir, Leilani, 155
Murray, Pauli, 150
music, 164, 166–67

N

NAACP (National Association for the
      Advancement of Colored People),
      110, 114, 161
Nanny, Queen, 58
Nanyehi, 61
Nash, Diane, 139
Native Americans, 76, 112, 116, 154
Navratilova, Martina, 171
Nazi Germany, 122, 124, 133, 134
NCAI (National Council of American
      Indians), 112

Nelson, Alice Dunbar, 114
New Deal, 117
Niagara Movement, 110
Nigeria, 149
Nightingale, Florence, 79
Night Witches, 126
Nikephoros I, Emperor, 45
19th Amendment, 88
niqab, 24
non-binary people, 141, 169
NOW (National Organization for Women), 150, 151
Nzinga, Queen Anna, 53

O

Odaenathus, King, 31
onna-bugeisha, 30
orphans, 101–2, 106

P

Paiute, 76
Pakistan, 172
Palmyra, 31
Pankhurst, Christabel, 83
Pankhurst, Emmeline, 83
Pankhurst, Sylvia, 83, 87
Parks, Rosa, 137, 138, 140
Parsons, Lucy Gonzalez, 92
Pascal-Trouillot, Ertha, 172
Paul, Alice, 85
Perdue, Bev, 155
Perkins, Frances, 118
Philippines, 60, 129, 172
Pike, Naelyn, 184
Prohibition, 113, 123

Q

Quran, 24, 80

R

Rainey, Ma, 115
Ransby, Barbara, 161
Ransome-Kuti, Funmilayo, 149
Raskova, Marina, 126
Reagan, Ronald, 156
Rebecca Project for Human Rights, 184
redress (reparations) movements, 156
Richards, Agnes, 144

Richards, Linda, 79
Riggs, Bobby, 171
riot grrrl movement, 167
Rivera, Sylvia, 143
Robinson, Amelia Boynton, 139
Rockhaven Sanitarium, 144
Roe v. Wade, 152
Rome, ancient, 15, 19–21, 31–32
Roosevelt, Eleanor, 117
Roosevelt, Franklin D., 118, 132
Ruth, Babe, 170

S

Saada Saar, Malika, 184
Sabina, Vibia, 15
SAI (Society of American Indians), 112, 116
Salt-N-Pepa, 166
same-sex relationships, 141
Sandberg, Sheryl, 176
Sanger, Margaret, 106–9
Sappho, 141
Saraswati, 43
Sargon of Akkad, 11
Sarmatians, 28
Sauromatians, 28
Schlafly, Phyllis, 151
Scholl, Sophie, 122
Schulman, Faye, 125
Sedgwick, Theodore, 62
Seneca Falls Convention, 64–65, 68, 74
Seokpum, Achan, 40
Seondeok, Queen, 40–41
settlement houses, 98–100, 101, 102
sexual harassment, 162
sexual revolution, 153
Shidzue, Katō, 109
shield-maidens, 18, 29
Shōtoku, Prince, 36
Silang, Diego, 60
Silang, Gabriela, 60
Singapore, 148
Singh, Sophia Duleep, 83
Sioux Nation, 76, 112
Sirleaf, Ellen Johnson, 173
SNCC (Student Nonviolent Coordinating Committee), 138, 139
social services, 98
Sparta, 14, 37

T

U

V

W

X

Y

Z

Text copyright © 2019 by Mikki Kendall
Illustrations copyright © 2019 by A. D'Amico

All rights reserved.
Published in the United States by Ten Speed Press, an imprint of
Random House, a division of Penguin Random House LLC, New York.
www.tenspeed.com

Ten Speed Press and the Ten Speed Press colophon are registered
trademarks of Penguin Random House LLC.

Library of Congress Cataloging-in-Publication Data
is on file with the publisher.

Trade Paperback ISBN: 978-0-399-58179-3
eBook ISBN: 978-0-399-58180-9

Printed in China

Design by Chloe Rawlins
Colors by Shari Chankhamma
Letters by Erica Schultz

10 9 8 7 6 5 4 3

First Edition